Conflict, Violence, and Displacement in Indonesia

Cornell University

Eva-Lotta E. Hedman, editor

Conflict, Violence, and Displacement in Indonesia

SOUTHEAST ASIA PROGRAM PUBLICATIONS
Southeast Asia Program
Cornell University
Ithaca, New York
2008

Cornell Southeast Asia Program Publications
640 Stewart Avenue, Ithaca, NY 14850-3857

Studies on Southeast Asia No. 45

Printed in the United States of America

ISBN: hc 978-0-87727-775-0
ISBN: pb 978-0-87727-745-3

Cover Design: Kat Dalton; photograph by Christopher Duncan.

TABLE OF CONTENTS

ACKNOWLEDGMENTS

In addition to the authors of individual chapters, there are a number of people who have contributed to the production of this volume. Gerry van Klinken, Geoffrey Robinson, Danilyn Rutherford, and John Sidel provided especially constructive comments on the manuscript, or parts thereof. Peter Carey, Graeme Rodgers, Jacqueline Siapno, and Riwanto Tirtosudarmo have also added perceptive insights at various stages of this project. They deserve special thanks, as do the anonymous readers of individual chapters, for their thoughtful criticisms and suggestions. As the editor, I remain especially grateful to the other authors, who have turned their distinctive perspectives on Indonesian politics and society to focus on this search for the dynamics of conflict, violence, and displacement.

At Oxford's Refugee Studies Centre, Kate Prudden lent early administrative support, and Corinne Owen offered kind assistance with the formatting of photographs. At Cornell's Southeast Asia Program, Managing Editor Deborah Homsher, assisted by Fred Conner, rescued displaced widows and orphans and more through painstaking editorial work on this manuscript. In addition to excellent editorial advice and assistance, Deborah Homsher also added her infectious enthusiasm and patient support to this collective project.

Many of the photographs and other illustrations for this volume have been provided by the author(s) of each individual chapter, as indicated elsewhere. In addition, the volume includes several photographs kindly provided by Gerry van Klinken for publication in the chapter by Hélène Bouvier and Glenn Smith. The arresting image on the cover of this volume is a photograph by Christopher Duncan, who has kindly allowed for its reproduction here. Special thanks also to Kat Dalton for the cover design.

The Andrew W. Mellon Foundation and the Refugee Studies Centre in the Department of International Development at the University of Oxford provided financial and institutional support, which helped sustain this international research and publications project.

Eva-Lotta E. Hedman
London, January 2008

Indonesia

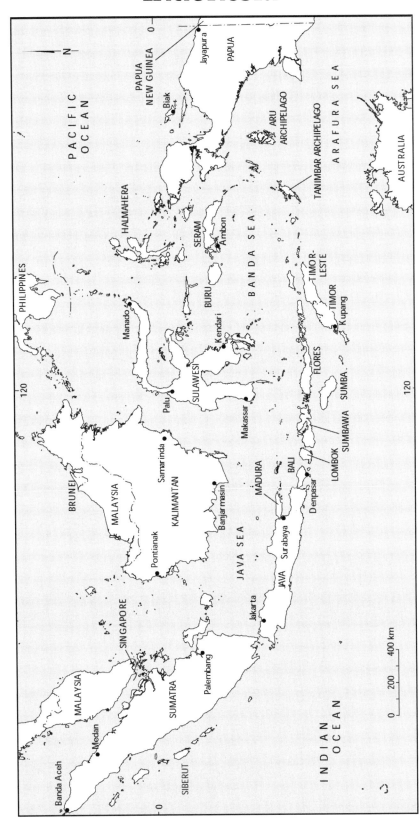

INTRODUCTION: DYNAMICS OF DISPLACEMENT IN INDONESIA

Eva-Lotta E. Hedman

There is a strong feeling within the Government of the Republic of Indonesia that a quick solution to the IDP [internally displaced person] crisis would help restore the dignity of the nation, and help resolve the conflicts that have caused displacement in various parts of the country.

> (UN Office for the Coordination of Humanitarian Affairs, November 19, 2002)

Why, many IDPs asked … have Poso District officials never come to major IDP locations to invite us back to our home areas? Is it because district leaders are still unable to guarantee safety and the rule of law? Or, is it really because they don't want some ethnic or religious groups to return and undo the "ethnic cleansing" and religious territorialisation that resulted from the regional warfare?

> (Cited in *Inside Indonesia*, January–March 2004)

In the wake of Suharto's long authoritarian reign, Indonesian politics and society have seen considerable realignment in the direction of democratization, demilitarization, and decentralization. As is well known, such realignments have also been accompanied by state-sponsored (para-)military campaigns in East Timor, Aceh, and Papua, and by murderous violence in the name of religion or ethnicity in parts of Maluku, Sulawesi, and Kalimantan. More commonly overlooked, perhaps, is the extent to which the emergence of a new kind of person—the internally displaced —in post-Suharto Indonesia has been symptomatic not only of conflict and violence, but also, in a sense, emblematic of the reordering of state power through processes of democratization, demilitarization, and decentralization, and the powerful effects thereof on "the national order of things."[1]

As suggested by the brief epigraphs above, the figure of the "IDP"—internally displaced person—was often referred to by Indonesian government officials as one requiring urgent ministrations for the sake of the "dignity of the nation." That is, while they themselves were no doubt mindful of the international human rights and humanitarian discourse on IDPs,[2] not least when addressing representatives of the United Nations Office for the Coordination of Humanitarian Affairs (UN-OCHA) in Jakarta, Indonesian government officials nonetheless revealed a more pervasive concern with displacement as a stain, something out of place in the body politic. Indeed, speculations about the "disintegration of Indonesia" aside, myriad forms of international and national non-governmental and governmental attention focused on IDPs in recent years have accompanied a kind of "forward movement" in the internal (re)ordering of state power, whether through coercion, consent, or some combination thereof, across different sociopolitical terrains.[3]

From the perspective of IDPs themselves, as suggested by the epigraph above, their displacement from local communities, and concomitant materialization as "IDPs" (or, in Indonesian, *pengungsi),* had morphed into a life on hold in "major IDP locations" carved out of the Indonesian body politic.[4] In the case of those displaced from local communities in Poso, cited above, they attributed this condition not only to the inability of district officials to guarantee protection and the rule of law, but also, significantly, to the unwillingness of such officials to see the new ethno/religious "territorialization" in Poso "undone." While waiting for Poso district officials to invite them to return, these IDPs, it would seem, were no longer at home in Indonesia, and, one might add, even in their IDP location sites, the very terms of hospitality—always already inscribed within (temporal and spatial) limits—signaled "a kind of ontological reduction as political beings."[5]

THE FIGURE OF THE *PENGUNGSI* IN INDONESIA

Indonesia's *pengungsi* constituted the single largest such population in the world by 2001—some 1.4 million IDPs, according to official figures cited by the office of the United Nation's High Commissioner for Refugees (UNHCR). Indonesia's *pengungsi* emerged as part of a wider global shift that saw the recorded number of internally displaced persons surpass the number of those seeking refuge across international

---

[1] Liisa H. Malkii, "Refugees and Exiles: From 'Refugee Studies' to the National Order of Things," *Annual Review of Anthropology* 24 (1995): 495–523.

[2] In this regard, *The Guiding Principles on Internal Displacement,* issued in 1998 by the United Nations Secretary-General's Special Rapporteur on IDPs, marks an important milestone.

[3] For a related argument, see Finn Stepputat and Thomas B. Hansen, eds., *Sovereign Bodies, Citizens, Migrants, and States in the Post-Colonial World* (Princeton, NJ: Princeton University Press, 2005), p. 2.

[4] The second citation in the epigraph is found in Lorraine V. Aragon, "Profiting from Displacement," *Inside Indonesia* (January–March 2004): 2.

[5] Peter Nyers, *Rethinking Refugees: Beyond States of Emergency* (London: Routledge, 2006), p. 83. See also Jacques Derrida, *Of Hospitality,* trans. Rachel Bowlby (Stanford, CA: Stanford University Press, 2000), pp. 361–62.

state borders in the aftermath of the Cold War.[6] Many observers have linked the rise of IDPs as a phenomenon in its own right—in Indonesia and elsewhere—to the proliferation of so-called "new internal conflicts" or "new wars" in the same period.[7] Inasmuch as these new wars have been seen to revolve around a politics of identity removed from the ideological and geopolitical considerations that propelled earlier rounds of militarized violence, displaced persons in the aftermath of the Cold War have appeared in many accounts as if "contaminated" with the communalism, or, in some formulations, primordialism, associated with such internal conflicts.[8]

Indeed, with the passing of the ideology and politics underpinning the international refugee regime during the Cold War, the question of recognition—recognition of those who flee, of the significance of flight—has become increasingly embedded within dominant national discourses (state religion, national culture) and state practices (sovereignty, noninterference). Viewed in this light, displacement points to failures of emplacement in nation and state, or, put differently, to "problems" of national (be)longing and state (dis)order, a world apart from Cold War discourses of "refugees voting with their feet," "refugee warrior communities," and, indeed, "regional conflicts"[9]—across borders, against dictatorship, and for democracy. In this vein, the experience of not being welcome, not being fully at home as a national citizen, has further resonance in the international system of states, as IDPs, in Indonesia and elsewhere, have been defined, at the same time, as persons "on the inside" of the borders and jurisdiction of the sovereign nation-state, and as persons "put out of place" of their "habitual residence." The defining experience of IDPs thus appears as a kind of captive dislocation rather than a politics of (be)longing—to an imagined community, or a future in "the free world," as it were.

At the same time, the experience of Indonesia's *pengungsi*, and their counterparts elsewhere, also suggests a more fundamentally refugee-like condition than commonly recognized. That is, as refugees find themselves uprooted from the territory of the state, ultimately, Hannah Arendt has argued, "it [is] a problem not of space but of political organization."[10] In a not dissimilar vein, internally displaced

---

[6] For an early account of this period, see Graeme J. Hugo, "*Pengungsi*—Indonesia's Internally Displaced Persons," *Asian and Pacific Migration Journal* 11,3 (2002): 297–331. In this volume, see Christopher Duncan's chapter, appendix, for a 2002 snapshot of the distribution of IDPs in Indonesia. Having declared the end of conflict IDPs in the country as of January 2004, the Indonesian government no longer issues national figures for IDPs. However, a recent report by the Internal Displacement Monitoring Centre estimates "[b]etween 150,000 and 250,000 still displaced by conflict in Indonesia at the end of 2006." http://www.internal-displacement.org/idmc/website/countries.nsf/Indonesia (accessed on July 30, 2007).

[7] See, for example, Donald M. Snow, *Uncivil Wars: International Security and New Internal Conflicts* (Boulder, CO: Lynne Rienner, 1996); and Mary Kaldor, *New and Old Wars: Organized Violence in a Global Era* (Cambridge: Polity Press, 2001). For a summary critique of the "new wars" argument, see especially Stathis N. Kalyvas, "Research Note: 'New' and 'Old' Wars: A Valid Distinction?" *World Politics* 54 (October 2001): 99–118.

[8] See, however, B. S. Chimni, "The Geo-Politics of Refugee Studies: A View from the South," *Journal of Refugee Studies* 11 (1998): 350–74; and, for a regional focus, Eva-Lotta E. Hedman, "Forced Migration in Southeast Asia: International Politics and the Reordering of State Power," *Asian Pacific Migration Journal* 16,1 (May 2006): 29–53.

[9] See, for example, Astri Suhrke, "Uncertain Globalization: Refugee Movements in the Second Half of the Twentieth Century," in *Global History and Migrations,* ed. Wang Gungwu (Boulder, CO: Westview Press, 1987), p. 227.

[10] Hannah Arendt, *The Origins of Totalitarianism* (New York, NY: Meridian, 1958), p. 294.

persons, even while retaining formal citizenship, may find themselves excluded from the very (local) space of sociality within which a set of institutionalized political mechanisms and practices mediate the exercise of (national) citizens' rights and, arguably, obligations. Inasmuch as IDPs, not unlike refugees, also find themselves in protracted situations of displacement, including in camps, problems of political access and representation faced by IDPs may be further compounded by a certain process of "normalization" in the "management" of such populations.[11]

In the contemporary Indonesian context, where the term *pengungsi* is used to refer to "refugee" and "IDP" alike, it is perhaps no coincidence that the targets of what has arguably remained the most "successful" case of ethnic cleansing—the Madurese of Central and West Kalimantan[12]—may also have been the most vocal in rejecting their designation as "IDPs." Indeed, many Madurese reportedly, and repeatedly, asserted their status and, indeed, their rights as national citizens of the Republic of Indonesia. Displaced from their homes in Central and West Kalimantan, with many subsequently encamped elsewhere, including as far away as Madura Island, where few had previously ever lived, these Madurese also found themselves largely ignored by the government in Jakarta, and commonly vilified in the national media. Unsurprisingly perhaps, Madurese, whose calls for recognition of their political rights had, in no small measure, failed to resonate with their own government—and, it would seem, with other Indonesian citizens—also gained a reputation for being difficult, demanding, and ungrateful in encounters with various (inter)national organizations administering humanitarian assistance to such displaced populations in "post-conflict" situations.[13]

As the most "failed" of Indonesia's *pengungsi,* the Madurese illuminate the close affinity of "IDPs" with refugees. On the one hand, the failure of the government of Indonesia even to acknowledge, let alone promote and protect, the rights of the Madurese, as national citizens, to freedom of movement within Indonesia, signaled a political disenfranchisement in its own right, a kind of internal exile not merely from a territorial space, but from an entire way of being, in state and nation. On the other hand, the failure of international organizations to distinguish between the limitations inherent in their own mandates to deliver humanitarian assistance, and the extent to which the concerns of Madurese "IDPs" were not reducible to such "needs," suggested a further displacement, a kind of misrecognition, twice over, as the Madurese emerged in public discourse as "failed refugees." Viewed thus, the Madurese failed to appear as "speechless emissaries" of suffering, or grateful beneficiaries of humanitarianism,[14] while, at the same time, the very politics of their

---

[11] On refugee camps, see, for example, Jennifer Hyndman, *Managing Displacement: Refugees and the Politics of Humanitarianism* (Minneapolis, MN: Minnesota University Press, 2000).

[12] On the 1967 Chinese purges in West Kalimantan, however, see further Jamie S. Davidson, "Violence and Displacement in West Kalimantan," this volume.

[13] See, for example, Hélène Bouvier and Glenn Smith, "Of Spontaneity and Conspiracy Theories: Explaining Violence in Central Kalimantan," in this volume, and Thung Ju Lan, "The Madurese IDPs and the Problem of Coordination" (unpublished paper presented at the International Association for Forced Migration Studies, Chiang Mai, January 5–8, 2003).

[14] For related arguments, see Liisa Malkki, "Speechless Emissaries: Refugees, Humanitarianism, and Dehistoricization," *Cultural Anthropology* 11,3 (1996): 385. For an early and critical formulation, see especially Barbara Harrell-Bond, *Imposing Aid: Emergency Assistance to Refugees* (Oxford: Oxford University Press, 1986).

(dis)placement and, indeed their embeddedness therein, remained, in no small measure, "displaced" even in refuge.

The Reordering of State Power, the Production of Refugees

It is not merely the scope and scale of recent displacement in Indonesia that demand further critical investigation, although they provide the point of departure for this volume. It is important to recognize as well that displacement, in the context of conflict and violence, has been an integral, if often overlooked, dynamic in the making of the Indonesian nation-state since Independence. While traces of forced migration can be found in the existing literature, a more sustained focus on the sites and modes of (internal) displacement promises a new, critical perspective on the nature and direction of Indonesian postcolonial state- and nation-formation.

As Benedict Anderson and Ruth McVey have argued, it is possible to identify a gradual but inexorable trajectory of increasing state power vis-à-vis society in Indonesia and, within the state, growing centralization of powers, reflective and reproductive of greater military penetration and control of Indonesian postcolonial politics and society.[15] Pointing to the discrete genealogies and "distinct histories, constituents, and 'interests'" of state and nation, Anderson traces the ascendancy of the postcolonial Indonesian state qua state over and against the legacies of a Revolution (1945–1949) characterized by highly localized popular resistance, and linked only by "a common vision of a free nation." In addition, he calls attention to the significant experiences of the early post-Independence period of parliamentary democracy (1950–1957), during which civilian and military bureaucracies and political parties enjoyed little institutional autonomy from the myriad—nationalist, religious, communal, and paramilitary—organizations and alliances active in Indonesian society at the time.[16] If the State of Emergency declared in April 1957 signaled a critical turning point in state-society relations in Indonesia, it was the subsequent shift to Guided Democracy (1959–1965), McVey argues, that paved the way for mounting military control over Indonesian society through an expansion of the military's activities in the economic and political spheres, and in the last years of this period, as noted by Anderson, the army had also established itself as increasingly powerful vis-à-vis all other branches of the state administration.[17]

The final ascent of the postcolonial incarnation of the old *beamtenstaat* and "its triumph vis-à-vis society and nation," Anderson argues, was achieved with the establishment of the New Order (1965–1998), which, notably, "never publicly proclaimed itself an emergency, provisional, or even tutelary regime," and thus offered "no prospects for a return to civilian rule or a restoration of representative

---

[15] Benedict R. O'G. Anderson, "Old State, New Society: Indonesia's New Order in Comparative Historical Perspective," in Benedict Anderson, *Language and Power: Exploring Political Cultures in Indonesia* (Ithaca, NY: Cornell University Press, 1990), pp. 94–120; and Ruth McVey, "The Post-Revolutionary Transformation of the Indonesian Army," Part I and Part II, *Indonesia* 11 (April 1971): 131–76, and *Indonesia* 13 (April 1972): 147–81.

[16] Anderson, "Old State, New Society," citations from p. 94 and p. 101. For an analysis of the Indonesian military during this period, see McVey, "The Post-Revolutionary Transformation of the Indonesian Army," Part I.

[17] These developments are analyzed with more nuance and detail in Anderson, "Old State, New Society," and McVey, "The Post-Revolutionary Transformation of the Indonesian Army," Part II.

government."[18] While the inception of the new regime in Jakarta involved considerable mobilization of civil and not-so-civil society alike in the mid- to late 1960s, the consolidation of the New Order in the 1970s saw the relentless narrowing of its political base—in society and nation—to "the charmed circle of its core supporters."[19] That is, the New Order concentrated unprecedented powers in the Indonesian military at the expense of an independent legislative and judiciary; it privileged state enterprises and multinational corporations at the expense of indigenous entrepreneurs; and it resorted to a range of repressive measures to curb freedom of expression, whether in print or broadcast media, public fora, or, indeed, elections.

Rebellion and Displacement

While this is surely a familiar enough narrative to many readers, what—and who—remains largely unseen is the large-scale forced displacement of civilian populations, ostensibly "at home" in Indonesia, that accompanied this process of postcolonial state- and nation-formation. This is evident from the earliest phases of post-independence reordering of state power in the archipelago in the 1950s. Indeed, with the formalities of independence achieved in the last month of 1949, the Indonesian state continued to face and to face down successive armed challenges to its claims to sovereign power throughout the decade that followed, prompting large-scale displacement of civilian populations. Such challenges ranged from the attempted secession by the "Republic of the South Moluccas" in 1950, to the regional rebellions of PRRI (Pemerintah Revolusioner Republik Indonesia, the Revolutionary Republic of Indonesia)–Permesta (Piagam Perjuangan Semesta Alam, Universal Struggle Charter) in West Sumatra and North Sulawesi from 1958 through 1961. Spanning more than a decade, the Darul Islam rebellions first emerged in West Java, and then in Central Java, South Kalimantan, South Sulawesi, and Aceh, with related "activity" reported elsewhere in support of an Islamic State of Indonesia (Negara Islam Indonesia) in the period 1948 to 1962.

While much scholarship to date tends to focus on the origins and dreams, as well as the wider political context and the military suppression, of the armed rebellions listed above, it is possible to glimpse something of the dynamics and experiences of displacement in the existing literature about these conflicts. Noting the "seriousness of the urban refugee problem in the early 1950s," for example, Geoffrey McNicoll also identified the following pattern of displacement associated with the Darul Islam campaigns and their suppression by government forces: " ... movement of families from insecure rural areas to the larger towns, with a tendency for the reverse movement to take place as soon as security was restored."[20] However, the massive influx of urban refugees resulting from such conflict and violence, especially in West

---

[18] Anderson, "Old State, New Society," citations from p. 109 and p. 114, respectively.

[19] Benedict R. O'G. Anderson, "Last Days of Indonesia's Suharto?" *Southeast Asia Chronicle* 63 (July–August, 1978), p. 10.

[20] Geoffrey McNicoll, "Internal Migration in Indonesia: Descriptive Notes," *Indonesia* 5 (April 1968): 49.

Java, also contributed to the rapid growth of some urban areas during the 1950s and 1960s, notably in the cases of Jakarta and Bandung.[21]

In West Java, the cradle of Darul Islam, the impact on local populations was "devastating," especially in the countryside, "where villagers were raided, in some regions quite frequently, goods and crops seized, and houses, bridges, mosques, and rice-barns set afire or destroyed."[22] A reported 52,672 people fled their homes or were evacuated in the last quarter of 1951, and "[f]rom 1955 to 1962 the annual number of evacuees fluctuated between 209,355 in 1962 and 303,764 in 1958, with an average of 250,000 per year."[23] Villagers were also caught between Darul Islam forces and Republican troops, "with both sides suspecting them of supporting the other and punishing them accordingly."[24]

In South Sulawesi, where the Darul Islam rebellion was also widespread and protracted, some areas saw a marked concentration of refugees. In mid-1955, for example, the whole of Sulawesi had 290,000 refugees, according to reports—"over 88,000 of them in Bone, over 96,000 in Luwu, and over 45,000 in Parepare."[25] While the Republican government provided some measure of food and clothing assistance to such refugee populations, their situation was reportedly "deplorable [with] people dying of hunger, and many others suffering from severe malnutrition and beriberi."[26] Affiliate movements in Central Java and South Kalimantan remained comparatively minor, but the Darul Islam rebellion in Aceh also generated considerable armed conflict and the displacement of an estimated 60,000 people to North Sumatra in its first year, in 1953.[27]

By contrast with the noted large-scale displacement of rural populations due to the Darul Islam rebellions and their armed suppression, it has been suggested, the PRRI–Permesta regional rebellions in Central Sumatra and North/Central Sulawesi "drew more support from the educated sections of the population, [and thus] probably had less impact on the rural population."[28] As noted by Naim, however, the PRRI rebellion coincided with an unprecedented increase in "the *merantau* flow" from West Sumatra, that is, the Minangkabau tradition of young men outmigrating from territory where land ownership has been regulated by matrilineal inheritance laws.[29] Audrey Kahin has underscored the extent to which conflict and violence shaped such nominally "voluntary" migration during this period:

> The PRRI rebellion and its defeat had sparked the largest exodus ever of Minangkabau from their home region. West Sumatran migrants spread across Sumatra, throughout the archipelago, and even to Malaysia, but the largest

---

[21] See T. Goantiang, "Growth of Cities in Indonesia, 1930–1961," *Tijdschrift Voor Economische en Sociale Geografie* 56 (1965): 103–8.

[22] C. Van Dijk, *Rebellion under the Banner of Islam: The Darul Islam in Indonesia* (The Hague: Martinus Nijhoff, 1981), p. 104.

[23] Ibid., p. 105.

[24] Ibid.

[25] Ibid., p. 201.

[26] Ibid., p. 202.

[27] McNicoll, "Internal Migration in Indonesia," p. 47.

[28] Ibid., p. 49.

[29] Mochtar Naim, "Merantau, Minangkabau Voluntary Migration" (PhD dissertation, National University of Singapore, 1973).

numbers went to the nation's capital ... Most of the migrants were petty traders and food-stall or restaurant owners.[30]

As indicated above, these rebellions saw large-scale and, at times, recurring forced displacement of civilian populations in many areas affected by fighting between Republican and rebel forces. Beyond the noted variation in terms of rural versus urban displacement during the rebellions pitting either Darul Islam or PRRI–Permesta forces against Republican troops, certain similarities in the dynamics of displacement across some of these rebellions also appear noteworthy, not least with reference to other forced migrations to follow elsewhere in the archipelago. On the one hand, flows of refugees sought "escape from violence"[31] in general, but displaced populations also tended to seek refuge under the protection of one or the other party to these armed conflicts, thus inscribing, however briefly and imperfectly, the territorial map of Indonesia with alternative organized and autonomous—"the techno-word is 'sovereign'"[32]—political communities. On the other hand, beyond the resourcefulness and relations of the displaced themselves, efforts to provide support and protection for the refugees remained largely embedded in the "partisan" loyalties of Republican and rebel supporters rather than in a more universalist commitment to the delivery of "humanitarian assistance," thus circumscribing these "refugee crises" as occasions for "statecraft" of a certain kind.[33]

While each challenge by armed rebel forces to the sovereignty of the unitary state of the Republic of Indonesia traced a distinct trajectory, these challenges also formed part of a larger push for the (contested) reordering of state power, reflected and reproduced through certain processes (administrative centralization) and institutions (military and civilian bureaucracies).[34] In the broader context of widespread mobilization by political parties and their affiliate organizations, the successful military suppression of these armed rebellions served to expedite the internal consolidation and centralization of the Indonesian Army as an institution. The declaration of martial law in 1957 signaled a turning point in terms of this (contested) reordering of state power, leaving the military with vast emergency powers, and rendering political parties and large state enterprises vulnerable to army control.[35]

---

[30] Audrey Kahin, *Rebellion to Integration: West Sumatra and the Indonesian Polity* (Amsterdam: Amsterdam University Press, 1999), p. 236.

[31] Aristide Zolberg, *Escape from Violence: Conflict and the Refugee Crisis in the Developing World* (Oxford: Oxford University Press, 1989).

[32] Clifford Geertz, "What Is a State if It Is Not a Sovereign? Reflections on Politics in Complicated Places," *Current Anthropology* 45,5 (December 2004): 578.

[33] For an analysis of refugees and statecraft, see Nevzat Soguk, *States and Strangers: Refugees and Displacements of Statecraft* (Minneapolis, MN: University of Minneapolis Press, 1999).

[34] See McVey, "The Post-Revolutionary Transformation of the Indonesian Army," Part I and Part II; and Anderson, "Old State, New Society."

[35] Indeed, the imposition of new restrictions on Chinese populations in Indonesia, and the exodus that followed, should be understood in this context. The 1958 Law on Citizenship also continued the pattern of stigmatization of Chinese immigrants to Indonesia, and their descendants, as an alien minority, and according to some estimates, more than one million (out of an estimated total population of 2.1 million) remained aliens, more than half of whom were effectively stateless. See Charles A. Coppel, *Indonesian Chinese in Crisis* (Kuala Lumpur: Oxford University Press, 1983).

Military Campaigns and Displacement

The gradual but inexorable trajectory of increasing state power vis-à-vis society gained further momentum in the 1960s, which also marked a "leap forward" for the state qua state in the (re)production of territorialized and nationalized boundaries through militarized conflict, violence, and displacement. If the origins of the military as an increasingly powerful centralized institution date back to the suppression of the internal armed rebellions of the 1950s, the Sukarno regime's external militarized campaigns of the early 1960s served to pave the way for military rule even further. The significance of these campaigns—against the Dutch in West New Guinea and the British in Malaya—for the rise of the military in Indonesian politics and society is evident from the career of Maj. Gen. Suharto, who, having participated in the suppression of the internal armed rebellions, went on to serve as commanding officer in both the West New Guinea and Konfrontasi (Confrontation) campaigns, and was also made the first commander of the army's new elite strike force, Kostrad (the Army Strategic Reserve Forces).[36]

The early 1960s saw the longstanding, "almost institutionalized," rivalry between the army and Sukarno give way to a common front—on the annexation of West New Guinea and, albeit briefly, on the confrontation with Malaysia—reinforced by shared ambitions that aimed beyond securing the sovereignty of the state within the confines of already established postcolonial borders.[37] In the case of West New Guinea, this common front allowed for the Indonesian military's invasion of the region in 1962, under Suharto's Mandala command, thus preparing for its annexation (as "Irian Barat," or West Irian) in 1963 and its subsequent integration into Indonesia through the UN-sponsored so-called "Act of Free Choice" in 1969. Having thus reestablished the outer perimeters of the old colonial map of the Dutch East Indies, Jakarta's incorporation of this territory anticipated the deep militarization and further entrenchment of the armed forces in this region, which has, in many ways, outlasted the Suharto regime itself. It also prepared the ground for one of the world's largest gold and copper mines, Freeport-Indonesia, a subsidiary of the American transnational mining corporation Freeport-McMoRan, and thus also for the Indonesian military's murky business of "protection" in the region.[38]

Indonesia's military campaigns and its neocolonial administration in "West Irian" anticipated dynamics of displacement, which, in many ways, have intensified since their early manifestation in the 1960s. The most easily recognizable form of such displacement involved trans-border crossings into neighboring Papua New Guinea, which shares a long land border with West Papua, and marked linguistic and other socio-cultural affinities. In the period between Suharto's Mandala

---

[36] For a revealing account of Suharto's career, see Anderson, "Old State, New Society," pp. 109–11.

[37] Audrey R. Kahin and George McT. Kahin, *Subversion as Foreign Policy: The Secret Eisenhower and Dulles Debacle in Indonesia* (New York, NY: The New Press, 1995), p. 221.

[38] Denise Leith, *The Politics of Power: Freeport in Suharto's Indonesia* (Honolulu, HI: University of Hawai'i Press, 2003), p. 3. In 1967, Freeport-McMoRan became the first foreign company to sign a contract with the new regime, and, in due time, it became Jakarta's largest taxpayer.

campaign in 1962 and the UN-sponsored "Act of Free Choice" in 1969,[39] almost four thousand West Papuans crossing the border were registered by the Australian Administration in Papua New Guinea, with the numbers peaking at 1,695 in 1969.[40]

In addition to such trans-border movements—which at times involved several thousand Papuans seeking refuge in Papua New Guinea, and, indeed, the establishment of a sizeable refugee settlement in East Awin under the auspices of the United Nations High Commissioner of Refugees—Indonesian rule over West Papua also prompted waves of internal displacement during military operations. Such operations included, for example, the strafing of communities near Enarotali in the mid-1960s, and military "sweepings"—house-to-house searches for activists and sympathizers of the OPM (Organisasi Papua Merdeka, Papuan Freedom Movement), carried out repeatedly from the time the resistance group was founded in the early 1960s.[41] Over time, and embedded in a context of deepening militarization, an even more pervasive pattern of internal displacement emerged in Papua due to the combined effects of government-sponsored relocation programs *(transmigrasi)* or the spontaneous migration of Indonesian citizens to the region, and the (en)forced relocation of indigenous populations *(relokasi)*.[42]

The West New Guinea and the Konfrontasi campaigns served, in distinct ways, to shape the social (re)production of state borders and national space in Indonesia through militarized conflict, violence, and displacement. In the case of the West New Guinea campaign, as suggested above, it prompted a creeping militarization of the long border with Papua New Guinea and the emergence of a growing and, eventually, so-called "protracted refugee situation" across this border, thus anchoring Jakarta's claims to the last remnants of the (former) Dutch East Indies colonial territory in new lived experiences of political boundaries and violent geographies on Indonesia's easternmost frontier. As noted elsewhere, moreover, the undeclared border war known as Konfrontasi prompted a new consciousness of the border between Indonesia and Malaysia and the wider social and economic effects thereof, as "people from across the border came to be viewed as outsiders rather than relatives."[43]

---

[39] See especially John Saltford, *The United Nations and the Indonesian Takeover of West Papua, 1962–1969: The Anatomy of Betrayal* (London: RoutledgeCurzon, 2002).

[40] Diana Glazebrook, "'If I Stay Here There is Nothing Yet If I Return I do not Know Whether I Will be Safe:' West Papuan Refugee Responses to Papua New Guinea Asylum Policy 1998–2003," *Journal of Refugee Studies* 17,2 (2004): 207. See further Beverley Blaskett, "Papua New Guinea—Indonesia Relations: A New Perspective on the Border Conflict" (PhD dissertation, Australian National University, 1989). For a review of Australian asylum policy, see David Palmer, "Between a Rock and a Hard Place: The Case of Papuan Asylum Seekers," *Australian Journal of Politics and History* 52,4 (2006): 576–603.

[41] See, for example, Robin Osborne, *Indonesia's Secret War: The Guerrilla Struggle in Irian Jaya* (Sydney: Allen and Unwin, 1985).

[42] See, for example, Leith, *The Politics of Power*, pp. 204–14. On the large-scale displacement caused by military operations in 1984, see especially Carmel Budiardjo and Liem Soei Liong, *West Papua: The Obliteration of a People*, 3rd edition (London: Tapol, 1988). For a recent overview of dispossession and forced labor, see also Elizabeth Brundige et al., "Indonesian Human Rights Abuses in West Papua: Application of the Law of Genocide to the History of Indonesian Control" (New Haven, CT: Yale Law School, the Allard K. Lowenstein International Human Rights Clinic, April 2004).

[43] Matthew H. Amsher and Johan Lindquist, "Frontiers, Sovereignty, and Marital Tactics: Comparisons from the Borneo Highlands and the Indonesia-Malaysia-Singapore Growth Triangle," *Asia Pacific Journal of Anthropology* 6,1 (April 2005): 95.

More generally, the Indonesian external militarized campaigns against the Dutch in West New Guinea and the British in Malaya in the early-to-mid-1960s anticipated the role of the military in the final demise of Sukarno's embattled regime and the inauguration of Suharto's authoritarian New Order. As for Konfrontasi, the army leadership's initial support for Sukarno's campaign against British designs for a postcolonial Malaysia that would encompass Malaya and Singapore, as well as the British territories of Sarawak and North Borneo (Sabah), allowed for the militarization of this conflict in its earlier phase. Even as the Indonesian military leadership drew back from the brink of a full-scale confrontation against Britain and Malaysia, who enjoyed US diplomatic support, the situation "provided army leaders with powerful arguments for deferring proposed cuts in Indonesia's military budget and for restoring as much as possible their partially lapsed access to martial law" at home.[44] At the same time, with Suharto as the deputy commander of the (late) Malaysia campaign and commander of Kostrad, Konfrontasi also provided the occasion for secret contacts among "a few of Suharto's top aides [and] British, Malaysian, and possibly American intelligence," who shared a growing concern about Sukarno and, in particular, his alliance with the Indonesian Communist Party (Partai Komunis Indonesia, PKI).[45]

COUNTER-REVOLUTION AND DISPLACEMENT

Militarized conflict, violence, and displacement in the (re)production of territorial state borders and sacred national space at the frontiers of postcolonial Indonesia in the 1960s also anticipated the final restoration of the state over and against society, through a military putsch at the center of power in Jakarta and the ensuing massacres of hundreds of thousands, or perhaps a million or more, alleged PKI affiliates and sympathizers across the densely populated agricultural heartlands of Indonesia. Critical scholarship has challenged the official narratives of the 1965 coup and 1965–66 killings at least since the circulation of the so-called "Cornell Paper" in a contested sub-field of inquiry in modern Indonesian studies.[46] However, the stories of the hundreds of thousands who survived, and those of their families and friends, colleagues, and comrades, have remained, in no small measure, inscribed within the political and social erasure effected by the administration of their de facto internal displacement from the body politic. Such displacement ranged from detention and imprisonment (with or without trial) in prisons and concentration camps, to designation as an "ET" (*Eks Tahanan-politik*, ex-*tapols*, "ex-political prisoner") lacking many basic civil rights, to other forms of dislocation from state and society. In the wider context of the Cold War, and in the absence of the kind of "regional conflict" dynamics and refugee movements, camps, and warriors spilling across nation-state boundaries that emerged elsewhere, governments in the region and beyond showed scant concern for the large-scale and myriad forms of

---

[44] Kahin and Kahin, *Subversion as Foreign Policy*, p. 222.

[45] Ibid., p. 223. See also Dewi Fortuna Anwar, *Indonesia in ASEAN: Foreign Policy and Regionalism* (London: Palgrave MacMillan, 1994).

[46] Benedict Anderson and Ruth McVey, *A Preliminary Analysis of the October 1, 1965, Coup in Indonesia* (Ithaca, NY: Cornell Modern Indonesia Project, 1971). For the most recent contribution to such scholarship, see John Roosa, *Pretext for Mass Murder: The September 30th Movement and Suharto's Coup d'Etat in Indonesia* (Madison, WI: University of Wisconsin Press, 2006).

displacement visited upon Indonesian citizens and society writ large in the aftermath of 1965–66. This state of "internal" and "international" affairs only changed somewhat as the—near-genocidal and unlawful—Indonesian invasion of East Timor in 1975 served to refocus international criticism of Suharto and the New Order in the name of universal human rights and the rule of law.

In 1975, official government figures indicating the number of Indonesian detainees ranged from 600,000 to 750,000, and Amnesty International estimated that some 55,000 to 100,000 *tapols* remained in detention without trial.[47] These figures do not include the many people—"how many will never be known"—who "died from torture, other forms of deliberate or arbitrary violence, hunger, or brutal over-work" in the first decade after the coup.[48] While the conditions to which detainees were subjected during their confinement in prisons and concentration camps have been documented in some detail,[49] perhaps the most powerful reminder of the very existence, as well as the irrepressible humanity, of those thus displaced is the extraordinary figure of the late Pramoedya Ananta Toer, author of *The Buru Quartet*, named after the notorious penal colony where he was confined to internal exile and forced labor under the New Order.[50]

While the Indonesian government introduced a "phased release programme" of untried political prisoners in 1977, and announced that all such *tapols* had been released by 1979, former political prisoners, or ETs, continued to face "severe institutionalized repression and victimization."[51] Indeed, hundreds of thousands of Indonesians who found themselves formally labeled as ET and subjected to the elaborate categorization of (former) charges and associated hierarchy of "graduated citizenship" were denied freedom of movement, association, expression, and/or access to employment in certain sectors upon their release, the government's official designation for release from prison—"return to society"—notwithstanding. Further compounding the banality of evil thus introduced through the bureaucratic machinery of the New Order state were the permutations over time in "the scope of vigilance, diffusion of procedure, and unstable clearance status." Such practices generated an increase in the number of actual and potential victims well into the 1990s, including through the "social contagion" visited on the family and friends, employees and students, of any ETs and the reinstatement of previously "cleared" or "rehabilitated" individuals as suspects.[52]

---

[47] Amnesty International, *Indonesia: An Amnesty International Report* (London: Amnesty International Publications, 1977), pp. 21, 41–44. The figure of 750,000 jailed or sent to concentration camps is attributed to General Sudarmo, head of Suharto's Kopkamtib, by Amnesty International General Secretary Martin Ennal, in *The New York Review of Books*, February 9, 1978, p. 44, cited in Kahin and Kahin, *Subversion as Foreign Policy*, p. 228. Amnesty International put the figure at one million in detention at the time.

[48] Julie Southwood and Patrick Flanagan, *Indonesia: Law, Propaganda, and Terror* (London: Zed Books, 1973), pp. 2–3.

[49] Hamish McDonald, *Suharto's Indonesia* (Honolulu, HI: University of Hawai'i Press, 1981), pp. 216–33.

[50] As noted by Joesoef Isak in the Epilogue to *The Mute Soliloquy*, Pramoedya was among the first to arrive on Buru after 1965 and also among the very last to be released from detention on this arid eastern Indonesian island some fourteen years later.

[51] Southwood and Flanagan, *Indonesia*, p. 3 and, see further, pp. 100–120.

[52] Ariel Heryanto, *State Terrorism and Political Identity in Indonesia: Fatally Belonging* (London: Routledge, 2006), p. 19.

Unsurprisingly, this formal bureaucratic machinery also produced certain effects that, while not officially endorsed by the New Order government, nonetheless served to reflect and reproduce its peculiar regime of internal displacement from the body politic through myriad informal arrangements with the powers that be and everyday survival strategies of "ex-*tapols*" or other "Others." On the one hand, ETs "regularly became convenient targets for further scapegoating and blackmailing,"[53] practices that continued, "especially at the lower levels of state administration and in areas away from the capital city,"[54] even after the government, in 1995, revoked the decree requiring village heads and local administrative officials to stamp ET on the identity cards of (former) political prisoners. On the other hand, there were also those who went underground, "changing their names and appearances, calling clandestinely on friends, often spending long periods as *gelandangan* [wandering, homeless people]."[55]

In the years following the 1965 coup and counter-coup, the Indonesian military underwent a massive "restructuring" under Suharto, which also served to reflect and reproduce the reordering of—authoritarian, centralized—state power under the New Order. In his efforts to consolidate control over the military, Suharto initiated purges within the army, and moved to curtail the autonomy of the air force, navy, and police. By the end of 1969, this process culminated in the "final integration of the armed forces under one single command," with every commanding officer in each of the four services appointed only after 1966.[56]

Not unlike previous rounds of consolidation and centralization of the armed forces in the 1950s, the developments identified above proceeded in the larger context of intensified military activity focused on the "internal security" of the state, and against the "enemy within."[57] If the suppression of regional armed rebellions had previously contributed to strengthening central control of the army, however, the massacres of hundreds of thousands—perhaps more than a million—(alleged) members or sympathizers of the (then legal) PKI and its affiliate mass organizations in a few short months in 1965 and 1966 served as the foundational violence for an entire authoritarian regime characterized by high centralization of state powers and deep militarization of politics and society.[58] In this vein, it is perhaps unsurprising that the very organization set up by Suharto in October 1965 to "direct the

---

[53] Ibid., p. 17. See also Brian May, *The Indonesian Tragedy* (London: Routledge, 1978), pp. 27–40.

[54] Ibid., p. 36.

[55] Robert Cribb, "Problems in the Historiography of the Killings in Indonesia," in *The Indonesian Killings of 1965–1966: Studies from Java and Bali*, ed. Robert Cribb (Clayton: Centre of Southeast Asian Studies, Monash University, 1990), p. 43.

[56] Harold Crouch, *The Army and Politics in Indonesia* (Ithaca, NY: Cornell University Press, 1978 [1988 ed.]) p. 306.

[57] On the political rivalry between the Indonesian army high command and the PKI, see McVey, "The Post-Revolutionary Transformation of the Indonesian Army," Parts I and II; Ulf Sundhaussen, *The Road to Power: Indonesian Military Politics 1945–1967* (Kuala Lumpur: Oxford University Press, 1982); and Crouch, *The Army and Politics in Indonesia*.

[58] On the role of the military in the massacres, see, for example, Geoffrey Robinson's important study of Bali, which shows that "the massacres started after and because elements of the state itself—particularly the local and national military commands—in alliance with powerful civilian political forces and with the support of key international actors, consciously sanctioned and encouraged the annihilation of a substantial segment of the population." *Dark Side of Paradise: Political Violence in Bali* (Ithaca, NY: Cornell University Press, 1995), p. 303.

obliteration of the PKI," Kopkamtib (Komando Operasi Pemulihan Keamanan dan Ketertiban, Command for the Restoration of Security and Order), emerged as the "central locus of power within the armed forces" under the New Order.[59] The New Order regime also saw the wider proliferation and institutionalization of domestic political surveillance and "special operations" in Indonesian politics and society, thus further strengthening the consolidation of state power.[60]

Secret Wars and Displacement

An extension of the anti-communist pogroms of 1965–1966, Indonesia's "unknown war" in West Kalimantan (1967–1973) also served as a dress rehearsal for the brutal invasion and occupation of East Timor in 1975 by the Indonesian military, with forced displacement and displaced populations emerging as new prospects for statecraft, of a kind.[61] Having declared West Kalimantan an "Operations Area" (Daerah Operasi) in August 1967, the military increased its presence and activities, including the deployment of a range of "counterinsurgency" tactics and strategies that would be employed again in subsequent Indonesian militarized campaigns. The significance of this war as a formative experience of irregular warfare for the (new) armed forces, and, more generally, for the state of emergency at the core of the New Order, is suggested by the fact that "[m]any of the army units, commissioned officers, and even tactics (such as the 'fence of legs') originally employed in West Kalimantan were to play a major role in East Timor."[62]

The war in West Kalimantan also involved the production and management of refugees, including the deliberate targeting of civilian populations for "relocation" and the "screening" of refugee camps for suspected rebels, practices that have since seen further elaboration as part of counterinsurgency campaigns in other military "operations areas." In the case of West Kalimantan, an estimated "100,000 ethnic Chinese were relocated from the rural interior to coastal cities and towns," some reportedly fleeing "under heavy duress, some of their own accord, while others were 'escorted' by the military."[63] With the military thus directly involved in the monitoring and transportation of displaced populations, local politicians also strove to establish influence in the governing of camps and reportedly "used disturbances in the camps caused by the arrival of supplies as an excuse to expel relief workers."[64]

---

[59] Anderson, "Old State, New Society," p. 119. Kopkamtib's dissolution in 1988 mirrored the decline of its commander at the time, Benny Murdani, the New Order's intelligence czar and Suharto's right-hand man until his fall from grace.

[60] For a useful overview, see Richard Tanter, "The Totalitarian Ambition: Intelligence Organisations in the Indonesian State," in *State and Civil Society in Indonesia*, ed. Arief Budiman (Clayton, Victoria: Monash University, Centre of Southeast Asian Studies, 1990), pp. 215–88.

[61] See Jamie Davidson and Douglas Kammen, "Indonesia's Unknown War and the Lineages of Violence in West Kalimantan," *Indonesia* 73 (April 2002): 55–87.

[62] Ibid., p. 86.

[63] Ibid., pp. 75 and 72. As remarked by Davidson and Kammen, "some Javanese, Malay, and Madurese also fled in fear, but soon returned to their homes or occupied Chinese land." Ibid., p. 72. They also note that Pontianak and Singkawang were major destinations for refugees from the interior, while the towns of Mempawak, Sambas, and Pemangkat received smaller numbers of forcibly displaced populations.

[64] Ibid., p. 74.

Against the backdrop of the 1960s military campaigns on Indonesia's postcolonial frontiers, the 1975 invasion of East Timor marked further developments in the nature and extent of conflict, violence, and displacement. There is evidence that, in the months leading up to the invasion, the government in Jakarta and the Indonesian military on the ground in West Timor, across the internationally recognized border with East Timor, engaged in a combination of public and covert strategies to draw thousands of refugees—whether as "political pawns" or "refugee warriors"—into the orbit of the New Order's influence as it sought to push beyond its established territorial boundaries.[65] In the wider regional context of the Cold War, the well-publicized information campaign to focus international attention on the refugees who were crossing the border into West Timor, where, according to Jakarta, "humanitarian relief" was provided at government expense, bore the unmistakable imprint of military intelligence and special operations. Indeed, the invasion followed the rise of military intelligence and special operations units, which gained influence during the consolidation of Suharto's grip on state power, and was preceded by a campaign of sorts from within the State Intelligence Coordinating Body, or Bakin (Baden Koordinasi Intelijen Negara) and Special Operations, or Opsus (Operasi Khusus), under Brig. Gen. Ali Murtopo, Suharto's closest political advisor at the time.[66]

As noted above, the Indonesian military invasion and subsequent occupation of East Timor relied on men and methods previously deployed in special operations and counterinsurgency warfare elsewhere, while also benefiting from the unprecedented and largely US-supplied addition of new military equipment and weaponry, to near-genocidal effect, at times and in places. In the aftermath of the brutal invasion, which saw tens of thousands fleeing towns and coastal villages for the mountains of the interior, some 40,000 combat troops were deployed in the Indonesian military campaign of "encirclement and annihilation" (1977–1979), which involved massive destruction to property, livestock, and livelihoods, and, deaths. According to contemporary local knowledge, "the more refugees, the more corpses."[67] With the number of dead estimated at 100,000 during this period, some 300,000 people displaced by fighting were also forcibly relocated upon surrender to the Indonesian security forces into so-called "transit camps" and "resettlement areas," akin to the "strategic hamlets" used by British forces in Malaya and by US forces in Vietnam. The Indonesian military had also developed the practice of forcible recruitment to form the dreaded "fence of legs," human chains in the line of fire, "forced to walk in front of units of soldiers, searching the countryside for

---

[65] See further Geoffrey Robinson, "People Power: A Comparative History of Forced Displacement in East Timor," this volume. Robinson also discusses the concurrent covert strategy to recruit East Timorese refugees in the camps for military training and subsequent deployment alongside Indonesian armed forces crossing the border into East Timor. Ibid. See also Damien Kingsbury, *Power Politics and the Indonesian Military* (London: RoutledgeCurzon, 2003), p. 95.

[66] Taylor, *Indonesia's Forgotten War*, p. 23. Opsus studies outlined the military's concern that Portuguese Timor posed a "security threat" and, thus, its preference for "incorporating" the territory with Indonesia. Ibid. See also James S. Dunn, *Timor: A People Betrayed* (Queensland: Jacaranda Press, 1983), p. 106.

[67] From interviews by Fr. P. Walsh, Jakarta, March 15, 1982 (Australian Council for Overseas Aid), cited in John Taylor, *Indonesia's Forgotten War*, p. 92.

Fretilin cadres."[68] As Indonesia sought to "normalize" its occupation, moreover, the countervailing dynamics of demilitarizing administration and legal rule, on the one hand, and militarizing East Timorese society, on the other hand, produced further rounds of conflict, violence, and displacement in a pattern that anticipated the relentless campaign of destruction unleashed during the year of the referendum in 1999.[69]

The (Old) New Order and Displacement

If the first two decades of the New Order saw increasing autonomy and assertiveness of the state qua state vis-à-vis society in Indonesia, the limits of this process had been reached by the late 1980s. This change was perhaps most apparent in the growing tensions between the military-as-institution, on the one hand, and the personal interests of Suharto and his family, on the other hand, with his children emerging as key figures shaping the Indonesian economy and colonizing the state. It was also evident more broadly in the "rise of capital" and the increasing subordination of the state—including its coercive apparatus—to the exigencies of economic growth and the interests of an entrenched oligarchy.[70] Thus, by the 1990s the role of the security forces no longer resembled that of a "ruling caste," as it were, but instead increasingly involved commanding officers and their men across Indonesia in such activities as safe-guarding large-scale manufacturing plants[71] and capital-intensive installations for natural resource extraction,[72] as well as serving as a "praetorian guard" of sorts for Suharto and his family. Indeed, during the "mature" New Order period, regional territorial military commands (Kodam) were immersed within complex local political economies across Indonesia, and elite strategic and special forces (Kostrad and Kopassus and, eventually, "integrated forces") were dispatched beyond Java for purposes of related "trouble-shooting," not least in zones of "special operations."

---

[68] Ibid., p. 117.

[69] This dynamic is demonstrated by Douglas Kammen, "The Trouble with Normal: The Indonesian Military, Paramilitaries, and the Final Solution in East Timor," in *Violence and the State in Suharto's Indonesia*, ed. Benedict R. O'G. Anderson (Ithaca, NY: Cornell Southeast Asia Program Publications, 2001), pp. 156–88. For an analysis of the dynamics of displacement during this period, see especially Robinson, "People Power: A Comparative History of Forced Displacement in East Timor," this volume. For essays of related interest, see Peter Carey, "Third-World Colonialism, the Geraçâo Foun, and the Birth of a New Nation: Indonesia through East Timorese Eyes, 1975–99," *Indonesia* 76 (October 2003): 23–67; and Amanda Wise, "Nation, Transnation, Diaspora: Locating East Timorese Long-Distance Nationalism," *Sojourn* 19,2 (2004): 151–80.

[70] See, for example, Richard Robison, *The Rise of Capital* (Sydney: Allen & Unwin, 1986), and also Robison and Vedi Hadiz, *Reorganizing Power in Indonesia: The Politics of Oligarchy in an Age of Markets* (London: RoutledgeCurzon, 2004).

[71] See especially Douglas Kammen, "A Time to Strike: Industrial Relations and Changing Class Relations in New Order Indonesia" (PhD dissertation, Cornell University, 1997).

[72] On Papua, see especially Leith, *The Politics of Power*; on Aceh, see especially Dayan Dawood and Sjafrizal, "Aceh: The LNG Boom and Enclave Development," in *Unity and Diversity: Regional Economic Development in Indonesia since 1970*, ed. Hal Hill (Singapore: Oxford University Press, 1989), pp. 107–23; and Tim Kell, *The Roots of Acehnese Rebellion, 1989–1992* (Ithaca, NY: Cornell Modern Indonesia Project, 1995), pp. 13–21.

Against this backdrop, as the role and significance of the security forces shifted under the maturing New Order regime, the late 1980s and early 1990s witnessed a final phase of conflict, violence, and displacement, most notably in Aceh, which emerged, alongside Papua and East Timor, as yet another officially designated "trouble spot" (*daerah rawan)*, and the target of massive military operations.[73] The resurfacing of a comparatively "miniscule" armed rebel movement, Aceh Merdeka, in 1989 triggered a massive response: the mobilization of some six thousand territorial forces for counterinsurgency operations through 1989 and the first half of 1990, and the subsequent deployment of an additional six thousand troops, including two battalions of Kopassus and other elite counterinsurgency units.[74] This substantial deployment of security forces anticipated "intensive surveillance, check points, dawn to dusk curfews, house raids, and arrests on a wide scale," as well as the further elaboration of methods employed elsewhere, such as the "fence of legs," "sweepings," and "mysterious killings."[75] Indeed, as argued by Geoffrey Robinson, "the regime's counterinsurgency repertoire had expanded considerably [and t]he availability of these techniques meant that a type of systematic terror was possible in the early 1990s that would have been difficult to institute in the late 1970s," when Aceh Merdeka first emerged.[76]

This proscribed "shock therapy" treatment for the second uprising served to produce many more refugees compared to the first rebellion (1976–1979), when displacement was largely confined to leading figures in the rebel movement (including Hasan di Tiro, who sought refuge in Sweden in 1979), along with supporters who escaped into exile in Malaysia. At the height of military sweeping operations in 1990, for example, "waves of young men from the affected villages made their way, mostly to the Klang Valley."[77] In 1991 and 1992, there were also reports of hundreds of Acehnese fleeing by boat across the Malacca Straits to Malaysia, where many were detained as illegal immigrants, and some were returned to Indonesia in violation of the principle of non-refoulement.[78] In June 1992, moreover, "forty-three Acehnese asylum-seekers entered the premises of the United

---

[73] See especially Geoffrey Robinson, "*Rawan* Is as *Rawan* Does: The Origins of Disorder in New Order Aceh," in *Violence and the State in Suharto's Indonesia*, pp. 213–42.

[74] Amnesty International, *Shock Therapy: Restoring Order in Aceh, 1989–1993* (London: Amnesty International, 1993). On the emergence of Aceh Merdeka in 1976, see Nazaruddin Sjamsuddin, "Issues and Politics of Regionalism in Indonesia: Evaluating the Acehnese Experience," in *Armed Separatism in Southeast Asia*, ed. Lim Joo-Jock with Vani S. (Singapore: ISEAS, 1984), pp. 111–28. For a more recent account of the introduction of the military operations code-named "Jaring Merah," or Red Net, and remembered in Aceh as "DOM" (Daerah Operasi Militer), see also Rizal Sukma, *Security Operations in Aceh: Goals, Consequences, and Lessons,* Policy Studies 3 (Washington, DC: East-West Center, Washington, 2004), pp. 8–11.

[75] Amnesty International, *Shock Therapy.*

[76] Robinson, "*Rawan* Is as *Rawan* Does," p. 232. Aceh Merdeka has become more widely known as GAM (Gerakan Aceh Merdeka, Free Aceh Movement).

[77] Diana Wong and Teuku Afrisal, "Political Violence and Migration: Recent Acehnese Migration to Malaysia," in *Three Papers on Indonesia and Displacement* (Jakarta: Ford Foundation, June 2002), p. 61.

[78] Malaysia is not a signatory to the 1951 Convention on Refugees or the 1967 Protocol, and makes no legal distinction between refugees and "illegal migrants." Regardless, the involuntary return of a person to a country where they remain at risk constitutes a violation of a norm of general international law, which is binding on all states.

Nations High Commissioner for Refugees in Kuala Lumpur asking for protection."[79] In 1994, the intensification of military operations prompted another surge in the forced displacement from Aceh and "forced GAM fighters themselves to flee, many of them with their families, to the Klang Valley."[80]

If the dynamics of military operations had profound effects in Aceh, they also exemplified a broader trend in the unfolding of conflict, violence, and displacement during the late New Order. This trend reflected the deepening rift between, on the one hand, Suharto and his Palace circle, and, on the other, senior active army officers "led by their doyen, General B. L. ('Benny') Murdani."[81] With the onset of Murdani's political decline in 1988, the Palace and its supporters moved to reassert central control over various "local mafias" of "lower- and middle-ranking, usually middle-aged, military personnel [who had enjoyed] the opportunity to build powerful long-term local bases in the regions, first as representatives of the Center, later as real-estate speculators, fixers, commission-agents, local monopolists, and racketeers."[82]

In the wider context of this process of "de-Benny-isasi" of the Indonesian military, the reordering of security forces and operations against such local mafias—ostensibly carried out to reassert central state control—also engendered distinct dynamics of conflict, violence, and displacement. In the case of Aceh, as argued by Robinson, the reemergence of an armed rebel movement and the massive military response were "stimulated by a conflict between the central military command and regional and police authorities"—a conflict that saw Regional Military Commander Major General Joko Pramono replaced and troops under his command dismissed on disciplinary grounds in the context of a centrally coordinated anti-narcotics campaign in 1989.[83] In East Timor, it has been suggested, one of the elements behind the Santa Cruz massacre in November 1991 was also such a local mafia, which had become the target of yet another centrally directed "clean-up" campaign, in this case involving disciplinary action against some three hundred military personnel by Regional Military Commander Brig. Gen. Rudolf Samuel Warouw in the comparatively brief period since his appointment in December 1989.[84] In Papua, the 1988 discovery of the world's richest copper-gold deposits in the Grasberg region had served to focus increasing military attention on the new economic opportunities in the Freeport area with "[c]ompeting business interests, legal and illegal, operated by … different units" of Kopassus, Kostrad, the Regional Trikora Military Command, and the elite paramilitary Police Mobile Brigade (Brimob), prompting "frequent

---

[79] Amnesty International, *Shock Therapy*.

[80] Wong and Afrisal, "Political Violence and Migration," p. 61.

[81] The Editors, "Current Data on the Indonesian Military Elite, *Indonesia* 48 (October 1989): 65–96.

[82] The Editors, "Current Data on the Indonesian Military Elite, July 1, 1989–January 1, 1992," *Indonesia* 53 (April 1992): 98.

[83] Robinson, "*Rawan* Is as *Rawan* Does," p. 235.

[84] The Editors, "Current Data on the Indonesian Military Elite, July 1, 1989–January 1, 1992," p. 98. As noted by The Editors, this campaign eventually achieved "a complete, massive purge of virtually all influential officers in the East Timor apparatus, at the Korem level, and within Dili itself, striking right at the heart of the mafia in a manner that had never been previously undertaken." Ibid., p. 100. Kammen also notes that the early 1990s saw "new central controls over combat troops posted in East Timor." Kammen, "The Trouble with Normal," p. 163.

clashes among them," but also, as of 1991–1992, "a more coordinated campaign of arrest, torture, and disappearances."[85]

Aside from the issue of "protection" and other predatory practices involving the security forces (which have remained enduring, if variable, features of the Indonesian economy), it has been argued that distinct changes to military doctrine and practice under the late New Order involved "the institutionalization of terror" and "the systematic and forced mobilization of civilians to serve as auxiliaries and spies in counterinsurgency operations."[86] These methods had far-reaching effects on the levels of violence and dislocation in society during this period of wider social mobilization across the Indonesian archipelago.[87] If forced displacement of local populations emerged as an integral aspect of such operations, the social landscapes thus targeted also emerged as sites for the strategic placement and public display of "bodies, parts of bodies, and the signs of bodies."[88] Commenting on Suharto's designation of such practices as "shock therapy" in reference to the so-called "Petrus" killings in major cities across Java in the mid-1980s, James Siegel has pointed out that this "therapy"—"to shock in order to cure"—was "directed not at criminals, but *at the general populace*."[89]

> The dead person was a notice posted to others. He was the essential element of Suharto's "shock therapy." His dead body displayed in public turned him into a messenger for his killers. The corpse was endowed with "death," which means the capacity to transmit "trauma" and to create "shock" ... The Petrus corpses, made into warnings, spoke; *but they spoke for the government*.[90]

Inasmuch as some of the methods that gained Indonesian security forces such notoriety during the late New Order recalled the Petrus killings, they suggest a similar drive towards the "deterritorialization of the power associated with

---

[85] Chris Ballard, "The Signature of Terror: Violence, Memory, and Landscape at Freeport," in *Inscribed Landscapes: Marking and Making Place*, ed. Bruno David and Meredith Wilson (Honolulu, HI: University of Hawai'i Press, 2002), p. 16. During this period, military operations in the Central Highlands also expanded, anticipating recurring cycles of conflict, violence, and displacement that would persist into the present era. See Richard Chauvel, "Refuge, Displacement, and Dispossession: Responses to Indonesian Rule and Conflict in Papua," this volume.

[86] Robinson, "*Rawan* Is as *Rawan* Does," p. 226. See also Tanter "The Totalitarian Ambition." In reference to East Timor, Kammen notes that under Prabowo's command, which began in 1993, the Special Forces "Group 3" "quickly became the new nerve center of ... a campaign that was losing even the most rudimentary trappings of a combat mission and was taking on the characteristics of a simple reign of terror." See Kammen, "The Trouble with Normal," pp. 166–67.

[87] See, for example, Adam Schwarz, *A Nation in Waiting: Indonesia in the 1990s*, rev. edition (Sydney: Allen & Unwin, 1999).

[88] Ballard, "The Signature of Terror," p. 16.

[89] James T. Siegel, *A New Criminal Type in Jakarta: Counter-Revolution Today* (Durham, NC: Duke University Press, 1998), p. 110, emphasis added. As noted by Siegel, the first edition of Suharto's *Autobiography* contained discussions of Petrus that have been excised from subsequent editions.

[90] Ibid., pp. 111–12, emphasis added.

'criminals' … and territorial communities, and its reterritorialization within the state."[91]

If the simultaneous (dis)appearance of bodies, in life and death, served to produce a strategic and symbolic transfer of power upward, toward the center of the late New Order regime, such a process was neither seamless on the contested grounds of "special operations areas,"[92] nor "functional" for the military as an institution. Indeed, the proliferation of such methods in the contested outer regions coincided with the ascent of Kopassus, which expanded exponentially from four thousand to seven thousand troops under Prabowo's command after 1995, and which filled the top echelons of the late New Order security apparatus with key appointments under Gen. Feisal Tanjung's tenure as commander of the Indonesian Armed Forces.[93] At a time when Suharto appeared to have weathered the economic crisis and political transition of early 1998, it was with the apparent instigation and orchestration of Lieutenant Gen. Prabowo, as newly appointed Commander of Kostrad, and his allies (including a close associate who was succeeding him to command Kopassus, and another, Maj. Gen. Sjafrie Sjamsoeddin, in charge of the Greater Jakarta Regional Command [Kodam Jaya]), that the rioting and the rapes unfolded in Jakarta, Solo, and a few other cities in mid-May of the same year.[94]

> Together with Jakarta-based *preman* and several hundred civilians brought in from as far afield as East Timor and Irian Jaya, these forces were then mobilized on May 12 and assigned targets for "riot" activities, including rapes of "Chinese" women. The military operation, under the rubric of a Gerakan 12 Mei Orde Baru (May 12 New Order Movement), was apparently intended to justify a harsh military crackdown in Jakarta and to precipitate both the immediate dismissal of [Armed Forces Commander] Wiranto and the elevation of Prabowo and his allies to the top command posts in the armed forces.[95]

Instead, the military stood aside, and Suharto stepped down, but not before some 150,000 residents (mostly Chinese Indonesians and Western expatriates) fled the country, mostly by airplane to nearby Singapore or Hong Kong, leaving behind some one thousand dead, and many others who had suffered beatings, rapes, and other

---

[91] Joshua Barker, "State of Fear: Controlling the Criminal Contagion in Suharto's New Order," in *Violence and the State in Suharto's Indonesia,* pp. 52–53.

[92] On such symbolic failures, see, for example, Ballard, "The Signature of Terror," and Nils Bubandt's exploration of "Ghosts with Trauma," this volume.

[93] See, for example, "Tergusurnya Para Jagoan Tempur," and related articles focused on Kopassus in *Tempo,* April 15–21, 2002. For a detailed account of Prabowo's reassignment from his East Timor posting to command the Special Forces Education Center in West Java, an appointment that involved overseeing the training of such troops for use in East Timor and Aceh, see Kammen, "The Trouble with Normal," p. 166.

[94] John Sidel, *Riots, Pogroms, Jihad: Religious Violence in Indonesia* (Ithaca, NY: Cornell University Press, 2006), p. 126. Citing the Jakarta weekly magazine *Tajuk,* Sidel recounts how "troops from Kopassus, Kostrad, and Kodam Jaya … had been assembled as early as March 1998 and readied for undercover operations by Prabowo and Sjafrie Sjamsoeddin. Ibid., p. 122.

[95] Ibid., p. 122. On May 12, 1998, there were shootings at Trisakti University that killed four students, and on May 13–15 the riots in Jakarta unfolded.

violations and massive destruction to property through burning, looting, and wreckage.[96]

As suggested above, the unfolding of militarized conflict, violence, and displacement during the late New Order had thus arrived at the center of power in Jakarta. With the 1990s witnessing increasing pressures on the state, new dynamics of intra-military rivalries had anticipated myriad forms of conflict, notably in areas designated for "special operations," such as East Timor, Aceh and, increasingly, Papua. As a result of intensified militarized counterinsurgency campaigns in such areas, an expanding and increasingly institutionalized "repertoire of terror" became available for emulation and adaptation elsewhere, as evident in the May riots in Jakarta and other major cities. Not unlike earlier rounds in the contested history of state- and nation-formation in Indonesia, the end of the New Order regime under Suharto in May 1998, and, indeed, the wider transition from authoritarian rule in subsequent years, was accompanied by considerable displacement, the dynamics and experiences of which will be explored in the chapters to follow.

Conflict, Violence, and Displacement after Suharto

The essays in this volume, individually and together, offer critical insights into the politics and experiences of displacement in post-Suharto Indonesia. Written by scholars whose research on Indonesian politics and society in many cases dates back to the New Order, these essays underscore the importance of interdisciplinary area studies for capturing a deeper sense of place in the—contested—geo-body of the nation, and, significantly, for highlighting the significance of dis-place-ment in the body politic. The volume also shows how different disciplinary perspectives, including comparative politics, history, sociology, and anthropology, can contribute to the generation of new research into and analysis of the dynamics and experiences of conflict, violence, and displacement in Indonesia and beyond.

In the first chapter, John Sidel revisits the inter-religious pogroms of 1999–2001 in Central Sulawesi, Maluku, and Maluku Utara, which left thousands dead, as well as hundreds of thousands internally displaced. Indeed, as Sidel shows, these pogroms were, in crucial ways, about displacement. Most obviously, the centrality of forced migration as an objective in these pogroms is evident in the strategies and outcomes of the violence. More subtly and yet critically important, Sidel argues, these pogroms were also about the displacement of internal anxieties regarding religious identities onto "others" in a dynamic that served to enable and impel the forced migration of people on such a massive scale. Beyond the concern with "psychosocial trauma and intervention" evident in the literature on forced migration, this chapter thus prompts further reflection upon the nature of subjectivity itself, and the attempts at restoration of "self" and "place" through violence in situations of changing social imaginaries and geographies.

In illuminating contrast to Sidel's focus upon the displacement of anxieties about religious identities, Jamie Davidson shows how the large-scale 1997 and 1999 violence and displacement in West Kalimantan emerged in the wider context of

---

[96] See Sidel, *Riots, Pogroms, Jihad*, pp. 121–25. See also James T. Siegel, "Thoughts on the Violence of May 13 and 14, 1998, in Jakarta," in *Violence and the State in Suharto's Indonesia*, pp. 90–123; and Jemma Purdey, *Anti-Chinese Violence in Indonesia, 1996–1999* (Honolulu, HI: University of Hawai'i Press, 2006).

national processes for the reinvention and revitalization of ethnic identities in Indonesia. Davidson argues that Dayak-Madurese violence, once the unintended consequence of Indonesian military counterinsurgency operations in the 1960s, came to fuel future episodes of violence, wherein constructions about the adversarial "other" and notions of "us" versus "them" crystallized and deepened. He also shows how the unresolved refugee crisis in the wake of the 1999 riots lay at the core of the violence in 2001. Read against the existing literature on refugee camps as near "total institutions," or, alternately, as "security threats," this chapter offers useful insights into the complex dynamics of political exclusion and social embeddedness shaping IDP camps and their residents' relations with locally franchised national citizens and political economies.

The three chapters to follow return critical attention to the dynamics and patterns of displacement in East Timor, Aceh, and Papua. Turning to East Timor, Geoffrey Robinson identifies patterns of displacement during the two periods that mark the beginning and end of the Indonesian occupation—the invasion and early occupation in 1975 through 1979, and the year of the referendum, 1999. Through a structured comparison of the nature, direction, and scope of forced migration across these two periods, Robinson marshals compelling evidence to show that, far from an inevitable byproduct of war, displacement resulted from deliberate political strategies deployed by key actors. The Indonesian military authorities and their proxies were particularly prominent among such actors, but, Robinson notes, the dynamics of displacement also reflected the role of pro-Independence forces, as well as powerful states and institutions during these periods. This chapter also highlights the significance of historical experience and memory, as it shows how the forced migration of 1999 was, in important respects, shaped by previous rounds of displacement during the period of 1975–1979.

Edward Aspinall explores similar dynamics in Aceh during three rounds of displacement between 1999 and 2004. Upon closer examination, Aspinall argues, the massive but mostly localized wave of displacement during 1999 proves to be not merely a fearful, but also a strategic response to armed conflict by affected populations. The remaining two case studies in this chapter turn to an analysis of practices of deliberate displacement, including the targeting of Javanese migrants by GAM (Gerakan Aceh Merdeka, Free Aceh Movement), and the relocation of entire villages to detention camps by the Indonesian security forces during martial law in 2003 to 2004. This chapter also directs analytical attention to the contested meanings of place—as securitized versus sacred space—and their significance for dynamics of conflict, violence, and displacement.

In the final chapter to focus on wider patterns of displacement in areas that have suffered from protracted militarized conflict, Richard Chauvel examines responses to Indonesian rule and conflict in Papua. In a useful juxtaposition to the previous chapters on East Timor and Aceh, Chauvel argues that displacement—both internal displacement and forced migration across the border with Papua New Guinea—serves as a barometer of political tensions and of the intensity of military operations in Papua. Noting the massive demographic transformation since the 1960s, moreover, Chauvel underlines how a deeper sense of dispossession and marginalization has fueled conflict, violence, and displacement in Papua. This chapter also highlights the importance of the international community in shaping local social imaginaries of independence, or *merdeka*, with particular emphasis upon the role of the United Nations.

Together, the five chapters introduced above show alternative and, at times, overlapping approaches to investigating dynamics and patterns of conflict, violence, and displacement. The chapters that make up the first half of this volume, individually and together, demonstrate the importance of focusing scholarly research on the (contested) structures of power and (rival) institutions of authority shaping the broader parameters of such dynamics and patterns. To that end, these first five chapters reveal how theories and methods at the core of political science, here notably and productively informed by comparative historical sociology and area studies, add a critical dimension to the study of forced migration.

In distinct ways, the remaining chapters in this volume shift the focus of analysis to bring into sharper relief the lived experiences and contested memories of conflict, violence, and displacement. To varying degrees and extents, the chapters that follow thus show how the effects of the very structures, institutions, and dynamics examined in previous chapters, while powerful, are neither seamless nor immutable but rather develop in and through myriad encounters with "IDPs" and other "concerned parties" in contexts of actual existing displacement. Inspired by the practices and insights of "thick description" and, more generally, ethnography, many of these chapters confirm the importance of a critical engagement with anthropology for forced migration studies and, indeed, for policy formulation and humanitarian interventions concerned with displacement and the displaced.

Returning to Poso, Lorraine Aragon reconsiders narratives of displacement in the wake of what she refers to as "the civil violence" of 1998 to 2002. Against the grain of official government and humanitarian discourses on displacement, Aragon traces multiple meanings attributed locally to place, as well as competing claims concerning who really was "in place," and, thus, "displaced" or "returned home" during the violence. Such diverging points of view, Aragon argues, not only lie at the heart of the conflict, but also have far-reaching effects on the protracted, and often seemingly endless, transformations of conflict evident in Poso. This chapter thus underscores the wider significance of public discourses about the legitimate "place-ment" of refugees and their rights of "return" for the prospects of curtailing further violence, as well as improving accountability and positive resettlement solutions.

In the next chapter, Christopher Duncan examines issues and concerns shaping the experiences of internally displaced persons from North Maluku, and juxtaposes the perspectives of IDPs themselves against those of the government officials they encounter in displacement. An illuminating complement to Aragon's focus on alternative, multiple narratives of dis-place-ment, Duncan's chapter highlights the powerful effects of development discourse and, in particular, the "IDP category" on Indonesian government officials. Notwithstanding the countless "IDP" registrations and surveys, Duncan argues, government officials made little effort to look beyond this ready-made category, and, in North Sulawesi, showed scant interest in making the connection between the presence of IDPs in places of refuge and the end of conflict in North Maluku. This chapter also points to the deeper resonance of such official discourses in the deliberations of people who have been displaced, as they make choices and develop strategies for a future inscribed, albeit not seamlessly, within a larger politics that seeks to end displacement, whether through "return, resettlement, or reintegration."

Revisiting conflict and displacement in Central Kalimantan, Hélène Bouvier and Glenn Smith note "the silence of the victims"—who were, with few exceptions, Madurese—in the aftermath of the large-scale violence in 2001 that left between five hundred and several thousand dead, thousands injured, and more than 150,000 internally displaced persons. In a critical reexamination of the causes and consequences of such silence, Bouvier and Smith direct attention not merely to Dayak communities and the media in the circulation of stories stereotyping the Madurese as "a group armed to the teeth and on the verge of taking over Central Kalimantan," but, also, to the numerous officials, researchers, and reporters who, in their efforts to document the violence, showed scant interest in the voices and experiences of the Madurese. As this chapter shows, the discourses and silences that inscribed this violence had far-reaching consequences for government policy, including the evacuation of nearly all Madurese from Central Kalimantan rather than the promotion of protective safe havens, the coordination of peace conferences, and the decision against assisting IDPs' return to Kalimantan in 2004 and 2005. In addition, these discourses and silences also had an impact on non-governmental organizations working with displaced Madurese and seeking to promote reconciliation in Kalimantan. This chapter thus underscores the wider significance of the production of knowledge about conflict, violence, and displacement for government policy and humanitarian interventions.

My chapter refocuses attention on Aceh in the early aftermath of the December 26, 2004, tsunami, which left some 150,000 dead or missing, and an estimated half million people displaced from their homes. As the tsunami also served to rupture the virtual closure of Aceh to the outside world, which had been effected since the Indonesian government declared martial law in May 2003, the rapid proliferation of international humanitarian organizations and a *reformasi*-like flurry of volunteers from across Indonesia brought into sharp relief the ambiguities and contradictions inherent in policies and practices concerned with displaced persons in the context of a militarized conflict area turned disaster zone. Of broader relevance for situations of complex humanitarian emergency, the chapter thus shows how old habits of control and surveillance served to circumscribe the nature and direction of government and other interventions, while also pointing to the role of IDPs in contesting official displacement discourse through collective action.

In the final chapter, Nils Bubandt examines narratives of spiritual revenge and the politics of memory in the wake of conflict, violence, and displacement in North Maluku between 1999 and 2001. As the global therapeutic concept of trauma and the occult figure of *Drakula* gained circulation among returning IDPs and other locals in the aftermath of the violence, Bubandt argues, they were incorporated into prior understandings of spiritual revenge and, thus, ways of thinking about the past in North Maluku. In this vein, narratives about traumatized spirits emerged as positioned ways of speaking about violence, self, and social morality. That is, the concept of trauma was altered radically and, in the process, inscribed within a memory politics very different from the global psychosocial discourse within which the concept originated. Against the dissemination of "trauma" as an accepted diagnostic device on a world-wide scale evident in humanitarian and development discourse, this chapter thus points to a critical but often overlooked dynamic of local appropriation at work.

Regarding the study of Indonesian politics and society in recent years, this volume thus seeks to make several interventions. First of all, existing Indonesianist scholarship on conflict and violence during the New Order or thereafter has tended to focus attention on violence as the "dependent" variable, the thing to be explained, notably in reference to the state and its agents of coercion, including paramilitary and other forms of subcontracted violence. By comparison, the essays in this volume tend to foreground the dynamics and experiences of displacement, across time and territory, and, in the process, to illuminate the nature and direction of conflict and violence at the margins of (contested) sovereignty, thus offering further glimpses into "the state of exception as a paradigm of government."[97] Second, the wider circulation of political discourses on "ethnic conflict," "Islamist terrorism," and, even, "failed states" from a broader "global" perspective have anticipated the appearance of Indonesia as yet another "case" in writings about such phenomena at a particular juncture in world historical time. In contrast, the present volume's scope for (comparative) investigation remains confined to territorial boundaries inscribed within the same overarching political organization—the Indonesian state (albeit at various levels and forms of governmentality), while also allowing for critical scrutiny of the contestation over claims to sovereign power within this realm, thus allowing more nuance and depth of analysis. Third, the mobilization of a massive transnational "humanitarian" machinery, with its own considerable complex of national and international, governmental and non-governmental, resources, networks, and discourses, has propelled an entire industry focused on "conflict and violence in Indonesia," including the so-called mapping of conflict and violence, the search for conflict intervention mechanisms, and the design of peace and conflict resolution programs. Against such efforts, which are arguably reflective and reproductive of a more pervasive conflict/violence discourse "grounded in a set of institutions that promotes its persistence,"[98] this volume serves as a reminder that the very processes involved in the production of knowledge about displacement cannot, by definition, remain somehow outside or above politics.

---

[97] Giorgio Agamben, *State of Exception,* trans. Kevin Attell (Chicago, IL: University of Chicago Press, 2005), especially pp. 1–31.

[98] Paul Brass, *Theft of an Idol: Text and Context in the Representation of Collective Violence* (Princeton, NJ: Princeton University Press, 1997), p. 29.

THE MANIFOLD MEANINGS OF DISPLACEMENT: EXPLAINING INTER-RELIGIOUS VIOLENCE, 1999–2001

John T. Sidel

Over the course of 1999–2001, a pattern of inter-religious violence unfolded in the provinces of Central Sulawesi, Maluku, and Maluku Utara that caused hundreds, indeed thousands, of deaths, and created flows of internally displaced persons (IDPs) numbering well into the hundreds of thousands. As the author has argued elsewhere, these pogroms of 1999–2001 represented a decisive phase in the shifting pattern of religious violence observed in Indonesia, from religious riots in 1995–1997 to religious pogroms in 1998–2001, and what might be glossed as *jihad* from roughly 2000 to the present.[1] Viewed from this comparative perspective, the inter-religious pogroms in Central Sulawesi, Maluku, and Maluku Utara must be explained in terms of the particular timing, location, perpetrators, targets, forms, and processes of mobilization associated with this phase of religious violence in Indonesia. Viewed through a zoom lens focused on the pogroms themselves, moreover, the very pattern of their unfolding—from initial outbreak, escalation, and spread in 1999 to gradual de-escalation by the end of 2001—also calls for close examination and explanation.

This essay will argue that the inter-religious pogroms of 1999–2001 in Central Sulawesi, Maluku, and Maluku Utara are best explained through a focus on *displacement*, in at least two different senses of the term. First and most obviously, these pogroms were "about" displacement in the sense that they concerned displaced *people,* as seen in the centrality of forced migration among the objectives and outcomes of the violence. As many observers have noted, the expulsion of thousands of residents from their homes, neighborhoods, and villages in Central Sulawesi, Maluku, and Maluku Utara constituted the primary means by which the violence spread and achieved its broadest consequences. Perhaps the clearest and most well-chronicled example of this process of violent displacement is Maluku

---

[1] See: John T. Sidel, *Riots, Pogroms, Jihad: Religious Violence in Indonesia* (Ithaca, NY: Cornell University Press, 2006).

Utara, as discussed in this volume and elsewhere by Christopher Duncan, Nils Bubandt, and other scholars.

Second, and perhaps more subtly, these pogroms were "about" displacement in the sense of displacement as it was articulated by Sigmund Freud more than one hundred years ago and rendered commonplace in psychology and social theory: displaced *anxieties*, externalized and transferred or projected onto objects "centered elsewhere."[2] Most accounts of the inter-religious pogroms in Central Sulawesi, Maluku, and Maluku Utara stress the conditions—including migration—that heightened tensions *between* Christians and Muslims in these provinces in the late 1990s. But alongside these seemingly "external" sources of tension and fear were "internal" anxieties *among* Christians and Muslims, anxieties about the boundaries and hierarchies associated with religious identities in these parts of the Indonesian archipelago, identities haunted by what Arjun Appadurai has called the "anxiety of incompleteness."[3]

This essay is intended to reveal the connections between these two meanings of "displacement" and to show how the latter form of displacement enabled and impelled the former. To be sure, there are other meanings of displacement, most obviously if one considers the diverse phenomenological experiences of those involved in forced migration in and beyond Central Sulawesi, Maluku, and Maluku Utara from 1999 onwards. Such meanings remain largely unexamined in this essay, given the very real limitations of the author's access to and understanding of such experiences. Instead, drawing on available ethnographic, investigative, and journalistic sources, the following analysis offers a more structuralist—some might say post-structuralist—account of the double imperatives of displacement in the inter-religious pogroms in Central Sulawesi, Maluku, and Maluku Utara in 1999 to 2001.

BACKDROP: RELIGIOUS UNCERTAINTIES AND ANXIETIES

The backdrop to the violence in Central Sulawesi, Maluku, and Maluku Utara was, of course, the ongoing transition from authoritarian rule to an open, competitive electoral system, and all the uncertainties and anxieties accompanying this transition. As could be expected, the effects of the first installation of a new president in three decades in Jakarta were soon to trickle down to the cities, towns, and villages of the archipelago in terms of access to state power and patronage. With the removal of the certainty and the centralization of state power that characterized the Suharto era, and their replacement by a transitional form of government moving towards competitive elections and the deconcentration and decentralization of state power, the fixity of the very hierarchy connecting locality to Center was undermined, as were the boundaries of the jurisdictions governed by those asserting authority within this hierarchy.

Under the New Order, the circuitries of power connecting villages to towns to provincial cities to Jakarta were centrally wired in the national capital and coursed through the military, the civil service, Golkar, various pseudo-parliamentary bodies, and schools and universities. Competition for power and patronage within the

---

[2] Sigmund Freud, *The Interpretation of Dreams* (London: Wordsworth Editions, 1997), p. 190.

[3] Arjun Appadurai, *Fear of Small Numbers: An Essay on the Geography of Anger* (Durham, NC: Duke University Press, 2006), p. 8.

political class was thus confined and channeled—vertically, as it were—within the state's coercive and ideological apparatuses, as rival networks defined by educational and religious affiliations and identities fought for coveted appointed positions (e.g., military commands, governorships, seats in various pseudo-parliamentary bodies) and associated perks (e.g., construction contracts and criminal franchises). Against this backdrop, the demise of the New Order and the promise of competitive elections on the horizon carried significant implications. Instead of individuated competition channeled vertically and confined laterally within the state, various streams or currents (*aliran*) within the political class now found themselves competing—collectively and horizontally, as it were—not (only) in and for the state, but (also) in and for society. Thus the boundaries of identities and interests in Indonesian society, long determined by a fixed, hierarchical source of recognition firmly anchored in the state and centered in Jakarta, were left in flux.

The implications of this loosening and shifting of boundaries were evident in a variety of violent new conflicts. In some cases, these were boundaries over property and territory, as seen in countless seizures of land and fights over control of mines, forests, and coastal shorelines. In numerous other cases, the boundaries concerned were those of local criminal rackets, with rival gangs in Jakarta and other cities initiating *antar-kampung* (inter-neighborhood) skirmishes to determine the extent of their claims over "turf" under conditions of indeterminate or fluctuating franchise. More broadly, with the deconcentration of power in Jakarta and the move towards decentralization in the provinces, the very boundaries of administrative units came into question, with local politicians vying for some control over the subdivision (*pemekaran*) of countless villages, regencies, and provinces in the months and years after Suharto's fall from the presidency.

In many cases, contestation was framed in terms of the boundaries outlining collective identities—whether cast in terms of community, clan, ethnicity, or religious faith—whose fixity was no longer assured. Against this backdrop, it is hardly surprising that much of the "horizontal" violence that began to unfold in 1998–1999 assumed the form of specifically *religious* pogroms. As is well known, religious faith had long served in Indonesia as the primary marker of public identities insisted upon—and enforced by—the state, and as a key determinant of point of entry into the political class. Not only was the ascension to the presidency of B. J. Habibie, a politician closely identified with Islam, thus experienced beyond Jakarta in terms of religiously coded local repercussions for the distribution of state offices and patronage, but the turn towards open politics and competitive elections laid open the question of the very basis of claims to religious authority and state power. If under a centralized, closed, authoritarian regime claims of representation had been imposed and enforced from above, now under conditions of political openness and competition the hierarchies and boundaries of religious authority faced unprecedented uncertainties. As argued below, these uncertainties generated anxieties whose displacement impelled the inter-religious pogroms in parts of Central Sulawesi, Maluku, and Maluku Utara in 1999–2001.

While heightened uncertainties and anxieties about identities and hierarchies—both religious and otherwise—were common throughout Indonesia during this transitional period, their capacity to generate inter-religious pogroms in parts of Central Sulawesi, Maluku, and Maluku Utara was enhanced by at least three features of these settings. First of all, these pogroms occurred along the boundaries between the officially recognized faiths of Islam and Christianity, with Protestant churches claiming sizeable congregations in these localities and constituting important alternative structures of authority and access to state power relative to those provided by their Islamic counterparts. Second, compared to the more economically "developed" and diversified setting of Java, with its clearer division between (predominantly Chinese) business and government, in the poorer and more peripheral regions of Central Sulawesi, Maluku, and Maluku Utara, access to the agencies of the Indonesian state was much more important for the accumulation of capital, status, and wealth, and local "business" and "politics" more fully overlapped. Third and finally, these local constellations of religious authority and political economy combined with unsettling events—the approaching elections of 1999, decentralization, and the redrawing of administrative boundaries (*pemekaran*)— to create tremendous uncertainty and anxiety along the local borders *and within the local hierarchies* of religious faith, not only among Islamic and Christian ecclesiastical establishments, but also among rival Muslim and Protestant networks of local politicians, businessmen, gangsters, civil servants, and (active and retired) military and police officers. These uncertainties and anxieties were not simply *inter*-religious in nature, but *intra*-religious as well. Indeed, as suggested in the analysis below, it was the displacement of anxieties essentially intrinsic and internal to religious identities and hierarchies onto ostensibly external enemies and aggressors that drove the pogroms in these localities.

CENTRAL SULAWESI

As a location for inter-religious violence in 1998–2001, the Central Sulawesi regency of Poso was notable for its role as a major "Outer Island" Protestant population center, and a hub for Protestant proselytization and political power, so that it acted as a center of Christian ecclesiastical activity and authority. The consolidation of Dutch control over this part of Central Sulawesi in the first two decades of the twentieth century had been accompanied, assisted, and in no small measure achieved by the activities of Protestant missionaries from the Dutch Reformed Church (and by other denominations such as the Salvation Army elsewhere in the province). While Islam was well established among the residents of the coastal areas of Central Sulawesi, it had largely failed to "climb" inland and upland, leaving the "animist" highlands of the province available for conversion to Christianity. Protestant missionary schools operating under the "Ethical Policy" of the colonial regime drew highlanders into their orbit with increasing success in the final decades of colonial rule, forging the crucial linkages between literacy, Protestant education, and entry into the state bureaucracy. These schools combined with the codification of customary law (*adat*) and the promotion of "indigenous" ethnic To Pamona identity to produce among highlanders very different kinds of supra-local connections and very different conceptions of collective identity from those emerging among the lowland, coastal Muslim population through *pesantren* networks, Sufi *tarekat*, the Hajj, and, increasingly, modern forms of Islamic education and association, most notably under the rubric of the Al-Khaira'at organization based in nearby Palu.[4]

---

[4] See Albert Schrauwers, *Colonial "Reformation" in the Highlands of Central Sulawesi, Indonesia, 1892–1995* (Toronto: University of Toronto Press, 2000).

This pattern persisted and deepened with Indonesian independence, under the rubric of the Gereja Kristen Sulawesi Tengah (GKST, Protestant Church of Central Sulawesi), established in 1947 and headquartered in the town of Tentena in the southern highlands of Poso regency. Still funded by the Dutch Reformed Church and assisted by foreign missionaries, the GKST evolved over the first half-century of independence into a complex state-like organization boasting more than three hundred congregations and an array of schools, hospitals, clinics, development projects, and other organizations by the turn of the twenty-first century. As the anthropologist Lorraine Aragon has noted, the Suharto regime appreciated the assistance of Protestant churches like the GKST in "creating nuclear family households, defining individual economic responsibilities, increasing ties to the national and global economies, introducing biomedicine, and expanding school attendance," and in promoting "the acceptance of national regulations, the use of money, government rhetoric concerning the benefits of progress, and regional record keeping."[5] Against this backdrop, the GKST continued to serve as a major channel for access to the state, through its network (*jaringan*) of school graduates entering the police, the military, the civil service, and Golkar. Indeed, as detailed by anthropologists who studied the church's history, the GKST itself evolved into a somewhat state-like set of local authority structures. The GKST's congregations were divided into evangelization groups composed of closely related families, which met weekly for ceremonial feasts and sermons by the church elders chosen by the governing body of the congregation. These church elders thus came to serve as lay preachers, authority figures within extended family circles, and as major local power brokers among a predominantly poor rural population, given their privileged access to the diverse resources, services, and networks of the GKST.[6]

Against this backdrop, the holding of genuinely competitive elections, the process of devolution of fiscal and administrative powers to the regency (*kabupaten*) level, and the shift from central appointment of regents (*bupati*) to selection by local assemblies (DPRD, Dewan Perwikilan Rakyat Daerah) all combined to create considerable expectations and anxieties with regard to the structure of religious authority and power in Poso from 1998 to 2001. The final years of the Suharto era—and the brief Habibie interlude—had witnessed in Poso increasing success on the part of Muslim political-cum-business networks in the regency in extending their presence and influence into realms previously dominated by Protestants. This success in Poso reflected both the national conjuncture (with significant political implications) and the local culmination of several decades of increasing Muslim integration into the market (e.g., in copra-producing coastal areas), into state educational institutions, including new local universities, and into the ranks of the local bureaucracy. By the 1990s, this trend was apparent both within the local corridors of the state, as ICMI- (Ikatan Cendekiawan Muslim Indonesia, Association of Indonesian Muslim Intellectuals) and HMI-affiliated (HMI, Himpunan Mahasiswa Islam, Islamic Students' Association) civil servants and politicians claimed positions and patronage powers once held by Protestants, and along the local circuitries of the

---

[5] Lorraine V. Aragon, *Fields of the Lord: Animism, Christian Minorities, and State Development in Indonesia* (Honolulu, HI: University of Hawai'i Press, 2000), p. 24.

[6] Albert Schrauwers, "Through a Glass Darkly: Charity, Conspiracy, and Power in New Order Indonesia," in *Transparency and Conspiracy: Ethnographies of Suspicion in the New World Order*, ed. Harry G. West and Todd Sanders (Durham, NC: Duke University Press, 2003), pp. 136–39.

market, as Muslim migrants (most notably Bugis from South Sulawesi[7]) established new money-lending and marketing networks and bought up land in the hills of the regency in the midst of a world-wide cocoa boom.[8] Researchers noted a pattern of land sales by families needing cash to fund their children's university education and to pay the bribes needed to obtain positions in the local bureaucracy.[9] Overall, these trends reproduced within the Muslim population of Poso similar patterns of exploitation and inequality, and parallel structures of power and authority, to those found among Christians in the regency. As for the impact of these trends on Protestant highlanders in Poso, Lorraine Aragon concluded:

> Family-based farming of cash crops also generated new wealth, but again mostly for ambitious Muslim migrants and urban merchants, including Chinese ones. Although Pamona and other highland Protestants did grow some cash crops such as cloves, coffee, and cacao, highlanders remained primarily subsistence rice farmers. Few became involved in market activities beyond the sale of small crop surpluses in exchange for basic supplies or cash needs. While Muslim Bugis or Makasar migrants became middleman traders or worked for private businesses through their patron-client networks, Protestant highlanders traditionally had no capitalist business experience and much more localized exchange networks. Many ran up high-interest debts to immigrant salespeople, whose kiosks offered credit, and so found their next season's produce already owed before harvest.
>
> Highlanders traditionally left their ancestral villages only for higher education, church employment, or civil service jobs, if they could obtain them. As non-Pamona bought up or were allotted lands through transmigration programs, many Pamona youths found themselves landless as well as jobless by the end of the Suharto regime. Opportunities for social mobility depended upon personal connections to members of the regional bureaucracy. Indigenous groups' access to positions remained available mainly to descendants of the precolonial nobility, and Protestants' ties to recognized aristocracies were fewer than those of Muslims. Although a small percentage of Protestant Pamona leaders did increase their economic standing dramatically during the New Order, the mass of Pamona and other highland Protestant farmers did not.[10]

---

[7] On Bugis migratory patterns and their consequences in Central Sulawesi, see Greg Acciaioli, "Principles and Strategies of Bugis Migration: Some Contextual Factors Relating to Ethnic Conflict," *Masyarakat Indonesia* 25,2 (1999): 239–68.

[8] On the effects of the cocoa boom on Central Sulawesi, see Tania Murray Li, "Two Tales and Three Silences: Critical Reflections on Indonesian Violence," paper presented at the conference on "Violence in Eastern Indonesia: Causes and Consequences," University of Hawai'i and East-West Center, Honolulu, May 16–18, 2003. The author is grateful to Professor Li for sharing a draft of this paper.

[9] See Arianto Sangaji, "Segregasi Masyarakat Poso," *Seputar Rakyat*, Desember 2003–Januari 2004, pp. 16–17; and George Junus Aditjondro, "Kerusuhan Poso dan Morowali, Akar Permasalahan dan Jalan Keluarnya," paper presented at a seminar on "Penerapan Keadaan Darurat di Aceh, Papua dan Poso?," held by Propatria in Jakarta on January 7, 2004, pp. 14–15.

[10] Lorraine V. Aragon, "Communal Violence in Poso, Central Sulawesi: Where People Eat Fish and Fish Eat People," *Indonesia* 72 (October 2001): 56.

Meanwhile, Protestant church leaders, politicians, businessmen, and gangsters in Poso in the 1990s had found an increasingly attractive alternative to Golkar in the Partai Demokrasi Indonesia (PDI, or Indonesian Democratic Party). The PDI had deep roots in Poso, incorporating the Sukarno-era Protestant party Parkindo (which polled 26 percent and won second place in Poso in the 1955 elections[11]) within its folds; the party held its annual national congress in the regency in 1997.[12] Thus the processes of democratization and decentralization in Poso came with the opportunity—for some, the imperative—of mobilizing Protestant voters to halt—and reverse—the apparent "religious" trends of the preceding several years, if not through Golkar then via the PDI-P (Parti Demokrasi Indonesia-Perjuangan, Indonesian Democratic Party of Struggle), headed by the popular figure of Megawati Soekarnoputri. Likewise, for members of local Muslim political-cum-business networks in Poso, the possibility that the "Muslim vote" would be fragmented, divided between Golkar, PPP (Partai Persatuan Pembangunan, United Development Party), the new Islamic parties, and even PDI-P, threatened a loss of control over the local assembly (DPRD) and, with decentralization, over key local executive posts as well.[13] Legislation creating a new regency of Morowali out of eastern Poso in September 1999 further narrowed the margin between the numbers of Christians and Muslims registered as residents—and as voters—thus heightening the uncertainty— and the urgency—of political mobilization along religious lines.[14]

However, the opportunity or imperative of mobilizing voters in Poso along religious lines in 1998–2001 came at a time when the established structures of local religious authority and identity appeared to be in danger of losing their certainty, their coherence, their distinctiveness, and their power. By the 1990s, migration patterns had made the town of Poso increasingly diverse, in terms of ethnicity, language, and religion.[15] As Lorraine Aragon noted:

> Protestants besides Pamona included Minahasans, Balinese, and Chinese as well as Mori, Napu, and Bada' people from within the regency. Muslims included Arabs, Javanese, Bugis, Makasar, Mandar, Buton, and Kaili people as well as Tojo, Togian (Togean), and Bungku people from the regency. The small Catholic

---

[11] Hasan, Darwis, Syakir Mahid, Haliadi, *Sejarah Poso* (Yogyakarta: Penerbit Tiara Wacana Yogya, 2004), p. 266.

[12] Schrauwers, "Through a Glass Darkly," pp. 129–32.

[13] Megawati's PDIP was especially popular in Bali, Central Java, and among Javanese communities in the so-called "Outer Islands" as well, thus raising the specter of a strong showing for the party among Balinese transmigrants and in the sizeable pockets of— overwhelmingly Muslim—Javanese immigrants who had settled in Poso.

[14] The creation of the Morowali regency appears to have reduced the Muslim percentage of the population of Poso regency from 63 percent in 1997 to 56 percent in 2000, with the Protestant percentage rising from 34 percent in 1997 to 40 percent in 2000. The remaining 3–4 percent of the population consisted of Catholics, whether of Chinese or Flores origin, and Hindu transmigrants from Bali. Compare: M. Hamdan Basyar, "Sketsa Kabupaten Poso," in *Konflik Poso: Pemetaan dan Pencarian Pola-Pola Alternatif Penyelesaiannya*, ed. M. Hamdan Basyar (Jakarta: P2P-LIPI, 2003), pp. 18–19; and Leo Suryadinata, Evi Burvidya Arifin, and Aris Ananta, *Indonesia's Population: Ethnicity and Religion in a Changing Political Landscape* (Singapore: Institute of Southeast Asian Studies, 2003), pp. 172–75.

[15] For a sketch of settlement patterns within Poso Regency, see Sangaji, "Segregasi Masyarakat Poso," pp. 13–17.

minority was comprised of Minahasans and Chinese, as well as migrants from former Portuguese colonies such as Flores. Balinese were the only Hindus.[16]

Thus the GKST, while still dominant among the To Pamona people of the Poso highlands, could no longer claim to speak on behalf of all Christians in the regency. Likewise the established mosque and school network associated with the Al-Khaira'at organization, with its headquarters and university in nearby Palu, now competed with local branches of national organizations like Nahdlatul Ulama, Muhammadiyah, and Persatuan Islam, Sufi *tarekat* like the South Sulawesi-based Khalwatiyya,[17] and other streams of Islamic devotion and affiliation for worshippers and pupils among Muslims of Javanese, Bugis, Makassarese, and other origins in Poso.[18]

Alongside the diversifying and destabilizing effects of immigration on religious affiliations and authority structures in Poso came more subtle—and in some ways more "subversive"—homogenizing local trends accompanying capitalist development, the expansion of modern education and communications, and the imposition of national state religious policies. For much as the local cliques of Muslim businessmen, bureaucrats, politicians, and gangsters within and beyond Poso in the 1990s resembled those of their Protestant rivals, so too did the local marketing and money-lending networks of (Muslim) Bugis entrepreneurs begin to mirror those of their (Christian) Chinese counterparts and competitors.[19] In the organization of religious life, moreover, further parallels emerged, as Christian and Muslim associations and schools alike worked to mediate between the needs of their respective "flocks" *(jemaah),* on the one hand, and the opportunities and pressures of state and market on the other. Thus, for example, the Al-Khaira'at school system had "modernized" over the years, a process that culminated in the formally recognized Universitas AlKhairaat in Palu, which offered degrees in agriculture, aquaculture, and medicine alongside its selection of religious studies courses. More broadly, Lorraine Aragon observed a "process of supra-ethnic convergence of local Christianity and Islam" during the course of her fieldwork in Central Sulawesi (mostly in neighboring Palu) in the 1980s:

> The longer I lived in Central Sulawesi, the more convinced I became that Christian and Muslim practices in Palu were conforming to each other. Christmas became, like the Muslim holiday in Lebaran, a weeklong visiting

---

[16] Aragon, "Communal Violence in Poso," p. 57. The 2000 census indicated that some 20 percent of the Poso population was "Javanese," with many found in rural concentrations of transmigrants outside the city.

[17] On this brotherhood, see Martin van Bruinessen, "The Tariqa Khalwatiyya in South Celebes," in *Excursies in Celebes: Een bundel bijdragen bij het afscheid van J. Noorduyn,* ed. Harry A. Poeze and Pim Schoorl (Leiden: KITLV Uitgeverij, 1991), pp. 251–69.

[18] On the diversity of religious practices and beliefs in South Sulawesi, for example, see Thomas Gibson, "Islam and the Spirit Cults in New Order Indonesia: Global Flows vs. Local Knowledge," *Indonesia* 69 (April 2000): 41–70.

[19] On the two-term entrenchment of the *bupati* of Poso in the 1990s, his ICMI affiliation and other Islamic associational links, his nepotistic personnel practices, and his patronage of local Muslim construction contractors and other businessmen, see Aditjondro, "Kerusuhan Poso dan Morowali," pp. 23–26; for a description of the *bupati*'s treatment of a prominent Muslim plantation owner and cattle baron in a rural area now part of Morowali regency, see pp. 32–33.

holiday where Christian and Muslim employees alike were invited to visit and eat at their superiors' homes. Christians who were invited to their Muslim coworkers' homes on Lebaran returned the invitations at Christmas, and vice versa. Common gifts such as jars of cookies, Western-style frosted layer cakes, or cases of imported soft drinks were exchanged both within and across religions at the major holidays.

As any visitor to Muslim regions of Indonesia knows, mosques of the past decades have used the miracle of electronic amplification to broadcast their five-times-daily calls to prayer throughout the surrounding community. In urban areas, these amplified chants in classical Arabic reverberate loudly in a manner that only the most hearing impaired could ignore. In the late 1980s, Christian churches similarly began to adopt the use of loudspeakers for their services. They then broadcast the ministers' words not only to their in-church congregations, but, like the mosques, also beyond the church walls to all those thinking they might sleep through the words of God.

Muslim services in Palu also began to include sermons comparable in format and length to those given in the Christian churches. One Protestant missionary wife claimed that local Muslim leaders were imitating her husband's sermon topics and delivery style. Even within Muslims' and Christians' minor discourses of rivalry, there was religious convergence. Christians disparaged goats as unclean Muslim animals, just as Muslims decried pigs as unclean Christian livestock.... Christian and Muslim institutions similarly contended to pull villagers away from their ancestral and family orientations towards compliance with a more remote state and God wielding more awesome powers. These common goals of modernization, at least in Central Sulawesi, made Christianity and Islam companions and peers as well as erstwhile adversaries.[20]

MALUKU AND MALUKU UTARA

As in Poso, the backdrop to inter-religious violence in Maluku and Maluku Utara in 1999–2001 was not only a long history of religious divisions, but also rising uncertainty, ambiguity, and anxiety with regard to religious boundaries and hierarchies. From the seventeenth century onwards, the Dutch East Indies Company (VOC, Vereenigde Oost-Indische Compagnie) brought Protestant missionaries in its wake, first to the island of Ambon and the fort settlement of the same town, and later to other islands of the Moluccan archipelago. Dutch missionary schools provided not only religious instruction but also practical education to Protestants in the Moluccas for the purposes of preparing low-level civil servants for the colonial regime. As the Dutch colonial state extended its hold over the Netherlands East Indies in the late nineteenth century and in the "Forward Movement" of the early twentieth century, and as the colonial bureaucracy expanded its functions and personnel under the Ethical Policy declared in 1902, so did the numbers of Protestant civil servants, teachers, missionaries, and soldiers leaving the Moluccas for other islands of the archipelago correspondingly increase.[21] Protestants from the island of Ambon were

---

[20] Aragon, *Fields of the Lord*, pp. 315–16.

[21] Richard Chauvel, *Nationalists, Soldiers and Separatists: The Ambonese Islands from Colonialism to Revolt 1880–1950* (Leiden: KITLV Press, 1990), pp. 25–35.

thus disproportionately well represented among the ranks of civil servants, professionals, and missionaries throughout the Dutch East Indies, and in particular in the Dutch colonial army, the KNIL (Koninklijk Nederlandsch-Indisch Leger, Royal Netherlands-Indies Army). The number of Ambonese Protestant recruits into the KNIL grew enormously in the late nineteenth century and early twentieth century, and the pattern of recruitment, organization, and quartering of soldiers "served to create a degree of competitiveness and a strong identification with the ethnic group and the status accorded to it by the authorities."[22] By the 1930s, an estimated 16 percent of the Protestant population of Ambon was living outside the Moluccas, and as clerks, professionals, and soldiers under the Dutch they and their families enjoyed a higher level of material welfare and a closer degree of identification with the colonial regime than did the Muslim residents of the island.[23] It was thus a group of Ambonese Protestants who had served in the KNIL who led successive local efforts to establish the Negara Indonesia Timur (State of East Indonesia), the Republik Indonesia Timur (Republic of East Indonesia), and, finally, the Republik Maluku Selatan (Republic of South Maluku) during the transition to Indonesian independence in the late 1940s and early 1950s. Yet despite their initial ambivalence about inclusion in the Republic of Indonesia, the "head start" enjoyed by such educated Ambonese Protestants was evident in their predominance locally (and, in relative terms, their prominence nationally) within the security forces, the civil service, the university belt, and the professional classes well into the Suharto era. This "head start" was, *inter alia*, a linguistic one. Since the early nineteenth century, a creolized Ambonese Malay had replaced local languages among the Protestant population in the South Moluccas, reinforced by "schools, sermons, [and] company directives," thus facilitating the adoption of the Malay-based national language Bahasa Indonesia in the twentieth century.[24]

Meanwhile, the termination of the Dutch clove monopoly, the collapse of the spice trade, and the relegation of the Moluccas to the status of an economic backwater combined to help establish a different, and more limited, pattern of extra-local linkages for Muslims in Maluku as early as the late nineteenth century. The phasing out of the clove monopoly in the 1860s and improved inter-island transportation in the late nineteenth century facilitated closer contact with Muslims elsewhere in the Netherlands East Indies, and small but growing numbers of Muslims began to leave the Moluccas as sailors, traders, and pilgrims. This pattern of slowly increasing circulation and interaction with Muslims from elsewhere in the archipelago began to draw the distinction between Muslim and Protestant elites in Maluku more sharply in the early twentieth century, as the former increasingly identified themselves in Islamic, and Indonesian, terms, while the latter tended to view their identities and interests as closely linked to the continuation of Dutch colonial rule.[25] Yet the limits of such patterns of supralocal circulation and sense of connectedness among the Muslims of the Moluccas were evident in the persistence

---

[22] Ibid., p. 52.

[23] Ibid., pp. 37–38.

[24] James T. Collins, *Ambonese Malay and Creolization Theory* (Kuala Lumpur: Dewan Bahasa dan Pustaka Kementerian Pelajaran Malaysia, 1980), p. 13.

[25] See Richard Chauvel, "Ambon's Other Half: Some Preliminary Observations on Ambonese Moslem Society and History," *Review of Indonesian and Malayan Affairs*, 14,1 (1980): 40–80.

of local dialects in Muslim villages, in sharp contrast with the rise of an Ambonese Malay lingua franca in Protestant areas of the islands.[26]

However, with independence and the defeat of the Ambonese Protestant-led Republik Maluku Selatan (RMS) in the early 1950s, and with the termination of Ambonese Protestants' colonial-era advantages within the bureaucracy and the armed forces in particular, Muslims in Maluku began to experience gradual upward social mobility along the pathways paved by their Protestant counterparts, through increasing access to education and employment opportunities within the Indonesian state.[27] The ascendancy of educated Muslims in Maluku into the political class accelerated in the Suharto era, with economic development, state expansion, and urbanization eroding the Protestants' hegemonic position, most notably in the city of Ambon, the provincial capital. By the 1990s, Protestants in Ambon and elsewhere in Maluku faced rising competition from Muslims in schools and in the Armed Forces, the bureaucracy, Golkar and the DPRD, and in business (both legal and illegal). Suharto's shift towards state promotion of Islamicization at the national level coincided with local demographic trends, as rising numbers of Butonese (and to a lesser extent, Bugis and Makassarese) immigrants from Sulawesi and high birth rates among local Muslims began to tip the population balance in favor of Muslims (59 percent province-wide in 1997), even in the capital Protestant stronghold of Ambon (42 percent citywide in 1997).[28]

Thus, as in Poso, local political-cum-business networks in the Maluku of the late Suharto era were incorporated into the national political class through a pattern of linkages defined—and divided—by religion. Indeed, just as Maluku's Protestant civil servants, Army officers, and members of Golkar engaged in intermarriage and nepotistic practices with their co-religionists in the universities, the professions, business, and the criminal underworld, so too did the province's Muslim political networks operate as channels for patronage and protection linking Muslim towns and villages around the province, Ambon City, and Jakarta. As Jacques Bertrand, a political scientist who conducted extensive fieldwork in Ambon, noted:

> The state sector became divided into sections controlled by each group. A particularly interesting example was the University of Pattimura (UNPATTI). The powerful Education Faculty (FKIP), one of the largest faculties in the university, was almost exclusively staffed with Christians well into the 1990s, while other departments included more Muslims. Within the regional and municipal bureaucracies, such tendencies were common. Christians resented the growing presence of Muslims in areas they previously controlled, while Muslims saw their advancement as a just redress since they had been previously marginalized in the region.[29]

---

[26] Collins, *Ambonese Malay*, p. 11.

[27] Christian Kiem, "Re-Islamization among Muslim Youth in Ternate Town, Eastern Indonesia," *Sojourn* 8,1 (February 1993): 92–127.

[28] Tamrin Amal Tomagola, "Ambon Terbakar," Februari 1, 1999, *Tempo*, pp. 24–25; and Riwanto Tirtosudarmo, "The Impact of Migration in Eastern Indonesia," *Jakarta Post*, April 6, 1999.

[29] Jacques Bertrand, "Legacies of the Authoritarian Past: Religious Violence in Indonesia's Moluccan Islands," *Pacific Affairs* 75,1 (Spring 2002): 67.

Against this backdrop, the resignation of Suharto and inauguration of B. J. Habibie as president in May 1998 carried particular significance for Maluku. Habibie, after all, had served throughout the 1990s as the head of ICMI, the Association of Indonesian Islamic Intellectuals, and under this national umbrella, well-connected Muslims in Maluku could be expected to enjoy considerably enhanced local advantages in terms of appointments to civil service posts, Army commands, seats in various parliamentary bodies, and university lecturerships, as well as preferential treatment for various business and criminal ventures.[30] Indeed, as in Poso, the last five years of the Suharto era had already witnessed marked trends along these lines, as a Muslim governor in Maluku began to fill the top positions in the local bureaucracy with fellow Muslim allies, cronies, and clients.[31]

Yet beyond the immediate implications of Habibie's rise to the presidency in mid-1998 for local Muslim and Protestant patronage networks, the approach of competitive elections in mid-1999 and the devolution of considerable powers to elected local assemblies legislated later that year represented a major challenge to existing religious identities, boundaries, and structures of authority in Ambon and elsewhere in Maluku. In obvious ways, local shifts in the distribution of state patronage and in the discretionary use of state regulatory power raised tensions along and across the borders between Muslims and Protestants, as did the impending shift to a system in which freely elected local officials would wield much more power over their constituencies. After all, the boundaries between Muslims and Protestants in Ambon and elsewhere in Maluku appeared to be sharply defined and securely fixed in spatial terms, in a pattern of segmentation into local units of official religious homogeneity.[32] Religious boundaries thus tended to conform to village boundaries, and even in those rare localities where religious diversity was found, segregated settlement patterns divided not only Muslims and Christians, but even Protestants and Catholics.[33] This pattern, observable in villages scattered throughout Maluku, as well as in urban neighborhoods (*kampung*) in the provincial capital of Ambon City,[34] was reinforced by government policies prohibiting inter-faith marriages, expanding religious instruction in schools, and promoting a pattern of recruitment into the bureaucracy through networks based on religious affiliation. In this context, competition for state offices, public works contracts, and legal and illegal business franchises was understood according to the zero-sum logic of a highly divided society. Given the considerable ambiguities about land titles and village boundaries in rural Maluku, gang "turf" in urban Ambon, and administrative units throughout the province, the uncertainties attending the regime change, the approaching elections, *pemekaran* (redistricting), and decentralization all made for

---

[30] S. Sinansari ecip, *Menyulut Ambon—Kronologi Merambatnya Berbagai Kerusuhan Lintas Wilayah di Indonesia* (Bandung: Mizan, November 1999), pp. 68–70.

[31] Bertrand, "Legacies of the Authoritarian Past," pp. 69–71. See also John Pieris, *Tragedi Maluku: Sebuah Krisis Peradaban* (Jakarta: Yayasan Obor Indonesia, 2004), pp. 222–30.

[32] Dieter Bartels, "Guarding the Invisible Mountain: Intervillage Alliances, Religious Syncretism and Ethnic Identity among Ambonese Christians and Moslems in the Moluccas" (PhD dissertation, Cornell University, 1977).

[33] Paschalis Maria Laksono, "Wuut Ainmehe Nifun, Manut Ainmehe Tilor (Eggs from One Fish and One Bird): A Study of the Maintenance of Social Boundaries in the Kei Islands" (PhD dissertation, Cornell University, 1990), pp. 123–24.

[34] David Mearns, "Urban Kampongs in Ambon: Whose Domain? Whose Desa?," *The Australian Journal of Anthropology* 10,1 (1999): 15–33.

heightened tensions along religious lines in the months following the fall of Suharto. The impending division of the province into predominantly Muslim (85 percent) Maluku Utara, and a rump Maluku with virtual parity between Muslims and non-Muslims (49 percent/50 percent) in September 1999 only exacerbated the problem.

Yet in perhaps somewhat less obvious ways, the shift to an open, competitive, and decentralized system of organizing power in Indonesia was also accompanied by heightened uncertainty and anxiety as to religious identities and structures of authority *within* the Muslim and Christian "communities" in Ambon and elsewhere in Maluku. Anthropological writings on the villages of Ambon, after all, stressed the persistence well into the Suharto era of religious beliefs and practices that transcended the Muslim-Protestant divide, patterns of enduring alliance (*pela*) and mutual assistance among villages of different official faiths, and understandings of local property and authority relations based on supra-religious customary law (*adat*) and aristocratic lineage.[35] Ethnographic work on other parts of Maluku likewise revealed a broad spectrum of diversity and change in the religious beliefs and practices of those registered as Muslims and Christians in the province, with "conversion" a recent and ongoing process for many official believers, even well into the 1990s.[36] Patterns of migration to and within Maluku—especially by (Muslim) Butonese from Sulawesi—were also cited by observers in the same period as increasing the diversity of religious practices in Maluku and heightening, "ethnicizing" tensions between both Christian and Muslim "natives," on the one hand, and immigrant "outsiders," on the other, over economic resources, property relations, village elections, and other issues.[37]

Against this backdrop, the dominant structures of power associated with Protestantism and Islam in Maluku were haunted by rising doubts and fears as to their authority, identity, and coherence, much like their counterparts in Poso. On the Protestant side, the Gereja Protestan Maluku (GPM, Maluku Protestant Church) greatly resembled the GKST in Central Sulawesi in terms of its internal authority structure and discipline, and its well-established links to state power. As one author noted, the GPM

> ... is by far the largest non-government organization in the province [of Maluku]. Its structure exactly parallels that of local government. Its youth wing, Angkatan Muda Gereja Protestan Maluku (AM-GPM), has thousands of affiliated branches.

---

[35] In this vein, see, in particular, Bartels, "Guarding the Invisible Mountain"; and Tri Ratnawati, "Interactions Between Adat and Religious Institutions and the New Order State: A Case Study of Two Islamic and Christian Villages in Central Moluccas," *Masyarakat Indonesia* 29,1 (2003): 1–22.

[36] On Muslims and Protestants in North Maluku, for example, see Kiem, "ReIslamization among Muslim Youths in Ternate"; Nils Ole Bubandt, "Warriors of the Hornbili, Victims of the Mantis: History and Embodied Morality among the Buli of Central Halmahera" (PhD dissertation, Australian National University, 1995); and Christopher Robert Duncan, "Ethnic Identity, Christian Conversion, and Resettlement among the Forest Tobelo of Northeastern Halmahera, Indonesia" (PhD dissertation, Yale University, 1998). On Catholics in Southeast Maluku, see Laksono, "Wuut Ainmehe Nifun," especially pp. 87–166, 171–178.

[37] See, for example, Franz von Benda-Beckmann and Tanja Taale, "Land, Trees and Houses: Changing (Un)certainties in Property Relationships on Ambon," in *Remaking Maluku: Social Transformation in Eastern Indonesia*, ed. David Mearns and Chris Healey (Darwin: Northern Territory University Centre for Southeast Asian Studies, 1996), pp. 39–63; and David Mearns, "Urban Kampongs in Ambon: Whose Domain? Whose Desa?"

All Protestant young people are socialized in the elements of an extremely formal religion through a constant round of activities that takes the dedicated believer away from home most nights of the week. Most prominent Protestant Ambonese are therefore also prominent church leaders.[38]

The establishment of the Gereja Protestan Maluku in 1935, the ensuing institutional detachment from the Dutch Reformed Church, and the end of Dutch rule in the 1940s had favored localizing trends and accommodation with non-Christian practices.[39] Yet expanding access to modern education and contact with the outside world combined with other processes—the increasing encroachment of other Christian denominations and the promotion of Islamic reformism in Maluku—during subsequent decades to raise concerns about the everyday religious beliefs and practices of those claimed as belonging to the church. As one anthropologist noted:

> After World War II some young Christian ministers were given the opportunity to study at prestigious theological schools in Europe and the United States. As these ministers gained leadership positions within the church, they were striving to achieve universally accepted standards of Protestantism and thus determined to "purify" Moluccan Christianity by ridding it of ancestor veneration and any customs contrary to Christian beliefs.[40]

Meanwhile, the Seventh Day Adventist Church had already established a small congregation in Ambon in the 1920s, and in the post-war, post-independence period, the GPM "saw a number of other Protestant denominations, mostly of evangelical and Pentecostal character, growing much faster. In psychological and institutional aspects the GPM was not yet fully on its way to abandoning the character of a dominant religion."[41] Over the years, the sizeable Catholic population in Southeastern Maluku had expanded, as had the numbers of Catholic migrants to Ambon City. Missionary activities in Maluku by Protestant churches from elsewhere in Indonesia and beyond likewise increasingly encroached on the GPM's established "turf."[42]

At the same time, the poverty and isolation of sparsely populated, archipelagic Maluku combined with the associational diversity and limited state institutionalization of Islam in the Netherlands Indies—and in early post-

---

[38] Gerry van Klinken, "Small Town Wars: Post-Authoritarian Communal Violence in Indonesia" (unpublished manuscript), p. 46. Many thanks to the author for making this important forthcoming book available, and for granting permission for the citation of this passage.

[39] On the establishment of the GPM, see Chauvel, *Nationalists, Soldiers and Separatists*, pp. 156–60; Theodor Muller-Kruger, *Sejarah Gereja di Indonesia* (Djakarta: Badan Penerbitan Kristen, 1966), pp. 83–97; and Th. van den End, *Ragi Carita: Sejarah Gereja di Indonesia* (Jakarta: BPK Gunung Mulia, 2001), pp. 158–68.

[40] Dieter Bartels, "Your God Is No Longer Mine: Moslem-Christian Fratricide in the Central Moluccas (Indonesia) after a Half-Millennium of Tolerant Co-Existence and Ethnic Unity," unpublished paper, 2000, p. 8.

[41] Karel Steenbrink, "Interpretations of Christian-Muslim Violence in the Moluccas," *Studies in Interreligious Dialogue* 11,1 (2001): 87.

[42] For a map of the US-based evangelical New Tribes Mission stations in Maluku in the 1990s, for example, see Duncan, "Ethnic Identity, Christian Conversion, and Resettlement," p. 106.

independence Indonesia more generally—to limit the possibilities for promoting universalistic understandings of the faith among the scattered and still mostly poorly schooled Muslims of the Moluccan Islands. As one observer claimed: "The degree of indigenization of Islam varied widely from village to village, but in one region it was carried so far that people ultimately came to believe that Islam was brought to the Moluccas by the Prophet himself. On the island of Haruku, the pilgrimage of Mecca came to be viewed as unnecessary, but was performed at a special sacred site in the mountains behind the villages."[43]

Over the three decades of the Suharto era, the expanding circuitries of the market, the state bureaucracy, and the school system began to propagate more modern understandings of Islam among Muslims in Maluku, as promoted by both the state's official policies on religion (*agama*) and the diverse outreach (*dakwah*) activities of various Islamic associations like Muhammadiyah and Al Khaira'at. Thus, as one historian already noted in the early 1980s: "A situation has therefore developed, in which, within both religious communities there has been pressure for reform. Under attack have been those elements of common *adat* heritage which Christians and Moslems share..."[44] These pressures, as the anthropologist Dieter Bartels further noted, went well beyond the strictly "religious" realm:

> The people battling in the political arena are often identical or allied with religious purists and fanatics within the religious structures of Islam and Christianity. These people are outward directed. That is, they tie in with other organizations on the national level and beyond. They perceive Islam or Christianity as universal truths and thus as mutually incompatible. Extremists among them demand the "purification" of religion from beliefs which are not in line with pan-Islamic or pan-Protestant beliefs. Thus they have launched attacks on beliefs that God is one and the same for Christians and Moslems, and they have demanded the discontinuance of ancestor veneration and most of *adat*—all of which would lead to a further weakening of interfaith ties.[45]

Against this shared backdrop of enduring concern about *adat*, the persistence of local aristocratic influence, and religious syncretism, and the rising ethnic diversification in Maluku, the hierarchies of Protestant and Muslim power in the province were notable for their increasing *similarities*, rather than differences. After all, in contrast with the final decades of Dutch rule in the archipelago, the half-century since Indonesian independence had witnessed the evolution of Muslim networks of power in Maluku strikingly similar to those established by their Protestant counterparts, through the modern school system, which led into the civil service and local legislative and executive offices, the police and military, the universities, the media, the professions, and the world of business and criminality. The same decades had likewise seen commensurate linguistic shifts in the direction of homogenization, with Ambonese Malay now serving—as it had for almost two centuries for Protestants—as a "lingua franca among Muslim speakers of different

---

[43] Bartels, "Your God Is No Longer Mine," p. 9. See also Keebet von Benda-Beckmann, "The Practice of Care: Social Security in Moslem Ambonese Society," in *Remaking Maluku: Social Transformation in Eastern Indonesia*, ed. David Mearns and Chris Healey, pp. 121–39.

[44] Chauvel, "Ambon's Other Half," p. 79.

[45] Bartels, "Guarding the Invisible Mountain," p. 326.

Moluccan languages and dialects," and Bahasa Indonesia increasingly used by Muslims and Protestants alike.[46] By the late 1990s, direct personal memories of the violent events of the transition to independence, when the mostly Christian forces backing the Republik Maluku Selatan (RMS, Republic of the South Maluku) had fought bitterly against the mostly Muslim supporters of integration into Indonesia, were increasingly distant and dying away with the aging men and women who had participated in the events of that era.[47] By the end of the twentieth century, moreover, more and more privileged Muslims in Maluku were attending the same state schools and universities, viewing the same television programs and movies, speaking the same *lingua franca* (or rather *linguae francae*), and jockeying for advantage within the same state and market circuitries as Protestants than ever before. By the mid-1990s, in the provincial capital city of Ambon, the newly built Ambon Plaza shopping complex combined Chinese, Bugis, and Butonese storefronts and drew Christian and Muslim consumers and flaneurs alike.[48] Thus, as in Poso, the attractive powers of the national state and the global market threatened, if not to dissolve, then to diminish the differences among the most privileged local representatives of the two religious faiths.

POGROMS AND FORCED DISPLACEMENT, 1999–2001

In short, it was against the backdrop of increasing ambiguity, uncertainty, and anxiety with regard to the structures and boundaries of religious identity and authority in Central Sulawesi, Maluku, and Maluku Utara that inter-religious pogroms in various localities in these provinces unfolded in 1999–2001. The dominant structures of religious authority in these provinces faced unprecedented uncertainty as to their strength, their solidity, and their claims on the local population, in the face not only of unsettling sociological trends but also of sudden political change. Under the Suharto regime, Protestant and Muslim hierarchies of authority had been subordinated to, and partially submerged within, a highly centralized authoritarian state, beneath which they found shelter, stability, and patronage. With competitive elections now determining the composition of local assemblies, and thus the selection of new mayors (*walikota*), regents (*bupati*), and governors (*gubernur*), and thus the distribution of patronage and power in Central Sulawesi, Maluku, and Maluku Utara, the period 1998–2001 broadened the field, the forms, and the increased fruits of contestation between these hierarchies, underlining the imperative of voter mobilization for gaining access to state power on the one hand, and for making claims to religious constituencies on the other.

In this context, struggles over the uncertain boundaries of "turf" were transformed into broader inter-religious conflicts between Christians and Muslims in Poso, and parts of Maluku and Maluku Utara. Such "turf battles" began with contestation over gang control over bus terminals in Poso town and Ambon City, for example, or, as in Malifut, Maluku Utara, with a dispute over the creation of a new subdistrict. Against the backdrop of the uncertainties and anxieties about religious

---

[46] Collins, *Ambonese Malay*, p. 13.

[47] See, for example, the account of embittered old men in a Muslim coastal village on the island of Seram, in Juliet Patricia Lee, "Out of Order: The Politics of Modernity in Indonesia" (PhD dissertation, University of Virginia, 1999), pp. 83–118.

[48] On Ambon Plaza, see Lee, "Out of Order," pp. 207–59.

identities and hierarchies sketched above, these "turf battles" came to be interpreted in religiously coded terms and to entail violent mobilization along religious lines. As such they crystallized into inter-religious pogroms. The reclaiming and redefinition of territory along religious lines drove a process of forced dislocation or displacement of religious "Others."

Indeed, displacement was intrinsic—and essential—to the *pogroms* in at least three ways. First and most obviously, the violence itself in large measure assumed the form of large-scale forced evictions of entire neighborhoods and villages through a combination of threats and intimidation, armed attacks, and arson. This pattern was apparent in the sustained inter-religious violence in Ambon City in January to March 1999, in the more episodic waves of violence in and around Poso in late 1998 and mid-2000, and in parts of Maluku Utara in the latter half of 2000. This pattern was also evident in the series of violent incidents perpetrated by armed Christian groups on Muslim villages in parts of Maluku and Maluku Utara in late 2000 and early 2001, and in the waves of attacks on isolated Protestant villages launched by Laskar Jihad and other armed Muslim groups in mid-to-late 2001 in Poso and earlier in parts of Maluku and Maluku Utara.

The Batu Merah neighborhood of Ambon after the first wave of inter-religious violence in the city in January–February 1999. (AP Photo, by Achmad Ibrahim, with permission)

In urban centers like Ambon City, evictions of entire neighborhoods were preceded by harassment and intimidation, and brought to culmination through violent attacks. In human rights groups' accounts of such "clearances" in Ambon City, for example, this process is said to have unfolded in many neighborhoods in the aftermath of the January 19, 1999, outbreak of inter-religious violence in the city, with homes stoned by gangs of youths night after night. So-called *posko* (command/communications posts) were established by Protestant and Muslim groups in neighborhoods across the city, with the avowed intention of "guarding each community against outside parties." But the nighttime stonings continued, and the *posko* soon evolved into nodal points for the mobilization of Protestant and Muslim groups, armed with crude weapons and prepared for attack. By February, this process had escalated in some parts of the city into full-blown armed attacks on vulnerable Protestant and Muslim neighborhoods. Crudely armed gangs, sometimes backed up by larger crowds of local residents and supported by elements of local army and/or police units, stormed into such neighborhoods, shooting, throwing various kinds of explosive devices, burning and demolishing homes, and killing or driving out the inhabitants who remained. Between January and March 1999, dozens of neighborhoods experienced this process, with thousands of homes destroyed and thousands more residents brutalized and forced to seek refuge among their co-religionists in Ambon City or further afield.[49]

In vulnerable rural villages, forced displacement was also often effected with great speed and apparent efficiency. Perhaps most emblematic of this form of forced displacement was the series of forced evictions imposed on Muslim villages in parts of Poso regency during the peak weeks of violence in June through July 2000. As recorded by human rights investigators, three separate residents of different Muslim villages reported a similar process:

> We were told to leave. The red [Christian] fighters came with lots of cars. I'm not sure if they had guns, but they had dum-dums, Ambon arrows, and bamboo spears ... First they burnt the houses near the road. We ran and hid and then they burnt the rest, but left the Christian houses. I don't know who they were. I just know my house is gone ...

> We were forced out of our house and told to gather in front of the mosque. They told us we were going to the subdistrict military command. But when we got to the mosque they herded us towards the Tangkora elementary school. We left midday and it was ten at night when we got there ... They kept us there for two days and two nights. They had us walk towards Kasiguncu, guarding us all the way ... Then we spent two nights in Kasiguncu. They took us to the edge of the city and retreated ...

> We were told to gather at the village hall by about one hundred men with masks and cloths over their faces. A truck came, and they had a list. They took away eight people ... At 2:00 we were made to walk. We saw a truck with two

---

[49] For a very detailed—if not entirely unbiased—account of this process, see *Laporan Hasil Investigasi Kasus Kerusuhan di Maluku* (Ambon: Yayasan Sala Waku Maluku, 1999). This report focuses almost entirely on Muslim attacks on Protestant areas, without commensurate attention to Protestant attacks on Muslim areas.

people in the back: her brother [indicates young woman] and another relative. He said tell my wife not to cry, we're just going to get some things in the next town. We never saw them again. We walked all the way to Mapane. We spent two nights there and then went by truck to Poso town ... [50]

In short, whether urban or rural, forced displacement figured prominently in the pattern of inter-religious violence observed in areas of Central Sulawesi, Maluku, and Maluku Utara in 1999–2001. Indeed, the eviction of entire religious communities from neighborhoods and villages lay at the heart of the very purpose and process of the violence itself. Looking back at the sheer numbers of houses destroyed and residents displaced, it is difficult to escape the conclusion that the violence served a means of effecting displacement, rather than displacement coming as a byproduct of the violence.

FORCED DISPLACEMENT AND THE SPREAD OF VIOLENCE

Second and somewhat less obviously, the forced displacement of hundreds, indeed thousands, of Muslims and Christians from their neighborhoods and villages played a crucial role in the *spread* of inter-religious violence from one locality to another in Poso, in Maluku, and in Maluku Utara. Such knock-on effects were arguably already evident in the outbreak of inter-religious violence in Ambon City in January 1999, just weeks after the arrival of Ambonese *preman* expelled from Jakarta after a major street fight in late November 1998. The fight, which occurred outside a gambling casino in the area of Ketapang in Central Jakarta, involved Christian and Muslim Ambonese gangs, local residents, and members of militant Islamic groups connected to the Habibie administration, and resulted in several deaths and the burning of seven churches.[51] Rumors that the riot had been deliberately instigated as part of a larger conspiracy spread rapidly in Jakarta and in Ambon, especially after the violent attack on a Muslim neighborhood in Kupang, West Timor, a week later, during a march organized by a Christian youth congress to protest the church burnings.[52]

Against this backdrop, the fallout from events in Jakarta began to trickle down to Ambon City, a process allegedly accelerated by the expulsion of dozens of Ambonese *preman* to their home province in time for Christmas and Ramadan, and amidst rising anticipation of the recently announced—and rapidly approaching—June 1999 elections. Thus violent competition over the fluctuating boundaries of power shifted "downwards," as it were, to local protection rackets in Ambon precisely as electoral mobilization was getting under way in a province where tight demographic margins between Muslims and Christians combined with the sociological and religious trends sketched above to produce considerable uncertainty and anxiety. As rival Christian and Muslim gangs in Jakarta and Ambon City had

---

[50] Human Rights Watch, *Breakdown: Four Years of Communal Violence in Central Sulawesi* (New York, NY: Human Rights Watch, December 2002), pp. 17–18.

[51] "7 Gereja dan 11 Mobil Dibakar," *Detik*, Nopember 23, 1998; "Mayat-mayat Jadi 14 Orang," *Detik*, Nopember 23, 1998; "Preman-Warga Bentrok, 6 Tewas," *Jawa Pos*, Nopember 23, 1998; "Bentrokan di Ketapang, Jakbar, 7 Tewas," *Republika*, Nopember 23 1998; and "Kerusuhan di Jakarta Enam Orang Tewas," *Kompas*, Nopember 23, 1998.

[52] Riza Sihbudi and Moch. Nurhasim, *Kerusuhan Sosial di Indonesia: Studi Kasus Kupang, Mataram, dan Sambas* (Jakarta: Grasindo, 2001), pp. 42–100.

long been part of competing networks of active and retired military officers, bureaucrats, businessmen, and politicians associated with Golkar, the possibility of a strong showing by the PDI-P in the upcoming elections foreshadowed not only mass defections by Christians (and potentially Muslims) but also a broadening of the arena and the weapons of contestation.[53] It was in this context that a second street fight, this time in and around the bus terminal in Ambon City in January 1999, grew from gang conflict over "turf" into full-blown inter-religious warfare.[54]

A ship in Ambon harbor overflowing with residents fleeing inter-religious violence in the city in March 1999. (AP Photo, by Charles Dharapak, with permission)

---

[53] On this dimension of the local scene, see Gerry van Klinken, "The Maluku Wars: Bringing Society Back In," *Indonesia* 71 (April 2001): 1–26: "Jaringan Provokator" and "Opek Merebut Birokrasi, Coker Menghunus Parang," *Tempo*, Maret 15, 1999, pp. 22–23.

[54] See "Jaringan Provokator Kerusuhan Ambon," *Tajuk*, April 1, 1999, pp. 19–23.

Large-scale displacement resulting from the violence in Ambon City created aftershocks elsewhere in Maluku.[55] Large-scale attacks across the religious divide in Ambon City and its environs continued sporadically into February 1999, spreading to the nearby Central Maluku islands of Haruku, Seram, and Saparua, and leaving dozens killed, hundreds wounded, and thousands of homes, shops, churches, mosques, and other buildings burned or otherwise destroyed.[56] By early March 1999, as this first phase of violence began to subside, more than one hundred casualties were reported, and as many as seventy thousand refugees were said to have fled Ambon.[57] By the end of 2000, as many as 140,000 IDPs were estimated to be seeking refuge from the violence within the province of Maluku, with tens of additional thousands fleeing to safe havens elsewhere in Indonesia. This flow of IDPs from Ambon and other early sites of violence—a flood of people "carrying with them," as an anthropologist working in the Banda Islands in 1999 noted, "stories, fears, and rumors"[58]—facilitated the spread of inter-religious violence elsewhere in Maluku.[59]

But it was in the newly created province of Maluku Utara where the role of forced displacement in the spread of the conflict was most fully revealed. In August 1999, fighting broke out in North Maluku, just a month before its official reconstitution as a new province and on the occasion of the formal inauguration of the new district (*kecamatan*) of Malifut in the regency of North Halmahera.[60] This new district was to consist of some sixteen villages populated by transmigrants resettled from the nearby island of Makian in 1975, as well as eleven additional villages identified with the more established local Kao and Jailolo ethno-linguistic groups. For years, the transmigrants' settlement and cultivation of land in the area had ran up against the resentment and resistance of the "indigenous" Kao and Jailolo, whose representatives' claims to customary (*adat*) land rights grew only more vociferous with the discovery of gold in Malifut by an Australian mining company in the 1990s.

This dispute acquired a strongly religious complexion, as the Makianese transmigrants were Muslim, while the Kao and Jailolo were predominantly Protestant. Malifut, moreover, had come to serve as a Muslim bottleneck choking off the southward spread of Christianity from predominantly Protestant North Halmahera, an expansion supported by the proselytizing efforts of the Evangelical

---

[55] Human Rights Watch, *Indonesia: The Violence in Ambon* (New York, NY: Human Rights Watch, March 1999), pp. 10–20.

[56] For contrasting accounts of the violence, see: Yayasan Sala Waku Maluku/Yayasan Lembaga Bantuan Hukum Indonesia, *Laporan Hasil Investigasi Kasus Kerusuhan di Maluku* (Ambon: Yayasan Sala Waku Maluku, 1999); Tim Penyusun al-Mukmin, *Tragedi Ambon* (Jakarta: Yayasan Al-Mukmin, 1999); and S. Sinansari ecip, *Menyulut Ambon: Kronologi Merambatnya Berbagai Kerusuhan Lintas Wilayah di Indonesia* (Bandung: Mizan, 1999), pp. 96–126.

[57] "Ambon Mencari Juru Damai," *Tempo*, March 8, 1999, p. 26.

[58] Phillip Winn, "Banda Burns," *Inside Indonesia* 61 (January–March 2000).

[59] Government of the Republic of Indonesia and International Agencies, *The Maluku Crisis: Report of the Joint Assessment Mission* (Jakarta: February 6, 2000), pp. 7–8.

[60] On the backdrop to the formation of the new district of Malifut, and on the subsequent pattern of violence in North Maluku in August–December 1999, see Tamrin Amal Tomagola, "Tragedi Maluku Utara," *Masyarakat Indonesia*, 25,2 (1999): 289–302; Chris Wilson, "The Ethnic Origins of Religious Conflict in North Maluku Province, Indonesia, 1999–2000," *Indonesia* 79 (April 2005): 69–91; and Christopher R. Duncan, "The Other Maluku: Chronologies of Conflict in North Maluku," *Indonesia* 80 (October 2005): 53–80. The paragraphs below draw heavily on these accounts.

Church of Halmahera (Gereja Masehi Injili Halmahera, GMIH) and the largely American-staffed New Tribes Mission based in the northeastern district of Tobelo.[61] The Kao and Jailolo thus won backing for their claims from Protestant politicians and the Sultan of Ternate, who counted on Christian support for his ambitions to assume the governorship of the new province, while the Makianese enjoyed the support of Muslim politicians in Maluku and Jakarta.[62]

Against this backdrop, a pattern of what Nils Bubandt calls "cascading" and escalating violence unfolded in North Maluku in the second half of 1999.[63] First, the scheduled inauguration of the new district of Malifut in August 1999 was marked by the outbreak of fighting between crudely armed groups from Kao/Jailolo and Makianese villages. The fighting persisted for several days, leaving a handful of casualties—and dozens of homeless or otherwise displaced families—in its wake. Violence recurred and escalated in October 1999, with a wholesale Kao and Jailolo attack that razed all sixteen Makianese villages, left dozens of Makianese casualties, and forced some sixteen thousand Makianese residents to flee to Ternate and Tidore.

Then, the presence of these Makianese IDPs combined with the circulation of a forged letter from the head of the GPM in Ambon to the head of the GMIH in Tobelo, calling for the Christianization of North Maluku and the "cleansing" of Muslims from the province, to set the stage for attacks on Protestants in Tidore and then Ternate in November 1999.[64] The violence in Tidore and Ternate, in turn, prompted mobilization by armed followers of the Sultan of Ternate and by forces loyal to his rivals for the governorship (including the Sultan of Tidore and a PPP politician who assumed the *bupati*ship of Central Halmahera), as well as the flight of Protestants from the two towns to safe havens in North Halmahera and North Sulawesi.

In yet another twist, late December 1999 saw groups of armed men from among these IDPs from Ternate and Tidore, and from local Protestant villages, launch attacks on Muslim villages in the predominantly Protestant North Halmahera district of Tobelo, where the headquarters of the evangelical GMIH was located. The attacks, which began on the day after Christmas and lasted into the first week of the new year, left hundreds of Muslim villagers in Tobelo and neighboring Galela dead (including more than two hundred slaughtered in a local mosque) and forced the flight of thousands more survivors.[65] By the end of January 2000, official sources estimated that more than 1,600 people had been killed in Maluku Utara since August 1999, and tens of thousands more had been displaced by the violence.[66]

---

[61] On the Gereja Masehi Injili Halmahera (GMIH) and the New Tribes Mission in Tobelo, see Duncan, "Ethnic Identity, Christian Conversion, and Resettlement."

[62] Tomagola, "Tragedi Maluku Utara," pp. 291–292. See also Smith Alhadar, "The Forgotten War in North Maluku," *Inside Indonesia* 63 (July–September 2000).

[63] On the pattern of "cascading" violence, see Nils Ole Bubandt, "Malukan Apocalypse: Themes in the Dynamics of Violence in Eastern Indonesia," in *Violence in Indonesia,* ed. Ingrid Wessel and Georgia Wimhofer (Hamburg: Abera Verlag, 2001), pp. 228–53.

[64] A copy of the forged letter has been reproduced in Henry H. Sitohang, Hidayaturohman, M. Dian Nafi', Moehamad Ramdhan, and Sabar Subekti, *Menuju Rekonsiliasi di Halmahera* (Jakarta: Pusat Pemberdayaan untuk Rekonsiliasi dan Perdamaian, 2003), pp. 175–78.

[65] On the massacre in Tobelo and Galela, see: "Kepolisian Benarkan 216 Transmigran Dibantai di Masjid Maluku Utara," *Republika,* Januari 17, 2000; "Perang Satu Keluarga Dua Agama," *Tempo,* Januari 23, 2000, pp. 26–27; "Berlindung di Hutan, Kondisinya Memprihatinkan; Tak Diketahui, Nasib Ribuan Muslim Tobelo," *Pikiran Rakyat,* Januari 30, 2000.

[66] "Suara Kecewa dari Maluku," *Tempo,* Februari 6, 2000, p. 23.

Finally, the massacre in Tobelo combined with a wave of attacks by Protestants on Muslims in other parts of Maluku to spur new forms of violent mobilization in avowed defense of Islam elsewhere in Indonesia. Fighting in Ambon City had broken out on Christmas Day 1999 and led to the burning of one of the GPM's most prominent churches in the capital by an armed Muslim crowd, followed by the burning of two mosques in the city by a similar Protestant mob later the same day.[67] Widely circulated media reports of this violence, which fell on a major Christian holiday and in the midst of the Muslim fasting month of Ramadan, had helped to precipitate the massacre in Tobelo, where tensions were reportedly already running high with the arrival of Protestant refugees from Ternate and Tidore the previous month. A similar dynamic was evident in the Central Maluku town of Masohi, where attacks by armed Protestant groups on Muslim villages in late December and early January left dozens of casualties and hundreds more homeless, violated, wounded, and otherwise traumatized by the violence. The alleged participation of Protestant police and military personnel (and the reported acquiescence of the Protestant *bupati*) in the violence in Masohi combined with the killings of twenty-seven Muslims in Ambon on Christmas Day, the massacre of hundreds of Muslim villagers in Tobelo, and the flight of tens of thousands of Muslim IDPs from Maluku and Maluku Utara to draw increasingly vociferous condemnations of Christian atrocities and expressions of concern for Muslim welfare in Maluku from Islamic organizations and political parties in Jakarta.[68] For example, Amien Rais, chairman of the People's Consultative Assembly (MPR, Majelis Permusyawaratan Rakyat), leader of the National Mandate Party (PAN, Partai Amanat Nasional), and long-time head of the modernist Islamic association Muhammadiyah, joined other leading politicians in calling for *jihad* to save Muslims in Maluku and Maluku Utara at a rally in early January in Jakarta attended by an estimated 100,000 militants.

This wave of Protestant violence against Muslims in Maluku and Maluku Utara also spurred both old and new forms of religious violence elsewhere in Indonesia. On January 17, 2000, for example, prominent Islamic leaders, including a dean from the local university, the heads of local Islamic associations and schools, the leaders of a local Islamic militia, and the Jakarta-based Islamic labor leader and ICMI member Eggi Sudjana,[69] held a *tabligh akbar,* or major public gathering, in a field in the city of Mataram, the largest urban center on the predominantly Muslim island of Lombok ("island of a thousand mosques") and the capital of the province of West Nusa Tenggara. The *tabligh akbar* was announced as a venue for raising funds for Muslim victims of the violence in Maluku and for expressing solidarity and concern among the faithful. But the event was preceded by the dissemination of a letter by some of

---

[67] On these events, see "Kerusuhan Ambon: Api Masih Berkobar di Hari Suci," *Tempo*, Januari 9, 2000, pp. 24–25.

[68] On the events of December 29, 1999–January 5, 2000, in Masohi, see Majelis Ulama Indonesia Kabupaten Maluku Tengah, "Laporan Khusus Kerusuhan di Masohi dan sekitarnya," Masohi, Januari 7, 2000. The accusations contained in this report were faithfully reported in "Pertikaian Masih Terjadi di Maluku; Bupati, Dandim, dan Kapolres Diduga Terlibat Penyerangan," *Republika*, Januari 13, 2000.

[69] Eggi Sudjana was a well-known Islamic activist since the 1980s, when he led a splinter group of the modernist Muslim university students' association HMI, which refused to recognize Pancasila as its founding principles. See Achmad Fachruddin, *Jihad Sang Demonstran: Pergulatan Politik dan Ideologi Eggi Sudjana dari era Soeharto hingga era Gus Dur* (Jakarta: Raja Grafindo Persada, 2000).

the organizers demanding that Christians in Lombok come forward to issue public condemnations of the atrocities committed by Protestants in Maluku in the preceding weeks of late December 1999 and early January 2000, and threatening dire consequences in the event of continuing Christian silence on the issue. An estimated two thousand Islamic activists attended the *tabligh akbar*, many of them sporting white bandanas with the inscription *Allahu Akbar* (God is Great) written in Arabic on their foreheads. After the gathering, some of these activists began to attack various buildings identified as belonging to the small Christian minority in Mataram, burning Protestant and Catholic churches, schools, shops, and homes over the next two days and driving some three thousand Christians to seek refuge in local police and military installations or in non-Muslim sanctuaries beyond Lombok, like Bali, Manado, and Papua.[70]

Thus, the wave of violence in late December 1999 and early January 2000 gave rise to calls for *jihad* in Maluku and Maluku Utara that resonated among many Muslims elsewhere in Indonesia and spurred the mobilization and deployment of Laskar Jihad units to the Moluccan archipelago in the spring of 2000. Indeed, it was this wave of anti-Muslim violence in Maluku and Maluku Utara that occasioned the very creation of Laskar Jihad, a well-organized paramilitary group whose operations in Ambon, North Maluku, and elsewhere in the Moluccan islands preceded and foreshadowed their arrival and activities in Poso more than one year later. Thus already in late January 2000, in the aftermath of the huge rally in Jakarta, dozens of Muslim volunteers were arriving in Ambon and other parts of Maluku to provide medical, logistical, and paramilitary support to their beleaguered co-religionists.

Laskar Jihad had been formed on Java in April 2000, and by May of that year an estimated three thousand Laskar Jihad recruits—and hundreds of other similar Muslim paramilitary forces—had reportedly arrived in Maluku, bringing with them military training, heavy automatic weapons, and sophisticated forms of radio communications, as well as close links with elements in the Armed Forces. Thus June and July 2000 witnessed a fresh wave of aggressive paramilitary attacks on vulnerable Protestant areas, including an assault on a Protestant village in Galela district abutting the GMIH stronghold in Tobelo district, North Maluku, and the razing of Waai, a Christian village sandwiched between two Muslim villages on the east coast of Ambon island. These assaults caused dozens of Protestant casualties and proved highly effective in "cleansing" thousands more Protestant residents from these border zones.[71] Even with the declaration of a civil emergency in Maluku by then president Abdurrahman Wahid in late June 2000, Laskar Jihad-led attacks on Protestant areas persisted, allegedly aided and abetted by elements of the Armed Forces. By early 2001, eight Protestant villages and towns in Ambon had been "cleansed" of Christians and occupied by Muslim forces. Hundreds, or perhaps even a few thousands, of Protestants living on small islands elsewhere in Central Maluku were reportedly forced to flee or to convert to Islam to insure their survival.[72]

---

[70] On these events, see Sihbudi and Nurhasim, *Kerusuhan Sosial di Indonesia*, pp. 106–22; and "Ketika 'Iblis' Berkuasa," *Tempo*, Januari 30, 2000, pp. 26–28.

[71] On this pattern, see International Crisis Group, *Indonesia: Overcoming Murder and Chaos in Maluku* (Jakarta/Brussels: International Crisis Group, December 19, 2000), p. 9.

[72] International Crisis Group, *Indonesia: The Search for Peace in Maluku* (Jakarta/Brussels: International Crisis Group, February 8, 2002), pp. 9–10.

While government forces launched a harsh crackdown on Laskar Jihad in Maluku in mid-2001, armed units associated with the group initiated a wave of attacks on Protestant villages in Poso in the latter half of the same year. The final few months of 2001 saw a wave of new armed attacks in Poso, now characterized by the use of automatic weapons and full-scale military operations across the religious divide. These attacks saw the mobilization of armed groups numbering in the hundreds and led to the razing of dozens of villages, which left scores of casualties and displaced hundreds, indeed, thousands, of residents. A human rights group based in Palu estimated that more than 140 people had been killed and nearly 2,500 homes destroyed by the end of 2001.[73]

FORCED DISPLACEMENT AND THE DECLINE OF LARGE-SCALE INTER-RELIGIOUS VIOLENCE

Third and finally, displacement played a crucial role in the transformation, de-escalation, and effective termination of large-scale inter-religious violence. The displacement of thousands of families caused by the destruction and burning of homes, and the flight of thousands more in the face of continuing intimidation and fear of further attacks, forced tens, indeed hundreds, of thousands of IDPs to relocate among their co-religionists, and thus reinforced—and simplified—pre-existing spatial patterns of segregation along religious lines.[74]

In many neighborhoods and villages in Poso, Ambon, and elsewhere in Maluku and Maluku Utara, Protestant and Muslim *posko* sprang up, as did elaborate local security arrangements for providing advanced warning of trouble, arming residents, and launching preemptive strikes against attacks by outsiders. Churches and mosques soon emerged as major nodes in these formations of violence, serving as important sites for paramilitary mobilization, planning, communication, coordination, and rearmament. This trend not only hardened the divisions between Christian and Muslim communities but further spurred the reconstitution of neighborhood and village gangs as crudely armed local militias, sporting variously red (Protestant) or white (Muslim) bandanas and other items of clothing to distinguish themselves as defenders of their respective religious communities and faiths.[75] In Ambon, for example, observers noted, "everyday social life is segregated: red market, white market, red and white speedboat quays, red and white pedicabs (*becak*), red and white minibuses, red and white banks, and so forth."[76]

---

[73] M. Hamdan Bashar dan Bayu Setiawan, "Rangkaian Peristiwa Kekerasan di Poso," in *Konflik Poso: Pemetaan dan Pencarian Pola-Pola Alternatif Penyelesaiannya*, ed. M. Hamdan Basyar (Jakarta: P2P-LIPI, 2003), pp. 48–49; Sinasari ecip, *Rusuh Poso Rujuk Malino* (Jakarta: Cahaya Timur, 2002), pp. 44–61; *Breakdown: Communal Violence in Central Sulawesi* (New York, NY: Human Rights Watch, December 2002), pp. 20–29; International Crisis Group, *Indonesia Backgrounder: Jihad in Central Sulawesi* (Jakarta/Brussels: International Crisis Group, February 3, 2004), pp. 11–14. For Laskar Jihad's own account of its activities in Poso during these months, see Dewan Pimpinan Pusat Forum Komunikasi Ahlus Sunnah Wal Jamaah, "Kronologi Poso Membara (Oktober 15–Desember 4, 2001)," www.laskarjihad.or.id, Desember 5, 2001.

[74] Aragon, "Communal Violence in Poso," pp. 60–64.

[75] For a detailed (if not disinterested) account of this process in one neighborhood in Ambon City, see Yayasan Sala Waku Maluku, *Laporan Hasil Investigasi*, pp. 41–42.

[76] Margaretha Margawati and Tony Aryanto, "Konflik Antaragama atau Politisasi Agama?," *Jurnal Antropologi Indonesia*, vol. 63 (2000): 124.

In addition, the paramilitary operations of Laskar Jihad in Poso in the latter half of 2001 and in Maluku and Maluku Utara from mid-2000 through mid-2001 heralded a pattern of effectively stalemated and subsiding inter-religious violence. By the end of 2001, the violence in these localities had effected a pattern of enduring religious segregation and simplification, with the Laskar Jihad-led assaults serving to eliminate some of the remaining anomalies of Protestant pockets inside—and impeding the connection of—Muslim zones.[77] By 2001, moreover, Protestant and Muslim villages and towns throughout many of these localities had come to feature "red" and "white" armed groups ready for armed mobilization and plugged into their respective interlocking directorates of local politicians, bureaucrats, businessmen, criminal networks, and retired and active police and military personnel. Local election results in the gerrymandered new regencies of Poso, Morowali, and Tojo Una-Una, and in the newly divided provinces of Maluku and Maluku Utara, also worked to clarify the new distribution of civilian-controlled state patronage along religious lines. Overall, by 2001 inter-religious violence had peaked in Poso, Maluku, and Maluku Utara, and had begun to subside. In subsequent years, incidents of armed combat across the religious divide in these localities were very infrequent and limited in their scope. These localities were occasionally troubled by drive-by shootings and other assassinations, as well as bombings and the discovery of explosive materials clearly intended for imminent use.[78] But overall, even with tens of thousands of IDPs still left homeless by the violence, and with the thorny questions of repatriation, compensation, and reconciliation left essentially unresolved, large-scale collective violence of a *pogrom*-like nature appears to have largely disappeared from Poso, Maluku, and Maluku Utara since the end of 2001.

In this way, the successful dislocation of thousands upon thousands of Muslims and Christians within and beyond Central Sulawesi, Maluku, and Maluku Utara in time helped to reduce the imperative of inter-religious violence and to restabilize competition and cooperation among the major hierarchies of religious authority in these localities. This reestablishment of equilibrium, of course, had been achieved at considerable cost and through the violent redrawing of religious boundaries and reconstitution of hierarchies of authority on both sides of the religious divide. Thousands are estimated to have been killed in Poso, Ambon, and various parts of Maluku and Maluku Utara during the peak years of violence in 1999–2001, with many more victimized by injuries and untold suffering, and with thousands upon thousands of homes and dozens of churches, mosques, and other buildings damaged or destroyed in the process. In addition, the violence forced several hundred thousand internally displaced persons to flee their homes, neighborhoods, and villages to seek refuge among their co-religionists elsewhere within Central Sulawesi, Maluku, Maluku Utara, and other provinces of the Indonesian archipelago.[79]

---

[77] See, for example, the illuminating religiously coded maps appended to Yanuarti et al., *Konflik di Maluku Tengah*, pp. 151–53.

[78] See, for example, Arianto Sangaji, "Pasukan Terlatih dan Perubahan Pola Kekerasan di Poso?," *Kompas*, October 17, 2003; "Upaya Perdamaian di Maluku Diwarnai Empat Ledakan di Ambon," *Kompas*, Februari 14, 2002; and "Maluku Utara diguncang bom," *Jawa Pos*, Juli 12, 2002.

[79] See, for example, the figures cited in Basyar and Mashad, "Pendahuluan," pp. 1–14.

Thus the pogroms proved effective in sharpening—and simplifying—the boundaries of religious identity and authority. These new conditions have been reinforced by obstacles impeding the repatriation of IDPs in all these localities and various gerrymandering schemes, most notably the scheme engineered by the majority-Protestant rump Poso regency—with less than one half of its original population—which hived off the two new, mostly Muslim, regencies of Morowali and Tojo Una-Una. The pogroms also proved instrumental for the reconstitution of local religious authority structures. Local Protestant and Muslim networks of politicians, businessmen, civil servants, policemen, military officers, and gangsters came to enjoy greater coercive powers within their respective religious communities, thanks to the evolution of policing and surveillance structures and the elaboration of arms smuggling and other illegal activities, all ostensibly defensive in nature and responsive to self-evident threats from without.[80] Thus the decline of large-scale inter-religious violence attested to the success of the pogroms in redrawing—and restabilizing—boundaries across the religious divide and reaffirming—and restrengthening—religious hierarchies and identities on each side.

CONCLUSION: DOUBLE DISPLACEMENT, 1999–2001

As argued in the pages above, the emergence, spread, transformation, and fading of religious pogroms in 1998 to 2001 owed much to displacement, in two senses of the word. First of all, the outbreak of violence owed much to the displacement of anxieties accompanying the major transition in Indonesian social and political life. This transition was one in which the forces associated with the promotion of "Islam" in Indonesian public life were first launched into the seats of state power in Jakarta, soon embattled from without and within, and eventually eclipsed and ousted from power. The effects of this precipitous "rise and fall of Islam" in 1998–2001 on the national political stage rapidly trickled down and came to affect the distribution of power and patronage in provinces, regencies, towns, and villages around the Indonesian archipelago. The local effects were especially destabilizing in localities where the national networks (*jaringan*) connecting local networks of politicians, civil servants, (retired and active) military and police officers, businessmen, and gangsters to Jakarta were defined and divided along religious lines, and where local boundaries of authority—and balances of power—were redrawn through *pemekaran*, the formation of new districts, regencies, and provinces (most obviously in Maluku Utara).

These palpable tremors of political realignments rippling across the archipelago were accompanied by deeper, perhaps somewhat less discernible, tectonic shifts in the very structures of religious identity, authority, and power in Indonesia. The loosening of the centralized authoritarian state's surveillance and control during the political liberalization initiated by Habibie in the latter half of 1998 called into question not only the established hierarchies of power and patronage in Indonesia, but also the very source and structure of recognition and identity for Indonesians around the archipelago. This state of uncertainty was profoundly destabilizing for religious institutions—whether ICMI, Al-Khaira'at, Gereja Kristen Sulawesi Tengah, or Gereja Protestan Maluku—which in one way or another had secured niches

---

[80] See, for example, Arianto Sangaji, "Memangkas Peredaran Senjata Api di Poso," *Seputar Rakyat*, Desember 2003–Januari 2004, pp. 18–23.

beneath and within the New Order state and thus kept at bay persistent questions about the boundaries of their authority and identity. This state of uncertainty was also profoundly destabilizing for many ordinary people.

As Patricia Spyer has argued, these religious identities, boundaries, and hierarchies had long rested on the logic of seriality, on "numbers, statistics, and the range of enumerative practices with which they are associated."[81] In this context, the competitive elections and decentralization that were already looming on the horizon in mid-to-late 1998 and came to replace centralized authoritarian rule in mid–to-late 1999 heightened anxieties about the numbers of the faithful—numbers of converts, numbers of voters—who could be claimed for each "flock" (*jemaah*).

It is thus against the temporal backdrop of this distinctive national conjuncture of 1998–2001 that the geographical distribution—and spread—of the pogroms in specific *locations* around the Indonesian archipelago during this period must be situated. Indeed, following the logic of seriality stressed by Spyer, it is striking how all the major episodes of communal violence during this period unfolded in provinces where the statistical distribution of religious faith was least concentrated, all of which were found in the cluster of eight provinces with between 30 percent and 85 percent Muslim populations—and electorates. According to the 2000 census, Maluku was only 49 percent Muslim after the creation of Maluku Utara (85 percent Muslim); Poso was only 56 percent Muslim, in 78 percent Muslim Central Sulawesi.[82] Thus the PDI had long-established roots in all of these localities, and the possibility of a destabilizing shift—of votes, DPR and DPRD seats, and eventually *bupati*ships and governorships—from Golkar to PDI-P loomed large on the horizon. All the sites of large-scale inter-religious violence in 1998–2001 were localities, in other words, in which high levels of electoral uncertainty prevailed.

In such settings, increasing apprehensions about the numerical—and electoral—strength of statistical religious "others" thus combined with abiding anxieties about the weakness and fragmentation internal to the religious "communities" themselves. The established positions of GKST and Al-Khaira'at in Poso were increasingly threatened over the years, not only by competition across the official religious divide but by rising ethnic, associational, and denominational diversity and fragmentation within their respective realms of pastoral care. Similarly, the ecclesiastical authority of their counterparts in Maluku ran up against the enduring influence of *adat* and aristocratic lineage, the proselytizing efforts of outside missionaries (evangelical Protestant, Catholic, and Muslim), and the destabilizing effects of immigration. Meanwhile, by the turn of the twenty-first century, the attractive powers of modern secular education, the national state, and the market had drawn increasing numbers of Christians and Muslims into their orbit, encouraging discernible trends towards cultural, linguistic, organizational, and social homogenization across the religious divide. These trends were perhaps most visible in everyday life in Maluku's

---

[81] Patricia Spyer, "Serial Conversion/Conversion to Seriality: Religion, State, and Number in Aru, Eastern Indonesia," in *Conversion to Modernities: The Globalization of Christianity*, ed. Peter van der Veer (London: Routledge, 1996), p. 191.

[82] Ananta, Arifin, and Suryadinata, *Indonesian Electoral Behaviour*, pp. 24, 53. Central Kalimantan and West Kalimantan, the sites of violent "ethnic cleansing" of immigrant Madurese communities in 1997, 1999, and 2001, were 74 percent and 58 percent Muslim, respectively The other provinces within this band of provinces were Jakarta (DKI), East Kalimantan, and North Sumatra, all of which merit further treatment as cases where communal violence did *not* occur during this period.

provincial capital city of Ambon, where Protestant and Muslim neighborhoods and houses of worship were often found in close proximity (as reports of the violence of early 1999 make clear), and where more and more Ambonese and migrants of different faiths mingled in the streets, the schools, the shops, and the offices of government with every passing year. Meanwhile, if in the 1955 elections the vast majority of voters in Poso and Maluku had backed "sectarian" political parties that were clearly identified with one or another religious faith—Masjumi for Muslims, Parkindo for Protestants—by the time of the elections of 1999, the avowedly ecumenical orientation of the two most popular parties—PDI-P and Golkar—signaled the possibility of overriding, if not erasing, religious differences in the political realm.

In such settings, the local ecclesiastical establishments had come to assume quasi-statal and para-statal forms, with religious identities intimately bound up with associational, educational, economic, and political hierarchies. In peripheral, less developed, "Outer Island" localities like Poso and Maluku, this pattern was particularly pronounced, in part thanks to the relatively modernized, rationalized, and capitalized structures of local Protestant churches, and in part because of the importance of the offices and resources of the state. As the anthropologist P. M. Laksono noted with regard to the remote Southeast Maluku district island town of Tual:

> Civil servants are the backbone of urban society. By the end of the 1980s nearly all the rupiah flowing into the district came from civil service salaries. Almost no rupiah came in outside the government budget. Agriculture is just subsistence. There is practically no export—just a little copra and marine products. The big fishing trawlers that frequent Tual harbor are Taiwanese and pay their money to Jakarta. The whole of society depends on the state—even if only as a labourer at a school building site.[83]

In such localities, moreover, religious institutions and identities had from their inception been "political" in the sense of close identification with religiously segmented networks connected to the state. As another anthropologist noted with regard to Protestant-Muslim conflict in Poso, "this fight is not about religious doctrines or practices, but about the political economy of being Protestant (or Catholic) and Muslim."[84] Likewise in Ambon and in other parts of Maluku, as the political scientist Gerry van Klinken concluded,

> …joining the Protestant or the Muslim community means being part of a network that not only worships God in a certain way but does practical things for its members—provides access to friends in powerful places, for example, or protection when things get tough. These networks extend up the social ladder to influential circles in Jakarta. And they extend downward to street level, where

---

[83] P. M. Laksono, "We Are All One: How Custom Overcame Religious Rivalry in Southeast Maluku," *Inside Indonesia* (April–June 2002). This argument was articulated earlier and elaborated in greater detail in Laksono, "Wuut Ainmehe Nifun," pp. 39, 75–84.

[84] Aragon, "Communal Violence in Poso," p. 47.

gangs of young men provide the protective muscle that an inefficient police force cannot provide.[85]

In this way, "turf wars" between urban youth gangs around bus terminals, competition among politicians over state offices, and the inauguration of a new district or province were religiously coded and interpreted in the light of the anxieties about religious boundaries, hierarchies, and identities described above. Neighborhood and village youth gangs—rather than students from religious schools—quickly emerged as the foot soldiers in the inter-religious policing and warfare. These gangs were defined and divided along religious lines and connected to the religiously segmented local networks of politicians, civil servants, retired and active military and police officers, and businessmen. In time, they were increasingly organized and equipped along paramilitary lines in the towns and villages of Poso, Maluku, and Maluku Utara.

If the displacement of anxieties about the "incompleteness" of religious identities, boundaries, and hierarchies prefigured the outbreak of violence, the forced displacement of neighborhoods and villages by armed groups across the religious divide promoted the spread, transformation, and, finally, deescalation of the violence. Indeed, as demonstrated most clearly in the events of 1999–2000 in Maluku Utara, the arrival of IDPs fleeing one site of violence often portended—if not precipitated—violence in would-be sites of refuge, creating a deadly contagion effect of a kind. Yet over time, in Poso, Ambon, and other parts of Maluku and Maluku Utara, the violent eviction of people from neighborhoods and villages also effected the spatial segregation and simplification of Christian-Muslim communities seen in other sites divided by inter-religious violence elsewhere around the world, producing an "interlocking binary spatial grid and inside/outside polarities," with the "proliferation of interfaces, the barricading, and the influx of refugee populations" reorganizing towns and villages into a highly militarized and religiously coded topography.[86] In these settings, such processes were accompanied—and expedited—by the reconstitution of the two opposing religious communities into militarized hierarchies organized and equipped for interfaith warfare. In a pattern reminiscent of shifts observed in other sites of sectarian violence elsewhere in the world, the years 1999 to 2001 in Poso, Maluku, and Maluku Utara thus saw a shift from more spontaneous rampages by crudely armed crowds to more carefully coordinated large-scale attacks by heavily armed paramilitary groups, and then a reversion to sporadic bombings, drive-by shootings, and quick raids and arson attacks across the well-established and tightly guarded religious divide.

Thus by the end of 2001, the large-scale collective violence between Protestants and Muslims of the preceding few years had run its course and subsided into small-scale disturbances to the formal and informal settlements that had crystallized in these religiously divided localities. In large measure, the fading of pogroms followed from the internal transformation of the violence itself, with the "successes" of forced displacement serving to (re)establish religious boundaries and hierarchies, and thus greatly reducing the uncertainties and anxieties so evident in 1998–99. In short, in its

---

[85] Gerry van Klinken, "What Caused the Ambon Violence?," *Inside Indonesia* 60, October–December 1999.

[86] Allen Feldman, *Formations of Violence: The Narrative of the Body and Political Terror in Northern Ireland* (Chicago, IL: University of Chicago Press, 1991), pp. 17–45, at p. 35.

double sense, and in diverse ways, displacement was a driving force of the inter-religious pogroms of 1999 to 2001 in Indonesia, prefiguring their inception, spread, and disappearance.

VIOLENCE AND DISPLACEMENT IN WEST KALIMANTAN

Jamie S. Davidson

INTRODUCTION[1]

The forms of violence in the ethnically diverse and resource rich province of West Kalimantan do not fit either of the two categories of massive regional upheaval examined elsewhere in this volume: non-separatist strife that first exploded in the post-Suharto state (Maluku Islands, Poso, and Central Kalimantan) or separatist-related violence suffered under the New Order (Aceh, Papua, and Timor), which, not coincidentally, then intensified following Suharto's fall in 1998. Only West Kalimantan experienced sustained, non-separatist bloodletting that spanned the entirety of the New Order. In fact, widespread riots again exploded less than a year into the post-Suharto era. In this way, the experience of West Kalimantan complicates claims that Indonesia's current regional conflagrations are merely an outcome of the instability of the incipient post-Suharto state or that regional bloodshed under the New Order was but a by-product of separatism. Moreover, disturbances in this vast province prove that in Indonesia religion is not the only marker of group identity with the power to mobilize antagonists. The simplistic national dichotomy of Islam versus Christianity does not provide a clear view of the divisions in West Kalimantan. In all, this case becomes crucial in the study of Indonesia's regional strife; comparative studies of this phenomenon must engage West Kalimantan's recurrent riots.

Rather than cover the political history of violence in West Kalimantan expansively,[2] this chapter examines the politics undergirding two recent incidents of

---

[1] This chapter is a revised version of the article "The Politics of Violence on an Indonesian Periphery," *South East Asia Research* 11, 1 (March 2003): 59–89. It has been revised for inclusion in this volume with the kind permission of the journal. The late Dan Lev, John Sidel, Billy Nessen, Laurie Sears, Steve Hanson, Jeremy Gross, Lotta Hedman, Portia Reyes, Deborah Homsher, and an anonymous reader from *South East Asia Research* read and commented on various parts of this essay. They enriched the analysis and rescued me from sophomoric blunders. Remaining deficiencies are attributable to the author alone.

[2] For expansive coverage, see Jamie S. Davidson, *From Rebellion to Riots: Collective Violence on Indonesian Borneo* (Madison, WI: University of Wisconsin Press, 2008, forthcoming).

large-scale civilian violence: the 1997 Madurese–Dayak riots and the Malay (and later Dayak)–Madurese episode of 1999. It also shows how the unresolved refugee crisis in the wake of the 1999 violence lay at the core of the city's cascading riots of June 2001. At the time, the violence was the apogee of a three-year saga of near catastrophic proportions, redolent of government corruption, ineptitude, intensifying urban economic competition, and the further dehumanization of a victimized population.

In this analysis, four interlocking mechanisms come to the fore. The first two are the specificity of local historical trajectories and the politicization of ethnicity. The third and fourth mechanisms are the complex interplay between elites and the routinization of violence among belligerents in the sparking of upheaval. In particular, I interrogate the rise of two unmistakable ethnopolitical movements that led to two instances of massive anti-Madurese violence. The Dayak movement stems from the 1997 clashes, while its Malay counterpart grew out of the 1999 killings.[3] Although they purport to have "local" orientations, in fact broader, national processes have also provided the opportunities and space necessary for these ethno-political revitalizations to flourish.

VIOLENCE AND THE NEW ORDER

Despite the troubled legacies of the colonial era and the Japanese Occupation during World War II, it was the tumultuous 1960s that most decisively determined patterns of ethnic conflict or cooperation in West Kalimantan. Hostility between Indonesia and the newly constituted Malaysian state—what President Sukarno believed to be a puppet regime masking Britain's neo-colonialist aims—put West Kalimantan on the political map. Fueled by Sukarno's anti-western New Emerging Forces and anti-Neoklim rhetoric, tensions soon escalated into sporadic combat, and the conflict known as Konfrontasi (Confrontation) began. From West Kalimantan, the Indonesian military conducted raids into the bordering Malaysian state of Sarawak. In September 1963, following the severing of diplomatic relations between the two countries, the raids intensified.

Under Konfrontasi, the Indonesian military trained and supplied two distinct yet related paramilitaries—the Malaysian Chinese Sarawak People's Guerrilla Force (PGRS, Pasukan Gerilya Rakyat Sarawak) and the North Kalimantan People's Force (Paraku)—to help destabilize and frustrate Sarawak's incorporation into Malaysia. It further mobilized thousands of "volunteers" (*sukarelawan*) comprised of local recruits and men from Java to act as raiders or border guards. But then came the military takeover of October 1, 1965, which created a political reversal with enormous implications for West Kalimantan.

The anti-communist Suharto moved swiftly to conclude Konfrontasi, but extinguishing its "remnants" on-the-ground would require large-scale bloodshed and nearly eight years of brutal military operations. With western-backed, reactionary regimes in Kuala Lumpur and Jakarta, the PGRS/Paraku found

---

[3] The third most populous ethnic group, the Chinese, are similarly enjoying an ethno-political revival. In contrast, this movement has gained strength from noninvolvement in violence. The fact that ethnic Chinese have not been victimized since 1967 is important, but beyond this paper's scope. Also, of the three movements, the Chinese example is the least "local," as Jakarta, not Pontianak or Singkawang, is the center of efforts to nullify discriminatory laws and restore full political rights to Indonesians of Chinese descent.

themselves unwelcome on both sides of the border.[4] Preoccupied with massacres in Java and Bali, military authorities in Jakarta did not begin to address seriously West Kalimantan's rebel problem until mid-1967. Military authorities insisted that rural Chinese villagers were supplying the rebels with goods necessary for survival. To eradicate these villages by forcibly moving their inhabitants to more manageable coastal and urban locales, the army deployed a well-known counterinsurgency tactic: drain the water so the fish can no longer swim. The water, of course, was the tens of thousands of rural Chinese villagers.

Here actions of the army commanders help explain the origins of the anti-Chinese purges, but the role of indigenous Dayak leaders accounted for their "success."[5] Regional officers and interested Dayak leaders helped to translate the virulent anti-communist environment (at both national and international levels) locally into an evident anti-Chinese sentiment. In the process, the rural Chinese were constructed as godless communists complicit with members of the local Indonesian Communist Party (PKI, Partai Komunis Indonesia) and the PGRS/Paraku. In October 1967, the military, with the help of the former Dayak Governor Oevaang Oeray and his Lasykar Pangsuma (Pangsuma Militia) instigated and facilitated a Dayak-led slaughter of ethnic Chinese. Over the next three months, thousands were killed and roughly 75,000 more fled Sambas and northern Pontianak districts to coastal urban centers like Pontianak City and Singkawang to be sheltered in refugee and "detainment" camps.[6]

By expelling the "communist" Chinese, Oeray and his gang sought to create a Dayak-dominated economic zone in the areas thus emptied out. They also intended to ingratiate themselves with Suharto's new regime. But another presence threatened to derail Oeray's plans, as migrant Madurese also began to settle the vacated lands. By December 1967, Dayak and Madurese clashed over the spoils of the expulsion.[7] An unintended consequence of the army's counterinsurgency operation, this outburst was the first serious Dayak–Madurese riot. Viewed against these little-known events,[8] West Kalimantan's recurrent violence, although lacking in separatist aspirations, proves to be more political than observers have thus far supposed.

---

[4] Meanwhile, several dozen members of the West Kalimantan branch of the Indonesian Communist Party (PKI), led by its chairman S. A. Sofyan, fled Pontianak to the Bengkayang area, a rural hinterland crowded with ethnic Chinese.

[5] It should be stressed that the purges were successful in expelling the rural Chinese; yet, in cutting rebel supply lines (the army's professed strategy) and in forming a Dayak economic zone (Oeray's plans), they failed miserably.

[6] These paragraphs are drawn from Jamie S. Davidson and Douglas Kammen, "Indonesia's Unknown War and the Lineages of Violence in West Kalimantan," *Indonesia* 73 (April 2002): 53–87.

[7] On the 1967 riot, see "'Tjina Hitam' Djuga Djadi Sasaran," *Kompas*, December 28, 1967; and Herman Josef Van Hulten, *Hidupku di Antara Suku Daya: Catatan Seorang Misionaris* (Jakarta: PT Grasindo, 1992 [translated from 1983 original]), pp. 295–97.

[8] This point is worth stressing. In recent essays by two prominent historians, neither the PGRS/Paraku rebellion nor the Chinese purges of 1967 is mentioned. See Anthony Reid's essay on the Indonesian history of anti-Chinese violence, "Entrepreneurial Minorities, Nationalism, and the State," in *Essential Outsiders: Chinese and Jews in the Modern Transformation of Southeast Asia and Central Europe*, ed. Daniel Chirot and Anthony Reid (Seattle, WA: University of Washington Press, 1997), pp. 33–71; and Robert Cribb's essay that traces the ideological and operational history of ABRI (Angkatan Bersenjata Republik Indonesia, Armed Forces of the Republic of Indonesia) from the revolution to the invasion of East Timor in December 1975: Robert Cribb, "From Total People's Defence to Massacre: Explaining

Minor Dayak–Madurese riots continued intermittingly in roughly the same areas from which the rural Chinese were expelled. A complex set of elements and circumstances insured that tensions remained strained and continued unabated. Here, I will address cursorily some of the more pertinent concerns. First, expulsions of rural ethnic Chinese, many who were small-scale traders and merchants, shattered the region's distribution network. It destroyed the local rural economy. Teams of government officials and Lasykar Pangsuma members were forced to traverse the area distributing foodstuffs to ward off famine.[9] Second, the excesses of the anti-Chinese mobilizations further destabilized an evidently militarized environment. An internal military report from 1969 describes northern Pontianak district as an area of "tumultuous conditions that is being exploited by instigators playing one ethnic group off another."[10] The report fingers the Lasykar Pangsuma as one of these instigators. Exploiting their mobilized strength, the militia tried to consolidate local control following the purges.

Another instigator was the Nahdlatul Ulama (NU). For one thing, during this period increasing numbers of Madurese migrants entered West Kalimantan. Most migrated to the region on their own, rather than as participants in any government relocation program—a phenomenon known as spontaneous migration (*migrasi swakarsa*). Madurese migration predates the New Order, yet the regime's policies— for instance, pouring substantial development monies into the province—facilitated Madurese migration by creating considerable job opportunities.[11] These infrastructure projects brought significant numbers of newly arrived Madurese, unfamiliar with local conditions and norms, to areas inhabited by Dayaks.[12] Meanwhile, this development furnished NU party organizers with opportunities to flex their electoral muscles. Electoral jostling and fractious "campaigning" would have been likely in 1968 and 1969. Debates in Jakarta on when and what form elections would take were well under way. Not until mid-to-late 1969 did Suharto's

---

Indonesian Military Violence in East Timor," in *Roots of Violence in Indonesia: Contemporary Violence in Historical Perspective*, ed. Freek Colombijn and J. Thomas Linblad (Leiden: KITLV Press, 2002), pp. 227–42.

[9] On the economic devastation, see "Masalah Perekonomian Jang Pelik," *Kompas*, December 14, 1967; and Garth Alexander, *Silent Invasion: The Chinese in Southeast Asia* (London: MacDonald & Company, 1973), p. 5. In fact, as late as 1971, news reports still commented on the near-famine like conditions of northern Sambas. See "Bahaja Kelaparan di Kalbar," *Kompas*, September 10, 1971; and "Penderitaan di Kalbar," *Kompas*, September 24, 1971.

[10] The report continues by describing a whirl of disconcerting rumors (*issue 2*) that "Dayas will attack Madurese ... Dayas will attack Malays (*Tjina Hitam*) [black Chinese]... [and] Catholics will attack Muslims." See "Rentjana Operasi Sapu Bersih III- Tahun 1969" (Pontianak: Laksus Pang Kop Kamtib Daerah Kalimantan Barat, n.d.), pp. 14–15.

[11] Projects first tackled the province's anemic infrastructure, which meant initiatives in road building. In 1971, the area had 1,830 kilometers of roads, of which 336 kilometers were asphalted. Within a short ten years, thanks to the physical labor of Madurese migrants, these numbers doubled and trebled, respectively. Hendro Suroyo Sudagung, *Mengurai Pertikaian Etnis: Migrasi Swakarsa Etnis Madura ke Kalimantan Barat* (Jakarta: ISAI, 2001), pp. 86–87, Table 3.12.

[12] Specifically, three important road projects were: the coastal Mempawah-Singkawang road, the inland Singkawang-Monterado extension, and the road connecting Bengkayang to the border (Seluas). On these road projects, see Government of Australia, Department of Foreign Affairs, and Snowy Mountains Corporation, *Preliminary Regional Survey for Road Network Identification in Kalimantan Barat-Indonesia: Volume 6: Roads and Transport* (Canberra: Government of Australia, Department of Foreign Affairs, December 1973).

top advisers begin to transform (Sekber) Golkar into its official electoral machine. As important, this period predates the depoliticization and "floating mass" policies of the New Order. In 1968–69, local party organizers most likely expected upcoming elections to be competitive, akin to those held in 1955.[13] It is within this context that this same military report noted above commented: "There are frequent local skirmishes between the Daya[k] and Madurese. These circumstances are used by the Madurese in their NU shirts to show off their mass support."[14] Although the report does not detail these "local skirmishes," evidently tensions remained strained and conflict was sustained.

At the same time, the local state apparatus did little to ameliorate tensions. Although New Order army officers were replacing civilian district executives (*bupati*),[15] lower-ranking Dayak civil servants unofficially aligned with Oeray and Partindo were still well represented in local bureaucracies.[16] These bureaucracies contained neither the institutional capacities nor possessed the required neutrality to help assuage the Madurese–Dayak dilemma. On the military's part, it was still focused on the communist insurgency—Sofyan was not killed until January 1974— and accruing handsome profits through "counterinsurgency" operations like logging. Not until the widespread Madurese–Dayak violence of 1979 in Samalantan subdistrict did the conflict attract the military's serious attention.[17]

Nonetheless, by 1979 numerous Dayak–Madurese clashes had already taken place. In this type of environment, a deepening mistrust, animus, and "routinization of violence" among Dayak and Madurese combatants coalesced.[18] Within a specific

---

[13] On this process, see Ken Ward, *The 1971 Election in Indonesia: An East Java Case Study* (Melbourne: Centre of Southeast Asian Studies, Monash University, 1974), Chapter 1.

[14] "Rentjana Operasi Sapu Bersih III–Tahun 1969," p. 15. The original reads: "sering terjadi bentrokan lokaal antara suku Daya contra suku Madura, maka kesempatan ini digunakan oleh suku Madura dan badju NU-nja untuk menundjukkan kekuatan massanja."

[15] With the success of the Unity Dayak Party (commonly abbreviated PD) in the 1958 regional elections, the party secured four district-executive (*bupati*) posts: M. Th. Djaman (Sanggau), G. P. Djaoeng (Sintang), J. R. Gielling (Kapuas Hulu), and Djelani (Pontianak District). By 1967, they all had been replaced.

[16] After Suharto banned the Sukarnoist Partindo, local military authorities coerced Oeray's followers to join IPKI (Ikatan Pendukung Kemerdekaan Indonesia, League of the Supporters of Indonesia's Independence). So, at this point, IPKI , not Partindo, may have been the relevant party.

[17] When it finally addressed the issue, it did so by forcing both sides to sign an ineffectual peace accord and by erecting a gaudy, thirty-foot monument. The statue's tribute to the official state motto, "Unity in Diversity" (*Bhinneka Tunggal Ika*), was a vain attempt in conflict resolution. In fact, the statue's ominous presence exacerbated the situation by monumentalizing the conflict and by announcing to all that a "problem" did indeed exist. The intractability of the conflict was ironically reflected in the statue's solidity and strength. On the 1979 episode, see Sudagung, *Mengurai Pertikaian Etnis*, pp. 126–27, 140–42; "Tragedi di Sambas," *Tempo*, December 8, 1979; and "Sumbang yang Pindah Karena Bentrokan Massal di Sambas," *Kompas*, November 19, 1979. The violence went unreported in the government-controlled, local daily, *Akcaya*.

[18] With regard to the protracted Sri Lankan Sinhala–Tamil conflict, Tambiah notes that one of the conflict's "diabolical byproducts" is "a *routinization* of violent action as the ordinary mode of settling differences rather than as a measure of last resort [italics in original]." S. J. Tambiah, *Sri Lanka: Ethnic Fratricide and the Dismantling of Democracy* (Chicago, IL: University of Chicago Press, 1986), p. 118. David Laitin posits a similar "culture of violence" in reference to the Basque separatist movement. See his "National Revivals and Violence," *Archives Europeennes De Sociologie*, vol. XXXVI (1995): 19, 26.

geographical location and among particular belligerents, as each moment of mayhem succeeded another, an internalization of violent impulses vis-à-vis a certain Other crystallized. These processes, ones internal to the conflict, may not have necessarily caused the violence, but they materialized as one of its unfortunate effects.[19] Madurese–Dayak fighting once more exploded in late 1983. In all, we do not know the precise number of Dayak–Madurese riots that had transpired prior to the widespread violence of 1997, although most locals cited a litany of real and phantom disturbances as proof that the Madurese were unwilling to assimilate and to adapt to local cultural conditions.[20] Undoubtedly, the dominant local discourse saddles the Madurese with blame for the habitual strife.

The conflagration of 1997 was the last in a series of exclusive Madurese–Dayak clashes extending from 1967. The intensity and expanse of the 1997 clash, however, far surpassed prior Dayak–Madurese incidents. In fact, at the time it was Indonesia's gravest communal conflict in nearly three decades. What accounted for the change? Why was this clash so much greater than previous local riots? Existing accounts that seek to answer these questions primarily suffer from two interlinked deficiencies.[21] First is that they tend to conflate explanations of the 1997 violence with references to the origins of Dayak–Madurese strife. We must, however, separate concerns that contributed to the 1997 affair—either its occurrence or scale or both—from ones that illuminate the birth of this conflict. Within the context of the 1997 clashes, what needs explaining is not why Madurese–Dayak violence per se exists—riots had taken place intermittently since 1967, as was demonstrated above—but why the 1997 affair was so severe. Second, prior explanations do not account for the temporal and spatial specificities of the conflict's history.

Below, I argue that the coalescing of a political consciousness among Dayaks, especially those of the province's western half, bolstered by the growth of Dayak-oriented non-governmental organizations (NGOs), was key. Although they neither incited nor engineered the violence, these activists fostered a complicated yet tangible awareness of deprivation among disparate communities. Tapping into a consciousness of Dayak grievance, they encouraged, facilitated, and provided the means by which frustration could be productively molded, articulated, and, ultimately, channeled to incite people to confront state authority. Having already touched on the conflict's origins and long duration, below I focus on why the intensity and expanse of 1997 far surpassed prior clashes. To do so, I engage local politics, the changing conditions of Dayak–state relations, and, more specifically, the coalescence of a political consciousness sparked and nurtured by Dayak NGOs.

---

[19] It should be noted here that as this kind of normalization takes root, elite manipulation and strategizing becomes less efficacious and necessary, as violence becomes the means through which specific groups come to resolve disputes.

[20] The then Governor Aspar Aswin's statement fingering the Madurese for the violence is illustrative. See "Aswin; Kerusuhan Dimulai Warga Madura," *Akcaya*, April 10, 1999; and "Gubernur Kalbar: Suku Madura Penyulut Rusuh," *detik.com* website, April 9, 1999.

[21] For a review of alternative perspectives in existing accounts, see Davidson, "The Politics of Violence on an Indonesian Periphery," *South East Asia Research* 11,1 (March 2003): 67–70.

RURAL POLITICIZATION AND THE GREAT RIOTS OF 1997

The year 1996 experienced a rash of riots across Indonesia, including the July 27 affair in Jakarta that was precipitated by the storming of the Indonesian Democratic Party's (PDI, Partai Demokrasi Indonesia) headquarters. Severe riots also broke out in the Java cities of Situbondo in October and Tasikmalaya in December. Cracks within Suharto's regime and concerns over its political future made these riots and a series of smaller outbursts possible; the regime's political legitimacy was on the wane. Yet, these riots paled when compared with the scale and intensity of what transpired in West Kalimantan. On December 30, 1996, in the area of Ledo—about 160 miles northeast of Pontianak City—a small scuffle between a few Madurese and Dayak youths broke out at a pop music (*dangdut*) concert, sparking wider clashes. Over the next two weeks, Dayaks killed about two dozen Madurese and torched nearly one thousand houses.[22] Another riot unfolded in areas intimately familiar with this kind of clash.

Three weeks later, after the violence had seemingly waned, two attacks ignited a much more deadly and widespread round of bloodshed. On January 30, 1997, a few Madurese attacked a Dayak female boarding house in Pontianak City. The following day in Peniraman (Pontianak district), a respected Dayak elder was pulled from a bus and murdered on the spot. This time violence spread rapidly and expansively to include Dayaks in the province's outer reaches. The riots spilled far beyond their geographical norm. When the mayhem finally subsided in early April, estimated death tolls ranged from 500 to 1,700, with Madurese accounting for the lion's share of fatalities.[23]

To explain the intensity and breadth of the 1997 clash, one must take into account the coalescence of a political Dayak consciousness sparked and nurtured by Dayak NGOs based in Pontianak City, led by the Pancur Kasih Foundation.[24] Although Pancur Kasih was founded in 1981, not until the early 1990s, when it was headed by interrelated Dayak NGOs under Pancur Kasih's umbrella, did members of the organization initiate a campaign of rural activism, advocacy, and agitation. Original NGOs included, among others, the Institute of Dayakology Research and Development (IDRD), the Institute for the Defense of the Talino Homeland (LBBT, Lembaga Bela Benua Talino), and the Community Based Forest Management System (SHK, Sistem Hutan Kerakyatan). They, along with the publication of their alternative news monthly, *Kalimantan Review*, were designed to meet this movement's needs.

These entities began to disseminate information, facilitate (and sometimes foment) local dissent, and fund traditional ceremonies. Indisputably, the situation was in flux and a politicization of the countryside was underway. These NGOs

---

[22] Here there is little space to detail the unfolding of the violence. See Human Rights Watch, *Indonesia: Communal Violence in West Kalimantan* 9,10 (September 1997).

[23] Moreover, it must be underscored that recorded death tolls for any single Dayak–Madurese clash—data that should be treated with suspicion—had never surpassed thirty.

[24] Originally founded by Dayak teachers to run a Catholic boarding school in Pontianak City, Pancur Kasih has blossomed into the province's most visible NGO. According to its 1999 figures, its credit union had some 270,000 members, including non-Dayaks, with a capital base of Rp. 137 billion. "CU 'Anak Nakal' Ekonomi Orba," *Kalimantan Review*, April 1999. Pancur Kasih also oversees some eighteen other semi-autonomous units—some of which receive international funding—whose activities range from advocacy and publishing to linguistic and community-based forestry research.

tapped into a large pool of frustration and grievances. With organized and sustained advocacy, they began to reawaken the political awareness of people who identified themselves as Dayak, as these NGOs strove to redress colonial and postcolonial wrongs.[25] Marc Edelman's discussion of the changing connotations of the term *agricultor* in the Costa Rican peasant movement of the 1980s is germane to what was happening to "Dayak" in West Kalimantan of the 1990s:

> ... the label *agricultor* increasingly took on a new meaning in local discourse ... [T]he term was suddenly being asserted in a new adversarial context assuming connotations of persecution and dignity, and becoming almost synonymous with a punishable offense.[26]

In particular, the role of media was formidable. Originally designed to publish current Dayak-oriented research, *Kalimantan Review* progressively evolved into an alternative news source that generally supported budding Dayak resistance. Besides its coverage of violent acts, its reports of small, peaceful protests—such as the submission of a letter of complaint to a subdistrict executive over a local development project—alerted distant Dayak communities to activities that had previously gone undetected.[27] While for the government-controlled local daily, *Akcaya*, notwithstanding one or two exceptions, these acts were immaterial, *Kalimantan Review* celebrated their efflorescence. In this way, the magazine helped to foster a notion of "simultaneity" (borrowing from Benedict Anderson's work on nationalism) among previously disparate groups.[28] With news reports in hand, Dayaks increasingly empathized with others' concerns and responses, a reaction which, in turn, engendered a thickening of reciprocal identification and an increase of coordinated action.

It would be disingenuous, however, to adduce that resistance only began once these NGOs were established. Despite the paucity of documented materials, reports indicate that a few cases did predate their founding.[29] Evidently, the frustrations of

---

[25] This brief account privileges the Dayak side of things at the expense of the Madurese because Dayak war parties were the determining factor in the intensity and expanse of the conflict.

[26] Marc Edelman, *Peasants Against Globalization: Rural Social Movements in Costa Rica* (Stanford, CA: Stanford University Press, 1999), p. 146.

[27] Some early cases of small-scale protests covered in *Kalimantan Review* occurred in Sekadau Hulu (Sanggau district) ("Kehidupan Masyarakat Dayak Desa Tinting Boyok dan Keberadaan PIR," *Kalimantan Review*, April–June 1994); in Sanggau Ledo ("Gua Maria Tetap di Merasap," *Kalimantan Review*, July–September 1995); and in Jelai Hulu (Ketapang district) ("Masyarakat Adat Tolak Proyek Perkebunan," *Kalimantan Review*, October–December 1995).

[28] Benedict Anderson, *Imagined Communities: Reflections on the Origin and Spread of Nationalism*, 2nd edition (London: Verso, 1991), Chapter 2.

[29] Activists recall an "incident" (*peristiwa*) that occurred in Ngabang (Pontianak district) in 1979 in which locals protested government-backed oil palm plantations. In 1981, five Dayak head villagers from Sayak subdistrict (Sintang district) met with the Head of the Sintang DPRD (Dewan Perwakilan Rakyat Daerah, the district congress) to demand compensation over the loss of nut trees felled by a logging company. "Ribuan Pohon Tengkawang Ke Kecamatan Sayan Di Tebang Pemegang HPH," *Akcaya*, April 8, 1981. At this time, this article, a small paragraph buried in *Akcaya*'s back pages, was an exceedingly rare article on Dayaks. And in 1984, Dayaks from Nobal (Sintang district) submitted a letter of complaint to the local bishop and *bupati* concerning a nearby transmigration site. Mill Rokaerts, *Tanah Diri: Land*

Dayak communities were not new. If not, what then was the purpose of establishing Pancur Kasih and its NGOs? New developments, however, were under way. Committed activists afforded local communities the external support needed to help organize sustained protest. And violence more regularly accompanied these protests, news of which was disseminated widely. Since the establishment of these NGOs, protests began to occur within a broader web of political activity and a rising collective political consciousness.[30] Two final striking incidents buttress the argument.

Roughly a quarter-century had elapsed since a Dayak last held a *bupati* post in a province where Dayaks account for some 40 percent of the population.[31] Accordingly, having faithfully delivered the Golkar vote, Dayak leaders began to press for representation. In 1994, the governor heeded their demands, and tapped L. H. Kadir—the then provincial head of village development (Kadit Bangdes) and the highest-ranking Dayak civil servant—for the Sintang *bupati* post. New Order district assembly elections conventionally rubber-stamped government directives; yet, in this case, district assembly members decided otherwise. They selected Abdillah Kamarullah, a Sintang Malay and head of the district's Development Agency Board (Bappeda).[32] Angered at the results, hundreds of Dayaks blocked the main road between Ngabang and Sanggau, smashing windows of passing cars. Notably, these events indicated a political reawakening (*kebangkitan*) and incipient revitalization under an increasingly distinct "Dayak" banner.[33] Large-scale street protests would also set a salient precedent.

Finally, blood spilled in Ngabang (Pontianak district) would set the stage for the fearsome raids on the security apparatus during the 1997 violence. In April 1996, about two thousand Dayak citizens angrily took to the streets, their outrage sparked by the kidnapping and beating of two locals by army soldiers two days previous. As the crowd approached the local military post, soldiers opened fire, injuring fifteen protesters and killing one.[34] For locals, this incident demonstrated ABRI's innate

---

Rights of Tribals, research report (Belgium: Pro Mundi Vita, 1985), p. 26. It is impossible to know how many likewise examples occurred.

[30] Lacking enough space to detail all incidents, I list here a sampling of sources, all taken from *Kalimantan Review*, that detail such incidents: "Warga Empurang Bakar Barak HTI Pt. Inhutani," January–March 1994; "Konflik Antara Masyarakat Adat dengan Perusahaan HPH dan HTI di Kabupaten Ketapang Kalbar," October–December 1994; and "Masyarakat Desa Belimbing Tolak HTI," January–February 1996.

[31] The *bupati* position, it should be noted, was accorded primacy as a coveted prize and a bellwether of change *before* the shift to regional autonomy enhanced political power at the district level, a development that has raised exponentially the value and prestige of these positions.

[32] "Terjadi Kejutan dalam Pemilihan Bupati Sintang," *Kompas*, February 12, 1994. In fact, the provincial Golkar board of directors accused Golkar members of the Sintang district assembly of "deserting" (*membelot*) Golkar and threatened to have them recalled. "Hasil Pemilihan Bupati Sintang Diprotes," *Merdeka*, February 16, 1994.

[33] Locally, this movement is often construed as a *re*-awakening, implicitly recalling the 1950s and the heyday of the PD (Partai Dayak), through which Dayaks were galvanized and organized at the provincial level.

[34] Six soldiers were prosecuted in a military court; sentences ranged from two to eleven months for their roles in the kidnapping and beating. None were prosecuted for shooting the protesters. "Sidang Lanjutan Kasus Ngabang; Memukul Jining, Dituntut 12 Bulan; JT Simanjuntak Dihukum 10 Bulan," *Akcaya*, August 2, 1996.

contempt for Dayaks. As significant, it buttressed their courage in confronting soldiers, a transformation that helps explain the aggressiveness shown by Dayaks who attacked military guard posts and roadblocks during the 1997 clashes.

REFORMASI AND MOVEMENT CONSOLIDATION

Unlike past violence, the 1997 riots spurred an impressive post-conflict mobilization, one aided greatly by national affairs. "Victory" had sparked Dayak self-assertiveness, particularly among communities in the province's western half, where violence was heaviest. One outcome was increasing public demands based on customary law (*hukum adat*) claims that fell outside the narrow limits imposed by the New Order. This nascent dynamic then metamorphosed into a bold political movement a year later, when the euphoria of the reform movement (*reformasi*) reached West Kalimantan. Fueled by the financial crisis that began in mid-1997, the movement that helped to topple Suharto in May 1998 had tremendous implications for the country's Outer Islands, where divergent parties translated various understandings of *reformasi* to suit local needs.[35] Forcefully and decisively, large numbers of rural Dayak—facilitated by some urban leaders—stepped into the space that had been opened by reform. Incessant protests and occasional violence by Dayaks have aimed to reverse long-standing economic, political, and cultural marginalization. Specifically, two principal short- to medium-range goals have been discernible: getting more Dayak into the province's highly prized bureaucracy, particularly in visible leadership positions; and pressing the government to recognize Dayak land rights. Both represent the ambition to claim a kind of redistributive justice.

Despite earlier instances of public protest, starting in late May 1998, nearly each week some form of visible protest against logging, plantations, transmigration, and productive forest sites—rural symbols of state-backed, large-scale capital enterprises—occurred. Listing all examples would be fruitless, but some notable ones were: on July 30 and August 6, 1998, more than a thousand Dayak demonstrated against the Wira Rivaco Mandum rubber plantation in Ngabang (Pontianak district). In the same district in August 1998, two logging bulldozers were seized. On November 25, 1998, more than five hundred locals protested at the Inhutani III plantation shouting "burn!" And in early February 1999, the Halisa and Alas Kusuma plantation companies in Ketapang district suffered fire damage caused by arson.[36]

Protests at district and provincial assemblies also became frequent. For example, on June 30, 1998, Dayaks held their first large-scale protest in recent memory at the

---

[35] The best account of these events across Java and the capital is John T. Sidel, "Macet Total: Logics of Circulation and Accumulation in the Demise of Indonesia's New Order," *Indonesia* 66 (October 1998): 159–94.

[36] All examples have been taken from *Kalimantan Review*: "Pembangunan=Penindasan?," September 1998; "Selama Ini Kami Ditipu Perusahaan," September 1998; "Pt. Rana Wastu Kencana Rampas Tanah Adat Dayak Bakati'," November 1998; and "Perusahaan Memelaratkan Orang Dayak?," January 1999. For the Alas Kusuma case, see also "Pembakaran Camp PT. Alas Kusuma Terus Diselidiki," *Pontianak Post*, February 9, 1999. To reflect the reform environment and distance itself from its New Order association, *Akcaya* has thus changed its name to *Pontianak Post*.

provincial assembly headquarters in Pontianak City.[37] And from October to December 1998, dozens of locals demonstrated at the Sanggau district assembly office to demand the recognition of their land rights.[38]

This mobilization most visibly crystallized over the question of representation in district executive (*bupati*) positions. Persistent demonstrations and occasional acts of targeted violence led to the selection of Dayak *bupati* in Sanggau (November 1998) and Pontianak (March 1999) districts.[39] Clearly, these mobilizations had convinced the government to take steps that would diminish the likelihood of more violence erupting "from below," possibly against the government itself. By mid-1999, Dayak civil servants filled four out of West Kalimantan's then seven *bupati* positions.[40] This was a remarkable development, particularly if we recall the exclusion of Dayaks from these posts under the New Order and the Kadir fiasco noted above.

Final points warrant mention before turning to the Malay ethnic revitalization. First, the linguistic, ethnic, and historical diversity of the "Dayak," a term that collects more than a hundred different sub-ethnic groups under its umbrella, is immense.[41] Second, and of related significance, "Dayak" reawakening has not been monolithic, but rather an amalgam of multifarious, sometimes contentious, collective perceptions and actions. For instance, rifts exist along party lines. In the 1999 general elections, Dayak personalities headed numerous parties, including the PDI-P (Partai Demokrasi Indonesia–Perjuangan, The Indonesian Democratic Party of Struggle, led by the late Rudy Alamsyahrum),[42] the PBI (Partai Bhinneka Tunggal Ika Indonesia, The Indonesian Unity in Diversity Party, led by the late Herbertus Tekwaan, Oeray's son), the PDI (Sebastiantos Khapat), and the PDKB (Partai Demokrasi Kasih Bangsa, The Love the Nation Democratic Party, led by Cosmas Damianus Yan Kay). Golkar also listed a Dayak, Arsen Rickson, as its legislative candidate from Sanggau district for the National Parliamant (DPR, Dewan Perwakilan Rakyat). These fissures ultimately contributed to a fractured Dayak vote, leaving many to joke warily that only in fighting the Madurese are Dayak united.

Finally, these movements have incurred occasional criticism from the very same Pancur Kasih NGOs that helped to spark their resurgence. Some activists fear growing ethnocentrism and an entrenched "culture of violence." They prefer to use legal, less violent methods and want to empower both Dayak and agrarian-based

---

[37] "Ini Dia...Reformasi Ala Masyarakat Adat Dayak Kalimantan Barat," *Kalimantan Review*, July 1998.

[38] "Ratusan Petani PIR Trans PT. Surya Deli Gelar Unjuk Rasa Di DPRD Sanggau," *Akcaya*, October 30, 1998; and "PT. MPE Telantarkan Petani," *Kalimantan Review*, January 1999.

[39] In the Pontianak district case, the assembly building was set alight by supporters of Cornelis, the then Dayak subdistrict head of Menyuke. Cornelis was not selected but this pressure "from below" enabled another Dayak, Cornelius Kimha, to be selected as *bupati*. Cornelis later became the *bupati* of the new Landak district, carved out of the original Pontianak district.

[40] Consonant with demands for regional autonomy, the number of districts in West Kalimantan has since increased to ten. There are, however, only eight *bupati* positions, for heads of Pontianak City and Singkawang are given mayoral status (*walikota*).

[41] Standard figure is 450. J. U. Lontaan, *Sejarah-Hukum Adat dan Adat Istiadat Kalimantan-Barat* (Pontianak: Pemda Tingkat I Kalbar, 1975), pp. 50–62. Yet, some elder Dayak claim the figure is closer to 145. The Institute of Dayakology (IDRD's new abbreviated name) is currently mapping the ethno-linguistic diversity of Dayak populations.

[42] Alamsyahrum's ethnic identity was controversial. Since he was a Muslim, the fact that he considered himself "Dayak" aroused the ire of many Dayak, who preferred to see him as "Malay."

non-Dayak *rakyat* (the people) alike. The destruction of the region's forests and the rapid acceleration of the establishment of new oil palm plantations hurt other similarly situated ethnic communities. Likewise, the ability of the newly appointed Dayak *bupati* in countering this New Order-inspired, capital-intensive transformation of West Kalimantan's economy is being questioned. What is the good of a Dayak *bupati*, they ask, if the forests continue to disappear, "development" strategies bring in more oil palm plantations, and capital continues to strip land from the *rakyat*? These are all well reasoned, but largely unheeded, concerns expressed to date.

"SAMBAS '99"

The threat posed by this Dayak reawakening precipitated a Malay counter-mobilization. Whereas under the New Order, specifically "Malay" organizations were rare, recently their numbers have mushroomed. While the Dayak movement was bolstered by the national euphoria of *reformasi*, the anticipation of regional autonomy has provided this Malay mobilization with an institutional impetus. To offset Dayak success, Malay leaders have sought to reassert their Malay-ness, to justify themselves as true native sons, and to position themselves to reap the short-term political and economic windfalls promised under decentralization. As it devolves substantial fiscal and administrative authority to the district level, regional autonomy has been seen as a promising antidote to the New Order's overly centralized and coercive rule.

Prior to the 1999 general elections, widespread violence again rocked Sambas district. In a national context, it was an incipient case of a kind of regional strife that came to dominate the early post-Suharto polity. Locally, however, in areas that had experienced recurrent bloodletting, the active participation of Sambas Malays in the riots made this incident unique. The background is as follows. On January 17, 1999, in the village of Parit Setia (subdistrict Jawai), some Malays beat a Madurese man from a nearby village who was accused of breaking and entering. In revenge, about two hundred Madurese raided Parit Setia on January 19 during Idul Fitri—the holiday marking the end of Ramadhan, the Muslim fasting month. Three Malays were killed in the twenty-minute-long attack.

For Malays, this attack vindicated the ubiquitous perception of the Madurese as arrogant, hot-tempered belligerents keen to take the law into their own hands (*main hakim sendiri*). Incessant bouts with Dayaks had given this view local currency, but this incident was perceived as different. In fact, Sambas Malays saw it as much worse. They argued that pious Muslims could not commit such acts on Idul Fitri; the Madurese had therefore proven themselves to be irreligious, savage. The actions of these Madurese served to further demonize and dehumanize the Madurese community in the eyes of local Malays, signaling an important change in consciousness that would later justify their expulsion.[43] Meanwhile, rubbing salt into

---

[43] In these circumstances, Tambiah notes that "an increasing alienation and polarization between the self as a 'son of the soil' and the other alien develops, and much that was previously shared now gives way to a suspicion-ridden separation and dehumanization of the other, so that to treat him as nonhuman and deserving of degradation and destruction becomes imperative and justifiable. So the aggressor community in attacking its enemy finally comes to perceive its actions as defensive and protective." Stanley Tambiah, *Leveling Crowds:*

Malay wounds, the Jawai subdistrict police dragged their feet on arrests. If the police will not protect us, Malays began to feel, then "we" will be forced to protect ourselves.

While government officials—both Malay and Madurese elite representatives—held meetings to ameliorate tensions, no retaliatory attacks were mobilized. Yet, during this lull, a new organization formed in Singkawang—The Communication Forum of Malay Youth (FKPM, Forum Komunikasi Pemuda Melayu), organized to coordinate Malay demands and efforts. FKPM would play a formidable role in the upcoming Malay mobilizations, but an important distinction requires elaboration. At this point, FKPM largely consisted of a group of retired civil servants and a group of "big men" (not youths) from Singkawang with underworld connections, some of whom have described their occupation as "contractor." The prevailing calm of elite level politics in Singkawang belied the reality on the ground, however. Tensions were brewing between Malay and Madurese youth in Pemangkat, Jawai, and Tebas subdistricts, the epicenter of the upcoming violence.

Here, organization and mobilization among youth gangs were enacted with impressive swiftness. Weeks prior to the outbreak of violence, strategies were discussed regarding how to best solve the Madurese problem. Young Malay men procured weapons, sharpened bamboo spears, got into shape (*mengisi badan*) in anticipation of clashes, and produced homemade shotguns from local smelts. They also patrolled neighborhoods at night to guard against Madurese reprisals. In all, they were preparing themselves but would not strike prematurely; they anticipated an opportune moment to come.[44]

The recklessness of some Madurese thugs soon presented these ready Malays with a moment to strike. On February 21, 1999, the stabbing of a Malay bus conductor in Tebas by a Madurese who refused to pay his fare ignited tensions. Over the next two weeks in Tebas and neighboring Pemangkat and Jawai subdistricts, sporadic fighting between Malay and Madurese gangs resulted in roughly two dozen deaths and tens of houses razed. Widespread violence was held in-check, however. Then, on March 16, a Dayak (Martinus Amat) was slain outside Pemangkat; this killing triggered direct Dayak involvement in the clashes. Galvanized by Dayak inclusion, Malay mobilizations grew apace. With Dayaks mobilized on the eastern front, FKPM commanders fanned the riots' flames north into areas that were hitherto peaceful, such as Sambas town and Paloh subdistrict. Some four hundred Madurese fled Paloh on boats to Kuching, Sarawak.[45] Meanwhile, by this time, some three thousand refugees (*pengungsi*) had arrived in

---

Ethnonationalist Conflicts, and Collective Violence in South Asia (Berkeley, CA: University of California Press, 1996), p. 284.

[44] Writing on ethnic riots, Donald Horowitz notes that "(R)iots are, for example, commonly preceded by a ... lull, a time of apprehensive quiet during which rumors and warnings may circulate ... while preparations for the attack go forward in inconspicuous ways." Donald Horowitz, *The Deadly Ethnic Riot* (Berkeley, CA: University of California Press, 2001), p. 16.

[45] The Sarawak government, not wanting an international refugee crisis on its hands, quickly returned the refugees to Pontianak. "Mereka Lari ke Malaysia," *Tempo*, April 5, 1999. As for the conspicuously delayed outbreak of violence in Paloh, a local commented, "I don't understand why this incident suddenly rocked Paloh. Here there is nothing that differentiates Malays and Madurese. They have assimilated well. Same for their economic status; there were no excessively wealthy Madurese." "Karena Isu Paloh Bergolak," *Suaka*, April 5–8, 1999.

Surabaya (East Java).[46] In early April, having completed their northern missions, FKPM commanders retraced their steps and sparked violence in the district's southern reaches, around Singkawang and in Sungai Raya subdistrict. Like its northern counterparts, Sungai Raya (and even Singkawang) had been peaceful until FKPM commanders decided to stir up trouble. In late April, another four thousand refugees had arrived in Surabaya.[47] By early May, with Madurese expelled from Sambas district, Malay and Dayak combatants ran out of intended targets, halting the mobilizations. All told, reports from this six-week-long orgy of violence contain gruesome and disturbing accounts of beheadings, mutilations, rape, deplorable attacks on refugees and hospitals, and shooting engagements between locals and crack troops (PHH, Pasukan anti Huru-Hara) brought from Java to contain the violence.

The sparking of the second round of violence and, in particular, Amat's controversial murder, raises several questions: who were the assailants? Did assailants act on their own or someone else's behalf? Was Amat targeted as "Dayak" or mistaken as "Malay"? Dubious eyewitness accounts finger Madurese attackers, claims that Madurese leaders refute. Would Madurese, already engaged in violence with Malays, deliberately precipitate Dayak involvement? Nonetheless, there were evident signs to suggest that at some point, most likely after the outbreak of violence, an intentional ethnic cleansing program, meant to be permanent, took shape.[48]

The first such sign was the conspicuous mobilization of Dayaks; "inviting" their support would facilitate an effort to focus greater violence against the Madurese.[49] Second, Malays razed dozens of Madurese mosques. In contrast, few if any mosques were affected during the 1997 riots, clashes between the mostly Christian Dayak and Muslim Madurese. Third was the total destruction of Madurese dwellings. Typically, the concrete foundations of homes that have been burned remain intact in these kinds of clashes. In the (new) Sambas district, however, extreme efforts were undertaken to remove these concrete foundations, as if those responsible were attempting to erase any reminders of Madurese presence.[50]

Last, and most evident, was the large exodus of Madurese from Sambas district. Local government officials and politicians wholeheartedly supported the exodus,

---

[46] "Warga Madura Dari Sambas Tiba di Surabaya," *Suara Pembaruan*, March 14, 1999.

[47] "Ribuan Pengungsi Asal Sambas Mendarat di Surabaya," *Republika*, April 29, 1999.

[48] Little evidence exists to establish ethnic cleansing as an intended, *a priori* aim of the violence. It was more likely an unintended by-product, materializing into a goal once the fighting had commenced. This substantiates Michael Mann's hypothesis (one of eight) on ethnic cleansing: "Murderous cleansing is rarely the initial intent of perpetrators." See Mann, *The Dark Side of Democracy: Explaining Ethnic Cleansing* (New York, NY: Cambridge University Press, 2005), p. 7.

[49] Having Dayak join the foray also would presumably divert attention from the fact that two Islamic communities were fighting. Islamic leaders in Pontianak City have admitted their embarrassment over this predicament. Interestingly, for the Dayak side, there are at least two points of view concerning their involvement. While some suggest that they joined (*bergabung*) with Malays, others insist that Dayak were merely defending their honor in the face of Amat's death. It was happenstance (*kebetulan*) that the Malays were already battling the Madurese.

[50] One historian of ethnic cleansing in Europe writes: "The intention of ethnic cleansing is to remove a people and often *all traces* of them from a concrete territory [emphasis added]." Norman M. Naimark, *Fires Of Hatred: Ethnic Cleansing in Twentieth-Century Europe* (Cambridge: Harvard University Press, 2001), p. 3.

which they perceived as a correction to decades of injustices.[51] Then there was the role the security apparatus played in the expulsions. Countering the once vaunted view of the military, some recent accounts have questioned the capabilities of the post-Suharto military in containing communal violence, especially in the Outer Islands.[52] Yet, the evacuations of Madurese from parts of West Kalimantan were conducted with exacting efficiency. In areas of ephemeral violence and in times of significant calm, security forces continued to evacuate Madurese. Although these actions might be characterized as germane and appropriate within the context of the situation, there were evident, and revealing, distinctions between the actions of local Kodam XII troops (and police forces) and the PHH troops brought to the province from Jakarta. The latter were most often responsible for confronting the rioters physically; they showed a certain restraint, notwithstanding possible overzealousness in some cases and probable human rights abuses. Yet members of the local security apparatus, who were often seen standing by idly while mobs rioted, were more likely to take up positions "safeguarding" Madurese property in order to resell it.[53] Following the numerous Madurese–Dayak clashes that had preceded this new eruption of violence—including the massive 1997 episode—most Madurese had returned home, often to rebuild razed homes. This time, however, things were different and much worse.

Nearly fifty thousand traumatized Madurese, escorted by military trucks and boats, arrived in Pontianak City and were placed in numerous holding camps, including sports stadiums and athletic fields. Refugee experiences have been diverse. First, some ten thousand Madurese from Bengkayang district were housed in camps outside Singkawang. Most Madurese from Sambas were escorted to Pontianak City. Second, a number of refugees were directed to holding areas outside Pontianak's camps. Perhaps as many as ten thousand were shipped and then housed in camps in East Java and Madura; an equal number found lodging in Pontianak. Of the latter, those better-off rented accommodations while others found shelter with families or friends. Also, not all refugees were Madurese. Dayak, Javanese, Bugis, and Malay spouses were involved as well. For the residents of Pontianak City, the lingering refugee crisis served as a reminder of violence past and a foreshadowing of violence to come.

---

[51] This was confirmed by my (and others') interviews with district assembly members and with officials in Pemangkat, Jawai, and Sambas subdistricts. For example: "There are no moderate views to be found; even schoolteachers and district chiefs are willing to stand beside a severed head and try to justify the butchery as a necessary response to long-standing grievances." *The Economist*, "Descent into Darkest Borneo," March 27, 1999. No one encountered defended the Madurese or held serious reservations concerning the violence.

[52] See Gerry van Klinken, "The Maluku Wars: Bringing Society Back In," *Indonesia* 71 (April 2001): 1–26; International Crisis Group, "Communal Violence in Indonesia: Lessons from Kalimantan," *ICG Asia Report*, No. 19, June 27, 2001; and Dini Djalal, "Front-line Friction; Conflict between Army and Police Spurs Separation," *Far Eastern Economic Review*, April 4, 1999.

[53] This exodus included thousands of cows owned by Madurese. It was reported that the cow population of Sambas in 1997 was 26,700. Although the precise, collective ethnic identities of the cows' owners are not known, it is widely believed the majority were Madurese. BPS Propinsi Kalimantan Barat, *Kalimantan Barat Dalam Angka* (Pontianak: BPS Propinsi Kalimantan Barat, 1998), p. 161, Table 6.3.1.

Refugees, Relocation, Riot

The provincial government was content to feed and to shelter the Madurese IDPs until after the June 1999 elections, evidently to avoid "unnecessary" controversies that might, in turn, disrupt the implementation of the election results. By election time, nonetheless, some eighty-five children had succumbed to diseases incurred from the camps' appalling conditions (*Pontianak Post,* June 14, 1999). Following the elections, the IDPs refused to be relocated to marshy, inhospitable sites some thirty miles south of Pontianak. They preferred to return to Sambas.[54] Leaving for Madura was never an option. Some 97 percent of the refugees were born in West Kalimantan.[55]

The deplorable conditions in the camps prompted little in the way of public outcry or sympathy. Madurese are not considered native sons and, as previously mentioned, a belief persists that Madurese belligerence is the root cause of the chronic unrest in West Kalimantan.[56] Although women, children, and the elderly made up the majority of the refugees, they were uniformly stigmatized as "Madurese" and thus considered responsible for their wretched fate. Accordingly, few (in some places *no*) local support groups formed to aid the refugees.[57] Local officials, who felt improvements to the camps' infrastructure would buoy spirits and provide incentives to prolong their stay, obstructed the efforts of international relief organizations. In this way, the camps' squalor was politically constructed.[58]

These decrepit conditions soon produced social ramifications. With disheveled facades and poor lighting, the areas surrounding the camps were soon deemed troubled and crime infested. In essence, camps in central Pontianak with permeable yet recognizable boundaries became Madurese ghettoes. Local newspapers did their part to reinforce these perceptions by featuring crimes that occurred nearby the camps; whether the perpetrators were refugees or not was usually obscure in the reports.[59]

---

[54] A survey conducted by a local Madurese organization in April 1999 found that 60 percent of respondents wanted to return to Sambas. See *Akcaya,* April 23, 1999. Two years later, a survey I conducted with the help of the Madurese student organization HIMMA (Himpunan Mahasiswa Madura, Association of Madurese Students) showed similar results: 66 percent (73 out of 110 respondents) wanted to return to Sambas; 31 percent were keen on remaining in Pontianak; 2 percent chose relocation; and 1 percent selected Madura as a preferred destination.

[55] This figure stems from the 2001 survey I conducted.

[56] The then Governor Aswin publicly pinned the violence on the Madurese. See *Akcaya,* April 10, 1999, and *detik.com* website, April 9, 1999.

[57] Islamic student groups engaged in a Herculean effort to provide necessities to refugees as they arrived in the camps. These were emergency measures, and the students lacked resources to sustain the effort. Later they raised sufficient funds to send some one hundred children to Islamic boarding schools (*pesantren*) in Java. A multi-ethnic collaboration of fifteen NGOs had formed an aid organization (LSM Peduli Kalbar). However, the effort was listless and accomplished little.

[58] On hand from the outset, *Medecins Sans Frontieres* (MSF) became the main pillar of non-governmental assistance. Projects concentrated on upgrading infrastructure, like sanitation facilities, rather than food distribution.

[59] See, for example, *Equator,* July 17, 2000, which includes a photo of a refugee camp, and *Pontianak Post,* November 15, 2000.

Against this backdrop, Pontianak City saw a three-day spate of "ethnic" violence in which refugee camps were occasionally targeted in late October 2000.[60] The city's economically and politically underprivileged—Madurese petty traders, *becak* (pedicab) drivers, and kiosk owners—bore the disproportionate brunt of the October riots. Another group of vulnerable Madurese—victims of the Sambas affair who had been housed in camps in Pontianak since early 1999—were likewise targeted, although this orgy of violence did not fundamentally involve the refugees per se.

IDP Madurese shacks outside Pontianak's badminton hall (GOR Pangsuma), mid-2000. (Photo by Jamie S. Davidson)

---

[60] The Malay–Madurese ethnic ascriptions of the violence masked a political tussle between the then Governor Aswin and provincial legislators who sought his ouster.

IDP Madurese shacks razed during the June 2001 riot, July 2001.
(Photo by Jamie S. Davidson)

Members of the Madurese elite also failed the refugees. Noteworthy was the duplicity of Sulaiman, West Kalimantan's wealthiest and most visible Madurese figure. Head of the leading Madurese organization, IKAMRA (Ikatan Keluarga Besar Madura, Extended Family Association of Madurese), Sulaiman was an infamous champion of Governor Aspar Aswin.[61] He also held contracts to help construct the relocation sites.[62]

The IDP presence in Pontianak created problems; the convenient combination of government incompetence, corruption, and vested interests made these problems into a crisis. Local officials inflated refugee rolls to increase the amount of central government subsidies circulating among their offices.[63] But corruption figured most prominently in the construction of the relocation sites. These projects would require thousands of new houses and miles of new roads, bridges, and irrigation ditches. It was a treasure trove to bureaucrats. Government departments fought amongst themselves for control of planning and construction. Atop the bureaucracy sat Aswin. His thirst for development monies was unquenchable—for instance, he implemented central government plans to give the Sambas and Pontianak district governments Rp. three billion apiece in construction subsidies. Tellingly, Aswin

---

[61] Accusations of Sulaiman's support of Aswin and his role in the October riots created a storm in the Madurese community. At a reconciliation meeting immediately following the riots, Sulaiman's leadership was seriously questioned. For accusations of Madurese leadership seeking material gain out of the refugee crisis, see Edi Petebang and Eri Sutrisno, *Konflik Etnik di Sambas* (Jakarta: ISAI, 2000), pp. 30–31.

[62] His enthusiasm for relocation could be gleaned from statements made in the press. For example, "[relocation] is a policy we respect and we put our full trust in the provincial government to carry it out." Cited in *Kompas*, April 22, 1999.

[63] "Jumlah Pengungsi Dimanipulasi Untuk Korupsi," *Kalimantan Review*, September/October 2001.

insisted that the monies be channeled to the district via provincial government conduits.[64]

Construction monies vanished at a remarkable rate. On-site investigations suggested that no more than one-quarter of budgeted construction funds for houses were actually used as they were intended. Meanwhile, officials recurrently falsified soil suitability reports. Again, the local press participated in this farce. It published pictures of proud Madurese settlers displaying their prodigious produce and ran disingenuous headlines like "Refugees in Tebang Kacang are a Success" and "4,000 Refugee Families want to be Relocated."[65]

The refugee "time bomb" to which the local press and aid workers had alluded finally exploded. On June 23, 2001, a robbery gone awry outside the city's sports complex (GOR, Golongan Olahraga) that housed several IDP camps resulted in the death of a young boy. The perpetrators were four Madurese youths, although whether they were IDPs was unclear. It hardly mattered. Their ethnicity and the crime's location signified "refugee" (*pengungsi*).

Beautification of the former GOR Pangsuma IDP camp, June 2005.
(Photo by Jamie S. Davidson)

---

[64] "Aswin Ingin Temui Gus Dur," *Pontianak Post*, January 29, 2000; and "Minta Kejelasan Penanganan dan Dana Rp. 3,6 M," *Pontianak Post*, February 5, 2000.

[65] For the photo, see *Pontianak Post*, June 3, 2001. These misleading headlines are from *Equator*, February 24, 2001, and March 9, 2001. The national daily *Kompas* was not above such commentary either, as suggested by photo captions identifying conditions in these designated locations as "*subur*" [fertile] and "*makin membaik*" [getting better] in *Kompas*, July 13, 2001.

Nearby locals mobilized at the GOR camps. The prominence of yellow among the crowd signified "Malay." A contingent of police officers kept them from invading the camps, but could not prevent the firebombing of the IDPs wooden shacks, hundreds of which were reduced to ashes. PFKPM (Persatuan Forum Kommunikasi Pemuda Melayu, Union of Communication Forums of Malay Youth) gangs then spread the violence, so that it consumed sites affected by the October 2000 riot. In particular, they torched scores of kiosks and lynched two *becak* drivers in nearby Flamboyan market. This time, thankfully, the violence dissipated quickly.

This June 2001 riot was limited in scope and largely spontaneous, but it exploded in a context of wider political and economic meaning. Rampant government corruption, intensifying economic competition between urban Madurese and Malays, and raw ethnic sentiments were all operative.[66] Finally, in April 2002, a few months before Aswin's second (and final) term was to expire, a deal was reached by which refugee families would receive varying amounts of compensation, based on their situations, to help them leave the camps.[67] A month later, refugees of their own accord began exiting the camps to build new homes and lives on the outskirts of Pontianak—a minor victory indeed.[68] A final cathartic explosion had been averted. While these Madurese are no longer in camps, they retain their IDP status until a safe return to Sambas is permitted.[69]

The urban dimensions of these two riots induced urgency among the province's elite to seek reconciliation, or at least minimize the likelihood of future outbreaks. Despite the massive size of the 1997 and 1999 incidents, the provincial (i.e., Pontianak) elite still tended to feel disconnected from the bloodshed and suffering that had occurred in the semi-rural districts. Moreover, no matter how extensive and horrendous, these affairs had disturbed but did not destroy the provincial economy.

---

[66] Malay elites protested that male IDPs working in construction sites were stealing jobs from Malays. Meanwhile, children from the camps sold newspapers on street corners, while hundreds of women were trucked from the camps to work in factories along Pontianak's periphery.

[67] According to Syamsuddin, formerly a well-to-do businessman from Sambas, an IDP and head of the Victims of Sambas's Social Violence Foundation (YKKSS, Yayasan Korban Kerusuahan Sosial Sambas)—the organization that represented the IDPs in negotiations—roughly seven thousand refugee families were accounted for in Pontianak (in and out of the camps). Families in camps were granted Rp. five million a piece, while those in resettlement sites received half this amount, based on the value of the houses they had been given. In total, the (central) government handed out some Rp. 4,5 billion for distribution to IDPs in Pontianak and those in relocation sites some one hundred kilometers south of the city. It remains unclear what percentage of the estimated 62,000 people were refugees. Syamsuddin stated that provincial officials essentially failed to address the IDP issue until a meeting with government ministers in Jakarta in September 2001. As government funding for resettlement sites had run dry, Syamsuddin noted, conceptions of the refugees as a "project" (*proyek*) were no longer feasible. Author's interview, Syamsuddin, Pontianak, July 18, 2002.

[68] Moreover, government officials also could no longer hold to the fiction that these sites were suitable for securing a livelihood. There was no choice but to accept relocation on Pontianak's fringes. Initially, there were a few reported cases of arson of new IDP houses, including the razing of some sixty houses west of Pontianak on July 12, 2002. To my knowledge, there have been no repeat occurrences since this incident.

[69] It appears that the refugees finally acquiesced once Indonesia's then vice president, a native son to West Kalimantan, Hamzah Haz, visited Pontianak to help broker a deal. See "Setelah Pengungsi Ditolak Kembali ke Sambas," *Kalimantan Review*, August 2002.

But now that Pontianak threatened to become the new locus of violence, the regional economy risked devastation. It would not survive a ransacking of Pontianak.[70]

With this in mind, elites sought to safeguard the gubernatorial succession. To be sure, an ethnically based power-sharing accord was in place; but again, it was Aswin who prevailed.[71] While the succeeding governor, Usman Djafar, is a Malay *putra daerah* (native son), he did not come from the provincial legislature. He is a businessman who had been residing in Jakarta. Moreover, his Dayak vice-governor, L. K. Kadir, had been a top Aswin assistant. Thus, it is perhaps unsurprising that Syamsumin, Golkar's candidate, finished a distant second in the December 2002 balloting, behind Djafar.[72]

POLITICAL REVITALIZATION AND *OTONOMI DAERAH*

The 1999 clashes precipitated a "Malay" reawakening, although its seeds had been sprouting prior to the violence. Threatened by Dayak mobilization, Malay leaders feared that they would be bypassed as groups jockeyed for positions that would gain them access to the new riches promised by regional autonomy. One need only recall the 1998–99 appointments of Dayak *bupati* in Sanggau and Pontianak districts to understand Malay elite anxiety. So, a "Malay" resurgence, fueled by violence against a vulnerable enemy to harness mobilization energies and to fortify identities, was perceived as an effective means to resist Dayak advances. Here, it must be underscored that anti-Madurese violence makes a claim on *penduduk asli* (indigenous people) status, the *sine qua non* of local politics under regional autonomy. In this way, the indigenous "Malay" is deemed the rightful challenger to the native "Dayak" in high-stakes, regional autonomy politics. Ultimately, whereas anti-Madurese violence involved subduing and expelling the Madurese, a project that entailed a necessary aggressiveness, the actual intended audience of this Malay outburst was the Malays' Dayak counterparts, whose prior mobilizations had placed the Malay elite in a defensive and reactive posture.

Under the auspices of regional autonomy, Sambas district was divided into inland Bengkayang and coastal Sambas districts. This was a crucial development.

---

[70] This fear was not wholly urban either. Pontianak is the linchpin for the distribution of goods throughout the vast province, and in the short two to three days during which the October riots paralyzed Pontianak, shortages in the countryside were noticeable. Prices spiked. The recent Dayak–Madurese bloodshed of 2001 in neighboring Central Kalimantan provided a haunting lesson of what could happen when a region's primary distribution center was destroyed. For months following the riots, denizens of upland Central Kalimantan suffered through famine-like conditions. News reports disingenuously blamed shortages on low rivers that had been reduced by drought, thus impeding the passage of goods. See "Bencana Kelaparan Ancam Warga Pedalaman Kalteng," *Kompas,* July 18, 2001.

[71] Previously, an informal, elite Malay–Dayak power-sharing deal had been struck. For district levels, *bupati*/vice-*bupati* positions were to feature Malay/Dayak (or Dayak/Malay) candidacies to ensure balanced representation. The *bupati* elections in Sintang, Ketapang, Kapuas Hulu, and Landak districts, which had been recently concluded, reflected this compromise. Moreover, because a Dayak, Oevaang Oeray, held the governorship prior to the New Order era (from 1960 to 1966), Malay elites insisted that it was time for West Kalimantan to have its first Malay *putra daerah* governor.

[72] It is also significant to note that Djafar is close to Hamzah Haz, who was vice president of Indonesia and national head of PPP (Partai Persatuan Pembangunan, the Unity Development Party) at the time. Haz visited Pontianak days before the election to campaign for Djafar. However, PPP controlled only six out of the forty-five seats in the provincial assembly.

Ideally, the split—a foregone conclusion by late 1998, yet officially implemented after the June 1999 elections—was envisioned as a way to create a Dayak-dominated Bengkayang and a Malay Sambas.[73] The latter was the more important issue. As for Bengkayang, it was irrefutable that Dayaks, although suffering from intra-elite friction, would rule Bengkayang. The *bupati*, the vice-*bupati*, and most of the district bureaucracy would be in Dayak hands. The politically limp Chinese were welcomed to inhabit Bengkayang town to help fuel the local economy. From economic, political, and demographic viewpoints, it was the rural Madurese, much more than the Chinese, who were perceived as threats to Dayak domination. But decades of violence have tempered this threat's potential; the 1997 riots were perhaps most effective in dampening the power of the Madurese. Although an unintended consequence, violence has authenticated Bengkayang as Dayak territory, a point that has been beaten into the Madurese, who, by and large, have come to accept it. Dayaks are the rightful heirs to Bengkayang. If certain uppity Madurese deem otherwise, Dayaks have proven repeatedly their willingness to battle and subdue Madurese challengers.

But for coastal Sambas, the situation was further complicated by the ambiguity of Malay domination. Malay leaders needed to stamp Sambas emphatically as its own, to demonstrate that Sambas is to the Malay what Bengkayang is to the Dayak. The threat the Madurese posed was not political in a formal sense. Their numbers remained too slight to upset balances in the district assembly, and Madurese leaders could not legitimately mount challenges for *bupati* or vice-*bupati* positions in the foreseeable future. For the Malay elite, the problem concerned "the street." Without Malay control of Sambas's gambling, extortion, and protection rackets, without Malay control of its crime, without respect from its police force toward Malays, without Malay control of informal service sectors like local transport, how could Sambas be considered "Malay"? In other words, as long as Madurese thugs roamed and operated in Sambas, Malay elite domination would be tenuous at best. Here, though seemingly immaterial, the stereotyped caricatures of Malays—in this case, at least Sambas Malays—as *"pengecut"* (chicken), *"krupuk"* (thin rice crackers), and *"penakut"* (coward) take effect. In an atmosphere where politics is determined by mobilizing masses and by controlling not only high-end business "concessions" but also low-end "informal" revenue sources, these disparaging tags weighed heavily. Malay leaders needed to prove themselves stewards of Sambas vis-à-vis the Madurese, and, more important, to demonstrate to the Dayak that "Malay" would formidably challenge "Dayak" for bragging rights. In the words of many Malay, they may be *krupuk*, but the longer it is fried, the harder *krupuk* becomes.

The forms this Malay revitalization has taken and its timing reflects its defensiveness against the looming Dayak "threat." The main features of Malay violence in Sambas—Madurese victims, beheadings, and trust in magical invulnerability (*kebal*)—were hauntingly similar to Dayak war practices. Malay responsiveness is also readily apparent in its organizations. When the Dayak movement began to coalesce following the 1997 violence, a Malay Cultural and Customary Council (Majelis Adat dan Budaya Melayu), mimicking the Dayak Customary Council (Majelis Adat), was established in Pontianak City to counter the growing abundance of Dayak customary law claims. The scope of customary law

---

[73] Although the elections were administrated under the old Sambas district, votes were tallied for each district so Sambas and Bengkayang districts could have separate district assemblies.

and its accompanying sanctions, Malay elites argued, was seeping beyond "traditional" boundaries and, as a result, being applied disproportionately to non-Dayaks. In mid-1999, another organization, the Malay Brotherhood Customary Council (Lembaga Adat dan Kekerabatan Melayu, known as Lembayu) formed to repel intensifying demands to place Dayak representatives in key governmental positions.[74] Lembayu later designated several Malay war commanders (*panglima*), again modeling their response on the Dayak example.

Not all aspects of this Malay revival merely imitate Dayak patterns, however. Most notably, the province's once-vibrant sultanates, dormant for decades, are being currently revived as centers of "Malay" culture. On July 15, 2000, Raden Winata Kusumah was installed as Crown Prince at the Alwadzi Koebillah palace (*kraton*) in Sambas, one of the first such ceremonies outside Java in nearly forty years.[75] Moreover, the rebirth of Pontianak's Kadriah *kraton* has been driven by the attempts of Malay elites to rehabilitate the name of Sultan Hamid II, Pontianak's last sultan, the titular head of the Special Region of West Kalimantan (Daerah Istimewa Kalimantan Barat) from 1945–1950. A well-known Dutch proponent and staunch supporter of the federal United States of Indonesia, Sultan Hamid II, was arrested in April 1950 for his role in "Turk" Westerling's failed putsch against the young Republican government.[76] Despite having for so long been branded a traitor and anti-republican by Indonesian historiography,[77] the late Sultan Hamid II has been refashioned as a local "Malay" champion, one who understood "regional autonomy" and the dangers of an overbearing political center long ago.

Yet, akin to the Dayak example, this Malay movement contains evident rifts. For example, within Sambas district, despite Crown Prince Kusumah's recent advance into the spotlight, he is not this movement's dynamic force; his location in quaint, quiet Sambas town and his lack of a strong grassroots following make that impossible. FKMP is the force. The influence FKPM gained in coordinating much of the violence has translated into political dominance of post-violence Sambas. Not incidentally, the center of this Malay movement coincides with the epicenter of the riots: Pemangkat, Tebas, and Jawai subdistricts, where FKPM's roots are deepest. The organization draws its strength from its urban and semi-urban networks of Malay youth and thugs (*preman*), who, with FKPM leadership overseeing their

---

[74] In particular, Dayak mobilizations surrounding the Pontianak District *bupati* fiasco (see footnote 39) precipitated Lembayu's formation.

[75] In the 1950s, the newly constituted republican government of Indonesia stripped the dozen or so sultanates in West Kalimantan of their authority, for they were seen as feudal holdovers and pro-Dutch. In Sambas, the district capital was moved from Sambas—the site of the *kraton*—to Singkawang. As for Raden Kusumah, commonly known as Wimpi, he was an obscure figure working in the Sambas district tourism office. The violence, however, catapulted him to become a recognized local figure (*tokoh masyarakat*) and spokesman for Malay concerns. At the same time, he has also been accused of facilitating some of the violent mobilizations, accusations he denies. See his interview in Petebang and Sutrisno, *Konflik Etnik di Sambas*, pp. 23–28.

[76] For an account of the abortive coup and Hamid's trial, see Persadja, *Proces Peristiwa Sultan Hamid II* (Jakarta: Fasco, 1955).

[77] In particular, see New Order history books where Hamid is derisively referred to as a "federal figure" (*tokoh federal*). Bagas Prama Ananta et al., *Sejarah Nasional Indonesia 3*, third edition (Klaten: PT Intan Pariwara, 1989), pp. 39–40; and D. Teguh Budi Pudya Rastanta et al., *Sejarah, 3a* (Klaten: Pt Intan Pariwara, 1994), pp. 64–65.

actions, have wrested control of rackets and operations from their Madurese counterparts, who formerly controlled such activities.

In addition to dominating Sambas's underworld, FKPM has extended its reach into the district's prized bureaucracy. Significantly, its backing of Burhanuddin Rasyid ensured him the Sambas *bupati* post, for which elections were held in May 2000. Because it is not a political party, FKPM's support for Rasyid was "informal," but decisive. Initially, the PPP and a coalition faction (Fraksi Gabungan) had nominated Rasyid (and his running mate, Prabasa Ananatatur). Rasyid's victory exemplified FKPM's local clout; candidates for Golkar and PDI-P, who together held the majority of the district assembly's seats, lost out.[78]

Finally, FKPM has been engaged in a turf war with Malay leadership in Pontianak City. To defend its independence, it has stymied efforts to form a hierarchical, provincial-wide "Malay" organization centered in the provincial capital whose leadership might then trump FKPM authority in Sambas.[79] In particular, FKMP has rejected the authority of Lembayu's *panglima* to interfere in Sambas. FKPM's leadership insists that it was the organization that expelled the Madurese through bloody intimidation, an "achievement" Pontianak Malays cannot claim.

CONCLUSION

West Kalimantan is a critical case in the study of Indonesia's regional violence. The long duration of its riots forces us to look beyond exigencies of the incipient post-Suharto state for factors that might explain the violence, and to investigate the ways in which the New Order anchored its centralizing authority in this particular locale. The regional bloodshed that has occurred says as much about the regime's demise as it does of its birth. The case of West Kalimantan also challenges current theories that posit outside forces, such as provocateurs (*provakator*), and/or the army as key instigators of strife. While broader national dynamics may spark similar regional upheavals—dynamics such as the ideological contexts that facilitate local constructions of Chinese as godless communists or Madurese as degenerate non-native sons—generally different eruptions of regional violence throughout Indonesia's periphery have had varied causes. Diversities of outcomes across and within these cases, including the absence of violence in places where one might expect it to occur, require elucidation. Even in West Kalimantan, districts that include sizable Madurese and Dayak populations, like Ketapang, have been free of massive, sustained civilian violence. In other words, local mechanisms are necessary to explain local outcomes.

---

[78] Out of forty seats, Golkar held thirteen, PDI-P had eleven, and the two fractions backing Rasyid accounted for twelve. This meant that cross-party voting was apparent in Rasyid's clear-cut victory.

[79] This unfolded at a conference in Pontianak City held in November 1999. A compromise was struck and a loose "communication forum" (rather than an organization) was established—the PFKPM (the Union of Communication Forums of Malay Youth). Branches were then set up throughout the province. Naming the new forum was a contentious process. The Pontianak faction wanted to replace "FKPM" because of its association with the anti-Madurese clashes. They knew their long-term adversaries were Dayaks, not Madurese. So, another compromise was reached: PFKPM. Syamsul Rizal, a Pontianak-based contractor with close ties to the then Governor Aswin, was named provincial head.

In 1967, in a specific geographic locale of relatively harmonious social relations, substantial army and local elite politicization of ethnicity was necessary to spark shocking violence against the ethnic Chinese, corroborating the claim that violence is not necessarily inherent in an ethnically diverse region. An unintended consequence of the army's counterinsurgency operations, Dayak–Madurese riots then fed succeeding episodes, wherein constructions of the adversarial Other and internalized notions of "us" versus "them" coalesced and solidified. This recurrent dynamic later exploded in 1997 amidst a (re-)politicized countryside fueled by local Dayak NGOs. Finally, local elites, such as those in the FKPM, emerged to alter significantly the forms that had previously defined the violence. Notably, this included the direct participation of Sambas Malays. The tremendous benefits regional autonomy could offer to those who controlled district bureaucracies motivated the FKPM to seek control of Sambas, which they managed through anti-Madurese violence, and, more broadly, it inspired this Malay organization to challenge previously mobilized Dayak interests.

Finally, bearing in mind the series of terrorist-related bombings since 2000 and the putative religious strife in the Maluku Islands and Poso (Central Sulawesi), this chapter has shown that, when viewed from the bottom up, the complexities of violence in Indonesia belie the Islam–Christian dualism that has overwhelmed conceptualizations of these conflicts. Alternative markers of mobilization have been and currently are available and exploited. Although Central Kalimantan's clash of 2001 was similarly deemed ethnic, ethnic violence should not be construed as an outlier restricted to Kalimantan. Most cases of strife in West Kalimantan, from the 1967 cleansing of ethnic Chinese to the 1999 Malay–Madurese violence, have multiple readings and causes. Class, party competition, gang turf wars, and patronage networks are all cleavages that illustrate noteworthy rifts within each putative ethnic or religious group, and that frequently cross each other, making interpretation—and resolution—more complex. Indeed, the refugee issue lay at the core of the cascading riots in Pontianak during June 2001. This eruption was the climax of a three-year saga of near catastrophic proportions, redolent of government corruption, ineptitude, intensifying urban economic competition, and the further dehumanization of a victimized population.

PEOPLE POWER: A COMPARATIVE HISTORY OF FORCED DISPLACEMENT IN EAST TIMOR

Geoffrey Robinson

Twice in its twenty-four years under Indonesian occupation, East Timor suffered the forced displacement of more than half of its population.[1] Between 1975 and 1979 at least 300,000 civilians were forcibly moved into "resettlement areas," where tens of thousands died of disease and malnutrition. In 1999, in the context of a historic UN-sponsored referendum that set the country on the path to independence, an estimated 400,000 people were forced to flee amid widespread violence by anti-independence forces.

The forced displacement of these two periods bore some intriguing similarities. Both occurred against the backdrop of major political transitions; in both the principal perpetrators were Indonesian military forces or their proxies; and in both the victims were predominantly villagers thought to be supporting pro-independence forces. But the events of 1975–79 and 1999 also differed in important respects. Perhaps most strikingly, the humanitarian consequences were very different. Whereas an estimated 100,000 of those displaced in 1975–79 died, in 1999 the displacement was for the most part quickly remedied through international humanitarian intervention, and as a consequence resulted in relatively few deaths.

There were also significant variations in the patterns of displacement *within* each of these two periods. In the earlier period, the displacement worsened dramatically after late 1977 when Indonesian forces, with broad international support, launched a brutal military campaign that entailed the massive bombardment of civilian populations. In 1999, the pattern of displacement became significantly more widespread and systematic after the vote on August 30, when international observers fled and Indonesian military authorities assumed full control of East Timor.

---

[1] As this article was nearing completion in 2006, East Timor experienced a third major wave of displacement. Against the backdrop of conflict between rival army factions that left dozens dead and which many feared might escalate into civil war, an estimated 150,000 people fled their homes.

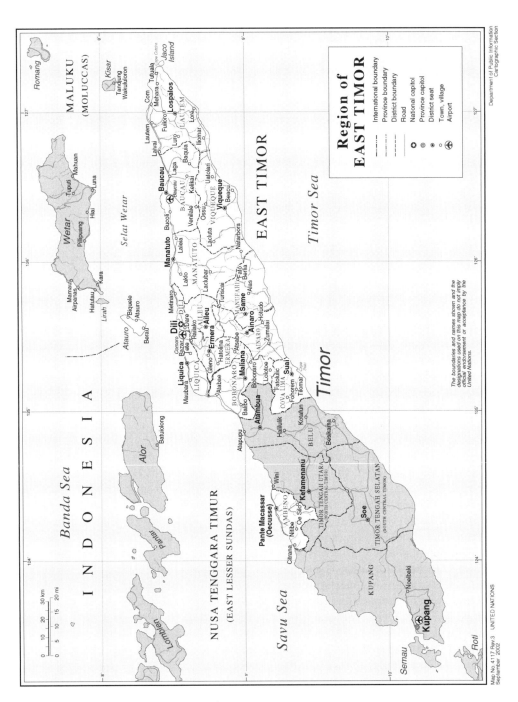

Based on UN map 4117, Rev. 3, September 2002.

What explains the marked similarities and differences in the patterns of displacement between and within these two periods? Why, in particular, were the humanitarian consequences of displacement so different in 1975–79 and 1999? What accounts for the similarities in the spatial distribution of displacement in the two periods? And why did the displacement worsen so dramatically over time within each period? This paper seeks to address those questions, while at the same time providing a detailed historical account of both cases of displacement.

The paper is structured chronologically, examining in turn the displacements of 1975–79 and of 1999. The discussion of each period is further divided to reflect and to underline significant changes in the dynamic of displacement within that period. To provide a basis for comparison between the two periods, and to highlight significant continuities and changes over time, each section is framed by the same set of questions: When did the displacement happen and how many people were affected? Who were the victims? Who was responsible? And, most importantly, what were the underlying patterns and dynamics of displacement?

The main argument advanced here is that the two main instances of forced displacement in East Timor were not, as might be supposed, the inevitable by-product of war. Rather, they were the result of the conscious political strategies employed by key actors, particularly Indonesian military authorities and their proxies, but also pro-independence forces, and powerful states and institutions. Significant variations between and within the two periods were, likewise, the result of changes in those strategies. A second and related argument advanced is that the displacement of 1999 was, in important respects, conditioned and shaped by the historical experience and memory of the displacement of 1975–79. Finally, the paper suggests that some differences in the pattern of displacement between the two periods may be attributable to broader historical changes in the discourses related to displacement, humanitarian intervention, and democratization.

Apart from offering insights into the dynamics of displacement in East Timor, I hope this comparative historical approach might also suggest conclusions about the causes and logic of forced population displacement more generally. The main hypothesis advanced here is that, wherever it occurs, forced displacement is typically the result of a historically contingent confluence of strategic political calculation and historical experience, and very seldom merely the inevitable result of violent conflict.

DISPLACEMENT, FAMINE, GENOCIDE: 1975–1979

The displacement that accompanied Indonesia's invasion of East Timor in 1975 occurred in three phases. The first, which entailed the movement of some ten thousand villagers across the border to West Timor, followed the outbreak of fighting between East Timor's two main political parties, UDT (União Democrática Timorense, Timorese Democratic Union) and Fretilin (Frente Revolucionária de Timor Leste Independente, Revolutionary Front for an Independent East Timor), in August 1975 and lasted roughly four months. The second phase, in which tens of thousands fled the main towns and coastal areas to Fretilin strongholds in the interior, began with the full-scale Indonesian invasion of December 7, 1975, and continued until late 1977. The third phase, which entailed the flight, and then surrender and forcible relocation into "resettlement areas," of some 300,000 people, and the death of perhaps 100,000, began in late 1977 and lasted until late 1979.

The main victims of displacement in all three of these phases were villagers accused of supporting Fretilin, or living in areas deemed to be Fretilin strongholds.

In all cases, women, children, and the elderly were prominent among the victims. In the first phase, from August to December 1975, those displaced were mainly villagers living in the western border areas. In the second phase, they were people from the main towns and coastal areas. In the third phase, the victims were overwhelmingly villagers from the interior of the country, where Fretilin had established its base areas (*bases de apoio*).

The principal perpetrators of forced displacement in this period were members of the Indonesian armed forces (Angkatan Bersenjata Republik Indonesia, ABRI). Locally recruited military units and military auxiliaries, known as Hansip, played a supporting role. Also instrumental in the dynamic of forcible displacement was the leadership of Fretilin and its armed wing, Falintil (Forças Armadas de Libertação Nacional de Timor Leste, Armed Forces for the National Liberation of East Timor). Particularly in the second and third periods, Fretilin strategy called for local populations to live and move with Falintil forces, an approach that subjected civilians to constant dislocation and hardship. Finally, by providing crucial political and military support for Indonesia's counterinsurgency campaign in East Timor, key states, including Australia, the United States, and the United Kingdom, shared responsibility for the displacement in all three periods, and for its terrible consequences.

PHASE 1: AUGUST – DECEMBER 1975

The initial displacement of some ten thousand people was set in motion by the brief armed conflict between the UDT and Fretilin that erupted after a UDT attempt to seize power in August 1975.[2] In the face of near certain defeat at the hands of Fretilin forces, some five hundred UDT and Apodeti[3] fighters and several thousand villagers from the border area fled into Indonesian territory. Their displacement was accelerated by armed Indonesian cross-border incursions that began as early as September 1975 and continued until late November.

Indonesian authorities exploited the presence of East Timorese refugees in West Timor in an attempt to justify the planned takeover of East Timor. They claimed that at least 40,000 East Timorese refugees had fled into West Timor—a figure at least four times greater than most independent estimates.[4] The presence of so many refugees, they said, was proof that East Timorese rejected Fretilin and preferred integration with Indonesia. And while outside observers raised concerns about the poor conditions in the refugee camps, Indonesian officials and media trumpeted Indonesia's role in providing humanitarian relief—and "vocational training"—to the refugees. These efforts, they insisted, were an indication of Indonesia's sympathy for its "brothers" in East Timor. Finally, the authorities used the 1975 refugee situation to disguise the dramatic build-up of Indonesian military forces in the border area, and the covert cross-border incursions it conducted between September and December 1975.

---

[2] On the August 1975 UDT coup and the situation at the border, see John Taylor, *Indonesia's Forgotten War: The Hidden History of East Timor* (London: Zed Books, 1991), pp. 50–54.

[3] Apodeti (Associação Popular Democrática Timorense, Timorese Popular Democratic Association) was a relatively minor party that advocated integration with Indonesia.

[4] Taylor gives the figure of 2,500 refugees and 500 UDT fighters. Taylor, *Indonesia's Forgotten War*, p. 53. Others cite higher figures, but none offers an estimate greater than 20,000.

The leader of the small Kota Party, José Martins, whose supporters had been among those who fled across the border in 1975, challenged all of these claims in a letter to the UN Secretary General in early 1976. "I wish to stress the fact," he wrote,

> ... that these people did not flee to Indonesian territory because they wanted to join Indonesia. They were just looking for a safe place until they could return to their homes. But they also fell into the hands of the Indonesian authorities; they soon realized that while seeking peace they found only maltreatment and misery. The refugees were either forced to take military training and fight against Fretilin, or to work without pay for the Indonesians ... Obviously, the Indonesian government was using the "40,000" refugees as a political weapon against Fretilin.[5]

Those allegations, dismissed by Indonesia as the ravings of a political opportunist, turned out to have more than a kernel of truth in them. Indeed, information contained in declassified government documents from Australia, the United States, and the United Kingdom show clearly that Martins was largely correct, at least in his claim that Indonesia was using the refugees as military proxies and as a political weapon.[6]

Australian government documents are especially revealing. They show that, as early as April 1975, Indonesia had embarked on a covert strategy that involved the military training of hundreds of East Timorese "refugees" and their deployment into East Timor alongside Indonesian forces. The provision of military training to these "refugees" was first reported by an Australian official who visited a refugee camp at Nenuk in April 1975, where he saw some two hundred young men undergoing what Indonesian officials said was "vocational training" in agriculture and carpentry. The Australian official had little doubt, however, about what was really going on. "It is difficult to avoid the conclusion," the report noted, "that this camp is involved in other activities besides agriculture and carpentry in spite of adamant statements by the Indonesian officials with whom Rodgers spoke that Indonesia was not involved in any way, or wish to become involved, in the military training of Portuguese Timorese."[7]

In June 1975, the Australian ambassador to Indonesia, Richard Woolcott, reported further details of Indonesia's covert military operation in which "refugees" played a central part. "Indonesia's covert activities in Portuguese Timor will be stepped up," he wrote, "as will the training of Apodeti leaders. 'Refugees' are being

---

[5] José Martins, letter to the UN Secretary General, April 29, 1979, reprinted in *East Timor, Indonesia and the Western Democracies: A Collection of Documents*, ed. Torben Retbøll (Copenhagen: International Work Group for Indigenous Affairs, 1980), p. 46.

[6] Many of the key US government documents can be found on the website of the non-governmental National Security Archive (NSA), at http://www.gwu.edu/~nsarchiv/. See especially: "East Timor Revisited: Ford, Kissinger and the Indonesian Invasion, 1975–76," at http://www.gwu.edu/~nsarchiv/NSAEBB/NSAEBB62/index2.html; and "A Quarter Century of US Support for Occupation," at
http://www.gwu.edu/~nsarchiv/NSAEBB/NSAEBB174/index.htm. For Australia, see Wendy Way, ed. *Documents on Australian Foreign Policy: Australia and the Indonesian Incorporation of Portuguese Timor, 1974–1976* (Canberra: Department of Foreign Affairs and Trade, 2000).

[7] Way, ed. *Documents on Australian Foreign Policy*, Document 126, April 15, 1975, p. 252.

prepared at Atambua to return to Portuguese Timor to play their part in persuading people to support integration."[8] A cable from Woolcott in early September 1975, moreover, revealed that the operation entailed deliberate deception regarding the identity and role of the refugees, in order to allow the covert infiltration of Indonesian troops into East Timor. The Indonesians "will replace some of the refugees forced across the border by Fretilin with well armed 'volunteers' who will provide backbone for UDT and other anti-Fretilin forces."[9]

In short, the Australian government knew that "refugees" were being used as a foil for a covert military operation to invade East Timor, but did nothing about it. And Australia was hardly alone. It is clear that other powerful governments, notably the United States and the United Kingdom, also knew very well what was going on at the border, but in order to maintain cordial relations with Indonesia, chose not to reveal what they knew or to make any effort to stop it.[10] On the basis of that evidence, it is reasonable to argue that those states were complicit in a cynical exploitation of humanitarian norms and in the terrible loss of life that inevitably followed.

PHASE II: DECEMBER 1975 – SEPTEMBER 1977

The second phase of displacement, from early December 1975 to late 1977, began in response to intensive Indonesian aerial and naval bombardment, and to widespread atrocities by Indonesian ground troops. Within a few days of the invasion, thousands of residents of the two main cities, Dili and Baucau, fled to the hills. For the next two years, Fretilin leaders claimed that some 80 percent of the population—then about 650,000—was living under its protection in "liberated zones" in the interior of the country. Although the precise figure cannot be verified, it is certainly true that Indonesian forces had great difficulty extending their control beyond the main towns and coastal areas.[11] Fretilin's control over much of the interior and the east ensured a reasonable supply of food and decent living conditions for the displaced population, despite the continuing war.[12]

---

[8] Ibid., Document 137, June 2, 1975, p. 267

[9] Ibid., Document 217, September 6, 1975, p. 392.

[10] Recently declassified British government documents reveal, for example, that British authorities were well aware of Indonesia's covert incursions and of its role in the murder of five western journalists in Balibo in October 1975, but sought deliberately to silence discussion and debate on the matter. See Donald Greenlees, "Complicity Shown in Timor Takeover," *International Herald Tribune*, December 1, 2005; and "Declassified British Documents Reveal UK Support for Indonesian Invasion and Occupation of East Timor, Recognition of Denial of Self-Determination, 1975–1976," National Security Archive (NSA), at http://www.gwu.edu/~nsarchiv/NSAEBB/NSAEBB174/indexuk.htm.

[11] According to a December 1976 report, prepared by Indonesian relief workers, "The total population of villages and towns occupied by the Indonesian forces amounts to 150,000 people." "Indonesian Relief Workers in Timor," *Tribune* (Australia), December 1, 1976.

[12] For a sympathetic personal account of life in a Fretilin-controlled area during this period, see Constancio Pinto and Matthew Jardine, *East Timor's Unfinished Struggle: Inside the Timorese Resistance* (Boston, MA: South End Press, 1997), pp. 41–59. Also see CAVR (Commission for Reception, Truth, and Reconciliation in East Timor), *Chega! The Report of the Commission for Reception, Truth, and Reconciliation Timor-Leste* (CAVR, n.d.), Chapter 7.3, p. 28 (www.cavr-timorleste.org/chegaReport.htm); and John Taylor, *Indonesia's Forgotten War*, pp. 79–82.

The widespread displacement of this period was primarily the consequence of an Indonesian military and political strategy that overestimated Indonesian military capability and underestimated the East Timorese capacity and will to resist. Indonesian military planners assumed, incorrectly, that a massive show of force would result in a quick capitulation by East Timorese forces. Displacement also stemmed from the Indonesian practice of moving those who had surrendered, or had been captured, into towns under their control, where their activities and movements were restricted.[13]

But the displacement of this period, and the next, was also the product of a strategy adopted by Fretilin's leadership, and maintained until late 1978, which called for civilians to live and move with Falintil forces.[14] The main base areas in which they lived, known as *bases de apoio*, were spread across the territory, with, at least one in each of Fretilin's administrative zones.[15] The strategy was portrayed, with some justification, as an effort to protect the local population from Indonesian attack. But it was, more than anything else, a political strategy, considered vital to Fretilin's political purposes and legitimacy.[16] The resistance leader, and later president of East Timor, Xanana Gusmão, explained the strategy as follows:

> The concept of *base de apoio* came about when the population ran to the hills after the Indonesians invaded on December 7 . . . Suddenly we were at war, but with the people among us. The concept was to build a foundation to provide political and logistical support, but mostly political support, which we could say was revolutionary.[17]

While it is true that many civilians followed Fretilin willingly, the strategy was not welcomed by all. Accounts provided to the CAVR (Comissão de Acolhimento, Verdade e Reconciliaçao de Timor Leste,, Commission for Reception, Truth, and Reconciliation in East Timor) reveal that some villagers were forced against their will to move in accordance with Fretilin orders, and that those who resisted were sometimes ill-treated or killed.[18]

Nor was opposition to the policy limited to anti-Fretilin elements. From the outset, some Fretilin and Falintil leaders believed that civilians should be permitted to stay in their villages and even to surrender to the Indonesians if they wished. As Indonesian military attacks on the *bases de apoio* intensified in 1977, even the party's president, Francisco Xavier do Amaral, came to advocate that view.[19] Most of the

---

[13] CAVR, *Chega!*, Chapter 7.3, pp. 21–25.

[14] The policy, first articulated shortly after the Indonesian invasion, was reaffirmed at a meeting of Fretilin's Central Committee in May 1976, and then formally abandoned at a meeting in late November 1978. See ibid.,,Chapter 7.3, pp. 25–27, 42, 49.

[15] For a list of thirty key base areas, see ibid., Chapter 7.3, p. 27.

[16] In its final report, the CAVR noted: "As conditions worsened and the bombing increased, many people wanted to surrender in order to save their lives and those of their families. They were prevented from doing so for political reasons. Fretilin believed that its political legitimacy would be undermined if people surrendered, and that encouraging people to do so was an act of treason." Ibid., Chapter 7.3, p. 31.

[17] Cited in ibid., Chapter 7.3, p. 25.

[18] Ibid., Chapter 7.3, pp. 20–21.

[19] Ibid., Chapter 7.3, p. 34.

party leadership, however, resisted, and accused those who advocated that position of treachery. Some of the dissidents were executed and, in September 1977, Amaral himself was detained, at least in part because of his position on this issue.[20]

The displacement in the period 1975 to 1977, finally, was facilitated by key western powers that offered vital political support to Indonesia at critical junctures and supplied most of the weaponry used in the invasion. On the political front, US President Ford and Secretary of State Henry Kissinger gave Indonesia the green light for invasion during a state visit to Jakarta in early December 1975.[21] Australian authorities likewise made it clear to the Indonesians that they would not interfere with the planned invasion.[22] For its part, the British government worked effectively to keep news of the invasion out of the press, and to limit criticism and action at the United Nations.[23] On the military side, some 90 percent of all the weaponry used in the invasion was supplied by the United States.[24]

PHASE III: SEPTEMBER 1977 – SEPTEMBER 1979

The third main phase of displacement began in 1977, with the start of a new, more intensive, Indonesian military campaign, and lasted through 1979. The new campaign—dubbed "encirclement and annihilation"—entailed the deployment of some forty thousand combat troops and the intensive aerial bombardment of one Fretilin base area after another, using low-flying counterinsurgency aircraft, such as OV-10 Broncos. Houses were burned to the ground, livestock were killed, and both crops and food stores were destroyed or stolen.[25]

In the face of these sustained attacks, the population abandoned what had been safe and productive areas, moved progressively eastward into steadily smaller and less productive areas, and finally surrendered.[26] The surrendered populations were then placed in transit camps and "resettlement areas," to ensure that they could not communicate with or provide food, medicine, or other assistance to Falintil forces.[27]

---

[20] Ibid., Chapter 7.3, pp. 19, 34.

[21] The key evidence to this effect is the record of the meeting between Ford, Kissinger, and Suharto in Jakarta on December 6, 1975. National Security Archive (NSA), "East Timor Revisited: Ford, Kissinger and the Indonesian Invasion, 197576," at http://www.gwu.edu/~nsarchiv/NSAEBB/NSAEBB62/index2.html.

[22] See Wendy Way, ed., *Documents on Australian Foreign Policy.*

[23] See "Declassified British Documents Reveal UK Support for Indonesian Invasion and Occupation of East Timor, Recognition of Denial of Self-Determination, 1975–1976," National Security Archive (NSA), at www.gwu.edu/~nsarchiv/NSAEBB/NSAEBB174/indexuk.htm.

[24] Benedict R. O'G. Anderson, "Testimony for the Subcommittee on International Organizations and the Subcommittee on Asian and Pacific Affairs of the Committee on International Relations of the US House of Representatives," Washington, DC, February 6, 1980.

[25] CAVR, *Chega,* Chapter 7.3, pp. 35–37.

[26] Ibid., Chapter 7.3, pp. 37–49; Taylor, *Indonesia's Forgotten War*, pp. 82–88; Pinto and Jardine, *East Timor's Unfinished Struggle*, pp. 60–78; and Paulino Gama, "The War in The Hills, 1975-1985: A Fretilin Commander Remembers," in *East Timor at the Crossroads: The Forging of a Nation*, ed. Peter Carey and G. Carter Bentley (Honolulu, HI: University of Hawai'i Press, 1995), pp. 97–105.

[27] For a description of the encirclement campaign, see Amnesty International, *East Timor: Violations of Human Rights* (London: Amnesty International, 1985), p. 29. Also see CAVR, *Chega!*, Chapter 7.3, pp. 37–49.

One account of the exodus from Remexio captures the sense of desperation felt by many civilians at this time:

> The Indonesian army was only about three miles away and everyone was in a panic. Everyone just tried to save his or her own life. That was the beginning of our long pilgrimage. We headed toward the east, along with hundreds of other people. As we moved, the Indonesian army constantly pursued us. Children, women, and men were dying on the way. Day and night we continually ran without knowing where we were going; we just followed the crowd. There was no time to bury those who died on the way.[28]

The encirclement campaign took its toll physically and politically. By early 1978, large numbers of people were suffering serious food shortage and illness, Fretilin's structure had started to break down, and tens of thousands of civilians had either been captured or had surrendered.[29] The campaign reached its culmination in October and November 1978, in a final massive assault on Mount Matebian in the eastern part of the country, where most of those under Fretilin control had fled.[30] In late November, as Indonesian forces closed in, Fretilin's Central Committee decided finally to abandon its policy of holding civilians in the base areas, and allowed them to surrender.[31] In the following weeks, thousands of civilians and some resistance fighters came down from Matebian and surrendered to Indonesian authorities.[32]

Surrender, however, did not bring an end to the suffering or the dislocation. Those who surrendered were immediately placed into scores of military-run "transit camps," and from there into "resettlement areas" (*daerah pemukiman baru* or *tempat pemukiman*). All told, the campaign of "encirclement and annihilation" resulted in the forcible relocation of at least 300,000 people into these camps.[33]

In the transit camps, the surrendered were registered and interrogated, often under duress. Those believed to be members of Fretilin or Falintil were detained, and sometimes killed.[34] From the transit camps, the civilians were sent to resettlement areas, of which there were at least 139.[35] Known locally as "concentration camps" (*campos de concentração*), the resettlement areas were akin to the strategic hamlets

---

[28] Pinto and Jardine, *East Timor's Unfinished Struggle,* pp. 60–61.

[29] Gama, "The War in the Hills," p. 100; and Pinto and Jardine, *East Timor's Unfinished Struggle,* p. 65.

[30] CAVR, *Chega!,* Chapter 7.3, pp. 41–44.

[31] Ibid., Chapter 7.3, pp. 42, 49. Resistance leader, Xanana Gusmão, later told the CAVR: "I regretted moving all those people to Matebian where it was impossible to cater [sic?] for them." Ibid., p. 42.

[32] Ibid., Chapter 7.3, pp. 50–51.

[33] The figure of 300,000 was given by the US Agency for International Development (US AID) in late 1979, on the basis of information provided by Indonesian military officials. See US AID, "Situation Report No. 1, October 19, 1979: East Timor, Indonesia—Displaced Persons." Taylor cites an official Indonesian figure of 372,921 people living in resettlement areas as of December 1978. Taylor, *Indonesia's Forgotten War,* p. 90.

[34] CAVR, *Chega!,* Chapter 7.3, pp. 52, 54–60.

[35] The CAVR provides a list of 139 camps, but says that the real number was probably higher. See ibid., Chapter 7.3, pp. 61–64.

used by US forces in Vietnam, and their purpose was similar: to control the population and separate it from the insurgents, whatever the cost.[36]

The objective of separating the population from the guerrillas was clearly spelled out in army training manuals for East Timor. Using the official term GPK (Gerakan Pengacau Keamanan, Security Disruptors' Movement)[37] to describe the guerrillas, one manual, instructed field officers to: "Physically separate GPK support by … moving to another place people with relatives who are GPKs still active in the bush, particularly those classified as leaders."[38] The manual further explained that those separated were to be moved to various secure locations, including the prison island of Atauro: "Evacuate to Atauro and other designated places the network of GPK support in the settlements as well as families of GPK not yet evacuated."[39]

The conditions in the resettlement areas were appalling.[40] Supplies of food and medicine were minimal, and residents were prevented from venturing outside a limited area to tend crops or harvest wild food. As a consequence, malnutrition and disease were rampant, and many thousands died.[41] Although precise figures are difficult to establish, it is now widely accepted that by late 1979 as many as 100,000 had died, the vast majority of them from malnutrition and associated disease.

Members of a delegation of diplomats and journalists who visited a resettlement area in Remexio in early September 1978, were shocked by what they saw. One of the journalists wrote:

> In Remexio as in most other towns the people are stunned, sullen, and dispirited. Emaciated as a result of deprivation and hardship, they are struggling to make sense of the nightmarish interlude in which as much as half the population was uprooted … The townspeople are undernourished and desperately in need of medical attention … The children in Remexio are so undernourished that one ambassador said they reminded him of the victims of an African famine.[42]

These revelations prompted calls for urgent international relief operations and stimulated small-scale humanitarian efforts by church groups. Nevertheless, it was a full year before Indonesian military authorities finally permitted two international agencies—Catholic Relief Services (CRS) and the International Committee of the Red

---

[36] According to the CAVR: "The camps were the central element of the strategy of the Indonesian military to control the population and isolate it from the East Timorese Resistance." Ibid., Chapter 7.3, p. 61.

[37] The acronym GPK was widely used during the New Order as a label for groups considered a threat to national security. While often translated as "Security Disruptors' Movement," the rhetorical meaning of the term GPK is closer to the English "terrorist."

[38] Tentara Nasional Indonesia, Korem 164/Wira Dharma, Seksi Intel, "Petunjuk Teknis tentang Cara Babinsa/Team Pembina Desa Dalam Membongkar Jaring Pendukung GPK," Dili, 1982.

[39] Ibid.

[40] CAVR, *Chega!*, Chapter 7.3, pp. 64–68; Amnesty International, *East Timor: Violations of Human Rights*, pp. 5, 64–71; Taylor, *Indonesia's Forgotten War*, pp. 64–68.

[41] The CAVR concluded that " … the Indonesian military failed to guarantee basic needs of those who did surrender, many of whom were seriously weak and hungry when they surrendered, and that without access to adequate shelter, food, clean water, and medical care in army-controlled camps, thousands died." CAVR, *Chega!*, Chapter 7.3, p. 52.

[42] David Jenkins, "Timor's Arithmetic of Despair," *Far Eastern Economic Review*, September 29, 1978.

Cross (ICRC)—to undertake systematic relief efforts in the area.[43] When it finally began in September 1979, that humanitarian intervention brought significant results, effectively ending the famine and dramatically reducing death rates.

That vital work, however, was carried out in the face of continuing restrictions by Indonesian military authorities. Among other things, the authorities prevented the agencies from distributing aid to people in areas outside Indonesian control. An East Timorese who worked with CRS at the time believed that the reasons for that restriction were clearly political:

> CRS was allowed to distribute food only to people in ABRI-controlled areas. We could not distribute to people in the mountains. ABRI did not want food distributed to people in the mountains because they thought that way they could force them to surrender.[44]

Such restrictions, and the long delay in permitting access to humanitarian agencies, highlighted a crucial aspect of the dynamic of forced relocation in this period: the Indonesian military considered the control of humanitarian relief to the displaced to be vital to its strategic and political objectives. As in 1975, such control was considered to be crucial in shoring up Indonesian claims to legitimacy in East Timor, and in limiting outside criticism of its actions there. The decision to grant limited access to relief agencies in September 1979 was part of the same dynamic. With more than half of the population secured in camps, and the armed resistance severely weakened, by late 1979 the military had achieved its main strategic objectives, and no doubt believed it could earn credit for assisting the suffering, without risking much in the way of outside scrutiny or criticism.

The strategic manipulation of humanitarian assistance and access was crucially aided by international actors, most notably the governments of the United States and Australia. Continuing a policy of deliberate silence concerning systematic violations of human rights by Indonesian forces, these and other states sought to suppress information regarding the widespread dislocation and famine in East Timor in the late 1970s.[45] According to one reliable account, the US ambassador to Indonesia, Edward Masters, failed to report the famine in East Timor for a full nine months after he had witnessed it firsthand.[46] And when the program of humanitarian assistance was finally set in motion in late 1979, key states sought disingenuously to portray it as evidence of Indonesia's sincerity in assisting the people of East Timor. Testifying

---

[43] The CRS program provided humanitarian relief to some 240,000 people, while the ICRC program focused on 60,000 people whose condition was considered most grave. CAVR, *Chega!*, Chapter 7.3, pp. 71, 74; Amnesty International, *East Timor: Violations of Human Rights*, p. 15.

[44] Gilman dos Santos, cited in CAVR, *Chega!*, Chapter 7.3, p. 76.

[45] Taylor writes: "Estimates of the many thousands of deaths resulting from Indonesia's occupation were dismissed, even though they were substantiated by varying sources, from the ICRC to the Catholic Church. The governments of the industrialized countries sought to minimize them to the greatest extent possible. For example, referring to allegations of genocide in East Timor, a US State Department report of 1978 noted that 'most of the human losses in East Timor appear to have occurred prior to Indonesia's intervention.'" Taylor, *Indonesia's Forgotten War*, p. 97.

[46] Anderson, "Testimony for the Subcommittee on International Organizations," 1980.

before Congress in June 1980, for example, assistant secretary of state for Asia and the Pacific, Richard Holbrooke, said of the humanitarian situation in East Timor:

> I am pleased to be able to report dramatic improvement in conditions with many areas returning to normal, and I wish to acknowledge and commend the excellent efforts of the international agencies, the Indonesian Government, and all those who have contributed to this effort which has resulted in the saving of many lives.[47]

Holbrooke was certainly correct in saying that the humanitarian situation had improved dramatically after the start of the relief operation. Although many East Timorese continued to suffer hunger and disease, by late 1980 the worst of the famine had ended. That success, however, was primarily the work of the international humanitarian agencies—*not* of the Indonesian government, or of unspecified others. Indeed, it had been achieved in spite of the restrictions imposed by Indonesian military authorities and in spite of the disgraceful code of silence maintained by its allies. To suggest that the Indonesian government deserved credit for the improvement diminished the extraordinary achievement of the international NGOs and obscured the fact that the Indonesian military was responsible for the humanitarian crisis in the first place.

Beyond such obfuscation, powerful western states contributed to the forced displacement and the humanitarian crisis through their continued provision to Indonesia of vital military aid and materiel. Between 1975 and 1979, US military aid to Indonesia totaled more than $318 million; and it spiked to more than $129 million in 1978, the year of the deadly "encirclement and annihilation" campaign in East Timor.[48] Especially important were low-flying aircraft, the OV-10 Broncos, which were ideal for counterinsurgency operations in difficult terrain. In February 1977, it was announced that Indonesia would be receiving thirteen of these planes with the help of US foreign military sales credits, and later that year at least six of them were reported to be operating in East Timor.[49] In January 1978, just as the encirclement campaign was getting underway, the US government announced the sale to Indonesia of sixteen F-5 jets, to be followed by sixteen A-4 bombers in August.[50] By one account, the introduction of these aircraft at this juncture tipped the military balance against Falintil and contributed directly to the massive population displacement and famine of 1978-79.[51]

In short, the massive forced displacement of 1975–79 was not the unfortunate but inevitable by-product of war. It was the consequence of the conscious political strategies of Indonesian forces, Fretilin leaders, and key international actors. More

---

[47] Cited in Joel Rocamora, "The Uses of Hunger," *Southeast Asia Chronicle* 74 (1980): 12.

[48] See Institute for Policy Studies, "Background Information on Indonesia, the Invasion of East Timor and US Military Assistance" (Washington, DC, May 1982).

[49] Taylor, *Indonesia's Forgotten War*, p. 84.

[50] Ibid., p. 86.

[51] Taylor writes: "The results of this rush to provide the Indonesian regime with the inventory necessary to intensify its campaigns in East Timor cannot be underestimated. Indeed, they appear, quite simply, to have heralded the move out of military stalemate. They provided the essential underpinning for the future successes of the campaign of encirclement and annihilation." Ibid.

specifically, the displacement of the population was a central element of Indonesia's military strategy for crushing resistance to its rule, and of Fretilin's political and military strategy of resistance. Both Fretilin and the Indonesian military evidently shared an understanding that control of the population was vital not only to their military success but, more importantly, to their political credibility and legitimacy.

Despite that similarity, the responsibility of the two parties for the displacement was very different. Indonesia used starvation and resettlement of the civilian population as part of a strategic campaign to crush the resistance. Fretilin's strategy was essentially a defensive one; without the Indonesian invasion, and without Indonesia's deliberate use of forced displacement, starvation, and resettlement, there is no reason to suppose that Fretilin would have moved the population to mountain base areas. The Indonesian strategy, moreover, relied upon overwhelming military force, rendering remote the possibility that the population movement was "voluntary" in any meaningful sense. Finally, while Fretilin essentially fought on its own, relying on the support of the local population (and some weapons passed on by sympathetic Portuguese officers), the Indonesian strategy of displacement was supported, both materially and politically, by key international actors, even when they knew its devastating human consequences.

DISPLACEMENT AS POLITICAL STRATEGY: 1999

The forced displacement of East Timor's population in 1999 occurred in two broad waves. The first, which took place before the UN-sponsored referendum on August 30, saw as many as 50,000 people displaced from their homes to other parts of East Timor, while a smaller number (c. 4,500) fled across the border to West Timor. The second, which occurred in the immediate aftermath of the vote, resulted in the displacement of at least 400,000 people out of an estimated population of 800,000. More than 250,000 of that number were forced across the border into West Timor and neighboring islands, while the remainder took refuge in the hills of East Timor and in other places considered safe, including churches, monasteries, and convents. Some 2,000 sought refuge in the UN compound in Dili and were later evacuated to Darwin, Australia.[52]

As in 1975, the victims of displacement in 1999 were primarily residents of villages considered sympathetic to the independence movement; fewer than 20 percent of the displaced were supporters of Indonesian rule. Villages in the westernmost districts, bordering West Timor, were especially hard hit, as were communities located on or close to major roads and/or ports. Many who had taken refuge from the violence in Catholic churches and other buildings were subjected to further attack and displacement. On the other hand, communities that moved or remained close to significant concentrations of Falintil forces were somewhat less likely to be subjected to forcible displacement.

In contrast to the earlier period (1975–79), the principal perpetrators of the acts that led to forced displacement in 1999 were not regular Indonesian forces but pro-Indonesian militia groups, such as Aitarak, Besi Merah Putih (BMP), and Mahidi, among others. Although Indonesian authorities insisted that the militias were

---

[52] For an account of the situation inside the UN compound at this time, see Geoffrey Robinson, "If You Leave Us Here, We Will Die," in *The New Killing Fields: Massacre and the Politics of Intervention,* ed. Mills and Brunner (New York, NY: Perseus Books, 2002), pp. 159–84.

independent, community-based, self-defense groups, there is now abundant evidence that they were mobilized, trained, supplied, and led by the TNI (Tentara Nasional Indonesia,, Indonesian National Army) and that they had political and financial backing from civilian authorities.[53] In short, the militias that carried out most of the violence in 1999, and which gave rise to the forced displacement of more than half the population, were proxy forces that allowed Indonesian authorities to maintain the pretext, at least for a time, that they were not interfering in the referendum process.

The shift from regular troops in 1975–79 to militia proxies in 1999 arguably reflected broader political developments, both in Indonesia and abroad, that dictated a new approach in East Timor. At home, Indonesian authorities were anxious to show that they were in step with the demands for democratization and civilian rule that had accompanied the forced resignation of President Suharto in May 1998. Internationally, the new government of President Habibie faced unprecedented demands from its allies, notably Australia, to resolve the East Timor issue peacefully. These pressures contributed to Habibie's surprise decision, in January 1999, to offer East Timorese a chance to vote on a proposal for "special autonomy." They also placed clear limits on the sort of methods that could be used to win that vote. The deployment of regular troops along the lines used in the late 1970s was clearly out of the question.

The May 5 Agreements, which spelled out the modalities for the referendum, likewise constrained Indonesian options for influencing its outcome. The accords stipulated that there would be a substantial international presence overseeing and observing the referendum. They also entailed an agreement that Indonesia would bear full responsibility for maintaining security, and that it would maintain strict neutrality with respect to the vote. Both of those conditions required that regular Indonesian forces would maintain a low profile, thereby making the use of proxy militia forces the most sensible option.

The use of militias in this context may also have been facilitated by the prevailing discourse of democratization circulating in Indonesia and beyond at this time. With its enthusiastic and uncritical celebration of "civil society," that discourse arguably opened the door wide for the mobilization of social and political groups, including vigilantes and militias, whose methods and purposes were decidedly "uncivil."[54] While such groups were not new to East Timor, it was conspicuous that in 1999 Indonesian authorities stressed that the militias had emerged spontaneously from the local community and that they deserved to be respected as expressions of the popular will. The dominance of the new democratization discourse gave those claims a new resonance and made it more difficult for opponents and outside observers to challenge them.

Although the militias and their Indonesian allies were the main perpetrators of the violence leading to displacement in 1999, pro-independence forces also bore some responsibility for the population movement. Falintil forces were responsible for the displacement of perhaps several hundred supporters of Indonesian rule in the first few months of 1999. The CNRT (Conselho Nacional da Resistência Timorense,

---

[53] For a complete account of militia ties to the TNI and other officials, see Geoffrey Robinson, *East Timor 1999: Crimes Against Humanity, A Report Commissioned by the UN Office of the High Commissioner for Human Rights* (Jakarta: Elsam & Hak, 2006), Chapters 6, 7, and 8.

[54] I am grateful to Eva-Lotta Hedman for drawing my attention to this possibility.

National Council of Timorese Resistance) leadership also influenced the spatial and temporal patterns of displacement later in the year by encouraging their own supporters to seek refuge near Falintil base areas, and by urging or instructing them to flee or return to their homes in accordance with the CNRT's political objectives.

Finally, as in the period 1975–79, displacement was crucially shaped by the actions and the rhetoric of key states and international institutions. The reluctance of key states to criticize Indonesia, or to insist that it rein in its security forces in East Timor, clearly facilitated the violence before the vote and significantly complicated efforts to respond to the violence in its aftermath. Moreover, as supporters and purveyors of the new democratization discourse, key states and international organizations helped to lend legitimacy to the dubious claims made on behalf of the militias by Indonesian authorities. In all of these ways, the international community arguably facilitated the violence and the massive displacement of 1999.

At the same time, international intervention was instrumental in stopping the violence, and reversing the forced displacement, within a few weeks of the vote. That outcome was partly the result of the unusual international media presence in East Timor in 1999 which, together with well-organized pressure from the Catholic Church and non-governmental organizations, forced key states to take action. The unusual swiftness of that international response also stemmed from significant discursive, institutional, and political changes in the realm of humanitarian affairs that had occurred since the late 1970s. By 1999, for example, the category of the Internally Displaced Person (IDP), virtually unknown thirty years before, was well entrenched, ensuring that forced displacement per se—and not just its consequences like disease and malnutrition—was readily identified as a problem and could be addressed at an early stage. The institutional mechanisms and logistical capacity for intervention were also substantially better developed in 1999 than they had been in the late 1970s, which meant that assistance could be rendered quickly and effectively. Finally, there was in 1999 a mood of openness to the idea of humanitarian intervention that had been decidedly absent in the period 1975–79. Against that background, political pressure for intervention could translate fairly quickly into effective action.

PHASE I: LATE 1998 – AUGUST 30, 1999

Forced displacement in the pre-ballot period stemmed primarily from a systematic campaign of violence by pro-Indonesian forces in perceived pro-independence strongholds. The violence took place under the cover of the government's campaign to "socialize" the proposed "special autonomy" option under which East Timor would remain under Indonesian rule. Depicted by government authorities as a community education effort, the "socialization" campaign was in reality a concerted propaganda offensive designed to pressure the population to vote for continued Indonesian rule. Official speeches at "socialization" rallies were filled with open and veiled threats of violence, such as: "If autonomy wins, blood will trickle. If independence wins, blood will flow!" These threats were underlined by the menacing presence of armed pro-Indonesian militiamen.[55]

---

[55] UNAMET, Humanitarian Affairs Office, "Preliminary Report on Humanitarian Issues," Dili, June 14, 1999, p. 4; Robinson, *East Timor 1999*, Chapter 2.

The physical appearance of the militias, as well as their weapons and their methods, appeared calculated to sow terror while obscuring the critical role of Indonesian forces behind the scenes and highlighting the ostensibly spontaneous and local character of each group. A small handful wore parts of Indonesian military uniforms, but most wore "civilian" clothing that symbolized their pro-Indonesia stance—red and white bandanas around their neck or head, and T-shirts bearing the name of their unit and a pro-integration slogan of some sort. Similarly, while a few militiamen had access to advanced weapons of the sort used by the TNI and the police,[56] the vast majority carried an assortment of low-tech weapons, including machetes, knives, spears, swords, rocks, and so-called "homemade" firearms (*senjata rakitan*). Despite their low-tech profile, these weapons could inflict serious wounds, and they had a terrifying effect. Just as importantly, they were useful in maintaining the fiction that the militias were independent, community-based groups with no formal ties to the Indonesian army. The same was true of the standard militia methods, which included house-burning, public beatings, decapitation, mutilation, and corpse display, and, towards women, sexual violence and rape.[57] These methods helped to create the impression of "anarchy," and thereby to distract attention from the fact that the violence was carefully organized, even calibrated, to terrorize supporters of independence.

An East Timorese man, armed with spears and a bow, cries after anti-independence militiamen burned down his house in Memo, East Timor, in late August 1999.
(AP Photo, by John Martinkus, with permission)

---

[56] A small number were seen with M-16s, SKSs, S-1s, and hand grenades, while a somewhat larger number carried Portuguese-era Mauser and G-3 rifles.

[57] TNI soldiers were also directly implicated in rape and sexual slavery. For further details see United Nations, *Situation of Human Rights in East Timor* (New York, NY: UN Doc. A/54/660, December 1999), pp. 9–11.

Significantly, the threats issued at "socialization" rallies, and in other contexts, too, often alluded to the violence that had engulfed East Timor after Indonesia's 1975 invasion. At meetings across the territory, the message was spread that if the vote favored independence, the violence that followed would be worse than in 1975.[58] The references to 1975 were evidently part of an official strategy to evoke historical experience and memory in the service of the pro-Indonesian cause.[59] By all accounts, such historical allusions had a powerful effect, stimulating fear among the population, thereby contributing to the dynamic of displacement. UNAMET's Humanitarian Affairs Officer, writing in June 1999, described the dynamic as follows:

> A view was put forward by some church leaders that the historical context of the problem in East Timor has led to a situation where the population is disproportionately sensitive to threats. Remembering the horrors of 1975–83 and being threatened that if they do not vote for autonomy an even worse situation will follow leads to a situation of near-panic driven fear which prevents the reasonable assessment of the likelihood of truth contained in the threats. Thus the effect of the threats is magnified.[60]

The strategy worked. Starting in late 1998, and reaching a crescendo in April 1999, the campaign of threat and violence caused residents of entire villages to flee to the forests or to neighboring towns. Many took refuge in places of worship, such as the parish churches in the towns of Liquiça and Suai. That was no coincidence. Since the late 1970s, the Catholic Church had become one of the few places of refuge for the displaced and persecuted, and by 1999 it had gained a reputation, not always deserved, for supporting independence.[61] Others sought protection in the homes of

---

[58] UNAMET, Humanitarian Affairs Office, "Preliminary Report on Humanitarian Issues," Dili, June 14, 1999, p. 5; UNAMET, Political Affairs Office, "Political Overview: Atambua, Cova Lima, Ainaro," Dili, June 15–17, 1999, p. 3; UNAMET, Humanitarian Affairs Office, "Preliminary Report on Humanitarian Issues, Subject: Update on Situation after Field Trip to Atambua, Suai, Fatumei, Ainaro," Dili, June 18, 1999, p. 5; UNAMET, Humanitarian Affairs Office, "Situation Report—Humanitarian Affairs," Dili, July 20, 1999, p. 9; UNAMET, Humanitarian Affairs Office, "Humanitarian Affairs Update," Dili, August 23, 1999, p. 1.

[59] The allusion to 1975 was evidently part of the official repertoire even before the "socialization" campaign began. Addressing a meeting of the pro-Indonesian youth group, Gada Paksi, in June 1998, the speaker of East Timor's Parliament, Domingos S. Mariano, said: "In my opinion, if there is a referendum, there will certainly be an even greater bloodletting than we had in 1975." See Tentara Nasional Indonesia, Dandim 1627 (Lt. Col. Endar Priyanto) to Danrem 164/WD and others, "Laporan Hasil Pertemuan di Gada Paksi," Dili, June 23, 1998.

[60] UNAMET, Humanitarian Affairs Office, "Preliminary Report on Humanitarian Issues, Subject: Update on Situation after Field Trip to Atambua, Suai, Fatumei, Ainaro," Dili, June 18, 1999, p. 5.

[61] Beginning in the late 1970s, Catholic Church leaders provided sanctuary to the victims of military operations and spoke out strongly against the occupation. The tone was set by Monsignor Martinho da Costa Lopes, an outspoken critic of Indonesian rule who was removed from his post as Apostolic Administrator in 1983. His successor, Monsignor Carlos Felipe Ximenes Belo, was expected to be more compliant. In 1989, however, he wrote to the then UN Secretary General, Javier Perez de Cuellar, decrying Indonesian violence and urging UN support for a referendum on East Timor's political future. For an account of the role of the Catholic Church during the Indonesian occupation, see Arnold Kohen, *From the Place of the Dead: The Epic Struggles of Bishop Belo of East Timor* (New York, NY: St Martin's Press, 1999).

prominent citizens in Dili and elsewhere. Shockingly, it was in these places of refuge—against those who had already fled their homes—that some of the most egregious acts of violence were committed in early 1999. Among the most notorious cases were two mass killings that took place in April. In the first, on April 6, at least sixty IDPs were killed by pro-Indonesian militias at the parish church in the town of Liquiça, while TNI and police forces looked on.[62] In the second, on April 17, militias backed by TNI and police forces killed at least twelve people who were among some 150 who had taken refuge at the Dili home of a prominent supporter of independence, Manuel Carrascalão.[63]

In addition to targeting IDPs in their places of refuge, pro-Indonesian forces sought to influence the vote by controlling, and disrupting, the flow of humanitarian assistance to the displaced. Government authorities clearly believed that the vote could be swayed by the strategic distribution of material goods to the population. For that reason, the authorities saw the distribution of aid by NGOs as a serious threat to its prospects in the referendum. That belief led naturally to a strategy of disrupting the distribution of humanitarian assistance by NGOs, and seeking to discredit NGO motives and credentials by linking them to Falintil. As UNAMET's Humanitarian Affairs Officer wrote in June 1999, the solution to the problem of displacement was complicated by the fact that Indonesian government and military authorities were "actively and systematically involved in the creation of a humanitarian problem, for political reasons."[64]

The central political importance of humanitarian assistance in the government's view was confirmed by a secret document that surfaced in Dili in mid-July 1999. Dated July 3, 1999, and entitled "General Assessment if Option I Fails," the document offered a candid assessment of the shortcomings of government strategy toward the Popular Consultation process. The author, Major General (ret.) H. R. Garnadi, was Special Assistant I to the Coordinating Minister for Political and Security Affairs, Lt. General (ret.) Feisal Tanjung, who led the ministerial group that oversaw Indonesia's strategy for the referendum in East Timor. After suggesting that the autonomy option was in danger of losing, Garnadi offered the following assessment and possible solution:

> The task of assuring the victory of Special Autonomy for East Timor is really not that difficult, because the political battle is for the poor, and their demands are very simple—they want food and medicine. Whoever can supply them with food and medicine will win their allegiance … We have been left behind in the effort to win the hearts of the people. Aid from foreign NGOs is waiting to be disbursed, and there is no doubt that it will be exploited by pro-independence groups. For that reason, the government's commitment must be confirmed through strengthening the pro-integration forces.[65]

---

[62] Robinson, *East Timor 1999*, Chapter 10.

[63] Ibid.

[64] UNAMET, Humanitarian Affairs Office, "Preliminary Report on Humanitarian Issues," Dili, June 14, 1999, p. 1.

[65] H. R. Garnadi, "Gambaran Umum Apabila Opsi I Gagal," July 3, 1999, pp. 2, 4.

If the Garnadi document revealed that the authorities sought to influence the population through the control of humanitarian assistance, other documents indicated that substantial resources were devoted to that effort, and that the highest-ranking military officers in the country were involved in it. In a secret telegram to Armed Forces Commander, Gen. Wiranto, dated July 6, 1999, Brig. Gen. Mahidin Simbolon (Chief of Staff, Regional Military Command IX) requested the immediate deployment of a Frost-type Navy vessel to transport rice to East Timor. The telegram explained that "the government must distribute rice to the population" because food distributions by some thirty-five NGOs were bound to influence the outcome of the referendum.[66]

The principal mechanism of control was the threat of militia violence against humanitarian workers. As a result of such threats, and some cases of actual violence, humanitarian agencies effectively ceased their activities outside of Dili for several months in mid-1999. In June 1999, UNAMET's Humanitarian Affairs Officer described the situation as it pertained to some three thousand IDPs in Liquiça:

> Local nuns supporting the displaced reported that forty-five children had died in the previous month. It was also verified that in the months previously anyone who had tried to assist the displaced with humanitarian aid had been threatened with death by the militia. The threats, and in some cases beatings, had been taken sufficiently seriously by the humanitarian community in Dili that the delivery of assistance had ceased for some months ... [67]

The most notorious example of this pattern in the pre-ballot period occurred in early July 1999, when armed pro-Indonesian militiamen attacked a humanitarian convoy. The convoy had stopped in the town of Liquiça after delivering food, clothing, and medicine to some seven thousand IDPs in the vicinity of Sare. Shortly after the convoy stopped, it was attacked by about a dozen BMP (Besi Merah Putih, Red and White Iron) militiamen, swinging machetes and knives and firing homemade guns.[68] One person was seriously injured in the assault, and the vehicles in the convoy were badly damaged. Indonesian police and TNI in the immediate vicinity did nothing to stop the attack. Suspicions of official complicity were confirmed by later events, most notably by the wholly inadequate police investigation of the incident.[69]

The attack of July 4 was met with a flurry of criticism from key states and international organizations, and for a time it appeared that the violence, the disruption of humanitarian assistance, and the targeting of IDPs might be brought under control. Apparently encouraged by the new situation, and also by the CNRT leadership, in mid-July thousands of IDPs began returning to their homes to register for the ballot. Within a matter of weeks, however, the violence had resumed and

---

[66] Tentara Nasional Indonesia. Kepala Staf Kodam IX/Udayana (Brig. Gen. Mahidin Simbolon) to Armed Forces Commander (Gen. Wiranto), Denpasar, July 6, 1999.

[67] UNAMET, Humanitarian Affairs Office, "Preliminary Report on Humanitarian Issues," Dili, June 14, 1999, p. 4.

[68] The BMP, based in the District of Liquiça, was one of the most notorious and violent of the more than twenty militia groups that emerged in 1999.

[69] Robinson, *East Timor 1999*, Chapter 10; UNAMET, Humanitarian Affairs Office, "Situation Report—Humanitarian Affairs," Dili, July 20, 1999.

fears of even worse violence after the ballot sent thousands of IDPs back into hiding. By late August, some 2,500 IDPs had taken refuge in the church in Suai, another 2,000 had fled to the mountains from the town of Maliana, 3,500 remained in the vicinity of Faulara, in Liquiça district, and an estimated 7,000 to 10,000 had gathered near the Falintil base area near Uaimori in Viqueque district.[70] Those who fled apparently understood better than some UNAMET analysts that the long-promised post-ballot violence would soon begin.

As this brief account indicates, the forced displacement of the pre-ballot period was not the inevitable result of armed conflict, but the consequence of the deliberate political calculations and strategies of Indonesian authorities, and the actions of their East Timorese proxies. First and foremost, displacement was the result of a strategy of intimidation designed to influence the outcome of the vote. Apart from overt threats and acts of violence, that strategy deliberately evoked bitter historical memories of 1975–79 as a mechanism to sow fear and encourage displacement. The strategy also entailed the control over the distribution of food and other humanitarian aid to the displaced in an effort to influence the outcome of the vote.

Yet if the displacement of the pre-ballot period was driven primarily by the strategic calculations of Indonesian officials, its spatial and temporal patterns were also shaped by other factors, including the posture of pro-independence forces and key international actors. From late 1998 through early 1999, for example, Falintil attacks and CNRT political mobilization prompted some 4,500 supporters of Indonesian rule to flee to Atambua in West Timor.[71] After April 1999, when Xanana Gusmão ordered pro-independence forces not to engage the militias or the TNI militarily, Falintil instead provided a safe haven for displaced villagers in their main base areas, especially in the eastern part of the country. Both Falintil and the CNRT leadership also appear to have been instrumental in encouraging the IDPs to return to their homes in mid-July in order to register, and then again to return home to vote in late August. In so doing, they arguably contributed to the process of displacement, and influenced its spatial patterns.

The role of the international community was similarly mixed. In the months prior to the deployment of UNAMET in June 1999, international attention to the plight of the IDPs was minimal, in part because key states were reluctant to alienate their allies in Jakarta. As a consequence, Indonesian authorities were free to carry out their strategy of forced displacement without hindrance. It was in that period that most of the pre-ballot displacement occurred and the worst of the attacks on IDPs were committed. That situation changed with the deployment of UNAMET and the arrival of hundreds of international observers and journalists, in June 1999. Thereafter, Indonesia's capacity to carry out its campaign of displacement was somewhat constrained. Nevertheless, international attention to the problem of displacement, and to militia violence more generally, was never sufficient to bring it to an end, with the result that the problem persisted right up until the day of the ballot.

---

[70] UNAMET, Humanitarian Affairs Office, "Humanitarian Affairs Update," Dili, August 23, 1999.

[71] UNAMET, Political Affairs Office, "Political Overview: Atambua, Cova Lima, Ainaro," Dili, June 15–17, 1999; UNAMET, Humanitarian Affairs Office, "Preliminary Report on Humanitarian Issues, Subject: Update on Situation after Field Trip to Atambua, Suai, Fatumei, Ainaro," Dili, June 18, 1999.

The effort to mobilize an international response to the violence was complicated, indeed almost completely undermined, by the May 5 Agreements under which responsibility for security during the referendum had been placed in Indonesian hands. Citing that agreement, Indonesian authorities insisted that they did not require—and would in fact resist—outside assistance in maintaining security. Despite mounting evidence of Indonesia's role in the violence, key states did not question that position and instead asked only that Indonesia fulfill its responsibilities under the May 5 Agreements. From the perspective of those states, particularly Australia and the United States, that arrangement served a useful purpose. It provided a plausible excuse *not* to intervene, at least until mid-September, when the violence became so serious that intervention became politically unavoidable.

PHASE II: AUGUST 30 – OCTOBER 1999

While forced displacement remained a significant problem throughout the months leading up to the ballot, its scale and humanitarian consequences in early 1999 paled in comparison to the displacement that followed the August 30 vote. The severity of the post-ballot violence and displacement was captured in a memo written from Dili by UNAMET's Head of Mission, Ian Martin, on September 13, 1999, just hours before UNAMET's evacuation to Darwin.

> … East Timor is in the midst of a serious humanitarian crisis. Dili town has been thoroughly destroyed. Up to half of the significant private buildings have been burnt down or affected by fire [and] the fittings and furniture of almost all houses have been looted. The population [of Dili], estimated at 100,000 has either been displaced or moved to West Timor (often forcibly) … Similar levels of destruction have been reported throughout western East Timor. There has been a massive outflow of IDPs who have dispersed throughout the countryside, reportedly into forest areas near known FALINTIL locations. A large concentration of IDPs, estimated at between 30,000 to 50,000, is confirmed to be concentrated in the Dare area … approximately 10 km south of Dili. Eyewitnesses report that these IDPs are in poor condition and are subsisting on foods foraged from the forest. Other suspected IDP locations are at Suai, Uaimori, and above Ermera town. Overall, it is estimated that only 200,000 of East Timor's population of 800,000 remain in their homes. Health systems have collapsed and it is reasonable to assume that many health facilities have been looted/ destroyed.[72]

Later investigations have confirmed this early assessment, while providing further details of the patterns and dynamics of the displacement. Those details suggest very strongly that the post-ballot displacement—both within East Timor and across the border to West Timor—was deliberately set in motion, and certainly accelerated, by Indonesian officials and their militia proxies. At the same time, the evidence suggests that, as in the pre-ballot period, the spatial and temporal pattern

---

[72] UNAMET, Special Representative of the Secretary General, cable to Vieira de Mello, United Nations, New York, on "Planning for Humanitarian Assistance Operations in East Timor," Dili, September 13, 1999.

of displacement, and its humanitarian ramifications, were also shaped by the policies and actions of the pro-independence movement, and of key international actors.

Residents of Dili aboard an Indonesian Police vehicle, in early September 1999. They were among more than 400,000 East Timorese forcibly displaced in the aftermath of the historic vote for independence. (AP Photo, by David Longstreath, with permission)

Major population movements actually began in the hours and days immediately after the vote, as East Timorese sought to avoid the acts of violence that most expected would follow the announcement of the result. Some came to polling stations laden with food and other supplies, so that they could flee immediately to the hills after casting their ballots. The displacement was accelerated by a campaign of intimidation and violence carried out jointly by militias and TNI soldiers. That campaign became even more furious with the announcement of the result on September 4. Across the territory, bands of militiamen and soldiers roamed freely through villages and towns, setting fire to homes and offices, selectively beating or killing pro-independence figures, and threatening residents, telling them that they must leave or suffer the same fate. TNI and police officials either took part in the violence, or appeared unwilling or unable to stop it.

The pattern comes through clearly in the personal testimonies of eyewitnesses. A young man described what he saw on the morning of September 4, at a church in Dili where many people had taken refuge:

> The Aitarak militias, the army ... and Brimob police in uniform arrived at the church with two big army trucks. They tried to get the refugees out of the church, but the refugees refused. Then they threw a grenade into the Portuguese headquarters [of the election observer delegation], which was further along, to frighten them ... I saw that the Brimob police and Aitarak militia had guns and were poking the refugees with them to force them onto the truck. People were screaming and were very upset. They filled up the two trucks with people and took them in the direction of Comoro ... The same thing happened at the seminary and school.[73]

Judging from their scope, their timing, and the broad similarities in method, the post-ballot evacuation operations must have been planned at the provincial level or higher. Some of the most powerful evidence to that effect lies in the behavior of the police and TNI during the evacuation of UNAMET personnel from their district offices in early September 1999. The events leading to the evacuations bore remarkable similarities and had the hallmarks of a well-planned psychological warfare operation. In every instance, the sequence of events began with militias roaming freely through the main town, more heavily armed than usual, shooting, setting fire to buildings, and killing. In every case, the TNI and the police either made no attempt to restrain the militias or actively assisted them. Within a matter of hours, the police in every affected district warned that they could no longer control the situation and recommended that all UNAMET staff relocate to the district police station. Once they had gathered UN staff in their stations, police suddenly announced that they would be leaving, and advised UNAMET to follow. Having no means of guaranteeing their own security, and cut off from all independent sources of information, district UNAMET officials had little choice but to go along. And so, in each case, they joined the police convoy out of town and back to Dili.

A UNAMET report about the evacuations from five separate district offices on September 3 and 4 concluded that the violence had been part of a "deliberate strategy to force UNAMET to withdraw from certain regions back to Dili."[74] In retrospect, it is evident that an important aim of that operation was to terrorize UNAMET international staff, and all other international observers, including NGO staff and journalists, with a view to making them leave the territory. And the

---

[73] Cited in Amnesty International, "East Timor: As Violence Descended: Testimonies from East Timorese Refugees," October 1999, p. 8.

[74] UNAMET, Political Affairs Office, "Incidents on 3 and 4 September which led to the relocation to Dili of UNAMET staff from Aileu, Ainaro, Maliana, Liquiça and Same regencies," Dili, September 4, 1999.

strategy worked. Within a few days of the ballot, the vast majority of foreign journalists, election observers, and NGO workers had left the country, and those who remained were trapped inside the UNAMET compound in Dili, where they were powerless to stop the violence. The removal of international observers at this critical juncture changed the equation dramatically: pro-Indonesian forces were now free to cleanse the countryside, and to target pro-independence supporters, with impunity.

In the face of the mounting violence, thousands fled to the hills and to places of refuge in the main towns, including churches, seminaries, and UN offices. Then, as in early 1999, those places of refuge were systematically attacked, and scores of displaced people were killed. In Dili, thousands of IDPs were forced at gunpoint from the ICRC compound and from the residence of Bishop Carlos Belo and on to waiting trucks. In the town of Maliana, militias and TNI troops assaulted thousands of IDPs who had gathered at the main police station, killing fourteen and forcing others to flee. In one of the most deadly incidents, at least forty people but possibly as many as two hundred were killed at the Catholic Cathedral in the town of Suai where thousands had taken refuge. In that case, too, the attack was a joint operation of militias, TNI, and police.[75]

A common pattern in many of these incidents was that TNI and police officials, as well as militias, warned local people that they would be killed—or that their safety could not be guaranteed—if they did not board the vehicles that had been readied for them. Faced with such threats, many felt they had no option but to comply, and so boarded and allowed themselves to be transported. In Dili, the key assembly points were the regional police headquarters (Polda) and the main harbor. At those sites, refugees were again systematically loaded onto trucks or ships and transported to West Timor and neighboring islands.[76] By September 13, less than two weeks after the ballot, there were an estimated 115,000 people in the camps, and by the end of the month that figure had jumped to some 250,000.[77]

These patterns strongly suggest that the massive displacement after the ballot was part of a deliberate strategy devised by Indonesian authorities. That conclusion is supported by documentary evidence discovered in late 1999. The relevant documents include a plan developed by the East Timor military command in July 1999, for "Operation Wira Dharma-99," and a police plan developed in August, dubbed "Operation Hanoin Lorosae II."[78] These documents describe plans for a massive post-ballot evacuation that accord very closely with the evacuation that was actually carried out. Those targeted for evacuation in the plans, for example,

---

[75] Robinson, *East Timor 1999*, Chapter 10.

[76] Robinson, *East Timor 1999*; Amnesty International, "East Timor: The Terror Continues," September 24, 1999; Amnesty International, "East Timor: As Violence Descended: Testimonies from East Timorese Refugees," October 1999.

[77] The exact number who fled to Indonesia was difficult to establish, mainly because they dispersed to so many locations. Early estimates were around 200,000, but a consensus later emerged that the number was closer to 270,000. See UNAMET, Special Representative of the Secretary General, cable to Vieira de Mello, United Nations, New York, on "Planning for Humanitarian Assistance Operations in East Timor," September 13, 1999; Amnesty International, "East Timor: Building a New Country Based on Human Rights," July 2000, p. 31.

[78] Tentara Nasional Indonesia, Korem 164/WD, "Rencana Operasi Wira Dharma-99," Dili, July 1999; Kepolisian Negara Republik Indonesia, Daerah Timor Timur, "Rencana Operasi Hanoin Lorosae II," No. Pol.: Ren Ops/04/VIII/1999, Dili, August 1999.

included 180,000 East Timorese, and roughly 70,000 Indonesian civil servants, soldiers, and police, and their respective families.[79] The total numbers of evacuees in both plans was about 250,000, or almost exactly the actual number evacuated. The police document also includes an intelligence assessment that predicts widespread destruction and violence in the event of a pro-independence victory.[80]

Australian soldiers count displaced East Timorese at a food distribution center in Dili, early October 1999. (AP Photo, by Maya Vidon, with permission)

---

[79] See Korem 164/WD, "Rencana Operasi Wira Dharma-99, Lampiran-D (Rencana Banmin), Sub-Lampiran-3 (Kebutuhan Angkutan)," Dili, July 1999.

[80] Kepolisian Negara Republik Indonesia, Daerah Timor Timur, "Rencana Operasi Hanoin Lorosae II," No. Pol.: Ren Ops/04/VIII/1999, Dili, August 1999.

Statements by senior Indonesian officials prior to the ballot confirm that there was official planning for a massive post-ballot evacuation. In August 1999, for example, Maj. Gen. Zacky Anwar Makarim and Col. Noer Muis both told UNAMET about official preparations for a large post-ballot evacuation. Col. Muis and Indonesia's Minister for Justice and State Secretary, Muladi, were also quoted in the press on the issue. Muladi reportedly noted the "strong possibility" of an exodus of some 223,000 people in the event of a pro-independence victory.[81] At a minimum, these documents and statements prove that the Indonesian authorities were being dishonest in assuring the international community that they would stay in East Timor and maintain order regardless of the outcome of the vote. Viewed together with the other evidence, they appear to confirm that the displacement was planned by Indonesian authorities at a high level.

But why would they do so? What was there to be gained by forcibly displacing the population on such a massive scale? Apart from considerations of revenge, there appear to have been two motives at work.

First, displacement served as the basis for later challenges to the credibility of the vote and demands for the partition of East Timor. In an echo of the claims made by Indonesian authorities in 1975, pro-integration leaders were quick to argue that the flight of so many people to West Timor was evidence of widespread support for Indonesian rule, and a rejection of the independence option. The flight of so many across the border was also evidence, they claimed, that the UN-sponsored vote had been rigged. Noting that the vast majority of those who fled were from the western-most districts, some argued that East Timor should be partitioned, with the western districts joining Indonesia. In a joint memoir about 1999, four senior Indonesian military officers, including Maj. Gen. Makarim, wrote: " ... the pro-integration side demanded that, if the results of the popular consultation proved unsatisfactory, East Timor should be divided into two parts, with an Eastern Sector under the CNRT and a Western Sector remaining as part of Indonesia."[82]

Second, again in an echo of 1975, the creation of a huge refugee population just across the border created abundant opportunities for undermining the new regime in East Timor. By controlling the refugee population—including their access to information, food, water, medicine, and other material necessities—Indonesian authorities would be able to disrupt and substantially impede efforts to repatriate East Timorese. In doing so, they would be able to weaken the political legitimacy of the new government, sow seeds of doubt and discord among East Timorese, and undermine efforts at reconciliation that were considered vital by the new regime in Dili. Controlling the refugees would also allow Indonesia to limit the ability and

---

[81] See *Sydney Morning Herald*, August 24, 1999; *Jakarta Post*, August 26, 1999; and *Media Indonesia*, August 27, 1999. Also see Ian Martin, *Self-Determination in East Timor* (Boulder, CO: Lynne Rienner, 2001), p. 82. Significantly, the figure 223,000 was almost exactly the number of evacuees estimated in the TNI's "Operasi Wira Dharma-99," excluding military personnel.

[82] Zacky Anwar Makarim, Glenny Kairupan, Andreas Sugiyanto, and Ibnu Fatah, *Hari-Hari Terakhir Timor Timur: Sebuah Kesaksian* (Jakarta: PT Sportif Media Informasindo, 2002), p. 380. The call for partition also appeared frequently in the Indonesian press. In October 1999, for example, a Kupang newspaper reported a militia leader, José Mauzinho Cardozo, saying that " ... the only just solution for East Timor was to divide the territory into two, with six districts belonging to the pro-integration side and seven to the independence forces." "Pejuang Timor Siapkan Intelijen Susup ke Timor," *Suara Timor*, October 25, 1999.

inclination of the new government of East Timor to push hard on the contentious questions of justice and reparations.

Whatever the reasons, early indications that the massive displacement and widespread violence were being orchestrated by Indonesian military authorities—or, at a minimum, that those authorities were unwilling to stop the mounting violence—helped to build an unusual consensus around an international military intervention in mid-September. Within two weeks of the ballot, the UN Security Council had agreed on that course of action, and just five days later a multinational force, known as INTERFET, was deployed in East Timor. Within a matter of weeks, the worst of the violence had been stopped, and major humanitarian operations were underway. Although East Timor had been reduced to a smoking ruin, by the end of October 1999 the vast majority of those who had fled to the interior had returned to their homes and had begun to receive humanitarian assistance in the form of food, shelter, and medical attention. In the absence of that swift and effective international intervention, the displacement might easily have given rise to a humanitarian crisis on a scale equal to or greater than that seen in the late 1970s.

Yet while international military intervention quickly changed the equation within East Timor, it did not immediately address the plight of those who had been forced to flee elsewhere.[83] On the contrary, the refugees in Indonesia faced perilous conditions long after the worst of the violence and dislocation within East Timor had been remedied. Poor sanitation, food and water shortages, lack of shelter, and minimal medical provisions all contributed to serious health problems in the refugee camps. As in the late 1970s, those problems were compounded by official restrictions on access to the refugees by humanitarian organizations and by repeated threats and attacks against their staff. As a consequence of those conditions, scores of refugees, many of them children, died in the first few months after their arrival.[84]

The most serious problem in the camps, and the root of most other problems, was that the pro-Indonesian militiamen who had terrorized the refugees into fleeing in September 1999 were also in the camps, where they continued to harass, threaten, and intimidate the refugees.[85] As they had done inside East Timor, the Indonesian authorities, including the TNI, made little effort to control the militias inside the camps. The predictable result was that they were free to harass and to commit serious acts of violence against the refugees, including rape, sexual slavery, and murder.[86]

Despite these considerable obstacles, and a lack of full cooperation from Indonesian authorities, international humanitarian agencies—led by the United

---

[83] The main concentrations of refugees in West Timor were near the border town of Atambua, which had long been a base area for pro-Indonesian forces and militias, and Kupang, the capital of Nusa Tenggara Timor province. Camps also sprang up in the district of Kefamenanu on the border. Several thousands also fled, or were transported, to other parts of Indonesia, including Flores, Alor, Sulawesi, Bali, and Java.

[84] Amnesty International, "Indonesia/East Timor: No End to the Crisis for East Timorese Refugees," December 1999.

[85] Komisi Nasional Hak Asasi Manusia, "Laporan Awal Komisi Penyelidik Pelanggaran HAM di Timor-Timur Tentang Tindakan Milisi dam Kondisi Hak Asasi Manusia Pengungsi di Nusa Tenggara Timur," Jakarta, November 1, 1999.

[86] Amnesty International, "East Timor: Refugees at Risk," October 6, 1999; Amnesty International, Indonesia/East Timor: No End to the Crisis for East Timorese Refugees," December 1999.

Nations High Commissioner for Refugees (UNHCR)—eventually managed to establish a presence in the main camps and to provide much needed assistance. Just as importantly, the UNHCR and the International Organisation for Migration (IOM) quickly set to work organizing a program of voluntary repatriation. The program was officially set in motion on October 8, 1999. By December, some 115,000 refugees had returned to East Timor, and by mid-2000 an estimated 175,000 had done so.[87]

Humanitarian and repatriation efforts suffered a temporary setback in early September 2000, when armed militiamen attacked and killed three UNHCR staff members in one of the camps in Atambua. The killings led to a temporary suspension of UNCHR operations. However, they also sparked an international outcry and placed renewed pressure on the Indonesian authorities to facilitate the safe return of the refugees. Repatriation was further encouraged by East Timor's president, Xanana Gusmão, who made a special appeal for their return. As a result of these combined efforts, by May 2002 the vast majority of refugees had returned to East Timor. Most of those who remained, an estimated 30,000, were former supporters of Indonesia, including militiamen, soldiers, and civil servants.

East Timorese man reunited with family. (AP Photo, by David Guttenfelder, with permission)

As this account clearly suggests, the massive displacement of the post-ballot period, like the displacement before the ballot, was not an accident of war, nor the unintended consequence of civil conflict. More than any other factor, it was the consequence of strategic political calculations by Indonesian military authorities. As

---

[87] Amnesty International, "Indonesia/East Timor: No End to the Crisis for East Timorese Refugees," December 1999; Amnesty International, "East Timor: Building a New Country Based on Human Rights," July 2000, p. 31.

in the pre-ballot period, however, the spatial and temporal pattern of the displacement, and its long-term humanitarian consequences, were also shaped by the strategic position of pro-independence forces and, even more importantly, by the posture of key international actors.

CONCLUSIONS

I began by asking why East Timor suffered two periods of massive forced displacement in just twenty-four years, and what might explain the marked similarities and differences in the patterns of displacement between and within those two periods.

The most basic answer to the first question, it should now be clear, is that forced displacement was not the incidental or inevitable consequence of armed conflict in East Timor, but an intrinsic element of the political strategies adopted by the Indonesian military and by East Timor's pro-independence movement. More specifically, the strategy of displacement appears to have been part of a political vision, shared by Indonesian and pro-independence forces, in which control over population, and not territory or property, was understood to be an essential element—perhaps *the* essential element—in establishing claims to political legitimacy, both domestically and internationally.

That shared political vision also helps to explain the extraordinary preoccupation on both sides with maintaining control over humanitarian assistance. Both sides, it seems, judged that the political opinion and allegiance of the population, and especially of the poor majority, could be swayed by the provision of food, medicine, and other material goods. Both were evidently convinced that their opponents would be able to use any available aid to strengthen their political and military position. And so, both fought bitterly for control of and access to that assistance, making it a central focus of political contestation. That contest over humanitarian assistance was essential to the dynamic of displacement and shaped its pattern.

Forced displacement in East Timor, I have argued here, was also crucially shaped by the actions of a handful of powerful states—notably the US, Australia, and the UK—and international organizations, particularly the UN. Key states were complicit in the massive forced displacement in the period 1975–79, through the provision of vital military material and political backing to the Indonesian regime. The same was true, though to a much lesser degree, in the pre-ballot period in 1999. By contrast, Australia, the US, the UK, and the UN all played critical roles in stopping the terrible violence of the post-ballot period and in mobilizing an effective humanitarian response.

In explaining the similarities between and within the two periods, the evidence also suggests the importance of the institutional repertoires and historical memories of the key parties to the conflict—the Indonesian military, the pro-independence forces, and the wider population. The forced relocation and control of the population was a central element of Indonesia's counterinsurgency strategy in the period 1975–79, and it remained so two decades later. The TNI did not employ forced displacement in all contexts, of course, but when confronted by the most serious threat to its political position in East Timor since 1979, military leaders once again adopted that course, albeit with some modifications. The same was true for Fretilin and the CNRT. The approach they adopted in 1999—encouraging civilians to move close to Falintil bases—was arguably part of a political repertoire inherited from the early years of the struggle.

It may also be the case that, as a result of the shared experience or social memory of 1975–79, massive population movement became part of the repertoire of the East Timorese population more generally in times of crisis. It was certainly striking that in 1999 such a large number of people moved so quickly, and with such evident purpose. To those on the ground, it appeared as though people knew what do, what to bring, and where to go—in a way that was not the case, for example, in New Orleans in the days before and after Hurricane Katrina in 2005. It does not seem unreasonable to suppose that the past experience of massive displacement, or at least a shared memory of it, somehow shaped and directed the patterns of displacement in 1999. That possibility would also help to explain why the spatial patterns of displacement in the two periods were so similar.

If the similarities between the two periods can be understood by reference to continuities in political vision, institutional repertoire, and historical memory, how do we account for the significant differences between the two periods? More specifically, how can we explain the vastly different humanitarian consequences of the two displacements? The evidence offered here points to the following possibilities.

First, and without question, the timing of international intervention was the crucial factor. In the period 1975–79, international humanitarian agencies were denied access to the displaced for a full four years, time enough for famine and disease to kill at least 100,000 people. By contrast, in 1999 international humanitarian organizations were relatively quick to arrive, reaching the displaced inside East Timor within a matter of weeks and those outside the territory perhaps a few weeks later. Despite the many difficulties, and the very considerable suffering of those who were displaced, this was an unusually swift and effective operation and arguably made the difference between a death toll in the hundreds and one in the tens of thousands. It is worth stressing that the deployment of international peacekeeping forces within three weeks of the vote, with the full backing of the UN Security Council, was instrumental in that process.

The very different humanitarian interventions in the two periods stemmed, in turn, from three significant differences in the international context. At the most abstract level, 1999 was something like the high tide of international sympathy for armed "humanitarian intervention." US President Clinton, UN Secretary General Kofi Annan, and countless other world leaders had expressed their strong support for this idea in the months preceding the crisis, so, despite some initial hesitation, there was an unusual openness to the idea when the crisis hit. The difference with the earlier period, when the notion of humanitarian intervention had scarcely been articulated, could hardly have been greater. Two closely related changes, which similarly facilitated swift international action, were the wide currency by 1999 of a discourse on IDPs, and vast improvements in the logistical and institutional capacity for humanitarian intervention.

International attitudes toward the regime in Jakarta, and toward its military in particular, were also very different in the two periods. In 1975–79, Indonesia was considered a vital anticommunist ally to the West, and its military was deemed worthy of robust political and material support. For those reasons, key Western powers chose not to interfere with Indonesia's genocidal campaign in East Timor; indeed, they helped to carry it out and to cover it up. Organized opposition to that approach from the Catholic Church and human rights organizations was still in its infancy and exerted relatively little serious pressure on those states. In 1999, by contrast, Jakarta's allies were only too familiar with the TNI's appalling track record on human rights—in part because of the work of the Church and of human rights organizations over many years—and were more concerned about Indonesia's financial and political stability in a post-Cold War, post-Suharto context. That made intervention much easier to contemplate in 1999 than in 1975–79.

Finally, from the perspective of international access and scrutiny, the situation could not have been more different in the two periods. In the earlier period, Indonesian military authorities were successful in limiting access to the territory to a handful of well-controlled official delegations. Those who did gain access were unable to move around or to speak freely with local people. In 1999, by contrast, there was a large, official UN mission, and literally thousands of international observers and journalists who fanned out across the territory, interviewing, recording, and photographing everything in sight. That level of scrutiny, and the resulting international media attention, severely constrained Indonesia's freedom of maneuver and, simultaneously, stimulated enormous political pressure on key governments and institutions (including the UN Security Council) to intervene when the situation degenerated in early September.

Apart from their importance in stimulating humanitarian intervention in September 1999, these aspects of the international context also help to explain a number of smaller, but still significant, differences in the patterns of displacement between and within the two periods. One of the most conspicuous differences between the two periods was in the methods used to move the population. In the earlier period, displacement was triggered by full-scale military operations, including aerial and naval bombardment, while in 1999 there were no major conventional military operations to speak of. Moreover, the main perpetrators in the earlier period were regular Indonesian forces, while in 1999 armed pro-Indonesian militia groups played a much greater role. Those differences arguably stemmed, in part, from the very different international context of 1999. Under pressure from allies to resolve the issue peacefully, and facing unprecedented international scrutiny on the ground, Indonesian military strategists understood that they could not use conventional military tactics to influence the outcome of the vote. The prevailing discourse of democratization, both in Indonesia and abroad, also suggested the need for a strategy that did not rely openly on military force. The use of ostensibly civilian, community-based militia groups and the reliance on deniable, low-grade violence were ideally suited to this new context.

Finally, why did the pattern of displacement worsen so dramatically in the later phases of both periods? The evidence presented here suggests that the tendency toward the displacement of ever-greater numbers of people was intrinsically related to a shared strategic political vision of population control that underpinned it. In 1975–79, Fretilin and the Indonesian military shared an understanding that control of the population was vital both to their military success and their political legitimacy. The result was a pattern of, forced displacement by both sides. As Indonesian forces began to overwhelm Falintil militarily in late 1977, however, they were able to pursue their strategic goal of population control to its logical extreme, leading to displacement on a much wider scale. Although the arena of conflict in 1999 was primarily electoral rather than military, physical control of the population remained central to the political vision of both sides, again resulting in widespread displacement. Prior to the ballot, displacement was part of the Indonesian, and to a lesser extent the pro-independence, strategy for influencing the outcome of the vote. When the Indonesian side decisively lost the vote, it deployed its military superiority instead to wreak revenge, to lay the basis for future challenges to the legitimacy of the outcome. It did so in accordance with its long-standing strategic vision—by forcibly displacing more than half of the population.

In short, to the extent that population displacement was the product of a common strategic political vision in which control over population was the central element, it tended inexorably to encompass an ever-wider swathe of the population. The difference in outcome between 1975–1979 and 1999 lay mainly in the presence of a force sufficient to interrupt that progression. Thus, in the earlier period, the ever-widening circle of forced displacement remained effectively unchecked until the political objective had been achieved in late 1979, and the result was an unprecedented humanitarian catastrophe. In 1999, the critical expansion came immediately after the August 30 vote, but was quickly halted by international intervention, thereby mitigating what might easily have been a far greater disaster.

PLACE AND DISPLACEMENT IN THE ACEH CONFLICT

Edward Aspinall

> We love our lives more than our possessions. We can get more possessions, but can we buy life?
> — Unnamed Javanese transmigrant, having just fled Aceh to the village of Setungkit, North Sumatra.[1]

Media and other popular accounts of civil wars sometimes portray displacement as being merely one of the tragic by-products of violence. Amid the chaos of conflict, unlucky citizens are caught in the crossfire. Victims of forces beyond their control, escaping cruel and capricious belligerents, they have little choice but to flee their homes. There is little rhyme or reason to displacement; it is merely one of the terrible consequences of war.

In fact, as we know from experiences in many places, displacement is often far from random or unpredictable. Instead, it occurs in clearly identifiable patterns that may shift dramatically over time. Nor is it often merely a peripheral side-effect of conflict. Rather, deliberate forced displacement can be central to the strategies of antagonists, who may seek to empty the landscape of rival populations or deprive their enemies of a support base.[2]

Such is also the first and main argument advanced in this chapter. The chapter presents an analysis of the patterns and dynamics of forced displacement in Aceh, the northern part of the island of Sumatra in Indonesia, where there was an intermittent armed conflict between 1976 and 2005. The conflict pitted an ethnonationalist insurgency, led by the Free Aceh Movement (GAM, Gerakan Aceh Merdeka), against the security forces of the Indonesian state. As this chapter shows, forced displacement was not a by-product of the conflict, but was instead central to it. Displacement developed into a strategy of war by the armed opponents in this protracted struggle, with the Indonesian armed forces at times trying to clear the countryside of the population in order to facilitate their counterinsurgency

---

[1] *Kompas*, June 29, 1999.

[2] See also Geoffrey Robinson, "People Power: A Comparative History of Forced Displacement in East Timor," in this volume.

operations. GAM was equally deliberate, and little less systematic, in its attempts to drive Javanese settlers from Acehnese territory.

The chapter also makes two additional arguments, which in different ways belie the image of displacement as simply an unplanned and chaotic by-product of war. The second argument is that, far from simply expressing the passivity and victimization of those who flee, displacement can also be a form of agency on their part.[3] For the displaced, flight can be an attempt to assert some control over their own circumstances amidst the disruption of war. More than that, however, displacement (at least in conditions of some political and media openness) can also be a highly politicized act, an attempt by civilians to protest against the actions of armed forces and to bring their own plight to the attention of wider audiences.

Third, the following analysis also suggests that displacement can be shaped by the views that the antagonists and civilians alike have toward *place*, toward the territory and landscape in which the conflict occurs. For many Acehnese nationalists, Acehnese territory is imagined as a sacred homeland, steeped in the blood of ancestor-martyrs, and pristine and unpolluted in its natural beauty. Indonesian security forces, by contrast, securitize space, breaking it into discrete territorial units and assigning personnel to collect systematic intelligence about the inhabitants who reside there as a central part of the effort to identify security threats and combat insurgents. During recent years of conflict, security forces divided the map of Aceh into "black," "gray," and "white" zones, suggesting different degrees of control by security forces and their adversaries. Both sides used displacement as an integral part of their strategies, but in ways that were very different and which reflected their different attitudes to territory and to the conflict in which they were engaged.

In seeking to illustrate different patterns of forced displacement in Aceh, and to explore the different strategic imperatives and attitudes to place that underpinned them, this chapter provides, first, an overview of the development of the conflict over the last three decades. This discussion introduces the ideologies and strategic thinking that motivated the belligerents to take action leading to forced displacement. The next section traces the changing nature of forced displacement over the duration of the conflict. The chapter then focuses on three distinct experiences of forced displacement that occurred between 1999 and 2004. This was a time when armed conflict reached levels not previously experienced since the 1950s. There was massive displacement, with several hundred thousand individual occurrences of people being forced to leave their homes (the total number of persons affected is difficult to calculate because many individuals may have been displaced on several different occasions).[4]

The first case study concerns a wave of massive but mostly localized displacement that occurred in 1999. This episode exemplifies some of the difficulties of interpretation that can present themselves when people flee their homes during armed conflict. At first sight, the events described are suggestive of a fearful

---

[3] David Turton, *Conceptualising Forced Migration*, RSC Working Paper No. 12 (Oxford: University of Oxford, Refugee Studies Centre, 2003), pp. 9–10.

[4] Different estimates were provided by various organizations. The US Committee for Refugees estimated that 200,000 people were displaced in 1999–2001: Eva-Lotta E. Hedman, "A State of Emergency, a Strategy of War: Internal Displacement, Forced Relocation, and Involuntary Return in Aceh," in *Aceh Under Martial Law: Conflict, Violence and Displacement*, ed. Eva-Lotta E. Hedman, RSC Working Paper No. 24 (Oxford: University of Oxford: Refugee Studies Centre, 2005), p. 7.

response by powerless civilians to violence by armed actors. A closer examination suggests that displacement also involved deliberate political intent and agency, even empowerment, on the part of the displaced. Second, the chapter looks at the practice of deliberate displacement engaged in by GAM insurgents. Their attacks on Javanese migrants and the consequent forced migration mostly flowed from a nationalist imagination of Acehnese space as vulnerable to desecration by polluting and destructive outside forces. Third, the discussion turns to the systematic and forced displacement by Indonesian security forces during martial law in the territory in 2003 to 2004. At that time, security forces temporarily relocated whole villages to detention camps, with the goal of separating insurgents in the wild spaces of Aceh's hinterland from their rural supporters.

ORIGINS OF CONFLICT AND CONFLICTING ATTITUDES TO PLACE

Aceh's most recent conflict can be dated back to 1976, when an Acehnese who for over two decades had been living in the United States, Hasan di Tiro, returned to Aceh, established GAM, and "redeclared" Aceh's independence. This movement was in different ways heir to earlier phases of conflict in the territory, including the very bloody "Aceh war" of the late nineteenth century, when Acehnese resisted the expansion of Dutch colonialism, as well as an Islamic revolt against the new Indonesian government in the 1950s. The focus of this chapter, however, is the period since 1976, especially the most recent post-Suharto conflict.[5]

GAM was in many respects an almost archetypal ethnonationalist movement. Most of the writings of Hasan di Tiro (himself the descendant of famous leaders of the war against the Dutch) and his followers stressed the glories of Aceh's history and the nobility of the Acehnese people. Their main ideological purpose was to highlight the distinctiveness of the Acehnese as a nation separate from and incompatible with Indonesians, and to assert their historic and sovereign right to an independent state. In particular, GAM literature (at least until recently) denigrated Indonesia as merely a cover for "Javanese" dominance; some of it disparaged the Javanese as an inferior people.[6]

---

[5] There is a growing scholarly literature on the origins and development of the conflict, making it possible to be brief here. See for instance: Eric Eugene Morris, "Islam and Politics in Aceh: A Study of Center-Periphery Relations in Indonesia" (PhD dissertation, Cornell University, 1983); Tim Kell, *The Roots of Acehnese Rebellion, 1989–1992* (Ithaca, NY: Cornell Modern Indonesia Project, 1995); Geoffrey Robinson, "*Rawan* is as *Rawan* Does: The Origins of Disorder in New Order Aceh," *Indonesia* 66 (October 1998): 127–156; M. Isa Sulaiman, *Aceh Merdeka: Ideologi, Kepemimpinan, dan Gerakan* (Jakarta: Al-Kautsar, 2000); Edward Aspinall, "Modernity, History and Ethnicity: Indonesian and Acehnese Nationalism in Conflict," *Review of Indonesian and Malaysian Affairs* 36,1 (2002): 3–33; Edward Aspinall, "Sovereignty, the Successor State, and Universal Human Rights: History and the International Structuring of Acehnese Nationalism," *Indonesia* 73 (April 2002): 1–24; Anthony Reid, "War, Peace and the Burden of History in Aceh," *Asian Ethnicity* 5,3 (2004): 301–14; Anthony Reid, ed., *Verandah of Violence: The Background to the Aceh Problem* (Singapore: Singapore University Press, 2006); and Kirsten E. Schulze, *The Free Aceh Movement (GAM): Anatomy of a Separatist Organization* (Washington, DC: East-West Center, 2004).

[6] See Aspinall, "Modernity, History and Ethnicity," pp. 3–33; and Aspinall, "Sovereignty, the Successor State, and Universal Human Rights," pp. 1–24.

GAM was also typical of ethnonationalist movements in that territory and landscape also figured prominently in its vision. Writing of nationalist movements in general, Anthony Smith suggests that:

> Whatever else it may be, nationalism always involves an assertion of, or struggle for, control of land. A landless nation is a contradiction in terms. ... the creation of nations requires a special place for the nation to inhabit, a land "of their own." Not any land; an historic land, a homeland, an ancestral land. Only an ancestral homeland can provide the emotional as well as physical security required by the citizens of a nation.[7]

GAM ideology was based not only on celebration of the Acehnese people, but also on strong attachment to an Acehnese homeland. After spending seventeen months in the mountainous and densely forested interior of Aceh, endeavoring to establish the nucleus of a GAM guerrilla force, Hasan di Tiro returned to exile, where he wrote *The Price of Freedom*, his "Unfinished Diary" of his time in Aceh. Much of it is filled with lessons about the glories of Aceh's history, and invective against the "Javanese-Indonesian" enemy. Important for our purposes, however, it also includes numerous reveries on the awe-inspiring beauty of Aceh's natural landscape. This landscape is not merely beautiful; for Hasan, it is also inscribed with memory and history. As he shifts camp from place to place, he frequently comes across old battlefields, hiding places, and, especially, graves, reminding him of earlier conflicts with the Dutch and the Republican government (which, for him, were merely earlier episodes in one continuous struggle to liberate Aceh from outsiders). He tells his followers:

> Memorize your history! It has been written, not by ink over the papers, but by your forefathers' blood over every inch of our beautiful valleys and breath-taking heights, beginning from our white sandy beaches to the cloud-covered peaks of Mount Seulawah, Alimon, Geureudông, Abông-Abông. Our heroic forefathers are not dead but merely waiting in their graves, all over this Blessed Land, to the Judgement Day, and in the meantime their spirits are watching you, their sons, yes, listening to what we are talking here and now, and watching you what you are doing with the rich legacy they had left for you and had sacrificed their lives to secure its safe passage to you. Would you be willing to sacrifice your lives too, in order to secure the transmission of this rich legacy to your children and their childrens' children. This Land of yours is a Holy Land—made Holy by the deed and by the sacrificed blood and lives of your ancestors—it is a Holy Land, not to be stepped upon it by the ingrate Javamen with their very dirty feet.[8]

Hasan di Tiro's purpose here is what Anthony Smith refers to as the "territorialization of memory."[9] He seeks not merely to impose duties on today's

---

[7] Anthony D. Smith, "Nation and Ethnoscape," in Anthony D. Smith, *Myths and Memories of the Nation* (Oxford: Oxford University Press, 1999), p. 149.

[8] Dr. Teungku Hasan M. di Tiro, *The Price of Freedom (The Unfinished Diary)* (Norsborg, Sweden: Information Department, National Liberation Front Acheh Sumatra, 1981), p. 69. English language expression in this and subsequent quotations is true to the original.

[9] Smith, "Nation and Ethnoscape," p. 152.

Acehnese by positioning them in a historical continuum with an eternal Acehnese nation, but also to infuse the landscape with the memory of the spilled blood of martyr-ancestors and turn natural locations into memorials to Aceh's heroic past. The land of Aceh becomes the exclusive inheritance, the birthright, of the Acehnese nation: "…you inherited your blood, this land, and everything in it, and on it."[10]

Hasan's position, that of the exiled romantic leader, was close to unique in the movement. A few of the movement's founders were members of Aceh's elite, but most of the foot soldiers and middle-ranking leaders were farmers, petty traders, and ordinary village youths. Hasan was especially enamored of the *pawang*, those forest guides who accompanied him in his travels through Aceh's high country. In his words: "*Pawang* is Achehnese title given to an expert in the affairs of mountains and forests… When you are in the forest of Acheh, you must always have at least one *pawang* with you at all time, otherwise when you have to move, planned or forced, you are certain to get lost. That is one of the great mysteries of the forests of Acheh."[11] It is these men who guide him through the mountains, often using an uncanny sixth sense. They know where the best locations for camps are, how to find jungle food, and where to run when pursued. This was the other side of GAM's attachment to place: rural people's intimate familiarity with local terrain.

The attachment of ordinary GAM members to the landscape was less romantic and poetic than Hasan di Tiro's. Yet most of the rural followers of GAM since 1976 also felt far more comfortable in Aceh's forests than both Hasan (whose diary is also full of stoic complaints about the rigors of jungle life) and their adversaries in the Indonesian security forces. Former GAM guerrillas whom I interviewed often recount tales of their ability to disappear into the jungles for months at a time, boast about their intimate knowledge of the healing properties and other uses of jungle plants, and recall wistfully their encounters with tigers and other wild beasts. They are also proud of their ability to elude Indonesian security forces because of their intimate knowledge of the terrain. Such local knowledge is an obvious advantage to a force that relies on the classic hit-and-run tactics of the guerrilla army, attacking their opponents on the roads or at their posts, and then melting into the forest. Little wonder that GAM sometimes became known in Aceh simply as the "mountain people."

If GAM's relationship to place fused ethnonationalist romanticism with local knowledge, what of the attitudes of GAM's main adversaries in the Indonesian state and security forces? Their relationship to, and conceptualization of, space and territory was very different. Various authors have argued that the transition to modernity, and the development of modern state institutions, has been associated with new attitudes toward space and new techniques for measuring and conceptualizing it.[12] Mapmaking, cadastral surveys, land registration, and other means of knowing territory have been central to the methods used by modern or modernizing states to develop systematic knowledge of their societies as part of the

---

[10] Tiro, *The Price of Freedom*, p. 67.

[11] Ibid, pp. 19–20.

[12] See for example: Winichakul Thongchai, *Siam Mapped: A History of Geo-body of a Nation* (Honolulu, HI: University of Hawai'i Press, 1994); and James C. Scott, *Seeing Like a State: How Certain Schemes to Improve the Human Condition Have Failed* (New Haven, CT, and London: Yale University Press, 1998).

attempt to control and remake them. The "repressive-developmentalist"[13] state of Indonesia's New Order was no exception.

Through the New Order years, especially the 1970s and 1980s, government and military officials were apt to see Aceh as one of Indonesia's remaining wild places, a rough, impenetrable, and backward frontier province in both physical and social terms. Local elites and national government officials were obsessed with breaking down Aceh's "isolation" and "backwardness" by modernizing it and integrating it more closely with the rest of the nation. They viewed Acehnese backwardness and narrow-mindedness as a cause of the Darul Islam revolt of the 1950s, and as an explanation for the troublesome nature of the population thereafter (especially its resistance to various capital-intensive natural resource projects). In this view, physical isolation and mental isolation were inextricably linked; state officials were especially distressed by the poor state of Aceh's transportation infrastructure, by the bad roads and the absence of ports and bridges that could link its scattered communities together and integrate them with the rest of the country. Golkar national chairperson, Amir Murtono, for instance, on one visit to Aceh in 1977, complained that it took him nine hours to go 200 kilometers by car.[14] In 1979 it was still reported that the only means of getting to the small town of Singkil, on the West Coast, was by sea.[15] Existing bridges and roads, most of which dated to the Dutch period, were frequently cut by landslides and floods. The railway system left behind by the Dutch, already damaged during the revolution and Darul Islam years, had fallen into disrepair.

State officials thus viewed building transportation infrastructure in Aceh as both a major goal of the regime's development effort and as a major measure of its success. Local newspapers throughout the New Order period frequently featured triumphant accounts of officials opening a new bridge, port, or road.[16] These attempts to open Aceh's physical territory were only one part of a wider effort to transform its social, economic, and cultural landscape as well, and to develop greater and more systematized knowledge about the territory and its inhabitants. Along with the roads and bridges (and natural gas plants and fertilizer factories) came the steady expansion of state institutions in even the more remote villages. So, too, came the appearance of ever more systematic ordering and intimate knowledge of the territory and its people, documented, for instance, in the regular "Aceh in Figures" (*Aceh dalam Angka*) reports released by the Regional Development Planning Board and Bureau of Statistics.

Of course, the New Order was not merely a modernizing regime; it was also a highly authoritarian one, in which the security forces played the major role, in their own terms, as the "stabilizer and dynamizer" of society. The foundation of the military's system of control was what it called its "territorial system." Under this arrangement, the entire Indonesian territory was divided into a system of hierarchically organized military commands, each responsible for progressively smaller territorial units, ranging from the Regional Commands (Komando Daerah Militer, Kodam), which were responsible for one or several provinces, down to the

---

[13] Herbert Feith, "Repressive-Developmentalist Regimes in Asia: Old Strengths, New Vulnerabilities," *Prisma* 19 (1980): 39–55.

[14] *Waspada*, January 30, 1977.

[15] *Kompas*, October 29, 1979.

[16] See for example, *Waspada*, February 27, 1977.

Subdistrict Commands (Komando Rayon Militer, Koramil). At the lowest level were the *babinsa* (Bintara Pembina Desa), Non-Commissioned Officers for Village Guidance, soldiers responsible for monitoring socio-political affairs in one or more villages. Most of the army's troops were assigned to the territorial commands, where they were distributed among the population. Officials justified this system by reference to the army's origins in local militias during the revolution against the Dutch, and by the resulting doctrine of "total people's defence," grounded in the logic that the best method for resisting foreign aggression was dispersed guerrilla resistance rather than conventional warfare.[17]

In reality, the primary function of the army's territorial structure was "to meet the constant demand for internal security operations [and] the imperatives of regime maintenance."[18] The various components of the territorial command structure were tasked with collecting intelligence on local communities, identifying and responding to potential threats to stability, participating in and monitoring the functioning of government, and generating popular legitimacy for the state by engaging in various civic functions. Indeed, military ambitions knew literally no limits: in the words of one New Order-era training manual, the military was responsible for "Territorial Guidance," which involved "all activities and efforts connected with the planning, arrangement, development, direction, and control of all the capacity of the territory, including all that is found in and on it."[19]

The key point, and the crucial connection to forced displacement, is that the military's territorial structure not only securitized space, it also gave the security forces confidence in their own detailed knowledge of the territory and population under their control. When combined with another crucial plank of military doctrine—the need to separate guerrillas from the local population in counterinsurgency operations—the ultimate result was deliberate and systematic displacement.

PHASES OF DISPLACEMENT

Forced displacement was not a prominent part of the conflict during its first phase, from 1976 to 1979. This was the period encompassing the establishment of GAM and the attempt to consolidate it as a guerrilla force in Aceh's highlands, as well as the army's "Operasi Nanggala" to destroy the movement. The absence of major movements of civilian populations in this period was partly because of the relatively small scale of the conflict. GAM probably had less than one hundred active participants at this time, and only a handful of weapons. Leaks from within its ranks quickly alerted the military authorities to the presence of Hasan di Tiro and his band of followers in Pidie's mountains. Troops moved quickly to cordon them off from surrounding villages. Large sections of Hasan's "Unfinished Diary" recount his band's desperate attempts to evade detection by these military forces, which were

---

[17] Robert Lowry, *The Armed Forces of Indonesia* (St. Leonard's: Allen and Unwin, 1996), pp. 25–30.

[18] Ibid., p. 94.

[19] Departemen Pertahanan-Keamanan, *Pengenalan Terhadap Masalah Operasi Keamanan Dalam Negeri, Operasi Teritorial, Pembinaan Wilajah, Teritorial dan Operasi Keamanan dan Ketertiban Masjarakat* (Staf Gabungan Teritorial. Biro Pendidikan dan Latihan Departemen Dalam Negeri, 1972), p. 17.

coming ever closer. From early on, it also became difficult for the rebels to supply their constantly shifting camp because the military was stopping and searching (and, according to Hasan, sometimes shooting) villagers bringing food and other material. GAM fighters made some attacks on Javanese transmigrant settlements, but it seems these did not result in the inhabitants fleeing, at least not for any length of time.

Mass displacement made its first appearance in the modern Aceh conflict in 1990. This occurred during a much more intense upsurge of violence that is now remembered as the DOM (Daerah Operasi Militer, or Military Operations Zone) period, which covers 1989 to 1998. The violence began with a few sporadic attacks on security forces and other targets by a new generation of GAM combatants, some of whom had received military training in Libya in the late 1980s. The period achieved its subsequent notoriety, however, as a result of the military response to these actions, which peaked between mid-1989 and about 1992. Security forces initiated a campaign of violence against insurgents and their supporters, including targeted abductions and killings, torture, beatings, and sexual assault. Most estimates put the number of civilians killed during this period at between one thousand and three thousand, though some Acehnese groups claim it was much higher.[20]

For the first time, from 1990 we see displacement of large numbers of people, including Javanese transmigrants. For example, *Editor* magazine reported that two hundred left their village and walked to the nearest bus terminal, explaining they wished to return to Java after being threatened by gunmen, and an even larger group of 130 families fled when their village chief was hacked to death.[21] However, the best-documented instances of forced displacement involved Acehnese people fleeing by boat, mostly from villages along the East coast of Aceh in Pidie, North Aceh, and East Aceh, across the Malacca Strait to Malaysia. This movement across the Straits began in late 1990.[22] Although precise figures are hard to obtain, by the mid-1990s GAM sources estimate that approximately three thousand Acehnese had fled to Malaysia,[23] although they were mixed with a larger number of economic migrants. Most of those who fled were from areas where support for GAM had been strong and military counterinsurgency operations had been fiercest. The very fact that those displaced felt they had to flee the country altogether, rather than simply leave the immediate vicinity of conflict, was itself one indication of the control exercised by the military throughout Aceh at this time, and the degree of its targeting of civilians. (Transmigrants, by contrast, during this phase of conflict rarely fled beyond Aceh's borders and were in fact usually returned quickly to their settlement camps, reassured with promises of military protection and, presumably, having very little say in the matter.) In conditions where the military (in the words of its commander-in-chief) required the community to provide assistance and "together with ABRI, seek and destroy the Security Disruptors' Movement wherever they may be,"[24] fleeing would have marked villagers as fearful of, and potentially unsympathetic to, the state's security campaign. It was thus hazardous to flee into adjacent territory,

[20] ICG (International Crisis Group), *Aceh: How Not to Win Hearts and Minds* (Jakarta/Brussels: Indonesia Briefing, 2003), p. 3.

[21] *Editor*, July 14, 1990.

[22] Amnesty International, *Indonesia: "Shock Therapy" Restoring Order in Aceh, 1989–1993* (London: Amnesty International, 1993), pp. 53–56.

[23] Interviews with GAM leaders in Malaysia, April 2004.

[24] *Suara Karya*, November 21, 1990.

which was also controlled by the security forces; leaving Indonesia was a safer option.

Forced displacement became a very visible part of the conflict in Aceh, however, only after the collapse of the Suharto regime and subsequent eruption of conflict in the territory. Displacement reappeared shortly after violence itself resumed in late 1998, and persisted even after negotiations in 2005 brought the conflict to an end. Coinciding with the resumption of violence in rural parts of Aceh, a full-scale displacement crisis occurred in Aceh in mid-1999 when over 100,000 villagers fled their homes to other localities within Aceh. At the same time, there were reports of large numbers of migrants from elsewhere in Indonesia, including participants in the government's official transmigration program, leaving the province (see below). Over the following four years, the number of displaced persons within Aceh fluctuated considerably. Displaced Acehnese villagers mostly did not leave their homes for more than a few weeks or months; even so, the total number of people displaced within Aceh rarely fell far below ten thousand at any one time.[25] Those who fled the province altogether, such as Javanese transmigrants, mostly did not return to their homes. A second major peak of displacement occurred from May 2003, when the government declared a "military emergency" in the province. Security forces deliberately relocated tens of thousands of people from their homes. Others fled under their own initiative, including at least 20,000 who went to Malaysia. The fluctuating nature of conflict-related displacement between 1999 and 2004 makes it difficult to provide a precise figure for the numbers of people involved, but overall it appears that several hundred thousand people were affected.[26]

In part, the increased levels of displacement were a result of the greater intensity of the violence. It was not simply that there was greater absolute loss of life, but also because of the greater parity, for a while at least, between the opposing forces. In the DOM period, GAM fighters were few in number and they were poorly armed. After a few initial surprise attacks, they had limited capacity to seriously harm the security forces. Conflict became very one-sided, and the majority of fatalities were villagers killed in reprisals or sweeps by security forces. After 1999, however, GAM expanded rapidly. Although it never matched the Indonesian army in armaments or manpower, it recruited many new members, raised funds, and purchased new arms.[27] Though depredations against civilians continued, and civilians still constituted by far the largest proportion of those killed, the security forces also suffered losses. Much of Aceh was transformed into a battlefield through which two opposing forces waged war. It was not a war of a conventional kind, however, but an intertwined conflict—guerrilla campaign and government dirty war—in which there

---

[25] OCHA Consolidated Situation Report 41,07 (September 14, 2001), for example, reports a drop from 18,656 to 8,962 total displaced people.

[26] This estimate does not include people displaced by the December 26, 2004, Indian Ocean tsunami, which killed an estimated 128,000 persons and resulted in approximately 500,000 people being displaced. Although the dynamics of the conflict in Aceh had an impact upon aspects of the management of this displacement crisis, tsunami-related displacement lies beyond the scope of this chapter. For a discussion of the politics of displacement in the post-tsunami period, see Eva-Lotta Hedman, "Back to the Barracks: *Relokasi Pengungsi* in Post-Tsunami Aceh," *Indonesia* 80 (October 2005): 1-19.

[27] Edward Aspinall, "Whither Aceh?," *Inside Indonesia* 62 (April–June, 2000): 6–7; Schulze, *The Free Aceh Movement*, pp. 17–19.

were few set-piece military confrontations, but many hit-and-run guerrilla attacks, reprisal killings, and bombings or burnings of buildings in the dead of night.

In a study based on a survey of three hundred IDPs in nine different camps in Aceh, Cynthia Buiza and Gary Risser concluded:

> … 61 percent of the total respondents in Aceh were displaced due to threats and orders to flee their villages by unidentified persons. The rest cited as the reasons for abandoning their homes direct orders from GAM to leave, burning of houses and property, being driven away by either soldiers or militia, and, for a small number, a generalized fear that if they did not leave, they would become the next targets.[28]

Fear of violence was thus the common motivating factor behind most displacement. Sometimes fear was prompted by direct intimidation, including "advance warnings from unidentified persons often wearing black masks," or by direct attacks on villages, involving the burning of villagers' homes and violent assaults and killings of villagers by TNI (Tentara Nasional Indonesia, Indonesian National Military), GAM combatants, or unidentified assailants. At other times, "merely reports of violence in a nearby village propelled families to run for their lives."[29]

To a large extent, then, mass displacement in Aceh resembles a dynamic familiar from most armed conflicts: "flight and fear" responses, where large groups of civilians flee from small groups of armed men.[30] However, the belligerents differed in their ideologies, strategies, and patterns of operation. GAM relied on its intimate knowledge of the terrain and its ability to melt into the local community; the TNI depended on its superior technical capacity and resources, and on its ability systematically to control territory and the populace by force. Each side also targeted different groups of civilians, leading to different patterns of forced displacement.

AMBIGUOUS EXODUS: DISPLACEMENT IN 1999

Mass displacement became a major feature of the Aceh conflict in May–June 1999. This was a time when violence was reviving. Following the collapse of the Suharto government in May 1998, for a brief period there had been considerable optimism in Aceh. There was dramatic liberalization of political conditions, public discussion of past human rights abuses, and government promises of restitution and reform. The calm did not last long. By the end of late 1998, a series of armed clashes between security forces and GAM insurgents was beginning. During the first months of 1999 there were well-publicized massacres and other human rights abuses by troops.[31] A series of "mysterious killings," attacks on the security forces, and other

---

[28] Cynthia Buiza and Gary Risser, *Anywhere but War: Internal Displacement and Armed Conflict in Aceh* (Bangkok: Jesuit Refugee Service Asia Pacific, 2003), p. 32.

[29] Ibid.

[30] Ali Aulia Ramly, "Modes of Displacement during Martial Law," in *Aceh Under Martial Law: Conflict, Violence, and Displacement*, ed. Eva-Lotta E. Hedman, p. 16.

[31] See for example: Human Rights Watch, "Indonesia: The May 3, 1999, Killings in Aceh" (1999: http://www.hrw.org/campaigns/indonesia/aceh0515.htm); Elizabeth Frances Drexler, "Paranoid Transparencies: Aceh's Historical Grievance and Indonesia's Failed Reform" (PhD dissertation, University of Washington, 2001), pp. 129–50; Amran Zamzami, *Tragedi Anak*

acts of violence had also begun in rural parts of Aceh.[32] Tensions were also rising in the approach to scheduled national elections on June 7, with GAM and various civil society groups calling for a boycott; the government viewed successful implementation of the elections as crucial for its own legitimacy.[33]

A family stands in the ruins of their home, burnt by government troops after a
fire-fight with GAM guerrillas, in Krueng Sabe district, West Aceh.
(Photo by William Nessen, with permission)

It was in this context that a new catch-phrase entered the political vocabulary in Aceh: "exodus" (*eksodus*). This word was used by the press, and sometimes by displaced people themselves, to describe a new pattern of mass displacement.[34] Suddenly, the entire population of a village, or sometimes clusters of several villages, would flee their homes *en masse*. Usually, they would move only a few kilometers, or a few dozen kilometers, sometimes on foot, sometimes by truck or other vehicle. The typical destination was the nearest subdistrict (*kecamatan*) capital, where they would set up camp in a mosque, school, university campus, or some other prominent public space. Local student groups or NGOs would quickly try to raise money and provide

Bangsa: Pembantaian Teungku Bantaqiah dan Santri-santrinya (Jakarta: Bina Rena Pariwara, 2001); and Jacques Bertrand, *Nationalism and Ethnic Conflict in Indonesia* (Cambridge: Cambridge University Press, 2004), pp. 173–81.

[32] See for example: *Media Indonesia*, July 1, 1999; *Waspada*, July 31, 1999.

[33] Edward Aspinall, "The 1999 General Election in Aceh," in *Pemilu: The 1999 Indonesian Election*, ed. Susan Blackburn, Annual Indonesia Lecture Series No. 22 (Clayton, Victoria: Monash Asia Institute, 1999), pp. 29–42.

[34] One newspaper reported a villager in Pidie saying, "Exodus again … exodus again," as 1,200 residents of the village of Lhok Keutapang packed up their belongings and fled: *Waspada*, June 28, 1999.

supplies for them. Ramshackle encampments of displaced villagers suddenly became a common sight in many small towns throughout Aceh.

The number of people on the move was considerable; certainly it was much higher than in any earlier phase of conflict. One local newspaper, for example, estimated that almost 100,000 people were internally displaced in May–June alone.[35] Six weeks later, the governor gave a figure of 165,000.[36] The pattern of displacement, however, was both sporadic and localized. Usually, displacement did not last long, with groups of IDPs staying away from their homes for a few weeks, sometimes only a few days, at a time. Displacement was also very geographically concentrated, with almost all of the displaced coming from the three districts of North Aceh, Pidie, and East Aceh, which had also been the traditional strongholds of GAM. Within these districts, population movement was also highly concentrated. For instance, in mid-June it was reported that there were some 26,000 IDPs from only forty-six villages in only three subdistricts in Pidie, with most of those—some 24,000—coming from the subdistrict of Bandar Dua.[37] A few weeks later, it was reported that there were 49,000 refugees from fifty-five villages in four subdistricts of Pidie.[38] Some subdistricts, consisting of a few dozen villages, were virtually emptied of their inhabitants overnight. And sometimes, the displaced gathered in large numbers in their places of refuge: at one point it was reported that about 26,000 refugees were collected around one mosque and one village prayer-house (*meunasah*) in Beureunuen, Pidie.[39]

Largely as a result of the much greater media freedom at this time, it is also easier to get a more precise picture of what motivated these villagers to flee. Sometimes, community leaders interviewed by journalists would merely say that they feared violence. More often, however, they explicitly said they were fleeing from the security forces. This was a period when the memory of DOM depredations was very fresh, and sometimes individuals told journalists that their fears had revived when troops entered their villages. As one displaced villager from the subdistrict of Teunom told *Tempo* magazine, when seventy-five soldiers set up a post in his village, local people believed, "That was a sign that there would be interrogations and abductions."[40] One village chief told reporters that the inhabitants of his village were still "frightened" of the military, especially after they began to threaten villagers after the disappearance of an intelligence officer.[41] Others complained even more explicitly about particular acts of violence perpetrated by soldiers, such as beatings of local people, the burning of homes, or theft of their belongings. As one displaced person called Abubakaruddin put it: "We were forced to flee because we were afraid of the security forces who were beating people [*main pukul*]."[42]

Another novel development was that the IDPs made explicit demands and sometimes appeared to be highly organized. Spokespeople for groups of displaced

---

[35] *Waspada,* June 28, 1999.

[36] *Republika,* August 12, 1999.

[37] *Waspada,* June 16, 1999.

[38] *Waspada,* July 7, 1999.

[39] *Waspada,* July 6, 1999.

[40] *Tempo,* June 28–July 4, 1999.

[41] *Waspada,* May 25, 1999.

[42] *Waspada,* July 5, 1999. See also. *Kompas,* July 12, 1999; *Waspada,* July 7, 1999.

villagers, or individual villagers interviewed by journalists, often insisted that they would not return to their villages until troops were withdrawn.[43] One group, for example, insisted that they would not go home until the UNHCR (United Nations High Commissioner for Refugees) arrived to take care of them, or at least until the authorities gave them "a security guarantee that they would not be intimidated by the TNI."[44] Another group of village heads, who were accompanied by student activists in a meeting with a *bupati* (district head), read from a statement they had prepared calling on the local Military Resort Commander to withdraw troops from their villages: "If the troops are not withdrawn we will not return to our villages," explained their spokesperson.[45] As the refugee crisis escalated, in a few cases leaders of the displaced communities negotiated with local TNI commanders, who eventually promised to withdraw military posts in order to convince villagers to return home.[46] Eventually, in August, an order was issued to pull troops back from the villages and large numbers of villagers returned home. The displacement crisis receded in intensity, though it never completely disappeared over the following years.

The wave of displacement in mid-1999 was very different from earlier experiences. In the DOM period, groups of individuals had furtively left their homes in the dead of night. They had tried to escape the reach of the authorities completely by fleeing to Malaysia. Now, although IDPs were obviously still fearful, whole communities moved *en masse* and did so in a sometimes public and politicized way. What explains this marked difference?

The first factor is that this wave of displacement came at a crucial juncture in the reviving military conflict in Aceh. The military's territorial structure, although not in a state of complete meltdown, was certainly in considerable disarray. In August 1998, General Wiranto had offered a begrudging apology on behalf of the military for abuses perpetrated during the DOM period. Hard figures are difficult to obtain, but it appears there was a substantial reduction in troops numbers (1999 was a year during which army resources were stretched thinly, with significant deployments to East Timor in the lead-up to that province's referendum on independent statehood at the end of August, as well as to sites of communal violence such as Maluku and West Kalimantan). There had been significant erosion of the capacity of the territorial structure at its base. During DOM, the army's territorial network had penetrated effectively down to the village level. From late 1998, the territorial structure came under extreme pressure. GAM was expanding rapidly, developing an alternative civilian governing structure, and launching more military assaults on government forces. There were assassinations of off-duty police and soldiers. Large numbers of their civilian informers and auxiliaries were also killed, presumably mostly by GAM. In a few cases, soldiers were pulled from vehicles and lynched by angry mobs. By mid- to late 1999, the administrative structures of the Indonesian state, and not just the military, were beginning to fail throughout rural Aceh. By the end of 1999, it was reported that most subdistrict offices were closed, as were district offices in Pidie and North Aceh, while that in West Aceh had been burned down. In the words of Sofyan Ibrahim Tiba, an academic from the Muhammadiyah University (and later a GAM

---

[43] For example *Republika,* July 2, 1999; *Kompas,* July 12, 1999.

[44] *Waspada,* May 31, 1999.

[45] *Serambi Indonesia,* July 1, 2005.

[46] *Serambi Indonesia,* July 1, 1999; *Waspada,* July 17, 1999.

negotiator), the "police and soldiers also cannot carry out any activities. They only have the courage to stand guard at their bases because if they go outside, they'll have problems."[47]

The mass exodus of villagers from May to June 1999 coincides with one of the first concerted attempts by security forces comprehensively to regain the ground they had lost, including by reinserting troops (mostly, at this stage, from the police) back into the villages. Of course, this effort was conducted with much arbitrary brutality. In the new conflict conditions, where security forces were themselves being targeted by frequent ambushes and hit-and-run attacks, they acted like an occupying army, with many recorded instances of collective punishment of villagers after armed clashes. The "exodus" of mid-1999 was an attempt by villagers to avoid such arbitrary violence, but it should also be viewed as a protest against the security forces' behavior and against their reappearance in villages they had previously abandoned.

This points to a second factor distinguishing the mid-1999 exodus from earlier experiences: the more open political climate and the obviously political motivations that undergirded the phenomenon of displacement itself. It has already been noted that the exodus was widely reported in the local, national, and international media, as were the stated motivations of those on the move and their criticisms of the military. This relative openness stands in contrast to the official silence and distortions that accompanied conflict in the early 1990s, and points to the fact that the crisis the Indonesian state faced in 1999 in Aceh was not primarily military but political. The state had experienced a collapse in credibility following the downfall of the Suharto regime. Almost immediately after Suharto resigned in May 1998, and well before the new wave of violence swept through rural Aceh, the media had begun publishing detailed investigations of past human rights abuses. From mid-1998, too, students and other groups were protesting against the government and military in Banda Aceh and other Acehnese towns. Coinciding with the rise of violence and the months of the exodus itself, a large student-led referendum movement rapidly gained momentum throughout Aceh. The climate of relative media freedom and political openness was not merely peripheral or coincidental to the exodus, but shaped it fundamentally. The new conditions afforded a measure of protection for fleeing civilians and provided a language for them to explain their motivations and express their views publicly. Doing this had been impossible during the DOM period, when those few individuals who managed to flee secretly to Malaysia were denigrated in the press back in Indonesia. Now, flight was not merely a means of self-preservation but also a means of protest.

Moreover, flight was more than a weapon of the weak expressing inchoate urges or elemental desires for self-preservation; the mid-1999 exodus was in some ways very overtly political. Displaced communities were often highly organized, appointing spokespeople to talk to the media and negotiate with local authorities. They were often assisted by student activists, who were at the same time involved in anti-military and pro-referendum campaigning. One local NGO gave a frank assessment:

> Based on the observations of activists and journalists in refugee sites at Ulee Glee and Peudada, a striking scene in every displacement camp is the flying of Free

---

[47] *Republika,* November 11, 1999.

Aceh flags and banners in English and Acehnese. At the Ulee Glee site there are banners reading "*No gun, no war, no Army Action, but freedom,*" "*We want UNO to come to Acheh,*" "*Good bye Indonesia*" [English in original]. They also shout out slogans about independence for Aceh. In Peudada, banners with similar sentiments are scattered around the displacement camp. There are indications these refugees are being organized by the Free Aceh group.[48]

Some commentators have argued that GAM organized the displacement in order to dramatize popular opposition to the military and to draw international attention to the plight of the Acehnese.[49] This may be so, and it may be that some of the people in the camps, while ostensibly fleeing from the military, were in fact equally fearful of GAM. Security forces were clearly of the view that the whole exercise was a result of GAM "intimidation" or "provocation."[50] Aceh's police chief warned that GAM operatives were disguising themselves among IDPs.[51] Security forces raided IDP camps, ripping down pro-referendum and pro-independence materials, and harassing, detaining, or beating activists who were assisting IDPs.[52] More commonly, they attempted to prevent villagers from fleeing their homes in the first place; forcing them to take side-streets and pathways to avoid guard posts.[53] It is an extremely difficult task, in fact, to disentangle the motivations of GAM (itself not a truly consolidated force at this point) from those of the ordinary villagers. While it is certainly likely that some of those fleeing did so under GAM's orders and felt they had little option, there is also plenty of evidence that the broader political goals expressed at the displacement camps were widely shared by many members of rural society.

Overall, the mid-1999 wave of displacement tells us to be careful about viewing all acts of displacement as merely unintended and horrific consequences of conflict. Displacement can be integral to conflict, a means for belligerents and civilians alike to express deeply held views and achieve strategic goals.

PURGING JAVANESE TRANSMIGRANTS

The next category of displacement also involved deliberate and calculated actions. Between 1999 and 2003, tens of thousands of Javanese and persons of Javanese descent were forced to leave Aceh by GAM and GAM sympathizers. It is not possible to interpret this flight as an act of protest by the displaced. It was instead the outcome of deliberate violence, intimidation, and attacks, which, in turn, were in keeping with GAM's ethnonationalist construction of Acehnese territory as the historic and exclusive property of the Acehnese.

Aceh's population is more ethnically homogeneous than many Indonesian provinces, but it is still mixed. Alongside several indigenous ethnic minorities, like

---

[48] Koalisi NGO HAM Aceh, *Pengungsi Aceh, Kehilangan Pemimpin Dan Terasing Di Tanah Leluhur,* June 17, 1999.

[49] Human Rights Watch, "Indonesia: Civilians Targeted in Aceh" (Human Rights Watch Press Backgrounder, 2000, http://www.hrw.org/press/2000/05/aceh05-back.htm).

[50] For example *Antara,* June 14, 1999.

[51] *Kompas,* July 29, 1999.

[52] *Media Indonesia,* July 25, 1999; *Serambi Indonesia,* August 23, 1999.

[53] *Waspada,* July 3, 1999, July 4, 1999.

the Gayo and Alas, there are also significant migrant groups, the largest of which is the Javanese, who make up probably around 10 percent of the population of four million.[54] Many Javanese, as well as members of other ethnic groups, had been moving to Aceh since the Dutch period. These early Javanese migrants and their descendants were especially numerous in the palm oil and other plantations of East Aceh, as well as the upland coffee-growing area of Central Aceh. Others were participants in the government's transmigration program, under which inhabitants of the densely populated areas of Java and Bali were moved to less developed provinces. The government viewed this policy both as a way to relieve population pressure in Java and Bali, and also as a means to further national integration and economic development of backward regions.

Aceh became part of the government's official transmigration program during the New Order, when in 1975 a settlement unit was opened in Cot Girek, North Aceh. As one exponent of the program put it that year, Aceh needed to "absorb as many transmigrants as possible" in order to "catch up" from its state of backwardness.[55] Over the following twenty-four years, a total of 126 transmigrant settlements were established in Aceh.[56] They accommodated almost 38,000 families, or 160,000 people in all.[57] Participants were placed in settlements separate from surrounding communities, effectively forming all-Javanese villages amidst indigenous populations. By the second generation, however, many of the inhabitants of such settlements (as with spontaneous economic migrants) were integrated relatively seamlessly into local communities, often having intermarried with locals.

In Aceh, however, the transmigration program did generate local resentment. In 2001, for example, the governor of Aceh, Abdullah Puteh, said bluntly that the cause of the conflict in Aceh was transmigration: "If the government does not quickly remove the transmigrants who originate from various places, the conflict in Aceh will not be solved."[58] As early as the 1970s there were reports of widespread Acehnese discontent with migration, though most of this was directed at the influx

---

[54] According to the 2000 census, Javanese make up about 16 percent of the population in Aceh. However, substantial care should be taken in using this figure, because only about 50 percent of the population of the province were directly interviewed by the census-takers in 2000 as a result of the poor security conditions prevalent at the time. See Leo Suryadinata, Evi Nurvidya Arifin, and Aris Ananta, *Penduduk Indonesia: Etnis dan Agama Dalam Era Perubahan Politik* (Jakarta: LP3ES, 2003), pp. 159–61. It is likely that most of those areas where census-takers could not operate were the predominantly ethnic-Acehnese GAM heartlands, and the proportion of ethnic Acehnese in the province is higher than the 50 percent figure given in the census. The proportion of Javanese may thus be proportionately lower; though the 16 percent figure does not account for the large number of Javanese who had already left Aceh by this time. Prior to 2000, questions about ethnicity were not asked in the census. Questions about language were asked, however. In the 1990 census, 65 percent of the population of Aceh spoke Acehnese at home, while 6 percent spoke Javanese. These figures are likely to be more accurate. These figures, too, would underestimate the numbers of both groups because a proportion of people of both Javanese and Acehnese descent (especially urban people, people in mixed marriages, etc.) speak Indonesian at home (13 percent of the province's population spoke Indonesian at home).

[55] *Waspada,* September 19, 1975.

[56] *Kompas,* June 29, 1999.

[57] *Analisa,* July 31, 2002; *Kompas* (June 29, 1999) gave the slightly lower number of 37,328 families.

[58] *Media Indonesia,* November 27, 2001.

of outsiders drawn to the petro-chemical enclave around Lhokseumawe, where it was commonly believed that non-Acehnese got the best jobs while the locals had to bear the costs, among them the appropriation of their land, for which they were poorly compensated, and environmental pollution.[59] However, GAM, with its ethno-nationalist framework for interpreting the Indonesian government and its policies, made opposition to transmigration central to its program.

In his "Unfinished Diary," Hasan di Tiro proudly recorded one of the first military actions taken by his new movement in 1978:

> The NLFAS [National Liberation Front of Acheh-Sumatra, Hasan's preferred name for GAM at this time] forces in Pasè Province attacked the Javanese settlers/colonization project (they called it "transmigration centre") at Aluë Meurieng. Four enemy buildings destroyed and three enemy soldiers killed. We suffered no loss.
>
> Our political objective is to discourage, and eventually to stop the Javanese settlers/colonizers/"transmigrants" from coming illegally (without our permission) to our country to devour our resources, to ruin our economy, to take away our jobs, to rob us of our land, and finally to constitute themselves as Javanese fifth columns in our midst, until our country can no longer be defended against Javanese aggression, and against Javanese takeover ... As Machiavelli had pointed out long ago, the cheapest way to colonize other's country was by sending in immigrants for they are less offensive to the local population, much cheaper than sending an army in uniforms, more loyal than soldiers, and easier to control.[60]

The depiction of Javanese transmigrants as an elemental enemy of Aceh's nationhood, and the subsequent targeting of this population by violent action, flowed directly from the movement's construction of Acehnese identity and its "territorialization of memory." GAM sought to develop a picture of the Acehnese people struggling to defend their ancestral lands and their very survival as a separate people. At the same time, the movement's leaders depicted the government as a vehicle for the interests of a hostile ethnic group, the Javanese. In this view, transmigrants were not poor peasants who were struggling to build a better life for themselves far from their homes, often with little say in their own fates and sometimes with little success (by the early 1980s, there were already many reports in the local press about the failure of transmigration settlements and the inadequate support the new settlers received).[61] Instead, transmigrants were agents of a deliberate government plan to rob the Acehnese of their birthright and to erase their knowledge of their heritage and separate identity. This view is articulated at great length in some GAM documents.

For example, a short book, *Malapetaka di Bumi Sumatra* (Calamity in the Land of Sumatra), written at the height of the DOM period by "Luth Ari Linge" (a pseudonym for Yusra Habib Abdul Gani, a former lecturer at Jakarta's Muhammadiyah University), depicts the "Javanisation" of Sumatra as having genocidal intent: "We will definitely be marginalized and become a minority, and

---

[59] Kell, *Roots of Acehnese Rebellion*, pp. 16–21.

[60] Tiro, *The Price of Freedom*, p. 330.

[61] For example *Waspada*, January 20, 1982, May 11, 1982, February 4, 1983.

the transmigrants a majority, as a result of the influx of these 'illegal aliens' in our own country, Sumatra."[62] Linge paints a sinister picture of a polluting Javanese presence:

> ... millions of hectares of the land of the peoples of Sumatra have been stolen ... our culture has been stained by Javanese culture [...] Are you aware of what is happening??? Our fertile land along the length of the island of Sumatra has been stolen by transmigrants from Java and Foreign Investors ... Are you aware of this??? That the "government" headquartered in Jakarta gives these transmigrants seedlings: Coffee, Tea, Oil Palm, Cloves, Rubber, Cacao, and fertilizer. Then they scoop up all the produce and enjoy it themselves [...] Are you aware of this??? Each of those transmigrants is given a ready-to-use house, built for their children and grandchildren on thousands of hectares of our own land [...] Are you aware of this??? Javanese transmigrants are marrying our Sumatran daughters and dragging and forcing them to live under Javanese culture; ... Are you aware of this???[63]

This vision of transmigrants as contaminants led to concerted attempts by the movement to purge the territory of Javanese. As noted above, GAM attacks on transmigrants began in the 1970s and resumed again in the late 1980s and early 1990s. They did not cause mass-scale dislocation, however, until the post-Suharto period. Reports of mass movements by transmigrants began in mid-1999, about the same time as the first (very different) wave of mass displacements of ethnic Acehnese villagers. The flow accelerated markedly approaching the December anniversary of GAM's declaration of independence, when GAM publicly called on transmigrants to leave. By this time, it was already being reported that many transmigrant settlements were lying abandoned, and the inter-island ferry and inter-province buses were packed with fleeing non-Acehnese.[64] Over the following years, there were sporadic reports of mass flights from transmigrations centers; for instance, in May 2001 five hundred transmigrants fled their homes in Geumpang in the Pidie district, and later the same month inhabitants of seven villages in West Aceh fled after GAM members burned several houses and threatened to shoot those who stayed one by one.[65]

Usually, displacement of transmigrants followed a consistent pattern. Armed men, sometimes wearing masks, would arrive at a settlement and simply tell the transmigrants that they had to leave. On·other occasions, villagers would find notices tacked on trees or doorposts. One such message shown to the author by a group of displaced transmigrants in Medan in early 2001 read in part: "Oh Javanese transmigrants who are on the land of Aceh-Sumatra, now take to your heels, do not stay in Aceh Sumatra. Complain to your King who tortures you." There were also

---

[62] Luth Ari Linge, *Malapetaka di Bumi Sumatra* (Medan: PT Kemalasari Enterprise, 1993), p. 3.

[63] Ibid., pp. 5–6.

[64] *Waspada*, November 18, 1999. As well as Javanese transmigrants, significant numbers of other migrants also fled the province. For example, military sources reported in late 1999 that about one thousand persons originally from the district of Dairi, North Sumatra, who had been working in Singkil, had been threatened and returned home (*Kompas*, November 4, 1999).

[65] *Waspada*, May 1, 2001; May 23, 2001.

many reports of attacks on property, especially the burning of transmigrants' homes at night, as well as physical violence and murders.[66]

Some of the transmigrants complained that they faced widespread hostility in Aceh. For instance, a leader of a group of transmigrants who had lived in the village of Bukit Makmur in East Aceh since 1983 explained to a journalist that "they had long been gripped by fear because they were not considered to be family [*saudara*], although they had continued to adapt and acculturate with local traditions."[67] More commonly, transmigrants told journalists that they simply did not understand why they were being made to flee and professed ignorance as to the causes of the conflict. Others complained that the security forces had been unable to protect them.[68] Some occupied local government offices and demanded to be assisted to leave Aceh.[69]

While most Acehnese villagers who fled military incursions traveled at most a few dozen kilometers from their homes, most transmigrants left Aceh altogether. By mid-2002, it was reported that more than 62,000 transmigrants had fled their settlements. The majority, about 37,000 people, had relocated to the neighboring province of North Sumatra, while twenty thousand went further afield to other provinces in Sumatra or Java, in many cases returning to their places of origin. The remainder had relocated to districts or towns within Aceh. It appears as if only members of the comparatively well-to-do minority were able to return to their places of origin; the majority stayed in Medan and other parts of North Sumatra, where they remained dependent on the meager support provided by the government and humanitarian organizations. By mid-2005, official sources indicated that as many as 130,000 transmigrants had fled the province since 1998.[70]

The fate of transmigrant communities was complex because collectively such communities became a site in which two conflicting visions of territory collided and fought for supremacy: GAM's ethnonationalist conceptualization of an historic homeland, as already discussed, and the TNI's vision of a landscape bureaucratically divided into military sectors on the basis of the "total people's defense" doctrine. From as early as 1989, there were reports that the military was helping transmigrant communities to organize into *wanra* (*perlawanan rakyat*, or people's defense units). These were essentially village civilian militia units, which were mobilized to defend settlements from GAM attacks, collect information, and otherwise participate in counterinsurgency operations. There was nothing especially unusual about this; on the contrary, mobilization of the population, including ethnic Acehnese, into civilian militias was central to military counterinsurgency strategy.[71] Members of transmigrant communities doubtlessly often felt very vulnerable, believed they needed to defend themselves, and were thus responsive to military initiatives to organize themselves into militias. When they did so, however, they confirmed GAM beliefs that they constituted a hostile force in the midst of the ethnic Acehnese, a

---

[66] For example *Kompas*, April 6, 2001, April 12, 2001.

[67] *Kompas*, June 23, 1999.

[68] *Kompas*, June 29, 1999.

[69] *Serambi Indonesia*, September 21, 1999.

[70] This figure was given by the acting governor of Aceh, Azwar Abubakar, when he called on transmigrants to return to the province after the signing of the Helsinki accord by representatives of GAM and the Indonesian government. See *Analisa*, August 30, 2005.

[71] Robinson, "*Rawan* is as *Rawan* Does," pp. 127–56; and Rizal Sukma, *Security Operations in Aceh: Goals, Consequences, and Lessons* (Washington, DC: East-West Center, 2004).

perception that accelerated the spiral of violence. This dynamic led to virtual ethnic civil war in some places, notably the Gayo highlands of Central Aceh, where large concentrations of ethnic Javanese had been cultivating coffee since colonial times. In June 2001, primarily Javanese and Gayo TNI-backed militias and primarily ethnic Acehnese GAM units attacked and burned rival villages, leading to considerable loss of life and the displacement of over ten thousand persons, of whom "5,758 alone came from the ethnically mixed subdistrict of Bandar."[72]

GAM leaders sometimes denied that their forces were responsible for attacks on Javanese transmigrants (in fact, there was a large volume of evidence suggesting their culpability). The post-1998 period was a time when GAM was reconfiguring its agenda in terms of human rights discourse, and the movement's more sophisticated leaders were aware that evidence of ethnic hostility could undermine their attempts to garner international support. Even so, GAM commanders continued publicly to call on Javanese to leave Aceh. GAM's military commander, Abdullah Syafiie, for example, in late 1999 stressed that he did not object to the presence of non-Acehnese in Aceh, but because GAM forces were fighting a war with the "Javanese-Indonesian" government, it might be best if they temporarily found a safer place to go: "We will not disturb them, but we are very fearful they will be harmed by provocateurs. We don't want GAM to be the scapegoat."[73] The well-known GAM commander Sofyan Dawood later responded to a TNI offensive by stating that all Javanese were used as "spies and intelligence agents" by the military and so: "We respectfully request our brothers from the Javanese ethnic group to immediately move."[74]

Some scholars have stressed the strategic nature of GAM's violence.[75] Certainly, the attacks on Javanese transmigrants can be seen as strategic insofar as an apparent (though in 1999–2004 largely undeclared) element of GAM strategy was to empty Aceh of the Javanese. The attacks, however, were also suggestive of a deeply held animus, an emotional response deriving from an ideology that transformed Acehnese territory into the exclusive and historic homeland of the Acehnese population and demonized Javanese settlers as agents of a hostile and threatening enemy. When the military organized them into militias, this deepened the perception in GAM ranks and among many other Acehnese that transmigrants were collaborators and informers, accelerating the dynamics of conflict and displacement.

MARTIAL LAW: DISPLACEMENT AS COUNTERINSURGENCY

In mid-2003 there was another wave of forced displacement in Aceh. This coincided with the declaration of a "military emergency" by the government following the breakdown of a short-lived ceasefire.[76] Large numbers of troops were

---

[72] Kirsten E. Schulze, "*Gerakan Aceh Merdeka*: Freedom Fighters or Terrorists?," in *Aceh Under Martial Law: Conflict, Violence, and Displacement*, ed. Eva Lotta-Hedman, p. 34.

[73] *Serambi Indonesia*, November 14, 1999.

[74] *Waspada*, April 23, 2001.

[75] For example Schulze, "*Gerakan Aceh Merdeka*," p. 34; and Kirsten E. Schulze, "Insurgency and Counter-Insurgency: Strategy and the Aceh Conflict, October 1976–May 2004," in *Verandah of Violence*, ed. A. J. Reid (Singapore: Singapore University Press, 2006).

[76] Edward Aspinall and Harold Crouch, *The Aceh Peace Process: Why it Failed* (Washington, DC: East-West Center, 2003).

transferred into the province, and Aceh's military chief was given martial law powers. Military commanders declared that the time for compromise was over and that they were going to destroy the GAM insurgency once and for all. A series of intensive military offensives began.[77]

As usual, figures are hard to ascertain, but tens of thousands of people were displaced during the military emergency and its immediate aftermath. One international NGO estimated that there were between 120,000 and 150,000 IDPs in Aceh between the beginning of the emergency and December 2004.[78] The coordinator of Jesuit Refugee Services in Aceh gave a figure of over 123,000 people displaced during the one year of the military emergency.[79]

Civilians hiding in the forest in the company of independence guerrillas in Sawang district, North Aceh. May 2003. (Photo by William Nessen, with permission)

Some of the displacement that occurred during this period resembled the spontaneous flight by communities of preceding years. Large numbers of villagers fled on their own initiative from security operations and the ensuing firefights. Provincial government officials reported that 23,397 people were on the move within a week of the declaration of martial law.[80] The political context was now very different, however, and the space to criticize the authorities had all but disappeared. Unlike in 1999, local newspapers rarely now reported on what motivated these villagers, or they used only vague and generic descriptors like "*kontak senjata*"

---

[77] On military strategy during this period, see Sukma, *Security Operations in Aceh;* and Schulze, "Insurgency and Counter-Insurgency."

[78] Hedman, "A State of Emergency, a Strategy of War," p. 9.

[79] Ramly, "Modes of Displacement during Martial Law," p. 13.

[80] *Kompas*, May 28, 2003.

("armed contact") to do so. Military commanders also made it clear that they did not approve of spontaneous flight that occurred outside their direction and control.[81]

There was also resumption of large-scale flight by civilians to Malaysia. By September 2003, four months after the declaration of martial law, UNHCR officials estimated that there were eight thousand to nine thousand persons from Aceh in Malaysia who might be of concern to them.[82] By March 2004, local human rights activists estimated that the figure was approximately twenty thousand.[83] As in the past, these refugees were mostly from areas where GAM had been strong. They reported they had fled in the face of considerable arbitrary violence carried out by government troops against civilians.[84] With the local media now controlled by martial law authorities, and local NGOs greatly constrained, the political space that had facilitated internal displacement as a form of mass protest in 1999 had disappeared. The fact that so many people fled beyond Indonesia's territorial boundaries, and thus altogether beyond the reach of the authorities, reflected the renewed advantage of the military on the ground.

However, a considerable proportion of the 2003–2004 wave of forced displacement was different from that in preceding years: most refugees now did not flee their homes on their own initiative, but were removed from them by military units. For decades, the TNI had aimed to separate insurgents from local populations in cases of internal conflict and had done so by seeking to surround and monitor civilians. It now took this strategy to its logical end by relocating civilian populations from their homes to place them beyond the reach of GAM.

The TNI's counter-guerrilla strategy had been honed during campaigns against rebel movements during the first three decades of Indonesia's independence. Even in decades-old military manuals, counter-guerrilla strategy was defined as involving a three step process: "Separation, Localization, and Destruction."[85] As summarized by one observer, all military operations in Aceh since the late 1970s had followed the same basic pattern:

> This military strategy sought, first, to separate GAM from the people and loosen its grip over them; second, to isolate GAM by severing its logistical and communication lines; and, third, to destroy GAM's military command and civilian infrastructure. The main challenge for the Indonesian security forces in all operations from 1977 to 2004 was to separate the insurgents from the population and to win the hearts and minds of the people.[86]

---

[81] The commander of the Teuku Umar Military Resort, for instance, told one group of village heads that in the event the military needed to take action against GAM in a particular village, the inhabitants should only leave if the military instructed them to do so: "It shouldn't be the *keuchik* [village head] who instructs the inhabitants to flee." *Serambi Indonesia*, June 3, 2003.

[82] Human Rights Watch, "Aceh Under Martial Law: Problems Faced by Acehnese Refugees in Malaysia (2004: http://hrw.org/reports/2004/malaysia0404/malaysia0404.pdf), p. 10.

[83] *Tempo*, March 23–29, 2004.

[84] Human Rights Watch, *Aceh Under Martial Law*, p. 10.

[85] Departemen Pertahanan-Keamanan, *Pengenalan Terhadap Masalah Operasi Keamanan Dalam Negeri*, p. 14.

[86] Schulze, "Insurgency and Counter-Insurgency," p. 248.

In describing their first and most basic task, military commanders sometimes used a metaphor drawn from numerous international experiences of guerrilla warfare: as one commander explained to his troops in late 2004, "… GAM and the community are like a fish and water. So long as there is water, the fish will live. But if the water is completely drained away, then the fish will die of its own accord. GAM cannot live without the support of the community…"[87]

In fact, separating the guerrilla fish from the water that enveloped them was no easy task. As we have seen, GAM fighters were deeply immersed in local communities and possessed intimate knowledge of Aceh's landscape. After the military emergency began, some Indonesian journalists who were "embedded" with security forces (in deliberate mimicry of the contemporaneous policy of US-led forces in Iraq) made some revealing observations about the difficulties troops faced in distinguishing between rebels and civilians:

> TNI soldiers have a phrase: "GAM has 'become fluid' [*sudah 'mencair'*]." It means that the members of the separatist group have gone into the villages and assimilated with the community. "They usually just hang out in the coffee shops, brother," explains a soldier in the Detachment IV command post. However, what often makes the soldiers angry is that, when members of the community are asked about GAM, they always reply that they don't know: "*hana tepu*" [in Acehnese]. "That's all they can do," complains a soldier from the Marines' 6th Battalion from Cilandak, "it's as if they don't understand Indonesian." Local people only want to speak in Indonesian if they are treated violently [*jika mereka dikerasi*].

> In addition, quite apart from separating GAM from the people, separating GAM from nature is also very difficult. For example, Detachment IV is responsible for an area the size of one subdistrict. On the map, their tasks are divided up among 17 x 4 quadrants, or map squares. One map square converted to the natural landscape is more than one hundred hectares. Such a great area has to be combed by only twenty-five people! The job of Detachment IV is to comb the areas where, according to intelligence reports, GAM are located. But it can be said that the accuracy of these reports is often only so-so … In addition, of course, they have to leave some of their soldiers behind to guard the areas that have already been searched. Who knows, GAM might outflank them and attack from behind.[88]

The perspective being reported here is obviously that of the military. No voices of the Acehnese are presented, except as a disembodied source of irritation for soldiers.[89] This perspective is revealing, however, because it provides some insight into how the dynamics of counterinsurgency operations, the frustrations so produced, and the attendant dehumanization of the local population could lead to

---

[87] This was expressed in the words of the outgoing commander of the Lilawangsa Korem, Colonel A. Y. Nasution. See *Analisa*, July 12, 2004.

[88] The author of this article was Adiseno, whose reports from Aceh included some of the most revealing observations of the dynamics of military operations in the province. See *Sinar Harapan*, May 27, 2003.

[89] For a critique of the Indonesian press reporting of, and middle-class attitudes toward, human rights abuses in Aceh, see James Siegel, "The Idea of Indonesia Continues: The Middle Class Ignores Aceh," *Archipel*, 64 (2002): 199–229.

acts of brutality against civilians. It is, of course, common in counterinsurgency warfare for troops who feel themselves vulnerable to constant attack from insurgents to commit abuses when they find it difficult to distinguish between combatants and ordinary citizens. This is not to suggest that human rights abuses in Aceh were merely the ill-disciplined acts of a few "rogue elements," as military apologists would have it. On the contrary, a wealth of analysis shows that human rights abuses against civilians were systematic and central to military campaigns.[90] In Aceh, "separating guerrillas from the population" often translated into torture of civilians to elicit intelligence, assassination of individuals suspected of assisting GAM, acts of collective punishment of villages in areas where GAM operated, and other abuses. By 2003, military commanders had become conscious that such acts often alienated the population, and they made some efforts to curb or disguise them. However, reports by journalists and human rights organizations suggested that arbitrary violence remained endemic.[91] Indeed, a pattern of systematic and forced displacement that was at its heart abusive became central to the military's campaign during martial law.

Despite the difficulties involved in fighting a foe with deep local roots, the military authorities believed they had a great advantage of their own: their institutionalized and systematic knowledge of the terrain and the population. As already discussed, through its territorial command structure the military authorities possessed not only a coercive apparatus that, theoretically at least, covered every inch of Aceh's territory, but also formidable mechanisms of surveillance through which to assess security threats in each community. As a result, even when the GAM insurgency was at its peak, military commanders often claimed detailed knowledge of their enemy. They would give very precise estimates of the number of GAM combatants and their weapons. More importantly, they also believed they possessed exact (or at least very solid) knowledge of the relative degrees of sympathy for the insurgency in all local communities. The authorities thus categorized Acehnese territory according to the degree of GAM influence: in "black" areas, GAM influence was supposedly great and the institutions of the Indonesian state did not function; "gray" areas had a significant level of GAM activity and government dysfunction; in "white" areas, GAM influence was minimal and government institutions functioned well. As interior minister, retired General Hari Sabarno, put it, the aim of the government was "to turn the gray into white and the black into gray."[92] Throughout the security operations from May 2003, the authorities precisely quantified the progress of the operations, both in terms of how many GAM combatants were being killed, weapons seized, and so on, as well as by measuring how much territory was

---

[90] Amnesty International, *Indonesia: "Shock Therapy" Restoring Order in Aceh*, pp. 53–56; Amnesty International, "New Military Operations, Old Patterns of Human Rights Abuses in Aceh (Nanggroe Aceh Darussalam, NAD)" (2004: http://web.amnesty.org/library/pdf/ASA210332004ENGLISH/$File/ASA2103304.pdf); Robinson, "*Rawan* is as *Rawan* Does," pp. 127–56; Human Rights Watch, "Indonesia: The May 3, 1999 Killings in Aceh"; and Human Rights Watch, "Indonesia: Civilians Targeted in Aceh"; Human Rights Watch, "Aceh under Martial Law: Inside the Secret War," (2003: http://hrw.org/reports/2003/indonesia1203/indonesia1203.pdf).

[91] ICG (International Crisis Group), *Aceh: How Not to Win Hearts and Minds*, p. 3; Human Rights Watch, "Aceh under Martial Law: Inside the Secret War"; and Amnesty International, "New Military Operations, Old Patterns of Human Rights Abuses in Aceh."

[92] *Kompas*, August 30, 2001.

changing from black through gray to white. Officials also released rough estimates of the proportion of the population who were free of GAM influence.[93] Of course, the quality of the military's intelligence was itself highly questionable, but it provided them with a high degree of confidence and a framework for planning and executing their operations.

It quickly became obvious that the TNI planned to use involuntary displacement as part of the counterinsurgency strategy in order to separate GAM from the population.[94] As military operations were launched, Aceh's governor announced that the provincial government was preparing eighty-five IDP camps in sixteen districts to cope with an estimated 120,000 displaced persons.[95] The next day, Minister of Social Affairs Bachtiar Chamsyah said the government was preparing to move 200,000 people from their homes in order to protect them: "We are waiting for an order from the military administration; should they want to comb a certain area in searches for rebels, we will move the local people from their homes."[96] It soon became obvious that not only humanitarian but also military goals were to be achieved by this process. Lieutenant General Sudi Silalahi, secretary to the coordinating minister for political and security affairs, was especially explicit: "First we will ask women and children to leave their houses. Then, we will ask unarmed men to do the same. The rest who stay behind must be those with arms."[97]

In a rolling operation over subsequent weeks and months, troops systematically emptied the population out of "black" and "gray" areas where GAM was believed to be strong. Reminiscent of the mass displacement of mid-1999, most displaced villagers did not move further than a few dozen kilometers. Usually they shifted to camps located within their district of origin, and they rarely stayed in the camps for more than a few weeks. Within two months, perhaps forty thousand individuals had been displaced, but the figures continually fluctuated.[98]

Unlike in 1999, however, when military authorities had condemned displacement as part of GAM's strategy, now they were the architects of the process (although they still continued to condemn, and tried to prevent, spontaneous movements of people). Villagers frequently reported that they were given no advance warning that they had to leave their homes. Often, they first found out about it when soldiers arrived in trucks and ordered them to depart. Residents often were forced to leave behind livestock and other valuable possessions. Sometimes, people working in the fields were stranded by the sudden exodus, in turn becoming vulnerable to accusations that they were GAM members, successfully "separated" from the population. Soldiers promised to safeguard residents' possessions in their absence, but when people finally returned to their villages, it often transpired that

---

[93] Sometimes these estimates were themselves very revealing, as when the commander-in-chief, General Endriartono Sutatarto, suggested that only 30 percent of the population supported the military emergency, while, "Perhaps another 30 percent support GAM and the remainder of 40 percent do not support GAM. That is already good." *Analisa*, November 21, 2003. Here the population itself was being categorized according to the black, white, and gray categories the authorities used to assess territory.

[94] See also Hedman, "A State of Emergency, a Strategy of War."

[95] *Analisa*, May 19, 2003.

[96] *Jakarta Post*, May 20, 2003.

[97] Sukma, *Security Operations in Aceh*, p. 26; also cited in Hedman, "A State of Emergency, a Strategy of War," p. 9.

[98] International Crisis Group, *Aceh: How Not to Win Hearts and Minds*, p. 4.

their homes had been looted, their livestock stolen, and their shops emptied. Sometimes, even the crops standing in their fields had been harvested. The identity of those stealing such material was rarely indicated, but senior military officers promised to punish soldiers responsible for such acts. From the start, government and military officials emphasized that displaced people would be well cared for. In fact, numerous media reports suggested that living conditions in the camps were often poor, and large numbers of displaced persons became sick.

As well as creating free-fire zones in areas from where civilians had been removed, the strategy of forced displacement served other purposes. Part of the explicit goal was to deprive GAM of its civilian support structure. As one officer in charge of removing the inhabitants of Desa Baru in the district of Southwest Aceh put it, the intention was to break the "logistics cycle" that supported GAM members, because "it was strongly suspected that local inhabitants had been providing logistics for members of the GAM group, including by cooking rice for them."[99] In conditions where the authorities (in the words of another senior officer) suspected GAM members of "uniting with the community and possibly uniting with the refugees," displacement also became a means to facilitate "screening" of the population.[100] There were numerous reports of individuals in camps being identified as GAM sympathizers and taken away for interrogation and punishment. Finally, communities held in camps were themselves required to participate in ideological training outlining the virtues of the Indonesian unitary state. The aim was to increase their "resilience" against the blandishments of separatism, so that, in the words of an officer addressing a group of IDPs, when they returned to their homes they would be "able to invite their relatives [i.e., those involved in GAM] to realize their errors and return to the bosom of the Indonesian motherland."[101]

Once initial assaults against GAM had passed and villagers were returned to their homes, the military also took steps to strengthen its territorial structure and its surveillance and control capacity throughout Acehnese territory. Military posts were established in villages in GAM areas, and officers told local inhabitants that they would remain in place so long as local people lacked the boldness to confront GAM themselves.[102] Thousands of noncommissioned officers were brought into Aceh to serve as *babinsa* and provide "guidance" at the village level. The goal was to saturate Aceh's territory with a military presence. The military would become, in the words of one supporter of the campaign, "fish" in the "water" of local society, effectively replacing GAM and so seamlessly integrated with the people that there would be no space left for GAM to operate.[103]

---

[99] *Serambi Indonesia*, August 29, 2003.

[100] *Serambi Indonesia*, May 27, 2003.

[101] *Serambi Indonesia*, September 2, 2003.

[102] See for example, *Analisa*, October 31, 2003. Sometimes, officers used graphic language to make this point. One local newspaper reported that the Deputy Commander of Operations, Brigadier General Safzen Noerdin, explained to a group of thousands of civilians in one GAM stronghold that "the TNI troops will never be pulled out from the interior of Sawang, North Aceh. TNI will only be withdrawn when the people in the Subdistrict of Sawang have themselves gained the courage to cut down [*membacok*] the GAM group or chase and capture them." *Serambi Indonesia*, September 3, 2003.

[103] This comment was from a local leader of the Pemuda Pancasila youth group in Central Aceh. See *Waspada*, July 13, 2003.

As some observers have noted,[104] the deliberate strategy to displace targeted populations practiced by the Indonesian military during 2003 to 2004 was reminiscent of earlier experiences in Southeast Asia. In the Malayan emergency in the 1950s, British forces had endeavored, with some success, to relocate peasants in strongly defended "new villages." This technique was later refined and practiced on a greater scale by United States and government forces in South Vietnam, whose use of coercion and incentives to move peasants to fortified settlements or "strategic hamlets" eventually generated considerable alienation.[105] The strategic goals of these early exercises in forced resettlement were similar to the later experience in Aceh; the motive was essentially to separate insurgents from local communities and deprive them of logistics and other support. There was likely an indirect thread connecting these different experiences, because counterinsurgency strategists had long viewed the successful separation of insurgents from surrounding civilian populations (as well as the need to win civilian sympathy by civic action programs) as a main reason for the British victory in Malaya, and as an important lesson of Vietnam. This lesson subsequently became a key plank of counterinsurgency strategy as it was taught in officer training schools everywhere, not least in the various US, Australian, and other schools where Indonesian officers themselves received training.

However, the strategy used by the Indonesian military in Aceh also had indigenous roots and followed national precedents. As noted earlier, the Indonesian military's own counterinsurgency doctrines, which ultimately could be traced back to its own much-mythologized origins in the 1945–1949 struggle for national independence, stressed that guerrilla forces depended on being embedded in local populations. The lessons taught by subsequent counterinsurgency operations were also important, including, most recently, the military's efforts to quell resistance in East Timor. In 1977–78, for example, following the army's "encirclement" campaign to destroy the resistance in mountainous areas of East Timor, the army moved an estimated 300,000 people to resettlement camps where "their inhabitants were prevented from traveling beyond the camp boundaries"; their goal was to cut off support to the insurgency.[106] The immediate backdrop of the campaign in Aceh during the military emergency in 2003–04 was the forced evacuation of hundreds of thousands of civilians from their homes and into West Timor in September 1999. Many of the leading army commanders in charge of the operations in Aceh had held positions of responsibility in East Timor during that exercise; some of them had been indicted by the UN Serious Crimes Unit.[107] But they were never punished by the Indonesian state and were instead placed in charge of a similar operation in Aceh.

CONCLUSION

Displacement was a persistent feature of the civil war in Aceh. Over the course of the conflict, but mostly in the period between 1998 and 2004, several hundred

---

[104] Hedman, "A State of Emergency, a Strategy of War," p. 11.

[105] Milton E. Osborne, *Strategic Hamlets in South Vietnam: A Survey and Comparison*, Data Paper 55 (Ithaca, NY: Cornell Southeast Asia Program Publications, 1965).

[106] John G. Taylor, *Indonesia's Forgotten War: The Hidden History of East Timor* (London: Zed Books, 1991), p. 88; see also Robinson, "People Power," in this volume.

[107] Human Rights Watch, "Aceh under Martial Law: Can These Men be Trusted to Prosecute This War?" (2003: http://hrw.org/backgrounder/asia/indonesia1003.pdf).

thousand people fled their homes out of fear or were forcibly removed from them. In Aceh, as in many other places around the globe, displacement is rightly seen as one of the more harmful results of armed conflict. This chapter has not focused on the human costs of displacement, but that does not mean they have been insignificant: the terror that prompts people to abandon their homes; the loss of possessions, land, and livelihood they experience when they leave; the disruption to employment, education, and family life they endure while separated from their homes; the poor health conditions, illness, increased infant mortality, and premature deaths that occur in displacement camps and on the road; all these horrors and more were central to the experience of displacement in Aceh. Nor has the chapter focused on the resilience of the displaced populations and the coping strategies they developed in order to secure a degree of normality amidst such disruption.

The analysis in this chapter, instead, has endeavored to understand the processes and ideologies that drove displacement in Aceh from 1976 into the twenty-first century. It has been argued that, in addition to being a by-product of conflict (it should be remembered that "fear and flight" displacement *was* a feature of the conflict in Aceh, though it has not been emphasized in this study), displacement was also central to the rationales that drove conflict. In part, this means that displacement was strategic and integral to the plans and methods by which the two sides tried to defeat one another militarily. GAM was responsible for deliberately displacing large numbers of civilians, especially Javanese migrants, as part of its plan to make Aceh ungovernable. In terms of scale, Indonesian military personnel were the main perpetrators of displacement. The military also conceived of displacement most purely in strategic terms, at times viewing it as integral to its effort to separate insurgents from the civilian population. While it was often the fruit of conscious strategic decisions, displacement also derived from a deeper level, where views about the proper political and social order mingled with those about place and territory. At this level, displacement resulted from ethnonationalist fantasies about a purified Acehnese ethnic homeland, on the one hand, and, on the other, from a modernist vision of a territory that could be completely known, ordered, and controlled by the state's security apparatus.

REFUGE, DISPLACEMENT, AND DISPOSSESSION: RESPONSES TO INDONESIAN RULE AND CONFLICT IN PAPUA

Richard Chauvel

In January 2006, Herman Wanggai, an activist and former political prisoner, and forty-two fellow Papuans sought political asylum in Australia. The outrigger canoe in which they landed on the other side of the Torres Strait flew the Papuan Morning Star flag and carried a banner pleading for freedom, peace, and justice. The banner also asserted that the Indonesian military was committing genocide in Papua. The quest for asylum was a political act designed to attract Australian and international attention to the struggle for Papuan independence. Two months later, there was a violent demonstration at Abepura, just outside the capital of Jayapura, which left five members of the Indonesian security forces dead. The demonstrators had demanded the closure of the giant Freeport copper and gold mine. Many of the demonstrators fled into the hills to escape the sweeping operations of the security forces and subsequently crossed over the border into neighboring Papua New Guinea (PNG).

These two cases are but recent examples of the displacement and demographic change that have been central features of Indonesian rule and Papuan responses to it. West Papuans' flight across the border into PNG began within weeks of Indonesia assuming administrative control in 1963. Today there are approximately 13,500 West Papuans living in exile in PNG. Not all Papuan flight from Indonesian security operations and political tensions has been manifested as flight across the border into PNG. Security operations some distance from the border more often have resulted in internal displacement. This paper will examine three recent cases of armed conflicts in Wasior and the central highlands that generated displacement of thousands of Papuans. There are similarities in the patterns of conflict that have triggered internal and external displacement, however, externally displaced refugees have tended to remain exiled from their homes for the longer term. Most of the Papuan political refugees who fled to PNG in the 1960s have not returned to Papua, and many involved in the large-scale exodus of the mid-1980s remain in refugee camps in PNG. Internally displaced Papuans are not confronted with the same logistical problems and ideological questions in returning to their original places of residence.

Herman Wanggai and his fellow asylum seekers followed a well-established political strategy of campaigning for independence from outside Indonesia. The most senior of the Papuan politicians of the last years of the Netherlands administration—Nicolaas Jouwe, Markus Kaiseipo, and Herman Womiswor—left with the Dutch and lobbied for international support for Papuan independence from a secure base in The Netherlands. They were followed in 1969 by Clemens Runawery and Willem Zonggonau,[1] who made an abortive attempt to present the Papuan case to the United Nations. The flight into exile of pro-independence leaders reflects not only the restrictions on political activities in Papua but also the importance of the international community in shaping how Papuans think of their struggle for independence. This reflects the role the United Nations played in brokering the 1962 New York Agreement, its subsequent supervision of the "Act of Free Choice" in 1969, and contemporary Papuan demands that the UN re-examine its acceptance of the results of the "Act of Free Choice." The common Papuan view that the "Act of Free Choice" was a denial of their right of self-determination found support in Pieter Drooglever's exhaustive study commissioned by the Dutch Parliament. Drooglever argued that: "In the opinion of the Western observers and the Papuans who have spoken out about this, the Act of Free Choice ended up as a sham, where a press-ganged electorate acting under a great deal of pressure appeared to have unanimously declared itself in favour of Indonesia."[2]

The paper will argue that these displacements, both internal and external, are barometers of political tensions and the intensity of military operations in Papua. This is a somewhat different pattern of displacement from the one evident during the military operations in Aceh, 2003–2004, where forced relocation of populations was part of the military's strategies. The displacement of Papuans, particularly activists, into PNG or the flight of asylum seekers to Australia is not the objective of Indonesian military operations, but rather something that the military has tried to prevent. The external displacement of Papuan activists and political leaders is a result of their own agency, not the most preferred option but rather one dictated by the political constraints the Indonesian authorities have imposed in Papua itself. That is to say Papuan activists have used displacement as a strategy through which to continue their political struggle.

External displacement of Papuans has highlighted the role that Australia has played as a "gatekeeper" for Indonesia in curtailing Papuans' ability to conduct an international campaign for independence using Australia as a base or a point of transit. The Papuan asylum seekers in Australia have been a considerable embarrassment to the Indonesian government and the focus of diplomatic tensions between Indonesia and Australia.

DISPOSSESSION: PLURAL SOCIETY, DUAL ECONOMY

The movement of Papuan leaders out of Papua has been important for how the campaign for independence has been conducted. The flight of refugees into PNG and the internal displacement of Papuans have alienated tens of thousands of Papuans

---

[1] Willem Zonggonau died in Sydney in October 2006. He and Clemens Runawery were conducting a pro-independence campaign.

[2] P. J. Drooglever, *Een Daad van Vrije Keuze: De Papoea's van westelijk Nieuw-Guinea en de grenzen van het zelfbeschikkingsrecht* (Amsterdam: Boom, 2005), p. 728.

from their means of livelihood and caused great material hardship. However, in terms of the scale of demographic change, it pales into insignificance when compared with the influx of Indonesian settlers into Papua. The massive demographic transformation Papua has experienced since 1963 has changed the dynamics of Papuan–Indonesian relations for all of Papuan society and has given Papuan nationalism a sharp ethnic expression. In 1960, the "Asian" population, mainly eastern Indonesians, Javanese, and Chinese, numbered just 18,600 out of an estimated population of 736,700, or 2.5 percent.[3] The 2000 Census indicated that the number of non-Papuans resident in the province was 772,684, or 35 percent. In the capital, Jayapura, the settler communities constitute about 68 percent of the population, as they do in Sorong and Fakfak.[4] The sense that indigenous Papuans have lost control of their own homeland to the Indonesians and have become marginal to Papua's political and economic life gives Papuan nationalism a strong ethnic expression. The Indonesian settlers are a major factor in the discussion in this chapter. However, unlike the Indonesian government and the Papuan leaders and activists, these settlers are not given sufficient voice and agency. This lack of focus on the Indonesian settlers reflects much of the public discourse and academic analysis to date on the conflict in Papua. This influx of migrants and the sense of dispossession and marginalization generated among Papuans by the migrants' presence serve to fuel the conflict with Indonesia and Papuan alienation from the Indonesian state. The refugee flow into PNG, internal displacement, and the flight of political leaders overseas are a consequence of conflict. The paper will argue that this sense of dispossession is much more broadly felt in Papuan society than is a sense of outrage over the displacement experienced by the Papuan communities that have lost their land to transmigration settlements.

In order to analyze the ways in which demographic change has shaped displacement and fueled conflict, it is necessary to examine the different ways demographic change has taken place. Indonesian settlers were a small but influential part of society in Papua under the Dutch colonial administration. Christians from eastern Indonesia—mostly Ambonese, Menadonese, and Keiese—served in the colonial administration as officials, teachers, missionaries, police, and military. Under Indonesian rule, settlement of Indonesians from elsewhere in the archipelago in Papua has taken two forms: government-organized programs of transmigration and voluntary, or "spontaneous," migration. Although "transmigration" is the term frequently used to describe the process, many more Indonesians have settled in Papua as a result of their own initiative than have relocated because they were sponsored by the government as transmigrants. In the period 1970 to 2000, transmigration resulted in the settlement of some 220,000 people. In the same period, over 560,000 people came to Papua as "spontaneous" migrants.[5] The government's transmigration programs ceased in the late 1990s as a result of the financial crisis and Papuan opposition. There are no signs that the rate of spontaneous migration has slackened. Indeed, the influx of "spontaneous" migrants is one of the most sensitive issues in Papuan politics and fuels the indigenous Papuans' sense of being

---

[3] Netherlands Government Annual Report to the United Nations on Netherlands New Guinea, 1960, The Hague, pp. 6–7.

[4] *Tifa Papua*, Minggu ketiga Mei 2002, p. 5.

[5] Rodd McGibbon, *Plural Society in Peril: Migration, Economic Change, and the Papua Conflict*, Policy Studies 13 (Washington, DC: East-West Center Washington, 2004), p. 23.

disadvantaged and marginalized. When two of Papua's senior religious leaders addressed the provincial parliament (DPRD, Dewan Perwakilan Rakyat Daerah) in June 2005, they asked rhetorically:

> Are you sending the migrants from outside because this is the only way to build our land? What is the purpose of sending the six white ships [Indonesian Royal Passenger Ship, paid for out of Special Autonomy funds] who every week bring thousands of migrants from Java, Sumatra, Kalimantan, Sulawesi, and Ambon to Papua? Is this what you call building Papua?[6]

The distinction between government sponsorship and spontaneous migration would be unimportant in itself except that these two groups of settlers have different ethnic and economic backgrounds and create quite different impacts on Papuan society. Government-sponsored transmigrants tended to come from the densely populated island of Java and were settled in rural areas in Papua. The migrants who came on their own initiative were more often from South Sulawesi—including Makasarese, Buginese, and Butonese—and elsewhere in eastern Indonesia. They tended to settle in urban areas and around resource projects. They were attracted by the economic opportunities of Papua's frontier economy.

The government's transmigration projects tended to be focused in particular regions of Papua. In the immediate areas near transmigration projects, the relative demographic status of the Papuans and non-Papuans changed over a short period, with the transmigrants quickly outnumbering the Papuans. For example, in Arso, located between Jayapura and the PNG border, in 1999 there were only 3,000 Papuans compared with 18,000 transmigrants. The late Michael Rumbiak, a Papuan demographer, argued that the local community was dominated by the transmigrants and the Papuans were displaced from their own lands and their culture overwhelmed by the Javanese. The economically weak Papuans, deprived of access to their land, were not capable of developing their own culture. Rumbiak observed that the transmigrants lived and worked by themselves, separate from the local Papuan community. Neither group had developed mechanisms of cooperation. Rumbiak concluded that "the transmigration program implemented over decades in Papua had not yet provided any positive direct benefit for local societies. The local society was isolated from the transmigrants because of differences in vision and culture."[7]

Transmigration intensified the competition for scarce resources, particularly land suitable for agricultural use. Examining land acquisition for transmigration settlements in Papua, Agus Semule calculated that 160,000 hectares of arable land had been appropriated. To put this into some perspective, this was three times the area used for the cultivation of sweet potato in 2000.[8] The large-scale land acquisition for the establishment of transmigration settlements was conducted with little regard

---

[6] Herman Saud and Socratez Sofyan Yoman, "Joint Statement on Regional Elections, Special Autonomy and the MRP," DPRD, Jayapura, June 9, 2005. MRP—the Majelis Rakyat Papua, Papuan People's Assembly.

[7] M. C. Rumbiak, "Migrasi Spontan dan Transmigrasi," unpublished paper, Fakultas Ekonomi, Universitas Cendrawasih, Jayapura, 2000, pp. 7–9.

[8] Cited in McGibbon, *Plural Society in Peril*, p. 22.

for Papuan *adat* (customary) law and communal land ownership (*hak ulayat*).[9] It is worth noting that the recognition of *hak ulayat* was central to the Papuan proposals for the Special Autonomy Law. Benny Giay, the Papuan theologian and intellectual, gave the displacement created by transmigration political expression when he wrote of the intimidation experienced by Papuans compelled to sign over thousands of hectares of land as part of the suffering—*Memoria passionis*—endured by the Papuan people during thirty-five years of Suharto's *pembangunan* (development).[10]

South Sulawesi entrepreneur of Papuan culture.
(Photo by Richard Chauvel, 2007)

The impact of the transmigration settlements on the Papuan communities in the immediate area is obvious. Yet, the scale and speed of the demographic transformation is most apparent in the urban areas. By 2000, Indonesian settlers constituted 66 percent of urban populations.[11] In 2000, Clemens Runawery observed the displacement of Papuans that had taken place in Hamadi, a suburb of Jayapura, in the thirty-one years since he went into exile. Filmed standing in the Hamadi market, he noted, "There is no place like home," but it was not the home he remembered. Runawery explained that Hamadi used to be a suburban paradise full of nice houses inhabited by Papuans. Hamadi was the dormitory suburb developed by the Dutch to house the emerging elite of Papuan government officials and politicians, people like Runawery himself. By 2000, it had become a market dominated by traders from South Sulawesi, including Buginese who owned shops

---

[9] Ibid., p. 20.

[10] Benny Giay, *Menuju Papua Baru: Berapa pokok pikirian sekitar Emanisipasi Orang Papua*, (Jayapura: Deiyai/Elsham Papua, 2000), p. 55.

[11] McGibbon, *Plural Society in Peril*, p. 26.

selling Papuan artifacts. As he paused to listen to the call to prayer from a nearby mosque, Runawery said, "Now you can hear Muslim sounds in the midst of what used to be Melanesia. So strange, but that is the reality."[12]

The spontaneous migrants have tended to settle in the urban areas of Papua. The census data cited above support the visual impression that Jayapura, in particular, is now an "Indonesian" city. Settlers have been economically successful. They dominate the city's economic life. The streets of Jayapura's central market reflect the economic hierarchy. The shops are owned by Indonesian Chinese and settlers of other ethnic groups. Settler traders run the market stalls in front of the shops. In front of stalls sit Papuan traders, mainly highlanders, selling small quantities of fruit and vegetables. The economic structure is even more starkly illustrated in the center of Jayapura. Next to the building that once housed the New Guinea Council, where the Papuan Morning Star Flag was raised for the first time on December 1, 1961, there is a supermarket and a Kentucky Fried Chicken outlet, unremarkable in Jakarta, but new in Jayapura. In the late afternoon and evening in the car park in front of the supermarket, Papuans are permitted to sell fruit, vegetables, and betel nut. One Papuan observer noted that the "… presence of the settlers has created a colonial economic structure, where only the traditional sector is run by the indigenous population."[13]

There is something of Furnival's plural society in Indonesian Papua. Just as Furnival observed of the pre-war Netherlands India, Papua has become "… a society, that is, comprising two or more elements or social orders which live side by side, yet without mingling, in one political unit."[14] Furnival contended that there was no social demand common to all sections of the plural society. The marketplace was the only common ground where all sections of the plural society met.[15]

In Papua, Indonesian settlers and Papuans meet in the marketplace, but it is a segmented and stratified market. This general "meeting place" has also become a site of conflict between the settler traders and Papuans. The markets symbolize the economic disparities between the communities. In 1984, the Hamadi market was the site of violent riots that helped trigger the exodus of Papuans into PNG, a development discussed in the latter part of this paper.

In April 2000, there were clashes between Papuans and Bugis–Makassarese settlers in Entrop, one of the principal market centers in Jayapura. Most of the people injured were traders from the Entrop market and Papuans from neighboring villages. In the clash, fire damaged much of the market.[16] In November 2000, the market at Abepura was the locale of a couple of violent clashes between Papuans and Bugis–Makassarese settlers. The first violence occurred when three Papuans (highlanders) refused to pay for a meal, sparking a fight in which the settlers, armed with

---

[12] Mark Worth, *The Land of the Morning Star*, Film Australia/Australian Broadcasting Corporation production, 2003. Broadcast, ABC TV, February 2, 2004. Clemens Runaweri had been permitted to return to Papua to attend the Kongres Papua in mid-2000.

[13] Jhon Wanane, Mth, "Politik Ekonomi dan Migrasi Bangsa Melayu di Tanah Papua," *Tifa Papua*, 11–16 Desember 2000, p. 6.

[14] J. S. Furnival, *Netherlands India: A Study of a Plural Economy* (Amsterdam: B. M. Israel BV, 1976), p. 448.

[15] Ibid., p. 449.

[16] "Pasar Entrop Jayapura Dibakar Massa," *Kompas*, March 26, 2000; "One Killed in Entrop Market Fray," *Jakarta Post*, March 28, 2000; "Market Fire Injures 11," *Jakarta Post*, March 27, 2000.

homemade weapons, wounded five Papuans.[17] The police account of the incident noted that disputes between the settlers and the Papuans were common around the market. "The migrants are usually vendors who work hard to earn their money, while some locals tend to extort money from them. In the Abepura case, the migrants fought back."[18] A couple of days later, another clash occurred involving larger numbers of Papuans and leaving sixteen people injured.[19]

Papuan streetsellers outside the supermarket. Dual economy and plural society in Jayapura.
(Photo by Richard Chauvel, 2007)

The security forces' sweeping operations following the Abepura demonstration in March 2006 set in motion the flight of demonstrators and students into the hills around Jayapura and over the border into PNG. It also changed the environment for those Papuans who remained in Jayapura. Socratez Sofyan Yoman, the leader of the Baptist Church in Papua, observed of Jayapura in the weeks following the riots:

> On public market and public shopping centre and public road no space for the Papuans, specially people from Highland. But, for the migrant they actually get more and more freedom for walking, for working and for speak and what else if they want. Because they get the best and strong protection from Indonesian

---

[17] ELS-HAM, "Insiden di Pasar Abepura," ELS-HAM report, November 11–12, 2000, Jayapura.

[18] "Papua Council Leaders to Go on Trial Soon," *Jakarta Post,* November 15, 2000.

[19] "Abepura Market Brawl Leaves 16 Injured," *Jakarta Post,* November 14, 2000.

intelligent, military, and police. The Indonesian intelligent, military, and police without uniform dominate in every corner of city, town, and villages in West Papua to spy the Papuan's activities. The Papuan are live under very strong pressure from Jakarta.[20] (English original)

The demographic transformation of Papua has created a complex pattern of displacement, marginalization, and isolation. The Indonesian settler-dominated urban areas have experienced rapid economic change and have become integrated into the modern economy of Indonesia and beyond. The Papuan bureaucratic, political, and professional elite form part of that urban society, but Papuans are a much stronger presence as employees in the government than in the private sector. Other Papuans live at the margins of urban society, more as observers than participants. In contrast, the regions where Papuans still constitute the vast majority of the population are the highlands, where there is an isolated subsistence economy. Highland societies are the most disadvantaged in terms of education and health. Some of these Papuan-dominated communities have been the sites for the political conflict and mass displacement discussed later in the paper. It is significant that civilian Indonesian settlers have been the victims of the conflicts in the central highlands and Wasior.

There is a touch of Boeke's "dual economy" in Papua. Boeke analyzed the segregation dividing the Western from the indigenous sections of the Netherlands Indies economy and noted that the division was based both on different socio-economic and cultural values and on spatial separation. In Papua, this second aspect of a "dual economy" is more clearly evident, as the Indonesian settler and Papuan economies are spatially separate from each other. Where the two economies do meet in the urban areas, the marketplaces are segmented and stratified.[21]

DEMOGRAPHIC TRANSFORMATION AND PAPUAN NATIONALISM

The demographic transformation has fueled Papuan resentment of Indonesian rule and given Papuan nationalism a sharp ethnic tinge. The sharp distinction Papuan nationalists make between Papuans and the Indonesians, the latter being known locally as "*amberi,*" had its origins in the Dutch period and related specifically to the role played by Indonesians as servants of the colonial administration. E. J. Bonay, one of the founders of the first Papuan nationalist political party and the first governor of Indonesian West Irian, argued that Papuans viewed the *amberi* as "accomplices" and "stooges" of the Dutch colonial government. *Amberi* treatment of Papuans was inhuman, because they looked down on Papuans as stupid, dirty, and curly haired. He asserts that the *amberi* sense of superiority had become even worse since 1963, as the Indonesians became the new colonizers of Papua. Thus, the conflict and antagonism between Papuans and *amberi* are legacies from the Dutch colonial past.[22]

---

[20] Socratez Sofyan Yoman, "Currently Situation in West Papua after and before Abepura Incident on 15th March 2006: Currently Situation in West Papua More Terrible and More Worst," Jayapura, email, March 30, 2006.

[21] J. H. Boeke, *Dualistische Samenleving*, 1930, p. 781, cited in Furnival, *Netherlands India*, p. 452.

[22] E. J. Bonay, "Sejarah Kebangkitan Nasionalisme Papua," unpublished manuscript, Wijhe, The Netherlands, 1984, p. 84.

Papuan children playing in front of the mural depicting the Indonesian liberation of Papua.
The mural and associated statue of Yos Sudarso are located in Taman Imbi, a square in central
Jayapura. (Photo by Richard Chauvel, 2007)

Bonay likened the Papuans' experience to that of the Native Americans in North
America, the Aborigines in Australia, and the Maoris in New Zealand. He said the
Papuan experience was even worse than these others, however, because the World
Bank had paid for the transmigrants' settlement, while in the New World the
European immigrants had at least been using their own capital. Bonay said the
"flood" of transmigrants had generated tensions between indigenous Papuans and
the settlers, as Papuans had been forced to leave the lands of their ancestors.[23]
Herman Wayoi, like Bonay a member of the 1960s generation of Papuan nationalists,
asserted in a presentation for President B. J. Habibie in February 1999 that:

> It was as if the Indonesian government sought only to "dominate"
> [*menguasai*] the territory, then planned to exterminate the ethnic Melanesians
> and replace them with ethnic Malays from Indonesia. Transmigration
> "proved" this impression; transporting thousands from outside to settle in
> the fertile valleys of the land of Papua.[24]

---

[23] Ibid., Bab 1, pp. 3–4.

[24] Herman Wayoi, "Kembalikan Kedaulatan Papua Barat, Pulang dan Renungkan Dulu," in
Dialog Nasional, Papua dan Indonesia 26 Februari 1999, ed. Agus Alua, Seri Pendidikan Politik
Papua No. 2, Sekretariat Presidium Dewan Papua dan Biro Penelitian STFT Fajar Timur
(Jayapura: Desember 2002), p. 64.

One of the delegates from Nabire at the Musyawarah Besar Papua 2000 (MUBES, Papuan Mass Consultation), of February 2000, made the connection between the demographic transformation of Papua and the demand for independence:

> Indonesians have never given Papuans a proper place. Because indeed they are Indonesians, and we are Papuans. We are murdered, enslaved, and colonized by Indonesians. In another ten years' time, Papuans will be finished, murdered by the Indonesian military. Because of that it is better that we just become independent.[25]

The *Pepera* (Act of Free Choice) monument in downtown Jayapura.
(Photo by Richard Chauvel, 2007)

ESCAPE TO CONTINUE THE STRUGGLE

This section of the paper will examine the flights into exile of Clemens Runawery and Willem Zonggonau in 1969 and that of Herman Wanggai and his colleagues in 2006. Although these two cases of flight were motivated by the desire to continue the campaign for independence overseas, the political circumstances of each were distinct, as were the position and status of the politicians in Papuan politics. Clemens Runawery and Willem Zonggonau fled Papua just before Indonesia conducted the "Act of Free Choice"; they were motivated by their conviction that they would be able to mount a more effective campaign against the Indonesian takeover of Papua from overseas rather than inside Papua itself. Shortly before their departure,

---

[25] Benny Giay, *Menuju Papua Baru*, p. 15.

Runawery and Zonggonau had been organizers and supporters of a substantial student demonstration against Indonesia's conduct of the "Act of Free Choice" in Jayapura. They had acted as intermediaries with the head of the UN mission, Ortiz Sanz, outside whose house the demonstration took place. Ortiz Sanz reputedly told them: "Your people and your leaders will be oppressed by the Indonesian authorities. It's up to you whether you make it [the demonstration] or not."[26] Runawery's and Zonggonau's opportunities for political activity had been curtailed since the end of 1968, when the Indonesian government-appointed provincial representative council (DPRD), of which they were prominent young members, had been abolished and they had not been appointed to the new council. Like other members of the Dutch-educated indigenous elite in Papua, Runawery and Zonggonau had both been members of Indonesian representative institutions and leaders of the OPM (Organisasi Papua Merdeka, Free Papua Organization). On arrival in PNG, they told Australian officials that, as leaders of the "West Irian" people, they wanted to ascertain the attitude of the Australian government to the independence of West Papua. Did Australia favor continued Indonesian control of West Irian? Did Australia favor an independent West Papua? Most importantly, they wanted to remain in PNG because they hoped to proceed to New York City, where they would present the case of the people of "West Irian" to the UN prior to Indonesia's scheduled implementation of the "Act of Free Choice."[27]

The Herman Wanggai group departed Papua in 2006, at one of the low points of the struggle for independence and during a period of tight political controls. Wanggai had been imprisoned on two recent occasions for nationalist activities. Since the end of 2000, with the detention of Theys Eluay and four of his Presidium[28] colleagues and then Theys Eluay's assassination in 2001 and the failed implementation of the 2001 Special Autonomy Law, both the nonviolent pro-independence and the pro-autonomy sections of the established elite had little to show for their strategies. Those members of the Presidium leadership who remained in Papua conducted few activities in the region, while the position and credibility of the pro-autonomy elite had been undermined by President Megawati's policies of divide and rule. Although Megawati failed in her ambition to divide Papua into three provinces, the establishment of a new province of West Irian Jaya in the western part of Papua and the proliferation of local governments has sharpened competition within the Papuan elite for bureaucratic and elected positions as well as control of increasing government revenues made available under decentralization. The elite and political organizations in Papua were much more united in 2000, with a seemingly dominant Presidium, than they were in 2005–2006. Wanggai was one of many Papuan activists preoccupied with the disunity and internal tensions; one of his objectives, when he chose to flee and live in exile in Australia, was to forge more unity in Papua's international lobby campaigns. The planning of the voyage took place over more than two years.[29] In Raymond Bonner's words, it was a "calculated

---

[26] Secret Report 801/5839, "Background and Motives of 11th April 1969 Demonstration in Jayapura, June 11, 1969," item 1969/1446, A452, NAA.

[27] Cable 1858, Canberra to Jakarta, May 11, 1969, TS 696/3/1 pt 3, A1838, NAA.

[28] The Presidium Dewan Papua (Papuan Presidium Council) was established in 2000, under the leadership of Theys Eluay and Thom Beanal. It was, briefly, the dominant pro-independence organization advocating a nonviolent struggle.

[29] Stephen Fitzpatrick, "Papuan Refugees Were Hand-picked," *The Australian*, September 25, 2006. http://www.theaustralian.news.com.au/story/0,20867,20470462-2702,00.html

and clandestine journey."[30] According to Wanggai's co-organizer, Edison Waromi, "We wanted to show the world a small picture of the terrible human rights situation across all of Papua. It was a tactical move in the struggle, to publicize the situation here."[31] According to a contemporary newspaper report, "This is part of the Papuan National Authority's international agenda. The asylum-seekers are intended to attract international attention. From the day of Papua's integration until today, it is militaristic."[32]

In each of these cases, the Australian government played a key role as gatekeeper, and its decisions influenced the effectiveness of Indonesia's ability to impose a political quarantine on Papua and Papuan strategies to escape isolation. The Australian ambassador in Jakarta, Gordon Jockel, saw Runawery and Zonggonau's escape as a "… clear and premeditated plan by West Irianese to cross into TPNG (Territories of Papua and New Guinea) illegally for political purposes." Jockel noted "… the possible serious consequences of the effect of the lobbying of these two West Irianese among African and other delegations in New York where they would represent a new and volatile element in the situation."[33] According to Jockel, Indonesian Foreign Minister Adam Malik feared the damage that Runawery and Zonggonau could wreak internationally to Indonesian interests. In contrast to the other exiles, they had come directly from Papua with firsthand stories and documentation and had the credibility of being "freedom fighters." They were not like the older exiles, living off Dutch money.[34] Australia responded to Malik's appeal to Jockel: "Can you not stop them?"[35] Runawery and Zonggonau ended up on Manus Island rather than New York.

With respect to the Herman Wanggai group, the Australian government's handling of the case created significant tensions in relations with Indonesia and rekindled domestic debate about Australia's refugee and asylum-seeker policies. The forty-three Papuans who reached Australia were granted temporary protection visas despite the Indonesian president's personal guarantee that their security would be safeguarded if Australia returned them to Indonesia. Indonesia withdrew its ambassador in protest. Although Wanggai does not have the status and influence Runawery and Zonggonau enjoyed among the Papuan elite, Indonesia was concerned by the ways the Herman Wanggai group in Australia had succeeded in attracting attention to the independence cause and displaying the symbols of Papuan nationalism. Because of the opposition from some government MPs and the opposition parties, the Australian government failed in its attempt to tighten up asylum-seeker processing procedures and to meet Indonesia's concerns by denying any future Papuan refugees the opportunity of using Australia as a campaign base. Some accommodation of Indonesia's concerns was achieved in the 2006 Framework for Security Cooperation Agreement. In the "Papua" provision of the agreement, Australia and Indonesia agreed to "… not in any manner support or participate in

[30] Raymond Bonner, "Long Trip by Sea and into a Political Maze for Papuans Seeking Independence," *The New York Times*, 15-4-2006. http://www.nytimes.com/2006/04/15/world/asia/15papua.html?_r=2&oref=slogin&oref=slogin

[31] Fitzpatrick, "Papuan Refugees Were Hand-picked."

[32] Sian Powell, "Papuans Upbeat on Bid to Gain Asylum," *The Australian*, March 20, 2006.

[33] Cable 1607, Jakarta to Canberra, June 13, 1969, Item 696/3/1 pt 3, A1838, NAA.

[34] Cable 1668, Jakarta to Canberra, June 18, 1969, Item 696/3/1 pt 3, A1838, NAA.

[35] Cable 1621, Jakarta to Canberra, June 14, 1969, Item 696/3/1 pt 3, A1838, NAA.

activities by any person or entity which constitutes a threat to the stability, sovereignty, or territorial integrity of the other Party, including by those who seek to use its territory for encouraging or committing such activities, including separatism, in the territory of the other Party."[36]

BORDER CROSSERS AND EXILES IN PNG

The demonstrators who escaped the security forces' sweeping operations by fleeing across the border into PNG after the violent demonstration at Abepura in mid-March 2006, around the same time as Wanggai, were political activists. However, the majority of these refugees differed from Wanggai and his group because their flight was not carefully planned with the objective of continuing the campaign for independence from exile. They escaped to avoid capture, imprisonment, or worse. A couple of weeks after the riots, the head of police in Papua, Drs. Tommy T. Jacobus, announced that, in anticipation of demonstrators attempting to seek refuge in PNG, border security had been tightened.[37] The police had a list of some nineteen people whom they suspected of being involved in the demonstration, and they were endeavoring to detain these individuals before they escaped into PNG.[38] A report of the Australia-based "Free West Papua Campaign" claimed that there were one hundred students from the Abepura demonstration residing in PNG by early July 2006.[39]

As noted earlier, there is a substantial West Papuan exile community of some 13,500 persons in PNG. The West Papuans are geographically dispersed, with 2,677 living in the East Awin camp in Western Province, about 5,000 Muyu located along the border in Western Province, 3,000 in Port Moresby and Lae, and 500 elsewhere.[40] In 2005 the UNHCR (United Nations High Commissioner for Refugees) gave the Indonesian refugee population in PNG, nearly all of whom were West Papuans, as 9,991.[41] The exile community had its origins in the 1960s, after Indonesia assumed control of Papua. It was in this community that Runawery and Zonggonau became prominent and successful members. The 1960s exiles could be divided into two groups: those who made their own way across the border and the "Dutch pensioners." The latter were Papuans who had worked with the colonial

---

[36] Article 2.3, Government of the Republic of Indonesia and Government of Australia, 2006, Agreement between the Republic of Indonesia and Australia on the Framework for Security Cooperation, signed November 13, 2006. http://www.dfat.gov.au/geo/indonesia/ind-aus-sec06.html

[37] "Pengamanan Perbatasan Diperketat," *Cendrawasih Pos,* March 29, 2006. http://www.cenderawasihpos.com/Utama/h.7.html

[38] "Seorang DPO Kasus Bentrok Abepura Ditangkap di Kotaraja: Dua Orang Lainnya Datang ke Polda Untuk Klarifikasi," *Cendrawasih Pos,* April 26, 2006. http://www.cenderawasihpos.com/Utama/h.1.html

[39] Nick Chesterfield, "Public Security Assessment & Intelligence Profile Mission: Sister Muruk 06: West Papua Border Mission, May/June 2006," www.freewestpapua.com, p. 14.

[40] Diana Glazebrook, "If I Stay Here There is Nothing Yet if I Return I Do Not Know Whether I Will be Safe: West Papuan Refugee Responses to Papua New Guinea Asylum Policy 1998–2003," *Journal of Refugee Studies* 17,2 (2004): 206; and Nic Maclellan, "Refugees: West Papua's Forgotten Asylum Seekers," *Australian Policy Online,* April 13, 2006, www.apo.org.au

[41] 2005 UNCHR Statistical Year Country Data Sheet—Papua New Guinea, 2007, http://www.unhcr.org/cgi-bin/texis/vtx/country?iso=png&expand=statistics

administration and were known to be anti-Indonesian and whose lives were thought to be in jeopardy if they had remained in West Irian. They were supported financially by the Netherlands government.[42] In 1973, four years after the "Act of Free Choice," when PNG was granted self-government, there were five hundred West Papuans who had permission to reside in PNG.[43]

In 1964, the Australian Department of Territories, which was responsible for administering PNG, distinguished two types of Papuan refugees: "political" and "nonpolitical." The "Dutch pensioners" were incorporated in the former group, but the latter also included political activists whose political activity took place after Indonesia assumed control. These people were to be returned to West Irian.[44] During the controversies over Runawery and Zonggonau's escape in mid-1969, Ambassador Jockel referred to the "tacit agreement" that had prevailed over the previous couple of years which determined that Indonesia would not question who was granted residence in PNG provided that "we [Australia] eliminate them from the area of effective activity against Indonesia."[45] This understanding between Australia and Indonesia was placed under great pressure as the exiles in PNG came to act as a vital conduit of information between Papua and the exiled leadership of Jouwe and Kaisiepo in the Netherlands. Foreign Minister Malik was convinced that Papuans were being trained in PNG.[46] The sensitivities were also evident on the Australian side, as one colleague remarked to Jockel: "... the last thing we would want would be an armed clash between the Indonesians and ourselves."[47]

The largest group that came to join the PNG exile community crossed the border in the mid-1980s. The movement of about eleven thousand Papuans across the border commenced in March 1984 in response to military operations, which in turn were Indonesian responses to OPM activities. This number included a group of about one thousand who crossed the border near Vanimo; this contingent included villagers from the border area, but also educated, urban activists, civil servants, and academics from Jayapura, Manokwari, Serui, Biak, and Sorong. International Commission Jurist interviews with the refugees cited human rights issues, discrimination against Melanesians, marginalization, and the impact of transmigration as reasons for their flight.[48] In contrast, the Muyu people, who lived along the central region of the border, had crossed the border into Western Province in much larger numbers (est. 9,435) in 1984–1985. Stuart Krisch argues that the Muyu fled because of the Indonesians' refusal to treat them as equals or establish reciprocal relations with them.[49] This explanation may not be phrased in the usual discourse of Papuan nationalism, but it nevertheless echoes Papuan descriptions of their relations with Indonesians.

---

[42] Klaus Neumann, *Refugee Australia: Australia's Humanitarian Record* (Sydney: University of New South Wales Press, 2004), p. 67.

[43] Ibid., p. 71.

[44] Ibid., pp. 67–68.

[45] Cable 1668, Jakarta to Canberra, June 18, 1969, Item 696/3/1 pt 3, A1838, NAA.

[46] Cable 1418, Jakarta to DEA, May 28, 1969, Item 3036/2/1 pt 13, A1838 T 184, NAA.

[47] TPNG Border Contingency Planning, meeting August 23, 1968, Item 3036/2/1 pt 9, A1838 T 184, NAA.

[48] Glazebrook, "If I Stay Here There is Nothing," p. 208; and John RG Djopari, *Pemberontakan Organisasi Papua Merdeka* (Jakarta: Gramedia, 1993), p. 125.

[49] Cited in Glazebrook, "If I Stay Here There is Nothing," pp. 208–9.

The distinction made in this paper between the elite political activists like Runawery, Zonggonau, and Wanggai, who left Papua to campaign for the independence cause overseas, and those who fled from Indonesian military operations should not be drawn too sharply. Diana Glazebrook's interviews with exiles in PNG show the importance of the political motivation in triggering the initial flight and how political considerations continue to influence the exiles' decisions to remain in PNG or return to Papua. If many refugees chose to return to Papua before *Merdeka* (freedom) had been achieved, this would signify that exile had lost its purpose and that there was no longer any hope of independence. Continuing to live in exile was a protest against Indonesian rule in Papua.[50] The provincial authorities in Papua are aware of the political nature of the decision confronting the West Papuan refugees in PNG. Barnabas Suebu, the recently elected governor of Papua, during a visit to PNG to mark the anniversary of its independence, appealed to his fellow countrymen to return to Papua and together build a new just, peaceful, and prosperous region. He said he would guarantee their safety.[51] Indonesia has continued to be interested in facilitating the return of Papuan refugees since the governor's visit. Agustadi S. P., the secretary of the security minister, announced in March 2007 that some two hundred refugees would be repatriated to Papua.[52] Berty Fernandez, the head of the Provincial Office for the Border and Regional Cooperation, explained that the repatriation would be conducted on a voluntary basis, without any pressure from the governments of Indonesia or PNG. Fernandez believed that the refugees wanted to return home because of the increasingly rapid economic development in Papua and the "conducive" security situation.[53] The relationship between political developments in Papua and decisions made by the Papuan exile communities in PNG is not merely a concern for the refugees and the authorities in Papua. Somewhat contrary to the proposition advanced by Berty Fernandez that the relative stability and prosperity in Papua has been a factor motivating the refugees to return, the UNHCR contingency plans show that the relationship between conflict in Papua and displacement in PNG is a significant factor in this organization's considerations:

> Its [PNG's] proximity and cultural ties to the Indonesian province of Papua means there is potential for a mass influx of West Papuan refugees. Given the continuing political instability and the security situation in Papua, regular revision of PNG's contingency plans and training of GoPNG officials is considered important.[54]

---

[50] Ibid., pp. 212–13.

[51] "Suebu Ajak Masyarakat Papua di PNG Mudik," *Gatra*, September 18, 2006, http://www.gatra.com/2006-09-22/artikel.php?id=97912

[52] "200 Warga Papua Akan Dipulangkan dari PNG: Agustadi: Masih Ada 25.000 Warga RI (Papua) di Sana," *Cendrawasih Pos* (www.kabar-irian.com). It is worth noting that the figures for Papuan refugees in PNG cited by Agustadi are more than double the numbers used elsewhere in this paper.

[53] "200 WNI yang di PNG Sedang Diidentifikasi," *Cendrawasih Pos*, March 24, 2007, (www.kabar-irian.com).

[54] UNHCR, "Country Operations Plan, Papua New Guinea, Planning Year 2006."

DISPLACEMENT WITHIN PAPUA

Conflict between the Indonesian security forces and Papuan resistance groups, as well as broader political tensions, have led to the displacement of Papuans within Papua. We have seen that when conflict and military operations occur near the border with PNG, the "displacement" that occurs generally involves flight across the border and subsequent exile in PNG. The pattern of displacement is different in places more remote from the border, where seeking sanctuary in PNG is a less practical option. Jayapura, the administrative and political center of Papua, has also been the locale of conflict. Because of Jayapura's proximity to the border, it is relatively easy for refugees from this area to cross that boundary line, as it was for Abepura demonstrators in March 2006. But there are many smaller, more remote towns and villages in Papua where violence has uprooted people who are unable to reach the border with PNG. Conflict sparked by military operations in many areas can lead to internal displacement, which often involves flight into the jungle since the poor transportation infrastructure in Papua makes longer treks extremely difficult.

In order to illustrate how the patterns of conflict in regions of Papua remote from the administrative and political centers have led to large-scale displacements in local communities, this paper will now examine two recent cases of Papuan resistance, Indonesian retaliation, and Papuan flight in Wasior and the Central Highlands.

WASIOR

The conflict in Wasior[55] became violent on March 30, 2001, after the killing of three non-Papuan employees of one of the logging companies operating in the area, PT Darma Multi Persada.[56] The killings occurred four months after the Indonesian government had brought to an end the period of relative political openness—the Papuan Spring—that had developed in the region after the fall of President Suharto.

The Wasior conflict illustrates how displacement is related to other aspects of the conflict in Papua. The dispute between the community and the logging company dates from the early 1990s. It was a struggle for control of resources and to determine how the resources were being exploited and for whose benefit. The local community felt that it had not been adequately compensated by the company for the timber and use of its ancestral lands. Amnesty International reported that:

> As was the case elsewhere in Papua and indeed throughout Indonesia, concessions were negotiated between the companies and the central government without any meaningful participation by members of the local population affected by the operations. Compensation for loss of land and livelihoods was low. Inadequate compensation, together with the impact of the logging on the

---

[55] Wasior is located in the southern part of Manokwari district, where the Birds Head is joined to the rest of Papua. The veteran Papuan nationalist Moses Werror sought to locate the Wasior conflict in the history of Papuan nationalism. Werror noted that Wasior was near where the Dutch missionary Izaak Samuel Keijne established his first school before the Pacific War and where Werror was a student in 1948. Keijne was the composer of what was to become the Papuan national anthem, "Hai Tanahku Papua." According to Werror, Keijne inspired his students with the ideals of Papuan nationalism. Email, Moses Werror, June 17, 2001, KABAR-IRIAN: [ID] "Situasi di Wasior" (www.kabar-irian.com).

[56] "Three Bodies Found in Manokwari" *Jakarta Post*, April 7, 2001.

environment, livelihoods, and local traditions has been the source of disputes between local people and the logging companies in the area.[57]

The International Crisis Group has argued that the struggle over land and natural resources is a key aspect of the conflict in Papua. From the perspective of the ICG, the Wasior conflict provided evidence for its contention that Indonesian security forces have a financial interest in resource exploitation, both through their direct involvement in logging and their collection of protection money paid by resource companies.[58]

The company reported that the attack on March 30 was the work of the National Liberation Army (Tentara Pembebasan Nasional, TPN). The Brimob (Police Mobile Brigade) operations that followed resulted in the killing of four people, and several others were wounded.[59] ELS-HAM (Lembaga Studi dan Advokasi Hak Asasi Manusia, Institute for Human Rights Study and Advocacy), the Papuan human rights organization, described the Brimob operations as "arbitrary action against the civilian population," noting that these operations included arrests, torture, and the killing of civilians.[60]

Reflecting this cycle of violence—Papuan resistance, Indonesian repression, followed by further resistance and more repression—on June 13, 2001, an armed group killed five Brimob members and a civilian.[61] The five members of Brimob were part of the security guard for the CV Vatika Papuana Perkasa, another logging company in the area.[62] In June and July, the security forces conducted "Sweeping and Clampdown" operations. It was these operations that resulted in large-scale displacement, disruption of economic activities, and the mistreatment of many in the local communities who had not been associated with the two violent attacks, treatment that violated their human rights. According to ELS-HAM, a local official of the GKI (Gereja Kristen Injili di Tanah Papua, Christian Evangelical Church in the Land of Papua) in Wondama, Wasior, reported that Brimob forces torched the houses of inhabitants of the villages of Senderawoi, Isui, and Wondiboy. While six families still remain in Wondiboy, all the inhabitants of the other two villages have fled to the forests. It is estimated that about five thousand civilians have fled their homes in Wasior. Witnesses and church officials have also reported that local residents were daily compelled by Brimob to collect food for them. The residents' social and economic activities (tending their gardens, hunting, fishing, attending school) were completely paralyzed, and everyone lived in a state of fear.[63] The

---

[57] "INDONESIA: Grave Human Rights Violations in Wasior, Papua," Amnesty International, September 30, 2002, http://web.amnesty.org/ai.nsf/Index/ASA210322002?OpenDocument &of=COUNTRIES\INDONESIA

[58] International Crisis Group, "Resources and Conflict in Papua," ICG Asia Report No. 39, Jakarta/Brussels, 13-9-2002, p. i.

[59] Amnesty International, "INDONESIA: Fear for Safety/Fear of Torture or Ill-treatment," June 8, 2001, Public AI Index: ASA 21/017/2001.

[60] ELS-HAM, Urgent Action No: 46/ELS-HAM Papua/VI/2001, Jayapura, June 19, 2001.

[61] ELS-HAM, 2001d–Urgent Action No: 46/ELS-HAM Papua/VI/2001, Jayapura, June 19, 2001.

[62] Amnesty International, "Impunity and Human Rights Violations in Papua," April 2002, AI Index: ASA 21/010/2002.

[63] ELS-HAM, Jayapura, issued the following Urgent Action on Monday, July 16, 2001: "Impact of Sweepings and Clampdown in Wasior, Manokwari, West Papua." See also the interviews

military operations appear to have continued for some months. Anthropologist Chris Ballard reported the discovery in September 2001 of Wellem Korwam's dismembered body floating in a river in the Wasior area.[64]

Although the security forces were not able to prevent some of the local community from fleeing into the jungle, they were able to control access to the community when church groups from Jayapura tried to offer assistance. The church (GKI) attempted to establish a pastoral team to look after its congregations in the area but was prevented from doing so by the local police.[65] Komnas-HAM (Komisi Nasional Hak Asasi Manusia), the Indonesian national commission for human rights, found that in the Brimob operations following the June 13 attack, four people died, six were tortured, one was raped, and five other people disappeared. "Those responsible for the crimes are fourteen members of the Papua police. Four of their superiors from the Papua provincial police were also responsible for not preventing or halting the crimes by their subordinates or having them prosecuted."[66]

As was the case with those who had sought refuge in PNG, internal displacement caused by the conflict in Wasior persisted long after the conflict ended. A year and a half after the killing of the five Brimob members and a civilian in June 2001, the *Cendrawasih Pos* reported that the residents of four villages in Wasior who had fled the conflict still had not returned. The residents had fled to Serui, Manokwari, Nabiri, Sorong, and Jayapura.[67]

THE CENTRAL HIGHLANDS

In the post-Suharto era, the central highlands of Papua have been a focus of conflict between the security forces and Papuans. Highlanders, particularly those from around Wamena, made a strong impression at the Kongres Papua of mid-2000, which, in retrospect, was the high point of the mobilization of mass support for independence during the "Papuan Spring." Delegates from Wamena had made a strong impression with their traditional attire and by the fact that many of them had walked the three hundred kilometers to Jayapura for the occasion. One of them told the Kongres, "I was born naked and brought up naked. I walked here from the highlands to the coast. Some of you came by planes and boats. I walked on my own two feet. I just want independence."[68] Propagation of the idea of independence following the Kongres seemed to have been most effective in the Baliem Valley, of which Wamena is the administrative center. Some months after the Kongres, a team of church and human rights leaders observed: "The element that most of all found a

---

conducted by Amnesty International of some of the victims caught up in the "Sweeping and Clampdown" operations. Amnesty International, "Impunity and Human Rights Violations in Papua."

[64] Chris Ballard, "The Denial of Traditional Land Rights in West Papua," *Cultural Survival Quarterly* 26,3 (Fall 2002). Ballard argues the murder was part of a series of vicious conflicts in the Wasior area, where timber companies, hiring elite police paramilitary troops for security, have been operating with little or no compensation paid to local communities.

[65] "West Papua: Brimob Violence Engulfs Manokwari," *Tapol*, the Indonesia Human Rights Campaign Bulletin Online 162 (August 2001).

[66] Muninggar Sri Saraswati, "Human Rights Commision Reveals Abuses in Papua," *Jakarta Post,* September 3, 2004.

[67] "Warga 4 Desa di Wasior Belum Kembali," *Cenderawasih Pos*, January 24, 2003.

[68] Mark Worth, *The Land of the Morning Star*.

place in the hearts of people of the Baliem [Valley] and Papua in general was that the demand for independence was non-negotiable."[69] In October 2000, Wamena was the locale of the greatest bloodshed and most serious political conflict resulting from the Indonesian government's determination to eliminate public display of the symbols of Papuan nationalism, particularly the "Morning Star" flag. The identification of highlanders as pro-independence hardliners, at least in the eyes of the security forces, was reinforced by the attack on the police station at Abepura on December 7, 2000.

In April 2003, Wamena again became the focus of conflict when the arsenal of the military post was raided by people thought to be members of the OPM. Some 29 rifles and 3,500 rounds of ammunition were taken away. Retaliation followed, and the Indonesian Human Rights Commission found many Papuans were harmed during what appeared to be well-prepared military operations against the OPM: nine people died during the operations in the villages around Wamena and thirty-eight people were tortured, while fifteen others were arbitrarily arrested during the raids. More pertinent to this study, thousands of residents were displaced from twenty-five villages near Wamena, resulting in the deaths of forty-two people in refugee camps.[70] The Catholic Commission for Justice and Peace likened the sweeping operations conducted around Wamena to those seen after the Abepura attack in December 2000 and Wasior in 2001.[71] The sweeping operations tend not to discriminate between those thought to be involved in Papuan resistance and non-involved members of the local communities.

MULIA AND THE PUNCAK JAYA

The town of Mulia is the administrative center of the district of Puncak Jaya. It is more remote from Jayapura than Wamena, located further to the west in the central highlands and to the north of the Freeport mine at Tembagapura. This next section of the paper will explore a pattern of conflict involving groups associated with the OPM, armed with traditional weapons and what they can capture from the TNI, and military operations that have led to the displacement of significant numbers and the disruption of economic and social life in the local community. The displacements of the local communities occurred in the last months of 2004 and again in early 2007. The OPM resistance has been capable of killing and wounding small numbers of security force personnel and killing small groups of civilians, mostly non-Papuans. Although the OPM operations have been small-scale and sporadic, they have persisted. The security forces have been incapable of capturing those whom they identify as being responsible for the resistance. The security forces recognized that they did not control some areas near Mulia.

The conflict was sparked off with the visit of a known OPM leader, Guliat Tabuni, to Mulia on August 17, 2004, Indonesian Independence Day. The security

---

[69] Tim Kemanusiaan 2001—Wamena Bagian Investigasi, "Peristiwa Tragedi Kemanusiaan Wamena, 6 Oktober 2000, Sebelum Dan Sesudahnya: Sebuah Laporan Investigasi," Jayapura, Januari 2001.

[70] Muninggar Sri Saraswati, "Human Rights Commission Reveals Abuses in Papua."

[71] Theo van den Broek, OFM, "Situasi Akhir Tahun 2003 Di Papua: Refleksi," Sekretariat Keadilan & Perdamaian (SKP), Keuskupan Jayapura, November 28, 2003 (www.kabar-irian.com).

authorities understood that it was Tabuni's intention to create disturbances and ruin the celebrations. The Baptist Church leader Socratez Sofyan Yoman offered another interpretation: that Guliat Tabuni had returned to the area to visit family graves and to settle a dispute about the use of his family's land. The head of the Puncak Jaya District government, Elieser Renmaur, attempted to contact Guliat Tabuni. Later there was an armed clash between Kopassus (Komando Pasukan Khusus, Special Forces Command) soldiers and Guliat Tabuni's group, in which two of the latter were killed and one of the soldiers was lightly wounded. Nothing further happened for nearly another month, when, on September 14, a minister from the Christian Evangelical Church Indonesia (GIDI, Gereja Injili Di Indonesia), Elisa Tabuni, was killed. The military assert that Elisa Tabuni was killed in a shoot-out between soldiers and the OPM, after the minister had been detained by the soldiers on suspicion that he was associated with the OPM. Elisa Tabuni was detained along with a younger man, who the military assert was carrying pro-independence material.[72] The military's version of these events is contested by Socratez Sofyan Yoman, based on the eye-witness account of Elisa Tabuni's son, presumably the younger man who figures in the military's account, who subsequently escaped. According to this report, Elisa Tabuni and his son, Weties Tabuni, were detained by soldiers and were asked about the whereabouts of Guliat Tabuni. They denied any knowledge of the OPM leader and after further questioning an angered soldier shot the minister.[73]

Another month later, on October 12, six non-Papuans were killed. They were transport drivers on the road between Wamena and Mulia, employed by PT Modern.[74] The Indonesian authorities asserted that Guliat Tabuni was responsible for this attack.[75] However, according to Socratez Sofyan Yoman, who visited Mulia ten days after the murders, there was some doubt about this, as there were two other groups that claimed to be OPM. Both of these groups seemed to have much greater freedom of movement than did the "OPM" unit led by Guliat Tabuni and were able to move in and out of the town of Mulia at will. According to Socratez Sofyan Yoman, five days after this murder the military launched operations against the local civilian population. The military operations involved both the deployment of troops and bombing from helicopters; this attack caused the members of twenty-seven church congregations to flee into the jungle.[76] The Indonesian version of these events

---

[72] "Team Formed to Investigate West Papua Shootings in Indonesia," transcription by BBC Monitoring Service (via *Joyo Indonesia News*) of an article from *Cendrawasih Pos*, October 29, 2004.

[73] "Pdt. Socrates Sofyan Yoman, MA: Kasus Puncak Jaya Murni Rekayasa Militer," Elsham News Service, November 3, 2004.

[74] Konferensi Pers Bersama, ELSHAM Papua, LBH Papua, Kontras Papua, Dewan Adat Papua, Gereja, dan Mahasiswa: "SOS: SBY lambat bertindak korban di Mulia, Puncak Jaya terus berjatuhan," Elsham News Service, November 17, 2004.

[75] Letter, Ramli Sa'ud, Minister Counsellor, Embassy of the Republic of Indonesia, London, to The Rt. Revd. R. D. Harries, Lord Bishop of Oxford, No. 47/IV/07/LON/05, June 30, 2005. Socratez Sofyan Yoman disputed this claim, arguing that Guliat Tabuni had not been able to operate in the area of the attack as it has been occupied by the TNI. Yoman asserted that the TNI itself was responsible for the attack. Letter, Socratez Sofyan Yoman to Minister Counsellor, Embassy of the Republic of Indonesia, London, July 22, 2005 (www.kabar-irian.com).

[76] "Pdt. Socrates Sofyan Yoman, MA: Kasus Puncak Jaya Murni Rekayasa Militer."

depicted fighting between the OPM and the TNI, as well as OPM attacks on and occupation of villages.[77] Writing in July 2005, Socratez Sofyan Yoman found that 6,393 people had been displaced as a result of the military operations launched in October 2004. These people remained in the jungle. He claimed that 78 Papuans had died in the jungle since that time because of starvation and illness. In addition, he asserted that 371 houses (*honai*) as well as gardens had been destroyed in the villages that were deserted by the residents who had fled the military operations.[78]

When Socratez Sofyan Yoman visited Mulia on October 21, 2004, he later told the Jayapura press:

> The first thing I witnessed was that the town was dead, social activity had completely stopped; government officials from the lowest to the most senior had fled the Puncak Jaya district. The local population also had fled into the jungle and the mountains as well as to the villages where they felt secure.[79]

Conflicts between the Indonesian security forces and the sections of Papuan society around Mulia resumed in the last months of 2006 and have persisted into the early months of 2007. The pattern of conflict became more complicated with the involvement of local political leaders, the first direct election (*pilkada*) for the head of the Puncak Jaya District government (*bupati*), and the establishment of "alliances" between OPM leaders and candidates in the election. Early maneuvering in preparation for the elections, together with the distribution of compensation funds resulting from the government's abolition of subsidies for petroleum products, appear to have acted as the trigger for the renewed violence. Throughout Papua, it has been common for the regional elections of the district government *bupati* to become the foci for political conflict. Mulia and the district of Puncak Jaya were not exceptions. What was more unusual was the involvement of OPM leaders and the security forces.

One of the candidates for head of the district government was the former head, Elieser Renmaur, a Keiese. As a non-Papuan, Elieser Renmaur faced the prospect that the DPRD of Puncak Jaya might disqualify him and thereby prevent him from being nominated as a candidate for the *bupati* election. According to a political report from the Kopassus unit based in Mulia, Elieser Renmaur attempted to mobilize support from a seemingly unlikely source: Guliat Tabuni, the OPM leader whose role in the earlier conflict in Mulia has been discussed above. The Kopassus report asserts that Elieser Renmaur held meetings in early October with OPM members, who pledged their support for his candidacy.[80] In June 2006, Guliat Tabuni had sent a letter to the Chair of the MRP (Majelis Rakyat Papua, Papuan People's Assembly) in Jayapura requesting that Elieser Renmaur should be reappointed as district head. The letter, written in formal bureaucratic Indonesian, using what purported to be OPM

---

[77] Letter, Ramli Sa'ud, Minister Counsellor, Embassy of the Republic of Indonesia, London, to The Rt. Revd. R. D. Harries, Lord Bishop of Oxford, No. 47/IV/07/LON/05, June 30, 2005 (www.kabar-irian.com).

[78] Letter, Socratez Sofyan Yoman to Minister Counsellor, Embassy of the Republic of Indonesia, London, July 22, 2005.

[79] "Pdt. Socrates Sofyan Yoman, MA: Kasus Puncak Jaya Murni Rekayasa Militer."

[80] Henri Mahyudi, Kapten Inf, Satgasban–4 Kopassus Pos-7 Mulia, "Koronologis aksi Anarkhis Massa Penerima Bantuan Dana Kompensasi BBM atau BLT di Distrik Mulia Kapbupaten Puncak Jaya," Laporan Khusus, R/01/LAPSUS/X/2006, October 15, 2006, p. 4.

letterhead with the insignia of the "Revolutionary Provisional Government of the Republik (*sic*) of West Papua," argued, inter alia, that the OPM supported Elieser Renmaur because Papuan leaders in Puncak Jaya were not committed to serve the people. They were corrupt. "They eat in Mulia, take their afternoon nap in Jayapura, and sleep in Jakarta."[81]

Elieser Renmaur's campaign coincided with the distribution of the compensation funds. The Kopassus report acknowledges the difficulties involved in distributing the funds, as some of the regions in Puncak Jaya were under OPM control, which meant that the monies for the poor in these regions had to be given out in Mulia itself.[82] The distribution of the funds, accompanied by large-scale consumption of alcohol, was followed by riots and the destruction of many government offices, houses, and other infrastructure in Mulia in October 2006. The Kopassus report asserts that the riots and destruction were provoked by Renmaur and his supporters, including the OPM.[83]

The violence continued, when, on December 8, Joko Susanto, a Kopassus soldier, and Tabias Sirgen, a retired military officer, were killed in Mulia. The security forces thought that the Guliat Tabuni OPM was responsible. On a hill within sight of the town, the Papuan Morning Star flag was raised. By coincidence, or otherwise, on the same day, Lukas Enembe, a highlander and former deputy head of the Puncak Jaya district and a candidate who had been narrowly defeated in the 2006 election for governor of Papua, announced his candidacy for the election in Puncak Jaya. In response to these developments, some of the residents of Mulia, especially the government officials, left by plane. Other residents were prevented from leaving by military roadblocks. On Christmas Eve, the Morning Star flag that had been flying just outside Mulia was replaced by an even larger and more conspicuous flag. According to a report of a church delegation, slogans attacking Lukas Enambe were shouted by OPM supporters in the vicinity of this flag.[84]

In early January 2007, military (Brimob) operations commenced with removal of the Morning Star flag. Gumi Morib was killed in these operations, and the traditional house of Laringgen Morib, a GIDI church leader, was burned. In response to the operations, large numbers of people fled into the jungle. The GIDI reported that 5,361 people had fled from its congregations.[85] It is worth noting that many of these people fled from regions near Mulia that the Kopassus document, cited above, described as being controlled by the OPM. A delegation of church leaders from Jayapura was told by local church leaders that the members of their congregations who had fled needed food supplies and medicines. The displaced people were living in fear of both the OPM and the Indonesian security forces.[86]

---

[81] Letter, Gen. Goliath Tabuni and Gen. Negoobet Tabinu to the Chair of the MRP, June 9, 2006, 201/TPN-OPM/PB/III/2006.

[82] Henri Mahyudi, Kapten Inf., Satgasban-4 Kopassus Pos-7 Mulia, "Koronologis aksi Anarkhis Massa Penerima Bantuan Dana Kompensasi BBM atau BLT di Distrik Mulia Kapbupaten Puncak Jaya," Laporan Khusus, R/01/LAPSUS/X/2006, October 15, 2006, p. 1.

[83] Ibid., p. 10.

[84] Ecumenical Council of Papuan Churches (Persekutuan Gereja-gereja di Papua), "Report on the Situation in Mulia," No: 005/PGGP/07/2.7, Jayapura, January 29, 2007, p. 3.

[85] Ibid., p. 5.

[86] Ibid.

An appeal by Sepnat Manufandu, one of the leaders of Foker, an NGO based in Jayapura, gives us a better idea of the dynamic of the military operations conducted in response to insurgent attacks on security forces, such as the murder of the Kopassus soldier and retired officer. Manufandu appealed to the OPM to acknowledge whether it was responsible for the murders. He did not want civilians to become victims of sweeping operations and indiscriminate detentions carried out in retaliation for such attacks. He pointed out that highlanders have very similar physical features, and it was difficult for the military to distinguish between civilians and separatists.[87]

The delegation of Jayapura-based church leaders, who visited Mulia in mid-January 2007, found that the conflict between the Indonesian security forces and the OPM had created an emergency humanitarian situation. The district administration in Puncak Jaya, preoccupied with the forthcoming election, needed the support of the provincial government to provide the necessary food and medical assistance to its citizens. The church leaders appealed to the security forces and the OPM to ensure the safe provision of food supplies and medical assistance to the displaced populations. They recommended that the number of security forces deployed in Puncak Jaya should be decreased so as to reduce the fear and trauma experienced by local communities, as well as the potential for further conflict.[88]

Perhaps reflective of the tensions in Mulia, on February 13 there was a shoot-out between Brimob and TNI units in front of the local government office that left one member of Brimob dead. The fight started after both soldiers and Brimob members had been waiting for a long time in a queue to get kerosene, and the supply ran out before one of the Brimob members was served. A verbal argument turned into an exchange of gunfire lasting ninety minutes. Government officials fled their offices in terror. The *Papua Pos* reported that a similar incident between Brimob and the TNI had happened in 2006 in Puncak Jaya.[89] The role of the security forces is central to some Papuan accounts of the conflict in Puncak Jaya, as many consider these forces to be more disruptive and provocative than helpful. For example, the Baptist Church leader Socratez Sofyan Yoman, who has closely chronicled the conflict in Mulia since 2004, argues that the military has fostered conflict in order to justify an increased military presence in the highlands. He claims the military has fostered "fake" OPM, who, for instance, were responsible for the flag-raising just outside Mulia. He cites a meeting on February 22, 2007, of the Puncak Jaya District government and council with the police and military at which it was agreed that eight new military posts would be established in Puncak Jaya.[90]

---

[87] "Pelakukanya Belum Tentu TPN/OPM," *Papua Pos*, December 28, 2006. http://www.papuapos.com/index.php?main=fullberita&id=1240

[88] Ecumenical Council of Papuan Churches, "Report on the Situation in Mulia," pp. 2, 6.

[89] "Tim Terpadu ke Mulia," *Papua Pos*, Februari 15, 2007. http://www.papuapos.com/new/index.php?main=fullberita&id=2113

[90] Email, Socratez Sofyan Yoman, "Laporan Khusus: Peristiwa 8 Desember 2006 Di Puncak Kumipaga, Puncak Jaya Murni Rekayasa Militer Bekerjasama Dengan Opm Binaan Militer," January 4, 2007. For an English language version, see Special Report: "The 8th December 2006 Incident in Puncak Kumipaga, Puncak Jaya Was A Manipulation Which Was Wholely [*sic*] Created By Indonesian Military And The Fake Opm (The Fake Free Papua Movement Armed Force) Trained By The Indonesian Military," https://lists.riseup.net/www/arc/ reg.westpapua/2007-01/msg00012.html); Socratez Sofyan Yoman, "Genocide, Military Operations & Islamization under Special Autonomy in West Papua," March 1, 2007. https://lists.riseup.net/ www/arc/reg.westpapua/2007-03/msg00019.html

At the time of this writing, in 2007, the humanitarian crisis created by the military operations and subsequent displacement of thousands of civilians has been at least partially resolved. Most of the refugees who fled the military operations have returned to their villages. The return of the refugees and the restoration of more peaceful conditions were related to the election for head of the Puncak Jaya District government, which was held on March 21. The provisional results were that Lukas Enembe had won with a substantial majority—74.9 percent of the vote.[91] This meant the defeat of Elieser Renmaur, the Keiese former district head, who was linked with the riots and destruction of infrastructure in Mulia in October 2006 and who attempted to mobilize support from the OPM.[92]

AD HOC CONFLICT, MASS DISPLACEMENT

The conflicts in Wasior and in the central highlands since 2001 have displaced about twenty thousand people. The scale of the displacement is substantial in relation to the size of the local populations. It is also substantial relative to the scale and intensity of the conflict that generated the displacement. If the intensity of the conflict is measured in terms of numbers of people killed, the conflict has been low-level and intermittent. The numbers of people killed in OPM attacks and in shoot-outs between the security forces and the OPM in Wasior and the central highlands were in the single figures, in marked contrast to the numbers of people displaced. However limited the capacity of the OPM appears to be, the Indonesian security forces have not been able to eliminate the OPM. In Puncak Jaya, the military has been able to identify the leaders of the OPM, and it recognized that some regions were controlled by the OPM.

The apparent incongruity between the relatively high level of displacement and the relatively low intensity of the conflict would seem to be related to the nature of the Indonesian military response. The immediate cause of displacement in Wasior and the central highlands has been the military sweeping operations that have rolled through local communities, capturing and punishing suspects without distinguishing between ordinary villagers and OPM activists and supporters. When villagers have fled from sweeping operations, the security forces have endeavored to restrict further population movements in the areas they controlled. The security forces have sought to limit the access of the churches and human rights organizations to the displaced populations as well as thwart efforts to provide humanitarian assistance.

Most of the displaced people were Papuans who lived in subsistence agricultural communities. The displaced lived in remote regions of Papua and enjoyed few educational opportunities and had negligible access to any government services. They were not the educated political leaders who escaped across the border into PNG and beyond with the objective of furthering the struggle for independence.

---

[91] "Enembe-Ibo Unggul dalam Pemilihan Bupati Puncak Jaya," *Tempointeraktif,* March 22, 2007. http://www.tempointeraktif.com/hg/nusa/papua/2007/03/22/brk,20070322-96091,id.html. The losing candidates had challenged the results. See "Saksi Nomor Urut 2 dan 3 Terus Datangi Panwas," *Papua Pos,* March 29, 2007 (http://www.papuapos.com/new/index.php?main=fullberita&id=2686)

[92] "Tetap Enembe!: KPUD Puncak Jaya Menangkan Sidang Pilkada," *Cendrawasih Pos,* May 3, 2007 (http://www.cenderawasihpos.com/Utama/h.5.html). On May 2, 2007, the High Court in Jayapura rejected the claims of Elieser Renmaur and the other unsuccessful candidates.

They represent another dimension of Papuan resistance to Indonesian rule. Their communities have supported the OPM. It was the OPM that created and sustained the resistance to Indonesian rule from the mid-1960s to the fall of President Suharto in 1998. Ironically, the OPM has continued the sporadic and localized resistance in the remote areas of Papua even after the Indonesian government has shut down nationalist politics in the urban areas of Papua.

The urban, Indonesian-educated elite that supplanted the OPM as leaders of the nationalist movement from 1998 has been represented in these remote regions of conflict and displacement by the Jayapura-based church leaders. The churches have congregations in the most isolated regions of Papua, including those controlled by the OPM in Puncak Jaya. Most of the Papuan accounts used in this discussion were taken from reports by the churches and church-linked human rights organizations. The churches have been nearly the sole channel of communication through which news of these conflicts and displacements have reached Jayapura and the world outside Papua. In these circumstances, it is not surprising that, in the minds of some Indonesian government officials, the churches and the OPM have been linked.[93]

The loss of life in the conflicts in Wasior and the Central Highlands has been modest. Wasior and the central highlands are regions of Papua where ethnic Papuans still form the majority of the population. However, in both regions civilian Indonesian settlers have constituted a significant proportion of the victims of OPM attacks. Another sign of the tensions generated by Papua's demographic transformation was the terms in which the election campaign for head of the Puncak Jaya district government was waged. The ethnic background of the candidates was an issue in the election.

INDONESIAN PRESSURE

This paper has attempted to relate displacement to some disparate patterns of conflict in Papua. A focus on displacement is useful for the way it illuminates those diverse patterns of conflict. The paper has argued that displacement both fuels the conflict and is a consequence of conflict. The radical demographic transformation that has taken place under Indonesian rule has displaced Papuan communities in areas occupied by transmigration projects, but for most of Papuan society there is a feeling of displacement that is perhaps better expressed as dispossession. Displacement touches many sections of Papuan society; those who have fled their homes include well-educated political leaders, who have sought to further their political campaigns outside Indonesia, as well as impoverished subsistence farmers living in the most remote regions of Papua, who have fled from military operations. Papuan political leaders who have gone into exile to further the struggle for independence have exercised agency not available to subsistence farmers in the highlands. Political leaders face a difficult choice: to choose exile or remain in Papua, where they must operate in a highly constricted political environment. To paraphrase Socratez Sofyan Yoman, Papuans live under great pressure from Jakarta. It is this pressure that provides the link between the various types of displacement discussed in the paper. Papuans' relations with Indonesians are often asymmetrical. The OPM is no match for the Indonesian military and police. Papuan subsistence

---

[93] Letter, Ramli Sa'ud, Minister Counsellor, Embassy of the Republic of Indonesia, London, to The Rt. Revd. R. D. Harries, Lord Bishop of Oxford, No. 47/IV/07/LON/05, June 30, 2005.

farmers and petty traders operate in a different sector of the economy from the Indonesian settlers. Except for the short-lived Papuan Spring, the Indonesian government has established and enforced the constraints on political activity. Displacements in its many forms are responses to this pressure.

RECONSIDERING DISPLACEMENT AND INTERNALLY DISPLACED PERSONS FROM POSO

Lorraine V. Aragon[1]

"Internally Displaced Persons" (IDPs) is a coldly bureaucratic and yet conceptually provocative term. Governments, NGOs, and international humanitarian organizations simplify their mammoth data collection and aid-distribution tasks by envisioning IDPs as a common category of people who share a set of specific problems. The latter include temporary or permanent loss of their houses, economic resources, and familiar environments. Such people often experience physical and mental trauma. Yet for all the common challenges faced by those in domestic flight, the category of IDP and the narrative framework it usually generates are problematic in several ways. Data from the Poso conflict disclose how competing narrative frames concerning the conflict's evacuees shape debates that directly influence consequent actions and accountability. My analysis is based on interviews, site visits, and other contacts made with diverse people who consider themselves as having experienced some form of displacement because of violence that began in Poso in December 1998. The "thick description" narratives included here enable my particular line of questioning and analysis, but also may aid future inquiries by other researchers asking different types of questions.

The way the category IDP conflates those fleeing natural disasters with those fleeing violence, even as it gives rise to prejudices by distinguishing all IDPs from other local citizens, has been explored elsewhere.[2] My focus here is concerned rather with implications loaded into the word "displaced," which can become a source of underlying arguments over prior and future rights. Those rights can be understood

[1] This research on involuntary migration was supported by a grant for research and writing from the John D. and Catherine T. MacArthur Foundation. Additional support on related projects was provided by the Wenner–Gren Foundation for Anthropological Research and the Koninklijk Instituut voor Taal-, Land- en Volkenkunde (KITLV). I am especially grateful to all those who shared their difficult experiences of the Poso conflict through narratives.

[2] C. Brun, "Local Citizens or Internally Displaced Persons? Dilemmas of Long Term Displacement in Sri Lanka," *Journal of Refugee Studies* 16,4 (2003): 376–97; Christopher R. Duncan, "Unwelcome Guests: Relations between Internally Displaced Persons and Their Hosts in North Sulawesi, Indonesia," *Journal of Refugee Studies* 18,1 (2005): 25–46.

in strictly territorial or property-ownership terms, or more broadly in terms of rights to regional or national citizenship. The narratives I present speak directly to both kinds of issues.

My observation is that people who fall into the Poso IDP category—or its Indonesian translation, *pengungsi*, literally "evacuee," or "those who flee"—are far more diverse in their circumstances and desires than generally imagined.[3] Below I introduce case examples and describe preferences for paths of flight and return, or "repatriation," to raise questions about the ideas of "displacement" and "replacement" in the Poso conflict. I contend that the prospects for curtailing future violence and moving toward accountability and positive resettlement solutions cannot be disconnected from narrative frames publicly advanced about the legitimate "placement" of evacuees and their rights of "return."[4]

Ideas about the "displaced" warrant reconsideration in the Poso case, but the broader categorical challenges apply to many more civil conflicts. By rethinking "displacement," we also are able to confront its implied antecedent "placement" (or "emplacement") and their frequently presumed consequents: "re-placement," "return," or, as it is commonly called in Indonesia, "repatriation" (*repatriasi*). The verb root, "displace," suggests that before their forced migration, the people involved once had a home or place where they clearly belonged. Yet it is exactly disputes over this issue that I would suggest lie at the heart of the Poso conflict. Perhaps more important, the disparate viewpoints that underlie these homeland disputes and implications for where refugees should go are an important rhetorical aspect of the conflict's protracted, and often seemingly endless, transformations.

This discussion bears in a more general way on migration policies, and on public debates about how migration or corrections to forced migration should be handled by government and multinational organizations. Liisa Malkki argues that nationalist discourses and most scholarship on the nation-state presume cultural sedentarism or rootedness. Those involved in territorial displacement or migration therefore frequently are marked as pathological and even potentially immoral.[5] Yet Indonesia is a place where an active cultural crossroads receiving many diasporas long preceded state-bounded and controlled territories. Upon this fluid situation, the post-colonial Indonesian government aggressively implemented inter-island migration, or "transmigration," as a national development tool.

Although Indonesian transmigration originally was conceived by the Dutch as a method to move poor and landless residents from overpopulated Java to less-populated outer islands, it was under the Suharto regime (1966–1998) that the

---

[3] The Indonesian term *pengungsi* also translates appropriately as "refugee." Although multinational aid organizations reserve the term "refugee" for those displaced across national borders, the Indonesian term makes no such distinction, and I will here use "refugee" in this general sense because it is, for present purposes, a less cumbersome and cognitively loaded term than IDP, the category under analysis.

[4] For related theoretical arguments, see Lorraine V. Aragon, "Mass Media Fragmentation and Narratives of Violent Action in Sulawesi's Poso Conflict," *Indonesia* 79 (April 2005): 1–55; and Elizabeth Drexler, "History and Liability in Aceh, Indonesia: Single Bad Guys and Convergent Narratives," *American Ethnologist* 33,3 (2006): 313–26.

[5] Liisa H. Malkki, "National Geographic: The Rooting of Peoples and the Territorialization of National Identity among Scholars and Refugees," in *Culture, Power, Place: Explorations in Critical Anthropology,* ed. A. Gupta and J. Ferguson (Durham, NC: Duke University Press, 1997), pp. 52–74.

government began to advance resettlement as a way to ethnically homogenize and boost the nation economically by moving "more advanced" Javanese as agricultural workers or migrant laborers for development companies into "backward" provinces populated by other ethnolinguistic groups.[6] Transmigration in Central Sulawesi, irrespective of the intent of particular migrants, rapidly accelerated deforestation, road building, voluntary migration, and land alienation—four developmental processes that contribute to increased communal tensions in Central Sulawesi and elsewhere. Those processes can be seen as part of a larger trend toward the marginalization of rural and upland regions that aids plantations and other development agendas.[7]

To complicate matters, members of some Indonesian groups, notably the Bugis of South Sulawesi, routinely describe migration as part of their pre-colonial ethnic heritage and portray themselves as avatars of the nation's development goals and majority religion, Islam. The post-1998 violence that occurred in Indonesia among some members of notably migratory groups, such as the Bugis, Butonese, Mandar, and Madurese, in opposition to some members of more sedentary non-Muslim groups who conceive themselves as "indigenous" (such as Pamona, Mori, and Lore), provides an additional opportunity to re-think the idea of "displacement" in relation to common assumptions about nation-state policies on ethnic minorities, migration regimes, ethnic nationalism, and the customary moral codes of religious networks.[8] Such re-thinking makes gradual penetration by the standardized infrastructure of the modern Indonesian state and global capital a more visible part of the sometimes rapidly changing social and ecological matrix within which post-Suharto regional frictions emerged.

The basis of my contribution here is fieldwork-based narratives from some Poso refugees that, added to the core tales one could anticipate, alter the picture of presumably "localized" or "in-place" Muslims and Christians who were alienated from their hometowns under duress during the 1998–2002 civil violence. Some of these cases complicate expectations oddly because the roots of these individuals seem less in the Poso District than in some other place with which they also have an ambivalent relationship. Other cases disturb the picture because the individuals technically left the Poso District *before* the violence began, even though they, too, now experience an inability to "go home." Thus, uncertainties arise about what "returning home" means. The arguments advanced by refugees and officials working with diverse assumptions about these concepts cannot be considered irrelevant to the prolonged violence in Central Sulawesi, although certainly that

---

[6] See Timothy Babcock, "Transmigration: The Regional Impact of a Miracle Cure," in *Central Government and Local Government in Indonesia*, ed. Colin MacAndrews (Singapore: Oxford University Press, 1986), pp. 157–89; and Riwanto Tirtosudarmo, "The Political Demography of National Integration and Its Policy Implications for Sustainable Development in Indonesia," *Indonesian Quarterly* 23 (1995): 369–83. Also, Rebecca Elmhirst, "Space, Identity Politics, and Resource Control in Indonesia's Transmigration Programme," *Political Geography* 18,7 (1999): 813–35.

[7] See also Tania Murray Li, ed. *Transforming the Indonesian Uplands: Marginality, Power and Production* (Amsterdam: Harwood Academic Publishers, 1999).

[8] For more details on ethnic diversity and the pre-Malino Accord Poso conflict phases, see Lorraine V. Aragon, "Communal Violence in Poso, Central Sulawesi: Where People Eat Fish and Fish Eat People," *Indonesia* 72 (October 2001): 45–79.

violence also has been compounded by government and legal failings, state agent greed, and exclusivist religious agendas among some participants.

The first word of the term "Internally Displaced Persons," signifying that those who fled are an internal or domestic state matter, indicates how much the IDP term is pinned to trust in the reality of national political borders and cozy assumptions about state sovereignty. Even national ethnic homogeneity seems tacitly implied. The persons at issue are displaced, but not displaced far enough to make them a clear and legitimate political concern of other states or other kinds of peoples. To take that last statement at face value would leave any scholar, government officer, or humanitarian aid worker in a state of deep misunderstanding (or denial) about the ethnic complexity and religiously transnational development of the Poso conflict, and the people who fled from it.

My goal here is not in any way intended to challenge the difficult and good work that humanitarian relief agencies do, and their obvious need to have a verbal category or conceptual image for deserving aid recipients. As many have noted, the label "IDP" allows for a much-needed measure of international legal protection for millions of people threatened within their own home countries. What I seek instead is to contribute a further effort to move scholarship on forced migrants to ethnographic zones beyond the statistics that tell us how many have fled and now reside in temporary or permanent resettlement locations. This shift in emphasis from unifying numbers and loaded categories to diverse experiences and narrative frameworks will contribute to an increased understanding of forced migration and regional identity—matters integral to the Poso violence, and perhaps many other contemporary civil conflicts elsewhere. A further possible contribution will be the elucidation of links between narratives about and by evacuees and political outcomes with regard to public accountability for violence and reparations.

BACKGROUND ON REFUGEE DISPERSALS AND NUMBERS

The resettlement of Indonesian Muslims and Christians from Poso has involved the overlapping influences of religious organizations, state politicians, Indonesian bureaucratic corruption, grassroots NGOs, and powerful international organizations such as the World Bank, the United Nations Development Program, Church World Services, CARE, and Mercy Corps. In most projects, however, resettlement patterns reinforced flight patterns that segregated Muslims and Christians. This left ethnic Javanese, Bugis, Gorontalo, and Arab Muslims in control of coastal centers and most regional government institutions, while indigenous groups of Protestant Pamona, Lore, and Mori became further entrenched in the interior mountains and rural villages. Many were left with less political representation beyond their immediate hamlet communities. Both coastal and highland communities, swelled by the addition of fleeing persons, became more religiously uniform or "purified" through fear, threats, and attacks on property and persons. This segregation process, like so many prior ones, was assisted by the Indonesian state requirement that all citizens have a religion from among the state-authorized choices listed on their national identity cards. To pass through a roadblock or to file an official form requires a documented religious identity.

The first time Poso City residents fled from hostilities, in December–January 1998, most headed to the Muslim-majority provincial capital of Palu, Central Sulawesi, or the Protestant-majority provincial capital of Manado, North Sulawesi.

Similar patterns followed in mid-April 2000. The third time, when tens of thousands more fled, was in May–July 2000. Violent militia attacks occurred again in several areas of the district throughout 2001 and 2002. Some villages, including a mixed-religion one I visited in the Tojo region during 2003, were burned up to five times. By this point, refuge destinations were more widespread and included South Sulawesi and Java, but the primary refuges of fleeing Muslims still were coastal towns on Sulawesi Island, while the primary refuges of fleeing Christians were either in North Sulawesi or the highland areas of Central Sulawesi, such as the mission towns of Tentena and Napu.

In sum, the successive peaks of Poso communal violence, revenge cycles, and subsequently more-organized militia attacks resulted in population dispersals that were patterned recognizably according to prior religious strongholds and migration chains. Within the province, Muslims generally fled toward and along the urban coasts whereas Christians fled to rural mountain villages. While this resulted in heightened Muslim-versus-Christian religious segregation in the province, the ethnic diversity within those two religious communities actually increased because ethnolinguistically diverse groups took refuge with their fellow Muslims or Christians.

After the government mediated the Malino Accord ceasefire agreement in December 2001, civil war between Muslims and Christians ostensibly subsided. Violence, however, did not fully cease. Rather, community-based fighting was replaced by periodic, premeditated attacks in the form of bombings, "mysterious killings," and revenge-linked village assaults. After 2002, the religious segregation and security situations were predictable and controlled sufficiently so that the number of people fleeing their homes for other regions declined significantly.

Following the Malino Accord, data on Poso's evacuees and their efforts to return to their prior villages were provided by the Indonesian government's Disaster and Refugees Coordinating Unit (Satkorlak) and the Central Sulawesi Protestant Church, with an overall profile presented by Human Rights Watch. Two months after the December 2001 Malino Accord and accompanying army–police security operation, about 10,000 refugees were said to have returned home. Roughly half of the estimated remaining 86,000 displaced persons within Central Sulawesi appeared to be Muslim, and roughly half Christian.[9] Although new episodes of violence often prompted those who had returned home to flee again, by mid-July 2002 the district social-welfare agency reported that almost 40 percent of the displaced had returned home: 43,308 of 110,227 people.

New official numbers of IDPs for Central Sulawesi (and other Indonesian conflicts) were compiled and reported by a joint Indonesian government Disaster Management unit (BAKORNAS-PBP, Badan Koordinasi Nasional Penanggulangan Bencana dan Penanganan Pengungsi, National Coordinating Body for Natural Disaster and IDP Management) and United Nations Office for the Coordination of Humanitarian Affairs (OCHA) team. Their report from a March 2003 site visit to the Poso District stated that a total of 31,326 families (comprising 143,354 individuals) had been displaced by the conflict.[10] That number represents *nearly half* of the

---

[9] Human Rights Watch, "Breakdown: Four Years of Communal Violence in Central Sulawesi," *Indonesia Report* 14, 9 (C), December 2002, p. 39.

[10] BAKORNAS-PBP and UN Office for the Coordination of Humanitarian Affairs 2003, "Joint BAKORNAS and OCHA Mission to Central Sulawesi, March 11–15, 2003." Report posted at www.db.idpproject.org.

population of the Poso regions affected by the violence.[11] The report from 2003, however, stated that nearly 75 percent of displaced people already had returned to their "places of origin" (107,283 of 143,354), which left only an estimated 36,000 within the district who still needed help with resettlement.[12] A 2006 official estimate pegged the number of IDPs or inadequately assisted people in Central Sulawesi at 40,000, with most living within the Poso District.[13]

Despite the seeming precision of those statistics, during the dangerous chaos and aftermath of Poso's fighting, the number of displaced persons would have been very difficult to record. Thus, the figures must be considered as rough estimates based on assumptions about average family size, tallies required from village or department heads, and so forth. The totals often appear to omit some of the kinds of people I met who fled to other provinces or islands, as well as those who took refuge individually in private homes with distant families rather than entering refugee camps or official resettlement areas. Those kinds of people were unlikely to be recorded or, as they complained to me, provided with any type of public acknowledgement or aid. In September 2003, one member of the Malino Accord aid-implementation team told me there were about 30,000 refugee families who still needed aid, which meant an estimated 90,000–150,000 individuals. The debates over totals therefore entailed often tacit distinctions among those people who had fled during attacks (and may or may not have returned one or more times) and those people registered to receive post-conflict aid at either old or new locations. Those numbers and distinctions are not ultimately separable from definitions of "places of origin" and appropriate places for "return."

THE MALINO ACCORD AND THE QUESTION OF RETURN

The Malino Accord mediated by the Indonesian government on December 19–20, 2001, marked an official end to community fighting between Muslims and Christians in Poso. It should be noted that the government-assembled delegate teams comprised mainly religious or militia leaders of Palu-based Muslims and Poso District Protestants. The central government thereby implicitly dismissed the importance of other types of citizens within the Poso District. In so doing, the agreement reified Muslim and Christian "sides" as if they were homogenous and united, which they had not been previously.

The agreement contains three points (6, 7, and 8) that speak directly but ambivalently to issues of post-conflict rights for refugees. Point 8, which calls for "returning all refugees to their respective places of origin" (*mengembalikan seluruh pengungsi ke tempat asalnya masing-masing*), is ambiguous, and it has been interpreted differentially. Point 7 states that all legitimate rights of ownership existing before the

---

[11] The total also is consistent with news reports from 2000–2002 that estimated IDPs at roughly 100,000–110,000 persons. Comparable religious segregation patterns resulted for the Ambon and Maluku conflicts, which produced an estimated 500,000 or more displaced persons. See Duncan essay, "Where Do We Go from Here? The Politics of Ending Displacement in Post-Conflict North Maluku," this volume.

[12] BAKORNAS-PBP and UN Office, "Joint BAKORNAS and OCHA Mission to Central Sulawesi."

[13] Norwegian Refugee Council IDMC (Internal Displacement Monitoring Centre), "Support Needed for Return and Re-integration of Displaced Acehnese Following Peace Agreement," www.internal-displacement.org, accessed July 26, 2006.

fighting should be reinstated (*Semua hak-hak kepemilikan harus dikembalikan kepada pemiliknya yang sah, sebagaimana adanya sebelum konflik dan perselisihan berlangsung*). Taking these two points together, most assume that Point 8 is an injunction to return all Poso District residents to the houses they fled between 1998 and 2002 or, if necessary, to new houses rebuilt on or near the sites where earlier ones were destroyed. That is likely what most of the Malino Accord's nearly fifty signatories intended, and it is the policy advocated by almost all NGO and government officials I encountered. It basically sets an unspecified date for the onset of violence during the 2000 to 2002 conflict period as a Day Zero, the goal being to restore people to their Day Zero situations.

By contrast, many other Poso District residents reasoned that if, after the fighting, a Protestant migrant to Poso City returned to his or her natal home in highland Tentena, or if a recent Muslim migrant or militia member fled back home to Java or South Sulawesi, they had in effect returned to their true "place of origin." For example, some Muslims in Poso City made it clear to me that they thought it proper that many Pamona and Minahasa Christians had returned (during the violence) to their respective ancestral homes in Tentena and North Sulawesi. By contrast, one Protestant claimed that a large number of the Muslims living in 2003 along the road between Poso City and Tentena arrived from South Sulawesi and Java *after* the fighting began. He claimed the Malino Accord thus specified that "they should be returned to their earlier situation, but [the Malino decree] was not being enforced" (*mereka harus dikembalikan ke situasi dulu tetapi tidak diterapkan*).

In other words, it became a matter of debate, in both theoretical and practical terms, for whom Poso City or locations in the surrounding Poso District really are "places of origin" (*tempat asalnya*). Despite recent pre-1998 migration trends that diversified the district ethnically and gave Muslims a slight population majority, Protestants were long established in the highlands while some Muslim communities were long-established on the coasts. So the issue is not just who belongs in the Poso District, but also *who belongs where*. Some exclusivist Protestants say that Poso was historically "a Protestant region" and should remain so, with Muslims returning to their "places of origin."

By contrast, Muslims say they have a perfect right to be Poso residents, and Malino Accord's Point 6 supports them by asserting that all citizens have an equal right to immigrate to Poso and stay in peace, respecting local customs (*Tanah Poso adalah bagian integral dari Republik Indonesia. Karena itu, setiap warga Negara memiliki hak untuk hidup, datang, dan tinggal secara damai dan menghormati adat istiadat setempat*). Some exclusivist Muslims then up the ante by claiming that Indonesia is a Muslim nation (or has a "Muslim culture"), and therefore it is the Christians, vestigial lackeys of the Dutch colonial empire and foreign missionaries, who really do not belong in Poso or anywhere else in the nation.

In a very Weberian sense, localized religious teachings have enhanced Protestants' and Muslims' divergent outlooks and economic strategies in Poso. Most Protestants' contemporary ethnic and social identities were constructed through their ancestry as rice farmers in the missionized highlands.[14] By contrast, many Muslim migrants' ethnic and social identities were constructed through chains of migration and complementary religious practices that support economic migration

---

[14] See Albert Schrauwers, *Colonial "Reformation" in the Highlands of Central Sulawesi, Indonesia, 1892–1995* (Toronto: University of Toronto Press, 2000).

with scriptures that deemphasize local land sacredness in favor of distant sacred sites in Saudi Arabia. These general differences in economic, ethnic, and religious backgrounds support refugees' varied decisions about "return," both why some were more inclined to return to pre-conflict locations than others, and why some argue that their groups are more justified than other people to return to those locations.

The infelicitous debates about places of origin often became moot in reality because the plan of returning everyone from Poso to his or her pre-conflict residence was impossible in many instances. Hostile new occupants, often refugees themselves, moved into prior house sites vacated during 1998–2002 fighting. For example, in the formerly Protestant neighborhood of Lombogia in Poso City, only families of Muslims whose adult women wore black full-body veils could be observed by mid-2003. Former residents who were lodging in the highlands said it was unsafe to return and they also had received no housing funds to do so.[15] Similarly, in the Dutch colonial mission town of Tentena, most former Muslim dwellings remained damaged and abandoned, with locals saying that prior owners had "gone home" (*pulang*) to Palu or Java.

Even in September 2003, public transport vehicles going north from Tentena were driven by Christians who deposited passengers at Kawua, four kilometers south of Poso City. In turn, transport vehicles from Palu or Poso City were driven by Muslims who would not drive south of Kawua, which was heavily guarded and monitored by security forces. As at dozens of other army posts, all vehicles were stopped and required to pay a fee. If anyone traveling did not have a residency identity card (marked with his or her religious affiliation), soldiers requested higher payments.[16]

Aside from the logistical difficulties of gathering refugee head counts for various villages and semantic difficulties of interpreting the Malino Accord requirements for "return," independent economic and political motivations for over-reporting or under-reporting refugees existed. In cases where aid funds were prorated according to the number of refugees, figures were apt to be inflated. By contrast, government officials directly responsible for the design and implementation of the Malino Accord were highly motivated to support its success with claims that violence had decreased and all displaced persons would be returned to their houses.

In late December 2001, the Indonesian government declared that all of the over one million persons displaced from the outer island regional conflicts would return or resettle by December 31, 2002, because that was when state aid would be terminated.[17] In fact, the target date arrived before many areas were safe, and the

---

[15] The misuse of refugee aid funds and conflict-related corruption are treated elsewhere, including in Lorraine V. Aragon, "Profiting from Displacement," *Inside Indonesia* 77 (January–March 2004): 14–15; and Lorraine V. Aragon, "Elite Competition in Central Sulawesi," in *Renegotiating Boundaries: Local Politics in Post-Soeharto Indonesia*, ed. Henk Schulte Nordholt and Gerry Van Klinken (Leiden: KITLV Press, 2007), pp. 39–66. The latter essay also covers the results of redistricting and decentralization initiatives and their links to the prolonged violence in Poso.

[16] Aragon, "Elite Competition."

[17] Christopher R. Duncan, "Confusing Deadlines: IDPs in Indonesia," *Forced Migration Review* 17 (2003): 35–36; and Duncan, "Unwelcome Guests," p. 26. See also Christopher Duncan, "Where Do We Go from Here? The Politics of Ending Displacement in Post-Conflict North Maluku," this volume.

government was forced to continue spending more aid for troubled regions such as Poso and Maluku.

I spent an afternoon in September 2003 arranging to interview Muslims and Protestants located at two separate refugee camps in the Poso District. Afterward I had an appointment to meet a Poso District politician who was involved closely with the Malino Accord and was on its implementation team. I asked the seasoned leader of an old Gorontalo migrant community based in Poso City which aspects of the Malino Accord he felt had been successful and where improvements might be made. He responded with assurance:

> If I am honest, Ma'am—and we want to be honest—not all the Malino Accord goals are 100 percent fulfilled. Some are only 10 percent fulfilled. Some are only 25 percent fulfilled. Some only 50 percent fulfilled, and some about 75 percent fulfilled. But the one goal that is almost 100 percent fulfilled is that all the people who fled already have returned home.

Were my ears still clogged from the last airplane ride? I seriously wondered if I had gone deaf but concluded I had not by looking at the gentleman's words, which I had transcribed fully in Indonesian in my notebook. Stunned, I sat quietly for the remainder of our meeting and listened to the politician describe how relations had so improved between Poso Muslims and Christians since 2000 that I now could safely tour and see for myself the reconstruction of the district. In fact, I had been driven through several neighborhoods in Poso City earlier that day and had marveled at the still devastated buildings and hostile graffiti.[18] A young man I met earlier claimed he was one of only three Christians who dared stay in Poso City at night, and that was possible only because he lodged with a Muslim-led NGO and was a little known recent migrant whose physical appearance allowed him to pass as a Muslim.

The Poso City politician later added that a very few refugees had not returned, but simply because their houses had not yet been rebuilt.[19] He assured me that the problem of safety had been addressed well and that the Poso citizenry was no longer susceptible to provocation. "Bomb explosions happen every day in Jakarta and the developed nations," he noted, as if violence were the new hallmark of Indonesian national development.

Afterward, the NGO colleague who accompanied me asked why I did not challenge the politician's statements. My companion perhaps thought me spineless. I responded simply that I sought information, not a combative exchange, and that once the politician spouted obvious lies there was not much more useful information I could expect from him. I also had been educated to show quiet respect for elders who granted me an audience.

But why, I persisted, was the regional spokesman lying to me? The only sense my several Muslim NGO colleagues could make of this attempted ruse was that an Indonesian cabinet minister recently had delivered a similar rosy story to the US Congress. Thus, they suggested, the regional official would not wish to contradict the cabinet minister's public claims, despite all local evidence to the contrary. The

---

[18] See Aragon, "Mass Media Fragmentation," pp. 45–52.

[19] The reasonable explanation of "no housing yet" is used differently by politicians minimizing security risks and by refugees fearful to return to their former neighborhoods but unwilling to say they don't want to live as members of a small minority among people of the other religion.

Indonesian government also likely sought to reduce the official number of displaced persons in order to end its aid commitments, even as some village heads sought to inflate the numbers to keep aid funds available. The half-truths pulled in both directions.

THE PUZZLE OF RETURN PREFERENCES

Although I began collecting data about those who fled and took refuge in private homes as soon as the Poso conflict began, I made two trips to Poso in June and September 2003 that were focused specifically on assessing refugee conditions at camps through site visits and interviews. At the end of my September 2003 trip, after interviewing roughly one hundred individuals, I found myself drawing a Chi Square chart of Muslims' and Christians' stated preferences about whether they did or did not want to return to their pre-conflict locations. Within each of the four squares I plotted lists of where groups of refugees I met were from, and to where they had fled. It was clear that almost all of the Protestants I interviewed expressed a desire to "return home" (*pulang*) to their pre-conflict neighborhood as soon as it was safe and otherwise possible to do so. By contrast, almost all of the Muslims I interviewed said they personally did not want to return to their former villages, but rather intended to forge a new livelihood at their current refugee location. Despite the incompleteness of my sample, I was struck by this clear trend.

I showed the rough sketch of my data to a Muslim colleague who had been part of a team studying and reporting on the conflict for several years.[20] He agreed that my chart accurately represented trends in return versus resettlement decisions that he, too, had observed. When I solicited my colleague's ideas for why this disparity existed, however, he provided a reason that was different than, although not mutually exclusive to, the line of explanation I was developing. He suggested that those whose losses, however great, were only of material property were far more eager to return home than those whose losses included physical injuries to themselves or their loved ones. Muslims, he stated concisely, had experienced more deaths and physical injuries than Christians, who had lost more homes and land.

Despite the lack of verifiable statistics on casualties, there is likely some validity to my colleague's thesis. Most public estimates concerning the over one thousand probable deaths through 2003 place the Muslim toll in the Poso conflict higher than that for Christians.[21] Moreover, Muslims who spoke negatively to me about returning to prior locations in Poso also often described the violence they had endured. On the other hand, some Protestant refugees also experienced violence and lost relatives, yet still they wanted to "return home" to Poso. After additional interviews and analysis, I concluded that interviewees' descriptions of their migration backgrounds and how they view their relevant social communities and "homelands" also can explain, with fewer exceptions, the disparities between the observed Muslims' and Christians' general return preferences.

---

[20] See S. Sinansari ecip, Darwis Waru, and Alip Yog Kunandar, *Rusuh Poso, Rujuk Malino* (Jakarta: Cahaya Timur, 2002).

[21] The problematic implications and debatability of Poso death-toll claims are beyond the scope of this essay, but there is further discussion in Aragon, "Mass Media Fragmentation," p. 51.

REFUGEE NARRATIVES ABOUT RECENT MIGRATIONS OR LIFELONG HOMELANDS

Although I revised interview questions and planned protocols on a case-by-case basis, my inclination to "first, do no harm" led me toward more of a listening approach than a data-driven inquisition. I generally allowed refugees' stories to unfold without interruption. I never took notes or photographs when I sensed the request might be unwelcome, and always only with verbal permission after an explanation of my background and research interests. When necessary, I made written notes just after, rather than during, meetings. Although I have been able to obtain longitudinal follow-up information about a few of the individuals I met (in one instance for a period of six consecutive years), in most cases what I learned about a person's situation concerns only one place at one particular time. Thus, the cases I present below carry importance comparable to that of a snapshot—that is, their value for scholarship is more exemplary than comprehensive, more qualitative than quantitative. I present them here, in as precise a form as readability allows, not to purvey them as accounts of "exactly what happened"—clearly some claims are less than credible—but to lay out for later analysis the kind of narrative forms or storylines that circulate among Poso refugees. I chose the narratives of these particular individuals based on their fullness and situational diversity, qualities I sought in lieu of the systematic data collection that was impossible under circumstances of research during violent times. For background, I add some context of our meetings, and information on camp or village conditions that I gleaned from NGO staff, government officials, or other refugee interviews.

A striking division among the narratives I heard was that between recent migrants, mostly Muslims, and those who identified themselves as indigenous people or lifelong residents who were "already Poso people" (*sudah orang Poso*). Many of the Muslim refugees I interviewed at either camps in the district or private homes outside the district had come to Poso as voluntary economic migrants during the 1990s. Almost invariably they would tell me about several locations on Sulawesi where they tried to make a living before they moved to the Poso District. These stories suggest that Poso had become a routine destination for a class of highly mobile but relatively poor, landless, and uneducated laborers by the end of the Suharto regime. In some cases, the migrant men had traveled with other family members. In other cases, they had ventured out on their own, marrying local women after their arrival in Poso. They usually settled near relatives from their home regions in South Sulawesi or Java, in keeping with familiar chain migration patterns.

Some migrants from South Sulawesi began as timber workers for new forestry concessions before saving enough money to buy land for cash cropping. In one case I was surprised by how a voluntary Javanese migrant who arrived without capital was able to obtain more than one hectare of land and over a thousand fruiting cacao trees in just a few years. This and other comparable stories suggested that Poso government authorities were supporting the arrival of voluntary migrants through the assisted allocation of fallow local lands that could be used for cacao tree seedlings.[22] None of the South Sulawesi or Javanese refugees I spoke with planned to

---

[22] More details on the 1990s cacao boom and land alienation are in Aragon, "Communal Violence in Poso," and Lorraine V. Aragon, "Migrasi, Komoditi Expor, dan Sejarah Perubahan Hak Pemakaian Tanah di Sulawesi Tengah," in *Berebut Tanah: Beberapa Kajian Berspektif Kampus dan Kampung,* ed. Anu Lounela and R. Yando Zakaria (Yogyakarta: INSISTPress, 2002), pp. 271–82.

return to their natal provinces, from which they had become estranged, *or* to return to their pre-conflict Poso locations. Instead they were seeking wage jobs at their post-2000 refuge sites in coastal Muslim enclaves of the Poso District.

Protestants I interviewed usually told a different type of story. Most had lived their entire lives in a single village or neighborhood of the Poso District, but there were class-based differences. Commoners who had moved had done so to work a spouse's ancestral land, while a few Protestant elite had moved to urban areas for education or civil-service jobs. Most displaced Protestants, however, were subsistence food farmers with a small area of their inherited fields reserved for cash crops. They noted that Muslim migrants increasingly arrived to buy land and cash-crop plots up to twenty times larger than the one to two hectares traditionally farmed for food by ordinary locals.

My ethnographic interviews with Muslim migrants and Protestant "natives" revealed how the outcomes of broader demographic and agricultural changes were diversely perceived.[23] Muslim migrants said they were "just trying to make a living," that in the Poso District there were large parcels of "empty" (*kosong*) forest land, which they had been able to make more productive and profitable. In their view, local Protestants had welcomed them into the region because they were hard workers, skilled at cash cropping, and able to introduce better prices for useful trade goods through their inter-regional migrant networks. Most migrants I spoke to claimed they had no idea their neighbors resented them until the very day they were threatened with violence and forced to flee.

Given the issue of trust, and its influence on open speech, I tried where possible to arrange interviews through friendships I had established from fieldwork well prior to the post-Suharto violence, as well as before post-September 11, 2001, wars.[24] I met additional Muslim and Protestant refugees through collaboration and travel with all-Muslim or Muslim-led NGO groups. Generally, the leaders of these groups were familiar with my academic work, or we were connected through older personal ties. I worked with groups based in Jakarta, Palu, and Poso City. The impressive staffs of these groups were able to facilitate visits to camps and village neighborhoods hosting significant numbers of refugees. I begin with excerpts from interviews with recent Muslim migrants, follow with those of "indigenous" Protestants, and then add some "betwixt and between" cases where Muslims' and Christians' claims to rights and land entail other ideological debates.

CASE 1: A MAKASSAR–BUGIS FAMILY THAT FLED FROM POSO PESISIR TO PALU IN 2000

In July 2000, I made a social visit to a Muslim Kaili family I had known closely for about fifteen years. Sometime after I arrived at their home outside of Palu, the mother mentioned that, by coincidence, they were sheltering a family of eighteen Poso refugees in a small house their family owned across the road. The refugees'

---

[23] I follow local use of terms indicating that someone is "native," "indigenous," or "original" (*asli*), recognizing that those categories are constructed, flexible, and political. Such terms connote a range of ideas: from alleged "first settlers," to the more vague and jingoistic "sons of the soil" (*pribumi*), to the simple reference to current residents descended from people with no other known origins.

[24] From 1986 to 1989 I lived continuously in Central Sulawesi conducting dissertation fieldwork and analysis. I made several other trips to the region before and after those dates prior to the Poso conflict, and repeated ones since then.

household centered around a marriage between a Makassarese man and a Bugis woman from Bone, South Sulawesi.

The Makassarese husband had come to the Poso District in 1994—just four years before the violence began—to work for a timber concession in the Poso Pesisir subdistrict. His Bugis wife and her mother then followed. There were now eighteen of them ranging in age from the elderly grandmother (the mother's mother) to a five-year-old child. They had resided in the village of Tokorondo, an older coastal settlement that had become heavily mixed with new Muslim migrants like themselves. The wages garnered from the husband's timber job had allowed the family to buy land to plant cacao trees. They said they thought their relations with their Protestant neighbors were good—until they heard news of the violence spreading from village to village along the roads out of Poso City at the end of June 2000. Then, suddenly, they did not know who was friend (*kawan*) and who was foe (*lawan*). The husband said that neighbors they had thought were their friends really were their enemies. Some told them to escape before they were physically harmed, and the family then "fled with just the clothes on their backs."

The family had heard from other refugees coming to Palu more recently that their cacao gardens had not been burned, but the fruits had all been picked, presumably by the Christians who invaded. The father said that the road from Poso City to Palu had been open again for one month but they were too angry and sick at heart (*sakit hati*) to return. He said he had heard that some rich Protestant Pamona person living in Jakarta was paying 250 million rupiah for each Muslim head taken by the Flores militia fighter, Tibo. Cornelius (a.k.a. Fabianus) Tibo, widely publicized as the "mastermind" of Poso's 2000 violence, was still at large on that date although he would be captured a week later.

The family displayed anger and even repulsion for the place and people of Poso (*orang Poso*). The father planned to look for work in Muslim-majority Palu instead. He said he was a skilled car mechanic and would pursue employment in one of Palu's many auto repair shops. The family had received no government aid, just help from the local Muslims into whose neighborhood they entered. Although I cannot verify what happened to this family after 2000, I observed the anguish they had experienced and noted that their bitterness against Poso Christians had made an impression upon my Muslim Kaili friends, who lacked any personal experience with the places or peoples of Poso. The family's stay in Poso had been only four years long, and there were no community roots there to make the family's "return" anything meaningful beyond the issues of lost crops, livelihood, and property.

CASE 2: A JAVANESE MAN WHO FLED FROM SINTUWU LEMBA TO PALU IN 2000

In September 2003, I accompanied a friend to visit a Muslim Bugis family in northeastern Palu. Refugees from the violence in Poso had come to inhabit some ramshackle buildings near their small wooden house. I was told that after the May 2000 killings of Muslims in the Javanese transmigrant village of Sintuwu Lemba (known more widely as Kilo 9), refugees from Poso just began showing up and camping under tarps around their solidly Muslim neighborhood in Palu. The family said that they and their ethnic Bugis neighbors took pity on the refugees, gave them food and occasional work, and helped them erect some simple wooden dwellings.

One Javanese refugee whom I met was originally from Jember, East Java. He was a voluntary migrant who followed on the heels of the more formal transmigration group to Kilo 9. He said he had only a grade-school education, and clearly he was accustomed to hard physical work outdoors. He told how he first landed by boat in Gorontalo, North Sulawesi, in 1996, but soon moved to Kendari, Southeast Sulawesi, then to Poso, Central Sulawesi. He entered the ethnically East Javanese settlement nine kilometers south of Poso City. Later, his Javanese wife and two children joined him. More people from his home area in East Java arrived later. But, he said sadly, only one of the eight comrades he knew from his home area survived the violence at Kilo 9.

Between his arrival in 1996 and the violence he experienced in May 2000, the young man said he had cultivated 1,500 cacao trees, which would cover about 1.5 hectares. He did not say how he came to own the trees, or the land on which they were planted. He did not speak at all about relations with local Protestants from nearby villages. He merely said he was caught in the May–July 2000 fighting around Poso and was captured three times by Christian militias, the last time being in the custody of the infamous Flores militia leader Tibo and his band of fighters.[25] He showed me small scars on his wrists where he said he had been bound with ropes. Ultimately, he was freed by an army company who transported and released him just south of Poso City. By then, however, he was separated from his wife and two children who, as it turned out, were rescued by Reverend Rinaldy Damanik, director of the Central Sulawesi Protestant Church Crisis Center evacuation team.[26] After much pleading, a soldier on a motorcycle took him to fetch his wife and children.

With his nuclear family reunited, the East Javanese refugee returned to Kilo 9 and rebuilt a home with government assistance. But, he said, his house was destroyed a second time in 2002, and he decided he did not want to live in Poso anymore. He was now working as a day laborer in Palu, clearly just scraping by.

The most notable part of the Javanese migrant's story was that he was an eyewitness caught in what is often called the Kilo 9, or Walisongo, massacre of May 2000. Out of curiosity, before he left I asked if he had a residence card for Kilo 9. He said he didn't have one for there but he had later obtained one for a Muslim neighborhood in Poso City called Gebangrejo. I knew the neighborhood and some of its young Javanese and South Sulawesi migrants— Gebangrejo was an area to where many formerly rural Muslim migrants fled. I glanced at the man's card, wondering whether he had ever had a legal residency card before the conflict. Poso City had become almost entirely Muslim after the violence, and efforts had been made to register both voters and potential aid recipients.

Although I do not know the current status of this refugee, his Bugis hosts later said that some of his East Javanese cohort had taken a three million rupiah (about US$300) payment from the government and returned to their natal home area near

---

[25] Tibo and two associates were arrested in late July 2000, and convicted and sentenced to death in 2001 for violent acts and provocation. After repeated failed legal appeals and several delays, the three men were executed by firing squad in Palu on September 22, 2006. For details, see Dave McRae, "Criminal Justice and Communal Conflict: A Case Study of the Trial of Fabianus Tibo, Dominggus da Silva, and Marinus Riwu," *Indonesia* 83 (April 2007): 79–117.

[26] Damanik was arrested and jailed in 2002 after being vilified in the press by some government and Muslim groups. See Aragon, "Mass Media Fragmentation" and Rinaldy Damanik, *Tragedi Kemanusiaan Poso* (Palu: PBHI & LPS–HAM Sulteng, 2003). Convicted of carrying weapons in his car during an evacuation effort, he was released after three years for good behavior.

Banyuwangi. Some others had returned to a rebuilt settlement at Kilo 9, while the rest had found work and stayed in Palu like the man described.

CASE 3: A MANDAR MAN WHO FLED FROM TENTENA TO THE CAMP AT MAPANE, POSO PESISIR

In September 2003, I visited the village and Muslim refugee barracks in Mapane, Poso Pesisir subdistrict. The women I saw in the old village were not wearing headscarves or specifically Muslim dress, but when we crossed the soccer field to the refugee barracks, all the women I saw were so attired. A government official later provided documentation that there were 409 households and 1,453 residents in Mapane. Given that Mapane had been burned once, all the residents were labeled as "those who already returned" (*yang sudah kembali*), while forty-three households, or 136 people, reportedly Protestants, were said not to have come back after the violence. The returned population was classified as 75 percent farmers, 10 percent fishermen, 10 percent civil servants, and 5 percent laborers.

I listened to the story of a young ethnic Mandar man born in Polmas, South Sulawesi, twenty years earlier. He had recently migrated voluntarily (*merantau*) to near Tentena. He said he was just a farmer, didn't know how to fish or trade, and had been given a plot of teak (*kayu jati*) by the regional government (*Pemda* or *Pemerintah Daerah*). But, he added, because the land was part of a conservation area, he owned no land title. Thus, the land that had provided his income actually was in a protected area and not legally his to return to. In 2000, his neighbors told him he had better flee. His uncle who stayed was killed. The man lost his house and everything he owned except a sack of rice. His house was destroyed as soon as he left it.

The author talking with refugee families at an army-built barracks for non-local Muslims in Mapane, Poso Pesisir subdistrict, September 2003.

The Mandar refugee said he did not want to return to Tentena, that it was better in Mapane with his "Bugis family." He was now farming the land of an ethnic Bugis government official. The official said that the biggest problem around the camp was a lack of work and land. "If the refugees had work, they would forget about revenge" (*Kalau mereka ada kerja, mereka akan lupa balas dendam*). While the official said there ultimately needed to be an end to financial aid, he also was adamant that post-conflict building projects such as the refugee camp barracks should have been carried out by locals, not army troops sent from Palu.

I met other refugees in the Mapane camp who had fled from Tentena, Pandiri, and Betalemba, all Protestant-majority highland areas. They were mostly ethnic Bugis migrants who had come voluntarily from South Sulawesi to farm cacao, or sometimes coconut, trees. One spoke of three hundred migrant families from Pandiri who, after being attacked and having their houses burned two times, had moved away permanently. Many had come with him to Mapane, although some dispersed through family connections to South Sulawesi, Kalimantan, and Malaysia. He said he had briefly tried working some fellow Bugis Muslims' wet-rice fields near Palu, but then returned to the Mapane camp. He stated that everyone in the camp did not want to return to prior (Protestant majority) residence areas even though they only had received about half of the government aid promised to them as camp residents.

CASE 4: A PAMONA WOMAN FROM LAGE, WHO FLED TO THE LATER CAMP AT TENTENA

In conjunction with Muslim NGO staff, I met with a Protestant NGO leader who worked at the Later refugee camp in Tentena. "Later" is an acronym for *Lapangan Terbang*, meaning "air field." The refugee camp was erected by refugees on a former Mission Aviation Fellowship (MAF) airstrip, existing on land owned by the synod of the Central Sulawesi Protestant Church (Gereja Kristen Protestan Sulawesi Tengah, or GKST). Once violence in coastal Poso began and thousands of Protestants flowed into Tentena, the church loaned the land bordering Poso Lake to accommodate the refugee population temporarily.

In September 2003, I spoke with several refugees living at Later Camp. One Pamona woman, who had lived her whole life in Batugencu, Lage, said her highland Protestant village was attacked on June 25, 2000, without warning. They had just finished the harvest festival when they heard that Poso City was in chaos. Suddenly they themselves had to flee. They received news from their neighboring village to the east, Sepe. The woman's family first fled west to Togulu, then south to Pandiri. In all these places, there were not many police to help, so they moved farther south in the mountains to Tentena.

This Pamona woman said she had tried to return home and rebuild, but houses in Batugencu were burned three times: in June 2000; on December 1, 2001; and then on July 22, 2002, when the neighboring villages of Sepe and Silanca were burned, too. The Batugencu church was burned twice and the third one was then built by the government. She said that in December 2001 even the security forces ran from the militias, because the outsider Muslim militias were more numerous than official forces. There were no deaths from her village, she explained, because there was no opposition. "We just ran," she said. If Batugencu became safe again, she wanted to go home (*kalau aman, mau pulang*).

Houses built by Protestant refugees on church-owned land by Poso Lake in Tentena.
September 2003. (Photo by Lorraine V. Aragon)

The woman said she had owned a cacao grove and dry- and wet-rice fields, but she was not "brave enough" to return and farm rice again. Instead, she was doing small farm labor jobs in Tentena, such as picking cloves on others' land. She lived just off these wages. She said the living allowance promised by the government (*Jaminan Hidup* or *Jadup*) had not yet been dispersed. Many had returned to Batugencu and rebuilt houses on their own from local forest timber, but she had not been able to afford that. Only about thirty people from her village ever received aid, and that was just a rice allotment after the first attacks in 2000. She summed up her view of government aid with a pun linking the Indonesian word for "promise" with the Pamona word for "lie." "These are not promises, but lies," (*ini bukan janji tapi janjee'*). "The point is," she concluded philosophically, "when there is money enough, I will go home. If there is chaos again, I will flee again."

CASE 5: A PAMONA WOMAN FROM TOJO, WHO FLED TO THE LATER CAMP AT TENTENA

I spoke to another Pamona woman at the Later Camp who had fled in mid-2000 from Galuga, Tojo subdistrict. Galuga is a coastal village that had been about 50 percent Christian (mixing ethnic Pamona, Mori, Toraja, Manado, and Sanghir) and 50 percent Muslim (mostly Bugis from Masamba, South Sulawesi). This mixed-religion village was located between two Muslim villages. In Galuga the woman owned gardens with cacao trees, capsicum peppers, and cloves, but her trees were all cut down. The attackers (*penyerang*) used chainsaws so that they could plunder her village's harvest quickly. They burned all the rice fields. It made residents "additionally resentful" (*tambah lebih sakit hati*) that their food was just burned, destroyed, in this way. Maybe, she said, the Muslims who had lost relatives in the prior days of violence were so mad that, when they found no people to hurt in her

Protestant village, they destroyed their own potential food. Cows were led away to be sold, pigs were killed and hung up in the church or in trees. But, she added with slight satisfaction, "They are the ones who smelled [the rotting carcasses]. We already had run away" (*Mereka yang cium. Kita sudah lari*).

The attackers, who were not recognizable (*tidak dikenal*), wore masks and arrived by boat from the Bay of Tomini. When attacked, she and her fellow villagers ran to the forests and stayed hidden in their gardens waiting for signs of evacuation vehicles (*kendaraan evakuasi*). People from Ampana (a Muslim center to the east) ran by. "We were squeezed," she said, "between two Muslim villages: Bambalo and Toliba, which were both Tojo and not attacked."[27] First her family fled west to Silanca where they had Protestant relatives. Then they moved further inland—up the mountains to Tentena.

Road sign in Poso highlands displaying Pamona motto *Sintuwu Maroso*, meaning "United We are Strong." After the violence, Pamona jokingly rephrased the motto as *Sintuwu Malonco*, "United We Flee." September 2003. (Photo by Lorraine V. Aragon)

The woman explained that "those of us who fled lived while those who fought died, victims on the fields of war" (*korban di lapangan perang*). Those who did not join the fighting but instead ran to the forest did not die. She said her group never directly faced enemy weapons, or maybe they, too, would have defended

---

[27] Muslim Tojo and Protestant Pamona share a common language and history, which has become divided only by ecological and religious separation. The recent emergence of this ethnic identity divide is discussed in Aragon, "Elite Competition."

themselves. The woman's explanation reinforced one of the many examples of humorous wordplay that Poso refugees invented to characterize their situation. The Pamona language motto of the Poso District, displayed on many outdoor signs and banners, is *Sintuwu Maroso*, meaning "United We Are Strong." After the conflict, many Pamona refugees say the motto runs, *Sintuwu Malonco*, meaning "United We Flee."

The woman explained that she wanted to return home, but she still felt too traumatized (*rasa trauma*). She said that five months after they fled in 2000, the subdistrict head (*camat*) invited refugees to return home because her village was not burned down—as many others had been. But less than one month later, Galuga *was* burned to the ground. Again, there were no casualties, but all property was destroyed. Then there was more destruction in 2002. Attackers first struck Silanca, to the west, then moved on to Galuga. The church and school were burned along with thirty homes that had just been rebuilt by the army.

The woman told how refugee men from Galuga go back there during the week to tend coconut trees, but they return to the Later camp on weekends to attend church and see their families. She said Galuga was now guarded by regional police from Pare-Pare (South Sulawesi), Kendari (Southeast Sulawesi), and mobile brigades from Papua. She said the security presence had improved the situation.

The Pamona added that, before the fighting, the village head of Galuga was Protestant, but he was "released" (*dibebaskan*) and the replacement was a Bugis Muslim from Masamba, South Sulawesi. No one from his office has come to invite the Protestants back. "It is said that he is afraid to come to Tentena because of the bats (*kelelawar*)."[28] She said that maybe local officials really feel they committed faults against the people (*ada kesalahan ke masyarakat*) and so they don't come to visit for fear they would get an earful. The woman claimed that only eighty-nine Muslim households (both pre- and post-conflict residents) now are registered as living in Galuga. The "original ones" (*yang asli*) are not registered. Now the village land is being used by Muslims there. Fewer than 50 percent of the former Christian households have returned and registered. But, she added, her mother's house is still not occupied by squatters because she possesses a legal certificate.[29]

The woman from Galuga then employed a metaphor I encountered repeatedly: that of refugees being needy children, unwanted by uncaring or neglectful parents. She asked rhetorically, "How can people return if their parents never visit them? We feel just like stepchildren (*Bagaimana orang masyarakat mau kembali kalau orang tua tidak pernah mengunjungi? Kita sudah anak tiri rasanya*). She continued by saying, "We can't return and camp in the church or school because they are burned. And we can't go sleep on the floor of the mosque, obviously."

---

[28] This is a gallows-humor reference to the Bat militia, a term for Protestant fighters, some of whom were led in mid-2000 by the Flores Catholic migrant Fabianus Tibo (see Aragon, "Communal Violence in Poso," pp. 66–67; and McRae, "Criminal Justice and Communal Conflict").

[29] The inconsistency here—concerning whether no Protestants are registered in Galuga or only less than half—is in the original. Also, this older woman refers to "her mother's house" not only because of the legal certificate, but also because homes in highland Central Sulawesi are traditionally passed through the female line. Despite the mention by many interviewees of the importance of legal land titles, there are genuine debates in Indonesia about whether it is easier for land to be confiscated by politically powerful outsiders when local individuals do, or do not, own certificates.

The Pamona woman said that of the two hundred Protestant families from Galuga residing at the Later camp, one hundred had received nothing from the Social Department (Depsos, or Departemen Sosial) and no promised living allowance (*jadup*), either. She said fifty-two families from Galuga want to build a new village near Tentena. The unoccupied land will be bought in installments (*dibeli cicilan*) by the refugees. But she said that she won't sell her unoccupied house land in Galuga because that is the "inheritance for her children" (*warisan anak*). Returning home, in this woman's mind, might be delayed even for a generation, but it would still come.

An NGO worker at the Later camp said there was no stigma in being a refugee in Tentena, that the situation was not like in Manado, North Sulawesi.[30] He was concerned, however, that Lake Poso was becoming increasingly polluted from the over five hundred resident refugee families and the wet-rice fields they had created nearby. The NGO leader said that those who could return to former locations should do so because land around Tentena is limited and shortages might give rise to more conflict. Ultimately, he concluded, everyone must go home. "All that remains needed is some process by which they can be returned home."

I heard repeatedly that all Pamona at the camps "want to return home but are not yet able to build houses" (*mau pulang tapi belum bisa membangun rumah*). Although often unstated, the obstacles clearly included safety as well as financial issues. Forty Protestants tried to return to the Poso City Muslim neighborhood of Kayamanya, but their new houses had been burned down. Because they felt greater safety in numbers, and their children had been attending Tentena schools, most were inclined to buy land around Tentena if possible. Thus, Protestant farmers reported a distinct desire to "return home," but because of the lack of safety and funds, many were hedging their bets with alternate plans to reside around Tentena.[31]

CASE 6: A PAMONA CIVIL SERVANT WHO FLED FROM POSO CITY TO TENTENA

I discovered in 2003 that many Pamona Protestants were "commuting" either weekly or daily between highland Tentena and their former towns or cities near the coast. At the Later camp, I was told that, three months earlier, there were only women and children there because the men had gone to tend crops at their former villages. By contrast, many Pamona civil servants who worked in Poso City before the conflict began now left there every night for safety.

When I visited a Pamona academic administrator at the Poso University (Universitas Sintuwu Maroso, or UNSINMAR) campus in Poso City, I was surprised to hear him exclaim, "I myself am a refugee." This man had been seriously wounded by gunshot in 2000 soon after he tried to mediate a campus dispute between some Muslim and Protestant youths. He had nearly died and was still visibly handicapped from his wound. He explained that now, six days a week, he spent several hours traveling each way to work at the university by day, and returned home each night to sleep safely at his house in Tentena. He said that all the Christian civil servants

---

[30] See Duncan, "Unwelcome Guests," and also Duncan, "Where Do We Go from Here?," in this volume.

[31] The NGO leader said some Muslims also returned to Kilo 9 (Sintuwu Lemba) and local Protestants were willing to receive them, but that, because of the traumatic events that occurred there, Muslims needed to be protected by security forces or Protestant guards. He said the rebuilt Protestant high school in Kasiguncu was being guarded by security forces and the Protestant Lombogia school will need protection, too, if it is ever rebuilt.

assigned to Poso City were forced to do that, and their salaries now mostly went to carfare. Many of the older Pamona civil servants, he said, simply retired to Tentena.

I was told by NGO workers in Tentena that about 75 percent of Protestants who fled from Poso City were civil servants. Many of them already owned land in Tentena because they were from older families native to the area.[32] But neighborhoods within Poso City were the hardest places for Christian refugees to return to. Along with some other now all-Muslim areas of Poso Pesisir and eastern Tojo Timur, the district capital of Poso City was considered too dangerous for Christians, and their house sites had been appropriated by Muslims, who also often were refugees themselves. The Pamona university official said that a lack of money, rather than Muslim squatters, was the major impediment to the rebuilding of his house in Poso City. He asserted that the government *could* evict the squatters, but even if they did, he still could not afford to replace what he once had.

CASE 7: A MINAHASAN WOMAN WHO FLED FROM POSO PESISIR TO MANADO

In Manado, North Sulawesi, in September 2003, I met a group of Minahasan and mixed Minahasan–Poso Protestant families who had fled Poso City and Poso Pesisir subdistrict to the west. An ethnic Minahasan woman leading one large refugee group said that there had been approximately 3,400 Christians who came from the Poso District by July 2000. Their numbers were now still over 2,000 in about 400 households. She said these refugees from the Poso District had never gone to camps or received any government aid, but just lodged with relatives in Manado where possible. The only aid they ever saw was delivered through church congregations when they first arrived. The refugees had done whatever work was available; women without capital just prepared and sold snacks. Three years later, her refugee association was writing a letter to the Social Services Department in Poso requesting aid, but they were well aware that success was unlikely, given the vastness of refugee needs and the department's reputation for embezzlement.

The woman bitterly told how her younger sister, who stayed in Betania Village in mid-2000 after others in her family left, was shot and killed. A younger sibling of her husband who lived in Silanca, Lage, was shot in August 2002. She noted that the army was transferred away from the village right after the shooting incident. Another of her younger in-laws was killed in highland Sangginora, Poso Pesisir, in 2002.

The woman said she had returned to visit her home village in Poso Pesisir in July 2003, and there was yet another mysterious shooting. "Maybe it is safe in the daylight," she said, "but there is still terror at night" (*aman mungkin siang tapi masih diteror kalau malam*). She said that government officials publicly called for refugees to return, but "whose neck will be the guarantee of our security?" (*leher siapa akan jadi kejaminan keamanan?*). "If Christians try to rebuild a roof on their Poso house by day, it will be stolen that night when they leave, so why bother?" she asked rhetorically.

The woman explained that she has Muslim as well as Protestant relatives. One of her grandparents' siblings converted to Islam after moving to a coastal community during the Dutch era. She said that when she talked to her former Muslim neighbors

---

[32] These facts are legacies of Dutch colonial policies, when aristocrats in the mission town of Tentena were provided with educational advantages and received many civil servant positions in the district.

and relatives in Poso Pesisir in July 2003, they said that they also are scared to go to their fields, which border Christian areas. Her Muslim relatives fled west to Pendolo during the fighting, but then returned and decided to send the jihadis who had moved in back to their own homes (*sudah dikasi pulang*). Local residents complained that the outside fighters were costly to "support" (*pelihara*, literally "to care of" like a pet or child) and also "they made jihad raping women" (*mereka jihad memperkosa perempuan*).

Her opinion was that Poso Muslims were divided on the issue of peace, that about 75 percent wanted peace and a return to normal business with Christians, while 25 percent did not. The latter, she said, were still emotional over Muslims' higher death toll, or else they benefited financially from the conflict or its favorable repercussions for Muslims. She noted that there were many new Muslim civil servants in Poso, especially pro-jihad Javanese, who took jobs that were vacated by fleeing Christians. Christian Chinese storekeepers fled, and Gorontalo Muslims just seized the abandoned shops, she claimed. She also described how Muslim Bugis migrants who formerly worked her family's wet-rice land in exchange for half the harvest now took it all.

The woman felt Poso District political leaders, both earlier Protestants and replacement Muslims, were to blame for the lack of security and the shifting inequities. She noted that the district head of Poso never once visited Manado to see his "children from the region" (*anak daerah*) after the conflict. He only visited those in Palu. She said this was because the displaced in Palu were mostly Muslims and he only wanted them to return.[33] While holding to the paternal kinship vision of politics so familiar in Indonesia, this woman presented Poso Protestants as unwanted children in Muslim-majority areas. By contrast, she claimed that the district heads from both Ambon and Maluku had come to Manado to visit their refugees.

She had heard from a cleric present at the Malino Accord negotiations that Muslims' demands (not accepted) had included prohibitions on Protestants eating pork and dancing their traditional dances. In her view, Poso's violence and displacement was a cultural attack against Protestants, which coincidentally also suited some powerful people's business agenda. As if echoing the conclusions of many NGO staff working in Poso, she said, "in an area of disturbance, there is money to be made" (*di daerah rusuh, ada uangnya*). She said that the security forces' inability to find what they term "pure criminals" (*kriminal murni*) who bomb churches in a tiny town like Poso suggests a desire to eliminate Christians.[34] They seem quite capable of finding criminal gangs deep in the jungles of Irian (now Papua), she noted. "Human rights for whom?" she asked rhetorically, "When Christians are killed, there are no human rights" (*HAM ini untuk siapa? Kalau orang Kristen dibunuh, HAM tidak ada*). Later, commenting on all the violence, she said with frustration, "in Poso, chickens are more valuable than people" (*lebih mahal ayam daripada orang di Poso*).

In this woman's view, the Malino Accord's Point 6, which says that all Indonesians have a right to live in Poso, was included because Bugis politicians want

---

[33] An independent source in Palu said that, although the Poso District head did come to Palu for provincial meetings, the public speeches he delivered in Palu never invited displaced groups to return. Rather, his office merely put announcements in the provincial newspapers declaring that everyone could return in safety.

[34] On the narrative significance of blaming "pure criminals," see Aragon, "Mass Media Fragmentation."

to control the economy of all of eastern Indonesia, not just their ethnic homeland of South Sulawesi. She noted that, unlike Chinese, Bugis migrants move into farming as well as trader roles, and they often pursue local girls. She claimed to have read a pamphlet spread among Bugis migrants that advised them to get a local girl pregnant and then ask for a face-saving marriage, which would provide access to land titles. If the girl's parents were not receptive, the pamphlet advised them to move elsewhere. The woman was outraged that this should be a condoned cultural teaching.[35]

The woman contrasted this alleged behavior by some Bugis migrants with that of Minahasan migrants to Poso. She said that although these migrants might have some Minahasan blood, they often had spent their whole lives in Poso and had buried their parents there. So, she concluded, "they are already Poso people" (*mereka sudah orang Poso*). She said the vast majority of Protestant refugees that had fled to Manado wanted to return to Poso—that the land, cacao trees, and property left behind were considerable—but they did not yet believe they would be safe.

After this Protestant refugee presented relentless accusations against the government and jihadists, I posed a question about Christian acts of violence such as the killings at Kilo 9. She answered simply, "We are not angels" (*kita bukan malaikat*). Despite biblical admonitions to turn the other cheek, she said, offering a metaphor I had heard before, when Poso Christians had been slapped twice (during the conflict's first two phases, in 1998 and 2000), there were no more cheeks left to turn. After that, she concluded, Poso Christians had to retaliate when provoked.

CASE 8: CHINESE–PAMONA FAMILY WHO FLED FROM POSO CITY TO PALU

In Palu during December 2004, I met several members of a Catholic family of ethnic Chinese, some of whom had intermarried with Pamona residents of Poso. They had lived as merchants in the Gebangrejo and Kasintuwu neighborhoods of Poso City until they were forced to flee in mid-2000.

They told me that one set of their Chinese ancestors had left Canton China and traveled via Manado to settle in Poso City during the colonial period. That original migrant couple remained Buddhist, but the children born in Poso converted to Catholicism. As one young member of the family had told me previously, the rituals and incense of the Catholic Church were more appealing to Chinese migrants than the stark practices of Dutch Protestantism.

The first Chinese migrant man soldered metal while his wife sold pork, sea-turtle meat, and a local liquor (*pongas*). Cantonese families, they told me proudly, were the original builders and "architects" (*arsitek*) of Poso City. One of the migrants' daughters married into an educated Chinese family that included the principal of Poso's Chinese school, which was shut down in 1965. During the Dutch period, they said, there were just a few migrants in Poso City: Chinese, Arabs, Bugis, and Gorontalo. These groups all lived harmoniously under the raja of Lage, who ruled indirectly for the Dutch.[36] The Chinese elders I met said several times that they

---

[35] A widely known aphorism among Bugis is that their success is based on knowing how and when to fight with "the three tips": the tip of their tongues, the tip of their penises, and the tip of their swords.

[36] A version of the apocryphal story of a colonial-era raja who admonished all migrants to Poso to live in harmony is related in Damanik, *Tragedi Kemanusiaan Poso.*

coexisted amiably with the original (Tojo) Muslim settlers and earlier Arab, Gorontalo, and Bugis migrants to Poso City; therefore, they never expected this violence.

A senior woman from the all-Chinese branch of the family said she had owned a general store in Poso City, but was forced to flee "with nothing" in 2000. She went first to Palu, then Surabaya, where she also had a house, and then back to Palu to open a new store. She said she still owned a house in Poso City but had no plans to go back. The house was being watched by a Muslim employee. I inferred that she might shift her sales business back in the direction of Poso City if it ever seemed safe again, but otherwise she would remain in Palu where she already had built a comfortable home and a retail business that sold expensive items such as gas cooking stoves on an installment plan.

A middle-aged man in the family was descended on his father's side from the same Cantonese Chinese builders, but his mother was a Pamona Christian. He had grown up in a mountain town north of Tentena, but then moved to Poso City for work. During the 2000 violence, this man lost his house in Kasintuwu near the Poso market terminal where he had owned a store.

No one in the family chose to relate details of the violence, but the man did offer a political analysis that included claims I had heard in various combinations from many kinds of people. He said all was fine in Poso City until the pre-conflict district head began to replace all the original (*asli*) officials with outsider Muslims. The district head was so corrupt that he was used by a powerful Bugis businessman to embezzle public funds. With additional money from Bugis and Tojo investors, they bought cacao and ebony seedlings. Then their cronies took residents' lands through directives implemented via official channels all the way down to village heads.

The Chinese–Pamona man then added several less widespread claims: that the murder conviction of the Catholic fighter Tibo and his two colleagues was a political set-up; and that the deaths of Muslims from Kilo 9 was not a slaughter, but the result of chaos and overloaded boats that capsized on the Poso River when panicking Muslims tried to flee. When I asked about the piles of skulls and mass graves depicted in mid-2000 newspaper photos, he claimed—somewhat improbably—that the images were taken from the fighting in Aceh.

The man concluded by saying, "whatever happens/happened, it is our region" (*Apa yang terjadi, kita punya daerah*). These were open words, with many possible connotations, but it seemed he felt that he and his Christian community still had domain rights from which they could be only temporarily displaced.

CASE 9: TWO BUGIS–RAMPI SIBLINGS WHO FLED FROM POSO TO NORTH SULAWESI

People caught in the Poso conflict who were in, or descended from, mixed-religion marriages provide theoretically challenging examples of how the "betwixt and between" often find themselves punished by the polarizing demands of violence. I met some Protestant women married perilously to Muslim men, and vice versa. Sometimes one member of the couple had to flee, either temporarily or permanently, so as not to be harmed by in-laws.

One particular case showed not the present threat for people in these mixed unions, but the trails of such hazardous pasts. I met a brother and sister who are fifth-generation descendants of a Muslim Bugis man who married a Protestant Rampi noblewoman in highland South Sulawesi. During the Darul Islam movement of the 1950s and 1960s, this mixed-religion couple fled north and took refuge among Protestants in Tentena. The family stayed there as devout Protestants. The sister had moved with her Protestant husband to North Sulawesi and then, during the Poso violence, found that she could not return. Her brother, who had served as a minister for the GKST church in the Poso highlands, traveled separately to another town in North Sulawesi.

The brother said that he and other Protestant church leaders around Tentena tried to keep Pamona refugees who arrived in 2000 from mounting revenge campaigns against Muslim villages back toward the coast, but ultimately they were unsuccessful. He said that because the government response was so blatantly pro-Muslim in the initial phases, eventually many highland Protestant congregations would not listen to pro-peace messages delivered in church. Rather, many local refugees felt that leaders of the GKST church were failing to defend local peoples' interests. Some even began to vote with their feet by converting to a more fervent and populist Pentecostalism.

Aside from refusals of cooperation from his own mixed local and refugee congregations, the minister brother received anonymous mobile-phone death threats and was "nearly killed." His sister said that the situation in November 2001 before the Malino Accord was extremely threatening for Protestants, a time when outsider jihadists proliferated and "posters of Osama bin Laden were everywhere." She had heard that there was a Rp.50,000 reward for taking the head of a Protestant minister, and one of Rp.25,000 for taking the head of an ethnic Chinese. She said she had no idea who offered those rewards. Such rumors of rewards for "enemy heads" were common among both Muslim and Protestant refugees, wrapping ancient Austronesian warfare traditions in new capitalist packaging designed to divide religious and ethnic groups.

CASE 10: A BALINESE TRANSMIGRANT MAN FROM POSO PESISIR WHO MOVED TO PALU

In December 2004, I met a man from a Hindu Balinese transmigrant family who had moved to the Poso District when he was a child. The man was currently living in Palu, where he had a Muslim Bugis wife and several children. Their marriage was in serious trouble, and they were discussing imminent separation, although I did not know that at the time of our first meeting.

The Balinese man's parents were from Tambangan, Bali, where they owned so little land that they asked the village head to sign them up for the government's transmigration program. They came to Poso City by a small boat along with about fifty others in 1979 when the man I met was just a ten-year-old boy. They were resettled with other Balinese in what came to be called Tambarana II, near the coast in Poso Pesisir. Tambarana I was a transmigration village that was assigned to Muslim Javanese. At the time his family arrived, the man said, there were few villages nearby and just poor dirt roads, traversed by oxcarts. He said that there was "too much forest": abundant ebony, mahogany, and other hardwoods. But they didn't know it was valuable. They just cut it all down for firewood and to clear the forest land for their wet-rice fields.

Starting in 1985 and 1986, cacao plants were introduced to the transmigrants by the government, but cacao prices were low, so people didn't bother with it much. They just put the seedlings they were given in their dry-crop fields. Only when cacao prices rose ten-fold, from Rp.1,100 per kilo to a peak of Rp.13,000 per kilo in 1999, did they pick and plant it like crazy.

The indigenous people (*yang asli*) of Poso didn't plant much cacao because they were unfamiliar with it. Then, during the 1998 financial crisis (*Krismon*), "those with cacao trees had their opportunity: in six months, you could buy a car" (*yang punya coklat ada kesempatan, enam bulan sudah beli mobil*). Now, the Balinese man said, it is easier to plant only cacao and stop growing rice. His family used to sell unhusked rice (*beras*) from their farm to other Balinese who were merchants. Now, he said, all the remaining forest at Tambarana has been cut to plant just cacao.

In Tambarana, he said, the Balinese and Javanese transmigrants had no problems with each other; their cultures and languages were similar. But the Javanese and local people... The sentence was never completed because the man clearly was uneasy speaking about the topic. He noted that the Javanese transmigrant village, Tambarana I, was "affected" (*kena*), but he said there was no problem at Tambarana II. Some Balinese Hindus from his village fled to Palu or Parigi for safety's sake, but then returned because security officials came there quickly (*petugas datang cepat*). His parents, who remained Hindu along with most of his siblings, still reside at Tambarana II. One of his siblings converted to Pentecostalism, while he became officially Muslim when he married. He met his Muslim wife after he came to Palu for schooling and she lived nearby. He said that he studied Islam in order to convert for his marriage, but he never could master Arabic and did not use his Muslim name.

It was unclear where the Balinese man might choose to live if his marriage did come to an end. He said Balinese transmigrants from Poso sometimes go back to Bali, but they then return to Sulawesi because work in Bali is so scarce.

CASE 11: A MORI-MINAHASAN WOMAN FROM POSO CITY WHO TURNED TO SOCIAL SERVICE

Because this essay is based on narratives of those still experiencing displacement, it does not adequately encompass information about the positive steps that have been taken to provide emergency aid, rebuild schools, and promote positive relations among Poso's fractious groups. For the sake of including a note of hope, however, I include here a final narrative about an individual whose refugee experience was not only of profound loss, but also of personal growth.

I encountered a mixed Mori–Minahasan Protestant woman who was born in Poso City but fled to Tentena when the killing began and her family's house was burned. The young woman, barely in her twenties, joined a voluntary refugee evacuation team. She told of sleeping many nights by the side of the road, waiting for a car to find her team and the families (both Christian and Muslim) that the team was guiding away from gunfire. She described carrying newborn babies, preparing food, and tending distraught women and elders. She said, "It was unpaid work and so it was pure of heart. Even if I could not save myself, one time in this life I have saved others" (*Itu kerja tanpa gaji jadi kerja tulus hati. Biar saya tidak bisa selamatkan diri, satu kali dalam kehidupan ini saya pernah menyelematkan orang lain*). She emphasized that it was the most important time of her life; that even if she never does anything else important on earth, she at least did that one thing: she helped save the lives of people in dire need. When I met her, she was working with a humanitarian NGO that integrated Muslims and Christians in the workplace and fostered inter-group communication. Like many Central Sulawesi NGO staff members I met, she had an unhealthy addiction to cigarettes and was working long hours for low pay. But she and her several mostly Muslim colleagues were exceptional in harnessing their own and others' refugee experiences to advance much-needed dialogues among the varied participants in Poso's violence. Only when more Poso refugees can even imagine similarly positive outcomes emerging from their experiences will it be possible to speak convincingly about Poso's social recovery.

REWRITING HISTORY AND ETHNICITY TO CLAIM DISPUTED TERRITORY

In addition to grief, trauma, anger, and fearful silences, communal violence can produce a reframing of participants' collective identities and historical perspectives. The following examples come from interviews I conducted in Sulawesi in May–June 2003, which I compared with narratives I heard during my 1980s–1990s fieldwork. The 2003 stories indicate how the experience of civil war transformed local versions of national and ethnic histories in unprecedented ways.

In the first case, I met with a group of eight young men, recent Mohammadiyah University economics graduates, who had begun a micro-credit NGO to help rebuild the economy of war-torn Poso City. Using funds that they received from a larger Muslim NGO in Jakarta, they were making rapid low-interest (2.5 percent), long-term loans to industrious (Muslim) people who had plans to start small businesses. The group's members were justly proud of their contribution to Poso City's economic recovery. There were no women in their NGO because they said they did not want to be distracted from their goals, and they did not want women in competition for scarce jobs in the city. The young men agreed that Poso Muslims and Christians wanted no more fighting. Unfortunately, they said, the post-Malino task force members are all corrupt, and everyone has lost respect for political and religious leaders. Army soldiers are involved in shady businesses and just get drunk in their free time. But, one said, "Things are better now, peaceful. If the Christians haven't come back to Poso City, it is mainly for economic or housing reasons. We have forgiven them."

The speaker told of forgiveness for the killings and neighborhood burnings, something very few Muslims or Christians I met were willing to do. On the other hand, he made the comment as if it were clear to all that only the Christian community needed to be forgiven. Shortly after I met the group, introductions began. As they told me, two were Javanese, two from Gorontalo (in northern Sulawesi), two from Makassar City (in South Sulawesi), and two from Sulawesi's offshore islands. They claimed that the ethnic diversity of their group—all from Muslim regions—was a reflection of the migrant population of Poso City itself. One said, "There are no original Poso people, other than people like us. There is no Poso language. We all speak Indonesian; that's it. Some of us were born here, some of us weren't, but we—or our parents—are all from someplace else." They claimed that Poso City had never been anything but a place occupied by migrants, mainly Muslims like themselves. This vision of Poso as a migrant frontier territory, to which all Indonesians from elsewhere can claim to be equal stakeholders, corresponds practically, if on a somewhat different political scale, with the official government position that all Indonesian citizens (except Chinese) are to be ranked as indigenous people.

In their listing of migrant ethnic groups in Poso, the young men mentioned two Christian groups: the Minahasa, from North Sulawesi, and the Pamona, from the highlands of the district. In their view, the Pamona in Poso City were just migrants like everybody else, not indigenous peoples or, as they said disparagingly, "they are not lords of the land" (*mereka bukan tuan tanah*). This was the viewpoint of some of Poso City's righteous winners. By 2003, Christian groups were negligible minorities on the coast with hardly any way to claim a stake in the political life of Poso City.

The young men's narratives fit nicely within the New Order state's pro-migration, pro-development discourse. But what, I wondered, would an indigenous Pamona person say to this type of revisionist history? What will future Indonesian government schoolbooks say about the region?

I heard a counter-narrative a few weeks later from two Protestants who were living outside the Poso District. These Protestants, one Pamona man and one Mori woman, were not war-displaced in the usual sense. They had migrated away from the Poso highlands for education and work, but then found it problematic to "return home" once the violence began. The young man said his family home and neighborhood were now so destroyed that he had nothing to go home to. They spoke of their people's "trauma," repeatedly using the borrowed English word.

They said that when the migrants (*pendatang*, literally, "new arrivals") first came into the Poso District, the "Poso people" (they clearly meant indigenous Protestants such as Pamona, Mori, and Lore) had given migrants access to spare fields. They saw this fallow secondary forest land "as a gift," they said, to make for good future relations. But the gift was betrayed. "They repaid us by driving us off our own ancestors' land," one said.

"But we will rise up again," the man interjected, "that is part of our culture." He then began an ethnic history, one that became mythic at times in its particular weaving of historical facts. He told how one sub-group of the indigenous Pamona (To Ondae) had a rebellious heritage, as they considered themselves to be aristocratic warriors and respected fighters, and he referred to an exemplary man from this group who was killed during the peak of battle in 2000. He said that men from this group repeatedly had led the indigenous mountain people to resist foreign incursions. First they fought the Dutch colonial soldiers, then the Darul Islam rebels in the late 1950s, now the rapacious, attacking migrants. They would continue to rise up this way. No peace agreements made in the coastal cities would ever work, he concluded, because "we have a problem up here." The young man had reconfigured nearly a century of past uprisings to make it appear that the successive historic resistance groups and their agendas were the same.[37]

The woman added that the Dutch Protestant mission and its local offspring church "kept us stupid." Here, too, was a different story than the usual one that claims the Dutch favored Christian converts. Some Poso Protestants were educated for civil service or church work, but most just remained small-scale subsistence farmers. Their Christian education, whether gained in elementary school or through church seminaries, never taught them how to compete in business, how to protect their land rights in the face of new rules, or how to cope with the changing religious politics of Indonesia.

When I mentioned that some Protestants I knew had been told by their ministers to face the violence by praying, the young man said darkly, "It seems God wasn't listening." This was a story from some of the righteous losers who migrated out of

---

[37] For the way this was done in Aceh by both Indonesian government authorities and GAM (Gerakan Aceh Merdeka, or Free Aceh Movement), see Drexler, "History and Liability."

the Poso highlands but then were forced to live as exiles. They did not feel they were full citizens in the Muslim-majority Indonesian nation.

At the end of our discussion, I raised the issue of casualties from the conflict and asked if Poso Protestants could accept that many Muslims also had been victims of terrible violence. I wondered if these Christians, too, could speak of forgiveness. The young man said that, intellectually, he knew this was true, but emotionally there was no way that Protestant highlanders could accept this because they feel they are the ones who were sacrificed.

CONCLUSION: NARRATING DISPLACEMENT, SELF, AND DIFFERENCE

The basic challenge of this essay has been to unsettle often overlooked assumptions and ideas about "IDPs," and the kinds of people who were displaced when the Poso conflict became increasingly polarized along Muslim versus Christian religious lines. Varying local interpretations of the Malino Accord ceasefire agreement reveal a measure of incomprehension among officials and evacuees, some of whom argue over the intentions of the agreement's less explicit and more internally contradictory points. What can be observed overall is a bureaucratic effort at reintegration or "repatriation" that effectively deepens prior segregation patterns.

Narratives about "displacement" and "returning home" define a set of expectations about how the violence in Poso should be resolved and adjudicated. I have sought to question unifying assumptions about "displacement" from Poso through narratives that make divergent claims about who really was "in place" initially, and thus truly "displaced" or "returned home" during the conflict. These claims, in turn, imply who should return to prior places or, by contrast, stay in the place to which they fled and where they currently reside. Such sites are now religiously segregated, but ethnically heterogeneous, pockets in the region.

Differences in Muslims' versus Christians' preferences for returning to prior neighborhoods or resettling at new refuge sites indicate variant attachments to particular livelihood strategies or ancestral communities. The refugee narratives presented also suggest the extent to which the Poso conflict became a battle that must be assessed, at least partially, in terms of competing territorial claims and civil rights among those who are recent migrants and those who claim to be natives. These zero-sum claims emerged in the late Suharto era as outer island forests became more potentially profitable for timber and export cash crops, and migrants, supported by pro-development government activities, penetrated both the rural agricultural sector and urban business-state collaborations. As is true in many regions of the world, new migrants were willing to purchase land, cut down the forests, and serve as a mobile labor force according to guidelines that local residents would never abide.

Before further analyzing what refugees I met did say, it is worth a moment to take notice of what they did *not* say. Many understandably were unwilling to discuss unpleasant details of their experiences in Poso. The suppression of fear and the silence of reluctant witnesses must be noted.[38] Evacuees also uniformly portrayed

---

[38] See Monique Skidmore, "Darker than Midnight: Fear, Vulnerability, and Terror Making in Urban Burma (Myanmar)," *American Ethnologist* 30,1 (2003): 5–21; and Kee Howe Yong, "Silences in History and Nation-State: Reluctant Accounts of the Cold War in Sarawak," *American Ethnologist* 33,3 (2006): 462–73.

themselves as clueless about the prior potential for violence in Poso, and the identity of their attackers.[39] Often refugees' life experiences were narrated within a list of places: where the person was born, moved, worked, and finally took refuge. Given the importance of place to ethnic identity and biography in Sulawesi, the names of these listed places may serve as shorthand narrative containers for the affect that often was not publicly expressed in terms of human individuals and loss.[40] For example, just the place name "Kilo Nine" (*Kilo Sembilan*) evokes anxieties about brutality and death. Other less infamous place names carry similar emotional baggage or, by contrast, represent nostalgic images of prior homelands in more halcyon times.

A few self-identifying indigenous Protestants displayed a residue of despair that had moved toward self-hatred. These individuals expressed a kind of "Pamona anti-Pamonaism" that blamed their own "bad culture" for human weaknesses, such as self-serving pride, greed, overindulgence in alcohol, and the inability to confront contemporary Indonesian political structures. Perhaps this is a stage of depression and self-reflection that is inevitable for the battered, but I could envision more violence or self-destruction ahead if such feelings were not addressed constructively. For a few scripturally-minded Christian refugees, flight had come to resemble the biblical Exodus from a natural homeland to which God promised that they would someday return.

Some Muslims also expressed misery and bitterness. A few spoke about the widely disseminated photographs showing corpses of Muslims brutalized in 2000–2001. Although extreme emotions and claims emerged from only a few individuals I met, attention to these kinds of narrative scripts are warranted to aid Poso citizens still living with anxiety, hostility, and periodic violence. Poso's sporadic revenge attacks and local jihadi movements surely have been bolstered by anxious and self-righteous narratives developed within the frustration of refugee camps and resettlement villages.[41] A more welcome result of refugees' trials, by contrast, is revealed in jokes and puns that use satire and laughter to frame hardships, and thereby make them more endurable.

Discussions by Poso refugees about rightful homelands to which certain groups could return—discussions about who belongs where—had a variety of religious, linguistic, and ethnic components. Some rural Protestants said Poso was a Protestant region, and therefore displaced Muslims should return to other "homelands." At the same time, some urban Muslims said Indonesia was a Muslim country so they had a right to be anywhere; it was Protestants who should accept Muslim majority demands or leave. Some Pamona Protestants said speaking Pamona (known as Bare'e in colonial Dutch literature) should be a litmus test for living in the region and "respecting local customs" as specified by the Malino Accord. By contrast, some migrant Muslims said there was no Poso language, that everyone in Poso City spoke only Indonesian.

---

[39] This position parallels mainstream mass-media accounts and law-enforcement policies focused on unknown provocateurs and unnamed "pure criminals"; see Aragon, "Mass Media Fragmentation."

[40] See Lorraine V. Aragon, *Fields of the Lord: Animism, Christian Minorities, and State Development in Indonesia* (Honolulu, HI: University of Hawaii Press, 2000), pp. 47–56; and Steven Feld and Keith H. Basso, *Senses of Place* (Santa Fe, NM: School of American Research Press, 1996.)

[41] See International Crisis Group, "Jihad in Central Sulawesi," Indonesia Backgrounder Report, February 4, 2004.

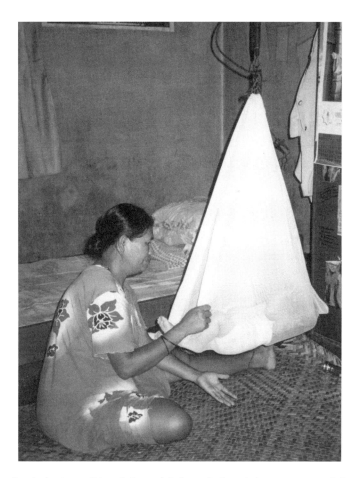

Woman tending baby in traditional Central Sulawesi sling. It bounces up and down in place rather than moving back and forth like those used by migrants from South Sulawesi. December 2004. (Photo by Lorraine V. Aragon)

There also were individuals who explained behavioral differences among indigenous and migrant residents with cultural analyses that posed no links to religious affiliation. During my visit to the Central Sulawesi Provincial Museum in Palu, a local Muslim Kaili staff member drew my attention to a display showing a Central Sulawesi baby swing. In Central Sulawesi, he pointed out, baby slings are attached to springs (originally rattan loops but now often coiled metal) that bounce the baby up and down over the same spot. Therefore, he said, Central Sulawesi people stay in their home villages and do not migrate. The man pointed out that in South Sulawesi, by contrast, baby swings are designed to move back and forth, so the adults of those ethnic groups (such as the Bugis, Makassar, and Mandar) travel back and forth in migration. His claim was one any student of Margaret Mead's "Culture and Personality" theories could appreciate.

The man's folk explanation, in fact, accurately indexes certain general differences of behavior and perspectives between Poso's recent migrant and long-term communities. Old place names in highland Central Sulawesi, such as Onda'e and Lage, are said to be drawn from Pamona names of trees that grew in these places, names that people also use to identify their communities. Highlanders' attachment to places concerns the trees and forest lands their ancestors first cleared for planting through rituals where public contracts with local land "owner" deities were announced. These places are also the sites where their forebears are buried and the sites of kin-group charter myths.[42] The fertility and productivity of land are linked conceptually to place-based life-cycle rituals, particularly mortuary events.

Because homelands are places guarded by their ancestors' spirits, particular land areas bear cosmological messages for many highland Protestants. A man in Tentena said that, after the conflict peaked, Lake Poso water levels rose and fell in unusual ways. When the violence was worst, crocodiles began to appear, a clear sign that elders' tales about crocodiles being the twin of humans and ominous signals were true. For his community, the uses of ancestral land and contemporary behavior have interlocked consequences. Most rural highlanders do not leave their natal homelands readily or permanently because their identities and moral principles are grounded, quite literally, in ideas about their land's vital qualities. Their subsistence farming sites and related agricultural rituals embody reminders of historical group narratives and moral principles.

By contrast, many recent migrants to Poso, mainly Muslims, have lived in several locations during the prior ten years, without establishing strong links to any particular lands or communities of the area. Their strongest social ties generally are to their families and fellow migrants. Their primary goals involve *the amounts of land and other capital they can obtain, not its exact location or social significance*. Hence the division between many Protestant highlanders focused on small plots of particular inherited land and Muslim migrants focused on obtaining higher yields from increasingly bigger plots in any area available for profitable cash cropping. As scholars of the Bugis have noted, financial success in migration is often key to raising one's status both in natal South Sulawesi communities and in new migrant locales.[43]

Migrants' narratives also corroborated reports by others that Central Sulawesi forest land, even sometimes legally protected conservation areas, was being turned over to migrants. These land transactions were aimed either at timber removal or the planting of high-value cash crops, such as cacao, that would be sold to businessmen, all transactions favored by political officials who stood to profit from road construction and increased land development using migrant labor. Both migrant and host communities have become enmeshed in collaborative relations with powerful forest-clearing businesses and government agents.[44]

Responses to these larger social processes of state and global economic penetration frequently are experienced and registered by Central Sulawesi residents as trespasses generated by ethnic or religious differences. Those observable cultural differences are then marshaled to explain migration frictions. Also rarely noticed following the violence is the way that fleeing Muslims have become dependents or clients of other Muslims—for example, Javanese the clients of Bugis, or Mandar the

---

[42] See *Founders' Cults in Southeast Asia: Ancestors, Polity, Identity*, ed. Nicola Tannenbaum and Cornelia Ann Kammerer (New Haven, CT: Yale Southeast Asia Program Monograph Series, 2003); and Lorraine V. Aragon, *Fields of the Lord*.

[43] See Greg Acciaioli, "Kinship and Debt: The Social Organization of Bugis Migration and Fish Marketing at Lake Lindu, Central Sulawesi," in *Authority and Enterprise among the Peoples of South Sulawesi*, ed. Roger Tol, Kees van Dijk, and Greg Acciaioli (Leiden: KITLV, 2000).

[44] See Anna Lowenhaupt Tsing, *Friction: An Ethnography of Global Connection* (Princeton, NJ: Princeton University Press, 2005).

clients of Kaili. Similar patterns hold for Christians, and may be further altering or fusing prior sectarian identities and religious orthodoxies as ethnic heterogeneity is collapsed within broader religious affinities.

In addition to offering differing ideological rationales about rights to land and cultural citizenship, refugees made pragmatic claims about what logistical obstacles prevented those who wanted to return home (or resettle to a new home) from actually doing so. The primary topics in these discussions, the inadequacy of safety and housing funds, routinely implicated the Indonesian government as negligent. As numerous reports attest, the Poso District government neither effectively prosecuted numerous cases of post-Malino violence nor dispersed funds designated for needy refugees. The former head of Poso District Social Services, Andi Azikin Suyuti, Central Sulawesi Governor Aminuddin Ponulele, and many other district officials have been implicated in misappropriations of refugee aid funds in amounts ranging from the equivalent of US$640,000 to US$18 million.[45]

Without adequate dispersal and use of rebuilding funds, Poso refugees found it difficult to return, resettle, or recover effectively from the devastation of the conflict. Security problems and financial obstacles to personal and community recovery have intensified anger and prolonged a minority's support of vigilantism in place of legal measures to address past inequities and crimes. Whether the Poso region is viewed by refugees as an ancestral homeland or a promising recent migration zone, secure houses, well-staffed schools, and civility from multi-ethnic neighbors are now needed by all to allow them to move beyond bitter experiences of violence as national or regional "stepchildren." New, public-minded government officials should take into account the region's particular history and cautiously rethink and amend resettlement and deforestation plans. Only then may displaced Poso residents again conclude that many diverse groups of people, with largely fluid boundaries, can belong there and live "in place."

---

[45] See "Central Sulawesi Governor Implicated in Graft," *Jakarta Post*, February 8, 2006; and Arianto Sangaji, "Masa Depan Poso Pasca-Koopskam," *Kompas*, July 17, 2006.

WHERE DO WE GO FROM HERE? THE POLITICS OF ENDING DISPLACEMENT IN POST-CONFLICT NORTH MALUKU[1]

Christopher R. Duncan

The various outbreaks of communal violence that plagued Indonesia at the end of the twentieth century displaced more than 1.3 million people throughout the archipelago. As these conflicts subsided, many individuals who had fled from their homes,returned to rebuild their lives. Thousands of others have chosen to start over somewhere else, and some have yet to decide whether to return. This latter group, numbering in the tens of thousands, has continued to challenge the Indonesian government well into 2007. Providing aid to these displaced persons has proven to be a financial burden to the Indonesian government, one that was increasingly difficult to justify as conflicts subsided. From a policy standpoint, government officials at all levels were confronted with a question common to many displacement situations around the world: When does displacement end?[2] How do local and national government leaders, as well as local community officials and the displaced themselves, decide when displacement is no longer an issue? The Indonesian government thought it could solve this problem via administrative fiat and initially announced an end to displacement, as of December 31, 2002. That strategy failed, however, and the country continued to address issues of conflict-induced

[1] This paper is based on fieldwork carried out in North Sulawesi and North Maluku from June 2001 through November 2002 that was sponsored by LIPI and Universitas Sam Ratulangi; and in North Maluku in 2005, sponsored by LIPI and Politeknik Perdamaian Halmahera. The research was funded at various points by the Anthropologists' Fund for Urgent Anthropological Research in coordination with the Royal Anthropological Institute and Goldsmiths College, the University of London, and a Research and Writing Grant from the John A. and Catherine T. McArthur Foundation. Additional fieldwork in North Maluku was conducted from 1995–1996, with additional visits in 2000, 2004, and 2006. Portions of this chapter were previously published in *Cakalele: The Journal of Maluku Studies;* the author thanks the editors of that journal for allowing the re-publication of some of that data here.

[2] For more on this debate, see Erin Mooney, "An IDP No More? Exploring the Issue of When Internal Displacement Ends," discussion paper for the "Brainstorming Session on When Internal Displacement Ends," Brookings–CUNY Project on Internal Displacement/Institute for the Study of Forced Migration at Georgetown University, Washington, DC, April 22, 2002.

displacement well after the artificial deadline had passed. Moreover, soon thereafter Indonesia also had to deal with the additional burden of the more than 500,000 people displaced by the 2004 tsunami in northern Sumatra.[3]

Table 1
Distribution of IDPs and refugees in Indonesia as of February 25, 2002

Relocated to (host province):	Number of IDPs	Fled from (home province):
Aceh	14,351	Aceh
North Sumatra	66,935	Aceh
East Java	169,837	Multiple regions
East Nusa Tenggara	80,000	East Timor
West Kalimantan	48,961	West Kalimantan
South Sulawesi	35,804	Central Sulawesi, Maluku, East Timor
Southeast Sulawesi	216,804	Maluku, East Timor
Central Sulawesi	85,899	Central Sulawesi
North Sulawesi	48,667	North Maluku, Central Sulawesi, Maluku
Maluku	336,814	Maluku, North Maluku
North Maluku	205,781	North Maluku, Maluku
Other*	88,273	Multiple regions
Total	*1,398,126*	

*Includes the provinces of Riau, Jambi, Lampung, South Sumatra, West Java, Central Java, Bali, West Nusa Tenggara, and Papua.
Source: World Food Programme/Vulnerability Analysis Mapping Unit. IDP Source and Recipient Regions, February 25, 2002. WFP/VAM: Jakarta.

Indonesian government officials focused mainly on the geographical location of displaced populations: where would they be when their status as IDPs (Internally Displaced Persons) was revoked? Indonesian IDPs were also concerned with figuring out their final destinations (in terms of where they would be when their IDP status ended). Would they return to their places of origin, relocate to a new locale, or integrate locally? The motives and concerns of IDPs and government officials are often at odds with one another when they are addressing these issues. For the IDPs, deciding upon a final destination is a difficult process fraught with many consequences for their current safety and their future prosperity. As a result, IDPs base their decisions on a number of factors that differ from family to family and from region to region. A partial list of these variables includes: safety, social support networks, employment possibilities, housing, government support, and educational opportunities for themselves or their children. Government officials have different motives. They are often focused on meeting the goals outlined in directives from

---

[3] The government does not consider those displaced by the tsunami as "internally displaced people," but defines them as "tsunami victims" (*korban tsunami*).

Jakarta or from provincial capitals concerning the return or integration of IDPs. At other times, they are concerned with the image projected by the continued presence of IDPs from their province who are living in camps, as many believe this image hurts their ability to attract investors.

Regardless of the rationales for their decisions, both IDPs and government officials must deal with the legacies of displacement and the economic and social challenges common to post-conflict communities. This paper examines the motives and opinions of IDPs from North Maluku concerning their futures and of the government officials whose job it is to deal with them. It will also explore how people who fled from the conflict in North Maluku are deciding whether to return to their homes and how they have been influenced by government policies. This essay focuses primarily on North Moluccan IDPs who fled to the neighboring province of North Sulawesi, but it also discusses other IDP populations from North Maluku.

THE CAUSES AND PATTERNS OF DISPLACEMENT IN NORTH MALUKU

An examination of the decisions that displaced North Moluccans have made (and continue to make) about their future must be based on an understanding of how the violence in North Maluku influenced patterns of forced migration.[4] These patterns determined when people fled their homes, who caused them to leave, and where they sought refuge. When ethno-religious violence began in Ambon, in January 1999, the northern part of Maluku province (what would soon become the new province of North Maluku) remained largely peaceful.[5] It was not until mid-August 1999 that violence between Makian migrants and indigenous populations erupted on the island of Halmahera, in the subdistrict (*kecamatan*) of Kao. Those clashes focused on government plans to create a new subdistrict of Makian Daratan from the southern half of the Kao subdistrict. This new administrative division would consist of all the Makian villages that were established in 1975 when the Indonesian government resettled the Makian to protect them from a predicted volcanic eruption on their home island. It would also include several indigenous Pagu villages and some villages from the subdistrict of Jailolo. The Pagu had no desire to be incorporated into this new subdistrict.

The violence in August lasted only a few days, but the problem remained unresolved. Disturbances broke out again in October 1999 and forced approximately fifteen thousand Makian to flee to the neighboring islands of Ternate and Tidore. Although the Kao–Malifut conflict initially revolved around ethnic differences, it soon took on a religious character. Since the Makian are Muslim and the majority of the indigenous people of Kao are Christian, the narrative of religious violence being used to describe the conflict in Ambon appeared to fit the situation in North Maluku as well. Furthermore, the appearance of a suspicious letter in Ternate and Tidore

---

[4] For a more detailed account of the conflict in North Maluku, see Christopher R. Duncan, "The Other Maluku: Chronologies of Conflict in North Maluku," *Indonesia* 80 (October 2005): 1–53. See also Chris Wilson, "The Ethnic Origins of Religious Conflict in North Maluku Province, Indonesia, 1999–2000," *Indonesia* 79 (April 2005): 69–91.

[5] For more on the Ambon (Maluku) conflict, see Gerry van Klinken, "The Maluku Wars: Bringing Society Back In," *Indonesia* 71 (April 2001): 1–26; Jacques Bertrand, "Legacies of the Authoritarian Past: Religious Violence in Indonesia's Moluccan Islands," *Pacific Affairs* 75,1 (Spring 2002): 57–85.

Map 1

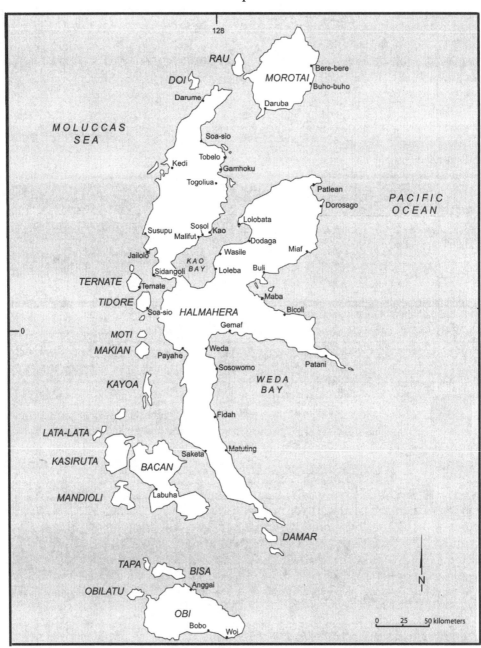

Map of Halmahera and surrounding islands (Province of North Maluku)

calling for Christians in North Maluku to cleanse the region of Muslims focused attention on religious differences and infuriated Muslims.[6] The resulting riots in early November forced approximately thirteen thousand largely Christian IDPs to flee to North Sulawesi and Halmahera. This violence was followed by attacks on central and southern Halmahera, causing thousands of Christian IDPs to flee to North Sulawesi and northern Halmahera. The conflict eventually spread throughout Halmahera and to the nearby islands of Morotai, Bacan, and Obi. When the large-scale fighting subsided in June 2000, few regions were untouched by the conflict and over 220,000 people (roughly 25 percent of the province's population) had been displaced from their homes.

People fleeing the conflict went to a number of places based largely on religious identification. North Moluccan Muslims fled primarily to the island of Ternate, the subdistrict of Galela (in northern Halmahera), the southern half of the island of Morotai, and the island of Bacan (see Map 1). The Christian diaspora was more widespread and covered at least four provinces: North Maluku, Maluku, North Sulawesi, and Papua. Within North Maluku, Christian IDPs were concentrated in the subdistricts of Tobelo and Kao (in northern Halmahera) and on the island of Rao (off the west coast of Morotai). Outside of the province approximately 35,000 mainly Christians IDPs were housed in North Sulawesi, and additional IDPs fled to Tanimbar, Seram, and Papua (Sorong and Manokwari).[7] There was also a small number of displaced people from Maluku who took refuge in North Maluku around the same time.

An important influence on patterns of displacement in North Maluku was that people fleeing violence in one part of the province often took revenge on minority religious communities in their place of refuge, causing the latter to flee to a new locale where they repeated the process. The most well-known example is the role that Makian IDPs from Malifut played in the displacement of several thousand Christians during the violence on Ternate. Similar events took place in Tobelo, where the presence of displaced Christians from Ternate and southern and central Halmahera increased tensions at the end of 1999 that eventually led to violence.[8] Muslim IDPs from Tobelo who fled to Morotai subsequently played a major role in the outbreak of violence there that led to the flight of several thousand Christians to Tobelo and elsewhere. This pattern of IDP-induced displacement continued to have ramifications in post-conflict North Maluku. People were hesitant to return home before other IDPs in their place of origin had left. In some cases their houses were occupied by other people, occasionally the same people who had played a role in their initial displacement. For example, Christians from Morotai housed in Tobelo were reluctant to return home before Muslim IDPs from Tobelo (who had played a role in their eviction) had left Morotai, but these same Muslims were averse to returning home until the various IDPs in Tobelo had been sent home.

---

[6] This letter is reproduced in full in *Halmahera Berdarah: Suatu Upaya Mengungkap Kebenaran*, ed. Jan Nanere (Ambon: Yayasan Bina Masyarakat Sejahtera dan Pelestarian Alam, 2000), pp. 68–73. See also Nils Bubandt, "Pamphlets, Rumors, and the Politics of Paranoia in North Maluku," in *What Went Wrong? Explaining Communal Violence in Eastern Indonesia*, ed. Joss Goss and Kirk Lange (London: Routledge, forthcoming).

[7] This list is in no way exhaustive. Small numbers of IDPs from North Maluku went to numerous other places, including Gorontalo, Makassar, and Jakarta.

[8] Duncan, "The Other Maluku," pp. 23–24.

Simplifications, Short Cuts, and Corruption: IDPs and Government Officials

Although Indonesia has seen internal displacement many times in its history, the government appeared unprepared, both logistically and conceptually, for the large number of people fleeing conflict throughout the country at the turn of the century.[9] IDPs were originally handled by the government agency that dealt with victims of natural disasters. Officials focused on meeting IDPs' basic needs (food, water, shelter, and clothing) and then expected to send them back to their places of origin once the violence had stopped, much as people would be returned to their villages after a natural disaster. IDPs were quick to point out the flaws in this strategy. People fleeing a flood can return once the water has subsided, but people fleeing from ethnic or religious violence can not return home simply because the fighting has stopped. It has stopped precisely because they are no longer there. Officials were seemingly unable or unwilling to make the connection between the presence of IDPs in their places of refuge and the end of conflict in North Maluku.

In North Sulawesi, most government officials working with IDPs made little effort to understand the situations of the thousands of forced migrants under their jurisdiction, or of the conflict that had displaced them. As I have discussed elsewhere, the reliance of government officials on development discourse and particularly on the category of "IDP" often hindered rather than helped their efforts.[10] The use of the IDP label appeared to absolve them from learning about the complexities or idiosyncrasies of individual IDPs or particular groups of IDPs (e.g., from certain villages or islands). All IDPs were considered to have essentially the same needs, wants, and motives. Officials didn't need to know about the plight or the history of various groups. All the government had to do was feed them, house them, and eventually move them elsewhere. Any attempt to do otherwise would complicate policy and, furthermore, directives from Jakarta did not mention the need to understand the historical background of the conflict. This lack of knowledge would subsequently have an impact on efforts by the government in North Sulawesi to return IDPs to North Maluku. Officials were often unaware of IDPs' original places of origin, where they were located, and the significance of those places in terms of conflict and post-conflict regional dynamics. This ignorance had ramifications for local governments in North Maluku as well as for the IDPs from North Sulawesi, some of whom were occasionally returned to places that were not their homes.

The lack of detailed knowledge about the plight of IDPs among North Sulawesi officials persisted despite several years of interaction. Even after they conducted

---

[9] For more on the history of internal displacement in Indonesia, see Graeme Hugo, "Pengungsi: Indonesia's Internally Displaced Persons," *Asia and Pacific Migration Journal* 11,3 (2001): 311–31; and Geoffrey McNicoll, "Internal Migration in Indonesia: Descriptive Notes," *Indonesia* 5 (April 1968): 29–92.

[10] Christopher R. Duncan, "Unwelcome Guests: Relations between Internally Displaced Persons and Their Hosts in North Sulawesi," *Journal of Refugee Studies* 18,1 (2005): 25–46. See also Roger Zetter, "Labeling Refugees: Forming and Transforming a Bureaucratic Identity," *Journal of Refugee Studies* 4,1 (1991): 39–62; and Liisa A. Malkki, "Refugees and Exile: From 'Refugee Studies' to the National Order of Things," *Annual Review of Anthropology* 24 (1995): 495–523.

numerous surveys, they continued to misunderstand the dynamics of the IDP situation in their province. For example, government officials assumed that IDPs who lived outside of camps in North Sulawesi were wealthier than those who lived in them. Officials believed that most of the IDPs who lived outside of the camps did so because they could afford to and thus needed less aid. However, the opposite was often the case. Camp residence was not determined by need, but was based on the date that IDPs arrived in North Sulawesi. The first groups to arrive were from Ternate and Tidore and consisted mostly of civil servants and urban traders, many of whom could find jobs in North Sulawesi. In contrast, later waves of forced migrants consisted mainly of farmers and fishermen from the islands of Bacan, Obi, and Morotai. These people had a harder time finding gainful employment in the urban milieu of Bitung and Manado. They also received less aid from the government and from nongovernment sources since they were harder to locate. Thus, those deemed more self-sufficient were often more in need of aid than those receiving it in the camps. The failure of officials to understand even this basic point about the settlement patterns of IDPs in North Sulawesi exemplified their general lack of knowledge and interest in the IDP situation beyond that required for the simple distribution of aid.

Government policy at the national level also often failed to distinguish between different groups of conflict-induced IDPs. This failure was exemplified when the government announced its plan in October 2001 for ending displacement. This strategy was aimed at solving the "IDP and refugee problem" by the end of 2002, when all of the displaced would lose their status as refugees or IDPs.[11] The Department of Social Affairs in Jakarta had devised the policy with little input from either the regions housing the IDPs or those from which the IDPs had fled. The policy contained no details on how the government would accomplish its goal other than providing three options for displaced populations: (1) return home (*pemulangan*), (2) empowerment in their place of refuge (*pemberdayaan*), or (3) relocation (*pengalihan*).[12] It also stipulated that all government aid to the displaced would cease at the end of 2002 because the government was no longer willing to provide aid specifically for forced migrants. Those still in need would be expected to rely on the regular social safety net. This new policy was greeted with confusion by many IDPs due to the vagueness of the plan and because it was announced at a time when people were still fleeing from sporadic violence in Poso and Ambon.

Although provincial and regional government officials had little input in the policy, they were responsible for coordinating its implementation. In North Sulawesi, the first move was to stop distribution of government-sponsored food aid. Many IDPs thought the aid had been stopped to encourage, if not force, them to

---

[11] The original document was released in October 2001 by the office of Jusuf Kalla, then head of the Department of Social Affairs. An English translation of this document titled "National Policies on the Handling of Internally Displaced Persons/Refugees in Indonesia" can be found in UN Office for the Coordination of Humanitarian Affairs, *Consolidated Inter-Agency Appeal 2002 for Internally Displaced Persons in Indonesia* (New York, NY and Geneva: United Nations, 2002), pp. 132–33.,

[12] For critiques of this plan, see Christopher R. Duncan, "Confusing Deadlines: IDPs in Indonesia," *Forced Migration Review* 17 (2003): 35–36; Patrick Sweeting, George Conway, and Nabila Hameed, "Promoting Sustainable Return and Integration of IDPs in Indonesia," *Forced Migration Review* 21 (2004): 39–41; and United Nations Commission on Human Rights, "Report of the Representative of the Secretary General on Internally Displaced Persons," (United Nations, February 12, 2001), pp. 19–25.

return to North Maluku, as well as to placate local residents who were jealous of the aid distribution. Government officials publicly argued that they urgently needed the resources to fund other social programs. In private discussions, however, officials often admitted that the growing tensions between IDPs and local community members had become a matter of concern and they would have liked to see most of the IDPs leave the province.[13]

If the government had been hoping to encourage the IDPs to go home by cutting off assistance, it had limited success. Corruption and mismanagement had depleted the aid to such an extent that most IDPs had learned to cope without it. Furthermore, church groups, NGOs, and others continued to provide support. Still, some displaced people from rural areas who lacked marketable job skills and elderly IDPs who were unable to do the manual-labor jobs available found it more difficult living in urban IDP camps once the aid stopped. As a result, the policy did hasten the return of a small number of IDPs, but in many cases it simply displaced them to other, more rural communities.

To make matters more confusing, the North Sulawesi government never presented the policy to IDPs in a clear or consistent manner, and I was unable to find evidence that officials had distributed copies of the policy to IDP camp leaders. Although civil servants visited camps to discuss the plan, they often presented conflicting explanations. Sometimes the same official would present differing versions at different times within the same camp. One of the IDPs' main concerns focused on how much financial support they would receive (both in cash and kind) when they returned to their villages in North Maluku since many of them would have to rebuild their homes. As with other aspects of the plan, budget figures were not made available to IDPs. This lack of transparency led to speculation about the amount each family would receive and increased the already high level of mistrust between IDPs and officials. Some officials reported that each family would receive Rp. 5.5 million in cash and materials, but rumors suggested amounts as high as Rp. 15 million. IDPs were prone to believe the higher amounts and blame the subsequent difference on corruption. They interpreted the confusion around the new policy in two ways. Some saw it as another example of the incompetence of the Department of Social Affairs. Others viewed it as an intentional plan by officials to sow confusion among IDPs so they could siphon off money and blame the IDPs if the policy failed.

The issues of money and aid were a constant bone of contention between government agencies and the IDPs. Officials frequently complained that the IDPs were greedy and trying to cheat the system by squeezing every rupiah they could out of the government and aid agencies. In response, the IDPs cited the corruption of officials, both real and perceived.[14] One of the more common forms of corruption required IDPs to forfeit a percentage of their aid for "distribution and administration" costs. For example, in 2004, when the Department of Social Affairs

---

[13] Duncan, "Unwelcome Guests," pp. 35–38. Similar tensions developed almost everywhere there were large concentrations of forced migrants. See Blair Palmer, "Migrasi dan Identitas: Perantau Buton yang Kembali ke Buton setelah Konflik Maluku, 1999–2002," *Antropologi Indonesia* 74 (2004): 94–109; and Jamie Davidson, "Violence and Politics in West Kalimantan, Indonesia" (PhD dissertation, University of Washington, 2002), pp. 373–88.

[14] "Korupsi Dana untuk Suksesi," *Forum Keadilan*, July 7, 2002, pp. 46–47; "Korupsinan Tak Habis-Habisnya," *Ternate Post*, June 25, 2002; "Bocornya Dana Pengungsi," *Ternate Post*, June 25, 2002; and "Dipertanyakan, Pemotongan Dana Pengungsi di Minahasa," *Komentar*, July 10, 2001.

handed out final payments to Christian IDPs from Ternate in Tobelo, the official distributing the money informed each family head (from several dozen families) that they would have to pay Rp.250,000 to cover the "handling costs." It was not only officials who cheated the system. On a few occasions, village heads in northern Halmahera removed the names of legitimate IDPs from aid rolls and replaced them with members of their own families. IDPs often worked the system as well. Some IDPs would register in multiple locales in an effort to increase the amount of assistance they received. Others would move from place to place, following the distribution of aid. They would join the government's resettlement schemes to get the aid, and then move back to Manado or Bitung. Some even went back and forth between North Sulawesi and North Maluku in an effort to maximize their take.[15] These IDPs argued that if they did not steal the money, then the officials from the Department of Social Affairs would. The perceived levels of corruption were so high on both sides that IDPs almost always assumed that they were getting less than they were supposed to receive, and officials assumed IDPs were always lying and trying to cheat the system.

THE POLITICS OF GOING HOME

The 2001 policy on IDPs seemed to afflict many officials in North Sulawesi and elsewhere with tunnel vision, as it appeared to prioritize sending IDPs back to their places of origin. As a result, officials focused on accomplishing this goal. They were not interested in the state of affairs of the places where they were sending the IDPs. Nor were they concerned whether authorities at those destinations could handle the influx of IDPs, or were even aware that they were coming. As one civil servant from the Department of Social Affairs in North Sulawesi explained: "Jakarta says the IDPs have to go home. We have to follow policy from Jakarta. The important thing is to send people to North Maluku." Another official simply noted: "We need to put these people on boats [i.e., we need to send them to North Maluku]." Because their superiors in Manado were unlikely to be concerned with whether the IDPs actually reintegrated successfully in another province, government representatives felt they would be judged simply based on the number of families that they shipped back to North Maluku.

As noted above, government officials in North Sulawesi and North Maluku tended to assume that IDPs could and should return to their homes in North Maluku. The presence of other IDPs in those locales, however, represented a major obstacle to returning displaced people to their places of origin. Most IDPs felt it would only aggravate tensions and could lead to further conflicts if they returned home under those conditions. One IDP from Ternate complained:

---

[15] It should be noted that this effort to gain access to aid was not focused solely on financial gain. At times it appeared to be a moral issue for some IDPs—they were intent on gaining the recognition and recompense they deserved from the government for the suffering they had endured. The actual monetary cost of securing the aid often outweighed the value of the assistance eventually received. IDPs were often aware of this imbalance from the start. For example, I met one man who had spent more than 150,000 rupiah in a futile effort to get a 50,000 rupiah payment from the Department of Social Affairs. He explained that the money was rightfully his as an IDP, and he was determined to press for it regardless of how much it cost him to get it.

We are not animals that can be shipped from one place to another. How can we go home and live in barracks while Muslims live in our homes? How will that make us feel? Everyday we wake up in an IDP camp and see people living in our houses. If I had to do that I would be very angry. Eventually I would get so mad I would shoot someone or attack them with a machete.

Large-scale coordination between regional and local governments could have facilitated the simultaneous relocation of IDP groups, but such coordination rarely occurred, and in some cases was even discouraged. The differing agendas of regional governments and what they perceived to be their best strategy for handling returning IDPs or reintegrating returnees further complicated the process. It often meant that host communities were doing their best to speed up the pace of IDP returns, while recovering home communities were trying to slow it down to ensure a smooth transition. The former were rarely sympathetic to the needs of the latter. For example, the Ternate municipal government paid no heed to requests from officials in Tobelo to repatriate displaced Muslims in stages. Muslim and Christian leaders in Tobelo had agreed that a gradual return of the thousands of IDPs from Ternate was the best way to ensure their peaceful reintegration into the community. The city of Ternate, in contrast, was interested in removing as many IDPs from Ternate as quickly as possible. The same could be said for the government of North Sulawesi; its primary goal was to return as many people to North Maluku as possible, regardless of where they were going or whether the target regions were able to cope with them.

A small ceremony at the Manado harbor marks the departure of a boatload of IDPs returning to North Maluku from North Sulawesi. The banner reads "The Departure of IDPs from North Maluku [presided over by] the Minister of Social Affairs, Monday, March 18, 2002." (Photo by Christopher R. Duncan)

The government's focus on returning people to their place of origin in post-conflict regions raised concerns about safety. How was it possible for IDPs or government officials to know when it was safe for the displaced to return? Having experienced the violence firsthand, IDPs tended to err on the side of caution. In contrast, government officials tended to make their decisions rather, arbitrarily. It was often evident that since their superiors in Jakarta had decided that IDPs needed to go home, all else, including the future safety of the forced migrants, was largely irrelevant. At times officials appeared to have a total disregard for the situation on the ground, often urging people to return to places at the same time that new IDPs, fleeing renewed hostilities, were arriving from those same locales. Furthermore, outside of North Maluku, officials handling the IDPs often knew very little about the conflict that had caused their displacement. This lack of knowledge exacerbated a credibility gap dividing, officials and the IDPs. IDPs wondered how the officials could judge the current situation in North Maluku if they did not understand the dynamics of the conflict that had caused them to flee in the first place.

An IDP from North Maluku waits in a Bitung IDP camp to be taken to the harbor to return to North Maluku. March 2002. (Photo by Christopher Duncan)

The way many North Sulawesi officials equated the cessation of hostilities with the ability of IDPs to return highlighted their lack of knowledge about the conflict. They presumed that once the actual fighting had stopped it was "conducive" for the IDPs to return to their villages. For example, in mid-2002 officials in North Sulawesi derided Christian IDPs from Ternate for not going home. They pointed out that the fighting in North Maluku had stopped in 2000 and conditions had been "conducive" for almost two years. In response, IDPs called the officials' attention to the presence of thousands of Muslim IDPs living in Ternate (who were themselves reluctant to go home to Halmahera), many of whom occupied the Christian IDPs' houses. IDPs also noted that (in 2002) Christians in Ternate could only attend church on a heavily guarded military base. These conflicting viewpoints stemmed from a significant difference in the terminology used by IDPs and government officials. Officials often spoke about whether the situation in North Maluku was "conducive" (*kondusif*) for IDPs to return. In contrast, IDPs were concerned with whether it was "safe" (*aman*) for them to return. Officials argued that this was a distinction without a difference, but IDPs saw it in another light. While both views took into account the end of hostilities, only the IDP view took into consideration whether their return would spark renewed violence. Furthermore, some officials seemed to have a completely different view of what was meant by "conducive." For example, many Christian IDPs wanted their churches rebuilt before they returned as signs that Muslims were willing to accept them. In contrast, a leading official in North Sulawesi said that not all of the IDPs could expect their churches to be rebuilt or even expect to be able to worship in public once they returned. He argued that conditions were conducive for them to return, but they would have freedom of religion "only in their own homes."

Government officials in some parts of North Maluku were also prone to declare a region safe in an effort to encourage IDPs to return home. They often based these declarations of safety more on administrative fiat than on the actual views of the local population. During a 2002 meeting between representatives of IDPs in North Sulawesi and provincial officials in Ternate, one IDP mentioned that his subdistrict head (*camat*) had advised Christian IDPs to wait a few more months before returning. The *camat* had warned that the local Muslim community was not ready for them to return. The head of the Provincial Coordinating Body for Disaster Management responded: "Who said that? He is not allowed to say it's not safe, of course it's safe." IDPs did not find this stance reassuring. Prior to this meeting, the IDP representatives had visited various places throughout the province to assess the situation, often accompanied by armed soldiers for their own protection. The need for an armed escort convinced most of the delegation that it was prudent to wait. Moreover, many of the officials who were telling IDPs that it was safe were often the same people who had promised to protect them in 1999–2000. As IDPs saw it, they were being asked to place their trust, and quite possibly their lives, in the hands of the very people who had failed them in the past. Both Muslim and Christian IDPs noted that, although conditions may look safe to officials from outside the village or town that the refugees had fled, the IDPs had lived through the violence and were still troubled by their past experiences. Many still did not trust their former neighbors, who had often turned on them during the conflict. Unfortunately, officials rarely took IDP fears or experiences of violence into account when discussing their return.

Despite these challenges, there have been a number of success stories, and the United Nations considers North Maluku to be one of the better examples of how to handle the return of IDPs.[16] One success has been the large percentage of Makian from Malifut who returned home by mid-2001. Relations between them and their neighbors in Kao have been peaceful. Pagu villagers from the Malifut region who fled to Kao have returned as well. A majority of people have also returned to their homes in the subdistrict of Galela in northern Halmahera. Most Muslim IDPs in

---

[16] Bakornas PBP, *Report: Follow-up Workshop on the Management of IDPs in Indonesia, Sukabumi, Indonesia,* June 19–20 (Jakarta: Bakornas PBP in Cooperation with UN OCHA Indonesia, 2003), p. 13.

Galela returned after the Christian communities were expelled from the region in mid-2000. By mid-2004, most Christian villagers in Galela had returned as well. A large number of IDPs have also returned to the islands of Obi and Bacan (in the southern part of the province). Many of these successes involve people returning to their homes in regions where there were not a large number of IDPs from elsewhere; thus they would not be competing with IDPs for aid, nor forcing those IDPs from their homes as returnees in Ternate, Tobelo, and Morotai were doing.

The changing political and administrative map of North Maluku has also affected the pattern of IDP returns, although less than some political scientists might argue. The impact of decentralization, however, has primarily been on the bureaucratic side of the equation, rather than among IDPs. In interviews, local officials said that the central and provincial government occasionally used the promise of regional autonomy to encourage or force local governments to deal with issues involving IDPs and reconciliation in a timely manner. Local officials worried that a poor handling of the IDP situation, or a return to violence, could possibly cost them their hoped-for autonomy as new districts (*kabupaten*). For example, in northern Halmahera, regional officials were informed that reconciliation and the smooth return of IDPs were vital to the ongoing redistricting process. Officials in Tobelo were supposedly warned that a failure to integrate Muslim IDPs successfully could lead to another town being chosen as the district capital. After these stories began circulating, a number of prominent individuals in Tobelo significantly changed the tone of their discussions about returning Muslim IDPs, as well as the way they would talk about the conflict in public. In contrast, rarely did IDPs in North Maluku or North Sulawesi mention decentralization as a concern in their decision-making process, other than to note that, in the case of Tobelo, regional autonomy meant more opportunities due to development and an expected plethora of civil service positions. They were often more concerned with presidential politics or those at the gubernatorial level, as they believed officials at those levels were the ones who could have an impact on preventing future violence.[17]

A Reluctant Success: Tobelo Muslims

Not everyone who returned home made that decision willingly. In some cases, government leaders lost their patience while waiting for IDPs to make up their minds. The Ternate municipal government, host to a large number of Muslim IDPs from Tobelo who were reluctant to return, exemplified this impatience. The ferocity of the violence in Tobelo made many Muslims from Tobelo reluctant to return. Moreover, the presence of several thousand Christian IDPs in Tobelo who had moved from elsewhere in the province, many of whom were living in abandoned Muslim homes, caused the displaced Muslims to think twice about returning. Muslims from Tobelo said they were not afraid of the locals, but of displaced Christians from elsewhere who were still upset about the conflict and might attack them. Furthermore, in the case of Tobelo proper, most of the Muslims had limited economic prospects, as Christians had taken over their previous occupations. Prior to

---

[17] The situation could be different in other provinces in Indonesia. For the impact of decentralization on the violence in Poso, see Lorraine Aragon, "Elite Competition in Central Sulawesi," in *Renegotiating Boundaries: Local Politics in Post-Suharto Indonesia*, ed. Henk Schulte Nordholt and Gerry van Klinken (Leiden: KITLV, 2007), pp. 39–66.

the conflict, Muslims constituted 95 percent of the laborers in Tobelo harbor and 90 percent of the traders in the market.[18] After January 2000, when Muslims fled the region, those jobs were taken over by Christians who were unlikely to give them up.

A policeman directs a Muslim IDP at the Tobelo harbor as she disembarks from the passenger ship that returned her from Ternate in September of 2002.
(Photo by Christopher R. Duncan)

By mid-2002, Ternate city officials and the local residents had lost their patience with the IDPs for a variety of reasons. The number of displaced in the city remained high, and many locals felt intimidated by what they considered the arrogant and violent nature of IDPs from Tobelo. The IDPs had demonstrated on a number of occasions when they felt their aid had been misappropriated, and at times these demonstrations had turned violent.[19] They were also known to react violently to

---

[18] Rudy William Tindage, *Damai yang Sejati: Rekonsiliasi di Tobelo, Kajian Teologis dan Komunikasi* (Jakarta: Yakoma-PGI, 2006), p. 40.

[19] For example, see "Bajingan Dibalik Pemulangan Pengungsi," *Ternate Pos*, February 27, 2001.

news of negative developments in Tobelo.[20] Such demonstrations upset local people and caused panic among the (largely Christian) Chinese business owners, who would temporarily flee. As they fled, they would order any ships unloading in the harbor to return to sea, to avoid being looted. As a result, workers at the harbor would lose wages. Locals also blamed the IDPs for an increase in the crime rate.[21]

Regardless of the reasons why IDPs had not returned to Tobelo, the national government's new policy provided Ternate city officials with an opportunity to return most of the Muslim IDPs. Over the course of a few days in September 2002, the city government shipped several thousand displaced people to Tobelo. This solved the IDP problem in Ternate, but seriously exacerbated it in Tobelo.[22] Thousands of displaced Christians still lived in Tobelo, and they had no plans to go home in the near future. To make matters more complicated, many of them were living in the houses of the Muslim IDPs who had just been sent home. The local government, already stretched thin coping with Christian IDPs and hundreds of Muslims who had returned on their own initiative, was now being told to take care of thousands of returning Muslim IDPs with little aid from the provincial or national governments. People in Tobelo were concerned that the influx of so many returnees in such a short time could lead to violence. Indeed, in June and August 2002 there had been brief clashes between Christians and returning Muslims to the north of Tobelo, and many thought the arrival of a large number of additional Muslims would exacerbate those tensions. Fortunately, the feared violence never broke out, and tensions eased as the Muslims slowly reintegrated back into Tobelo society.

WE WON'T GO HOME AGAIN: CHRISTIANS FROM TERNATE AND TIDORE IN NORTH SULAWESI

In contrast to the relatively successful large-scale return of Muslims to Tobelo, efforts to encourage displaced persons who had fled Ternate and Tidore to return to their previous homes were less successful. During 2001–2002, most of those IDPs swore they would never return to either island and were instead making plans for their futures either in North Sulawesi or on Halmahera. Unlike reluctant IDPs from other regions who eventually changed their minds and returned home, many of those from Ternate and Tidore have continued to maintain this stance. The IDPs' reasons for not returning to Ternate and Tidore initially revolved around the large number of Muslim IDPs there, many of whom were occupying their homes. Yet once the Ternate government uprooted and returned the majority of these Muslim IDPs to locations where they had lived previously, or they left on their own, Christians still remained reluctant to go back. Although a number of Christian IDPs have returned to Ternate, the vast majority have not. On Tidore, virtually no Christians have gone back, and various sources claim that the local government still says, albeit off the

---

[20] "Refugees Attack North Maluku Governors Office," *Antara*, August 8, 2002.

[21] "Pencuri Teri dan Pilatu Raksasa," *Ternate Pos*, October 10, 2000. For a similar claim in North Sulawesi, see Duncan, "Unwelcome Guests," p. 35.

[22] This movement of IDPs to Ternate also went against the provincial government's policy that sought to remove IDPs from Tobelo prior to sending those from Ternate home. See Gubernur Maluku Utara, *Kebijaksanaan Percepatan Pemulangan Pengungsi Tahap I dan Rencana Tahap II Tahun 2002 Program Pemulangan Pengungsi di Propinsi Maluku Utara* (Ternate: Kantor Gubernur Maluku Utara, August 19, 2002), pp. 2–3.

record, that the people of Tidore are not ready (*belum siap*) for the Christians, always a small community, to return.

Christians from Ternate who have not gone back often cite the "radicalization" of the city that they believe has taken place since the conflict as one of their main reasons. During the conflict, some Muslims in Ternate had supposedly, for a time, hung a banner at the entrance to the harbor saying "Welcome to the Islamic city of Ternate" (*Selamat Datang ke Ternate, Kota Islam*), and IDPs returning from visits to Ternate reported a new atmosphere in the city that reflected the sentiments of that banner even if it had long since disappeared. According to them, the conflict had turned Ternate into a more conservative and less tolerant place. Billboards and murals glorifying Osama Bin Laden and other Muslim icons were visible in parts of Ternate and Tidore, which some Christians found disturbing. A number of large mosques were under construction in various parts of town, and city planners appeared to be redefining the skyline. Rumors (albeit unsubstantiated) that the city government would eventually implement *shariah* law also made Christians reluctant to return.[23] People cited new legislation forbidding the sale and consumption of alcohol as a precursor to the eventual implementation of Islamic law.

The most common reason IDPs gave for not wanting to return to Ternate was that they did not feel welcomed by the Muslim population. They were not directly threatened or told to leave, but rather, they said, the town did not have the same sense of hospitality that it had prior to the conflict. Christian IDPs claimed that former Muslim friends no longer wanted to associate with them and would ignore them or pretend not to recognize them in passing. The lack of warmth that Christians experienced in their relations with their former Muslim neighbors created a sense of mistrust and unease that discouraged many Christians from moving back into their former homes. Many of these former residents concluded that they did not want to return to a community that considered them an unwelcome minority, particularly to a place where they had been chased out based on this minority status. They noted that the Muslims had resorted to violence in the past, and nothing prevented them from doing so again.

The reluctance of some Christians to return to Ternate and Tidore was not due entirely to fears of future conflict. Civil servants and teachers who had fled from these islands had been able to find employment in Manado and had no financial need to go back. A perceived sense of religious discrimination in North Maluku created another incentive for civil servants to stay in North Sulawesi. Many Christians felt that their religious affiliation limited their chances for advancement and promotion in many parts of North Maluku. Whether this discrimination was real or simply a perception remains undocumented, but it was a common complaint among Christian civil servants throughout North Maluku. It was one reason many chose to move to Christian-majority areas after the conflict. In addition to mentioning economic prospects, people cited the better educational opportunities for their children that were available in North Sulawesi. Although Ternate is generally perceived to have the best schools in North Maluku, people consider its schools to be inferior to those in Manado. High school graduates also had more educational

---

[23] Many Christians from North Maluku interpreted the implementation of Islamic law in Aceh and the subsequent stories about the closure of several churches as a possible sign of the future in Ternate. Movements to reinstate the Jakarta Charter also made some people nervous.

opportunities in North Sulawesi, whether at one of several established universities or numerous professional schools.

Other IDPs did not return to Ternate because they had already sold their homes there and had no place to live. In the months and years immediately following their flight, many IDPs felt they would never be able to go back to Ternate and live in peace. They also needed money to meet their basic needs. As a result, many decided, some reluctantly, to sell their homes. Finally, a number had never before lived in a town, like Manado, with a Christian majority, and they found the experience agreeable. They enjoyed the increased comfort level that they felt when they practiced their faith and celebrated religious holidays. The addition of this factor to the other factors—better schools and better economic conditions—made Ternate less than appealing, regardless of safety concerns.

AMBIGUITY AND AMBIVALENCE: RECONCILIATION IN NORTH MALUKU

One aspect of facilitating the return of IDPs involved efforts to prevent future conflict and bring about reconciliation between the two religious communities. Government officials, local leaders, and NGO workers consistently talked about the importance of reconciliation for the return and reintegration of IDPs and the future stability of North Maluku, yet they rarely clarified exactly what they meant by it. For the most part, government or military-sponsored efforts consisted of short ceremonies, often *adat*-themed communal meals, with speeches declaring that reconciliation had taken place. At other times, local officials hoped to institute reconciliation by simply telling people they needed to forget about the violence. For example, in Galela (in northern Halmahera) during 2002, local officials told communities that they must accept that the conflict had been "the work of God" and thus neither side was to blame. They hoped this declaration would lead to a reconciliation between the two sides and prevent future violence. This explanation was not well received. As one Christian man in Galela said:

> We are shocked that the government says we cannot blame anyone, and that we have to look at this as the work of God. You can call a famine, a drought, or a natural disaster the work of God, but social conflict is different. If a river turns to blood, you can say that is a curse sent by God, but the Muslims clearly invaded us. How can you say that is the work of God? Why do we have to share equal blame?

Officials' insistence that "all is well" and that people needed "to forget the past and look to the future" did little to improve relations between Muslims and Christians. This policy of forgetting occasionally increased resentment among community members, particularly those who saw themselves as victims of the violence. Regardless of local reactions to this strategy, it appears that local governments in North Maluku are not seeking to identify perpetrators of violent acts during the conflict or their victims. The government most likely fears that any attempt to label or prosecute individuals for their actions during the conflict would lead to new outbreaks of violence directed at both government officials and the security apparatus, as well as renewed ethno-religious conflict.

In addition to the limited attempts by the local government, some local and international NGOs also made efforts at reconciliation. They tried to facilitate reconciliation throughout the province with a variety of methods, including seminars and multi-day workshops. Many people in North Maluku pointed out that these meetings were rather pointless as the people who attended the workshops and forums were precisely the people who *wanted* reconciliation. The people who refused to reconcile and who refused to attend such workshops were the ones who might have benefited from such activities. Ironically, on one occasion in August 2002, while an international NGO was holding a reconciliation workshop in Tobelo, some recently returned Muslims burned down a local community college and numerous houses before being chased off by local militia, who then proceeded to attack and burn down Muslim homes to the north of Tobelo.[24] The discourse of "reconciliation" coming from government officials, NGO workshops, and seminars was hard to avoid in the years right after the conflict. People often complained about the constant talk of reconciliation by officials in public settings, officials who many felt were being disingenuous. Some even accused officials and others of using the discourse of reconciliation as a way to make money. People who took part in these workshops were often paid for their time, and also gained access to NGO staff, which, some argued, allowed them to compete more effectively for future contracts, grants, or staff jobs in these same NGOs.

The local government in Tobelo (in northern Halmahera) appears to be less cynical and hopes to stimulate reconciliation by reviving local interest in *adat*. Officials and local elites argue that more than thirty years of New Order religious policy led people to identify themselves with their religion (as Muslim or Christian) rather than by their ethnic identity (as Tobelo). They hope the revival of *adat* will encourage people to see themselves as Tobelo Christians and Muslims rather than as Muslim Tobelo or Christian Tobelo and make them less susceptible to religious-based provocation. However, others dismiss this revival of *adat* as an elite initiative unlikely to have a significant impact on intra-group relations.[25] Critics point out that the leaders who promote this *adat*-based reconciliation strategy often use more divisive rhetoric when speaking to audiences from their own religious tradition. Others fear that an emphasis on *adat* will simply shift the focus of future conflicts to ethnicity.

Although reconciliation has taken root in several places and among various individuals, the more common situation appears to be one of tolerance rather than reconciliation.[26] Most communities accept that Muslim or Christian IDPs have returned to their community or will eventually do so. They are willing to accept the return of these IDPs, but many on both sides still view the other with suspicion. For example, although a large number of Muslims have returned to Tobelo, the community in general remains segregated, and many people still talk in private of their dislike and mistrust for the other religious community. Furthermore, not all IDPs who have returned to their homes wish to live in mixed communities. In some instances, returning minority communities have established new villages a short

---

[24] "Dua Desa di Tobelo Rusuh, Puluhan Rumah Dibakar, 1 Tewas," *Komentar*, August 8, 2002; and "N. Maluku Violence Leaves One Dead," *Jakarta Post*, August 9, 2002.

[25] Tindake, *Damai yang Sejati*, pp. 110–11.

[26] For examples of locally initiated attempts at reconciliation, see "Jemaat Duma Sumbang 50 Juta untuk Mesjid Dokulamo," *Sangkakala: Media Informasi dan Komunikasi GMIH* [Tobelo] 2 (May 2006): 4; and "Muslim-Kristen di Maluku Utara Bahu-Membahu Mewujudkan Rekonsiliasi," *Berita Oikoumene* (June 15–July 15, 2006): 41–42.

distance from their previous homes but within walking distance of their gardens. For example, Muslim returnees to the village of Tatam in Central Halmahera established a new settlement of Tatam Islam a few kilometers from the village of Tatam rather than move back into the village. Similar developments have taken place in Jailolo, Oba, and elsewhere.

The secretary of the Adat Council (Indonesian, *Dewan Adat*) leads the 2002 Independence Day celebration ceremony in Tobelo. Many in Tobelo believe a revival of *adat* could help prevent future conflict. (Photo by Christopher R. Duncan)

RELOCATION AND TRANSMIGRATION

Not all IDPs wanted to or could return to their pre-conflict homes for a variety of reasons. Families that decided to relocate had two options: they could move independently to a place of their own choosing or they could take part in one of the government-sponsored resettlement schemes, usually the government's transmigration program.[27] IDPs who relocated independently went to a number of places. Many Christian IDPs from Ternate or from other Muslim-majority areas of North Maluku moved to Tobelo and surrounding villages. Tobelo was an attractive destination because many Christians wanted to live in a Christian-majority community. They also chose Tobelo due to the perceived security of the region and the economic opportunities available there. Some Makian IDPs who did not wish to return to Malifut returned to the island of Makian, which the government had "re-opened" with much fanfare in June 2002.[28] Other Makian moved to Bacan or parts of southern Halmahera, where many had planted gardens prior to their resettlement in 1975.[29] A number of Muslim IDPs relocated to the village of Togoliua, south of Tobelo, in the subdistrict of Tobelo Selatan. This village had been destroyed during the violence, and many of the villagers had been killed. A number of people relocated there to increase the population so as to make it a viable settlement. Others took advantage of unclaimed land, or married into families who had returned.

One interesting aspect of this process, as IDPs searched for new homes, was the use and influence of recruitment, as members of particular communities encouraged families to move to their village or region in an attempt to increase the population of their religious community. The largest example of this recruitment was the effort undertaken by some of the Christian elite in Tobelo to encourage IDPs from Ternate, Tidore, and elsewhere to move to Tobelo, rather than stay in North Sulawesi or return to their former homes. They argued that the future of North Maluku lay in Tobelo and it would be easier for IDPs to find employment there. They sought to entice civil servants and other skilled labor to Tobelo to spur the economic growth of the region. They also noted that Tobelo had never been taken by Muslim forces during the conflict. Some smaller communities elsewhere in the province tried to recruit Christian IDPs to provide manpower for possible future conflicts. In 2002, I met a delegation from a Christian village in central Halmahera who were recruiting Christian IDP families to move to their village or neighboring villages to increase their population size, as a defense against potential future violence. They argued that since they lived near several large Muslim villages, they needed to augment their population for their own protection.

IDPs who did not want to relocate independently could participate in the government's transmigration program. For IDPs from North Maluku, the government's relocation option meant taking part in one of several transmigration

---

[27] The Indonesian transmigration program moves landless peasants and other impoverished rural and urban populations (usually from the overcrowded islands of Java, Madura, and Bali) to the more sparsely populated parts of the archipelago. As part of this program, the Department of Transmigration builds new villages (i.e., transmigration settlements) to house these government-sponsored migrants. The Indonesian government gave the Department of Transmigration the task of resettling IDPs and refugees from the various conflicts that plagued Indonesia at the end of the twentieth century. See Christopher R. Duncan, "Die neue Existenzberechtigung: Transmigration, Wiederansiedlung und interne Zwangsvertreibung in Indonesien," *Südostasien* 3 (2005): 47–50.

[28] The island of Makian was evacuated in 1975, as described above. After that time, some people slowly moved back to the island in small numbers, but since the island was officially closed there were no public services. The government reopened the island with the issuance of SK Bupati No 284/2002. For more on the reopening of the island, see "Dibuka Setelah Seperempat Abad Ditutup," *Ternate Pos*, July, 2, 2002.

[29] For more on Makian migration patterns, see Ronald Lucardie, "Spontaneous and Planned Movement among the Makianese of Eastern Indonesia," *Pacific Viewpoint* 26 (1985): 63–78.

projects in North Maluku or North Sulawesi.[30] In North Maluku, the Department of Transmigration built one transmigration site in 2002 on the island of Mayu (also known as Batang Dua) in the Moluccas Sea between Sulawesi and Ternate. The Department of Transmigration moved forty Christian families (IDPs) with fishing backgrounds to this new settlement. Within the province of North Sulawesi, the government built two transmigration sites for IDPs in 2002: Kakenturan Dua, in the western part of the district of Minahasa; and Serey-Sangkilang, in eastern Minahasa.[31] Conflicting land claims plagued both of these projects, and local officials warned of the possibility of violence between IDPs and local populations if the projects went ahead as planned, which they did.[32] The anger in those cases was directed at the government, however government officials and NGOs worried that it could just as well be vented on the IDPs.

Outside of the transmigration program, the provincial government of North Sulawesi built a resettlement site for IDPs in the village of Pandu, behind the city of Manado. City officials originally designated the site as temporary housing for IDPs from North Maluku, and families were to be granted use rights over the houses, not ownership. After the North Maluku IDPs had gone home, the houses would be available for IDPs from future conflicts or natural disasters. The government wanted to avoid placing IDPs or refugees in camps in the city in the future. Conflicting land claims plagued this project from the start.[33] Local residents were angry that land they had been using was seized by the government for the project. To stem the problem of jealousy among poor segments of the local community, some people were granted land on an adjoining plot, but they did not receive houses. In addition, many IDPs who claimed houses in the site continued to live in the city, and locals were upset by the sight of hundreds of vacant houses that they were not allowed to use. At various points, these tensions broke out into violence, resulting in the destruction of resettlement houses and physical attacks on IDPs. Regardless of those conflicts, a large number of IDP families decided to stay in Pandu and still lived there in October 2007.

THE INTEGRATION OF IDPS

Despite the government's efforts at all levels to send IDPs home, it was clear that a significant number would not be returning to their place of origin or relocating elsewhere. Many have decided to stay where they had lived for the last several years.

---

[30] Javanese transmigrants from North Halmahera who were taken back to Java were given the option of joining other transmigration projects throughout Indonesia. Based on interviews with returned Javanese transmigrants in November 2005, it appears that some took these opportunities and moved to other places, such as Kalimantan. For example, in the transmigration settlement of Markati, in North Halmahera, the village head estimated that only about 60 percent of the Javanese had returned by the end of 2005.

[31] There were eight other transmigration sites proposed for IDPs, but their present status remains undocumented. See "Sekilas tentang Lokasi Transmigrasi Betelen," *Suara Pengungsi* 2 (September–October 2003): 8–10.

[32] "Warganya Butuh Pemukiman, Pemkab Bolmong Tolak Transmigrasi," *Komentar*, August 10, 2001; and "Kadistrans Bantah Menyerobot Lokasi Transmigrasi Likupang," *Komentar*, July 30, 2002.

[33] "Hari Ini Warga Pandu Demo," *Manado Post*, November 14, 2001; "Gubernur 'Kalah' Kasus Pandu," *Sulut Post*, August 31, 2002.

In North Sulawesi, the government had concerns that if too many IDPs stayed in Manado or Bitung, social conflict could develop. They based those fears in part on low-level tensions in North Sulawesi that had developed shortly after the arrival of the IDPs in November 1999. Officials voiced these fears of future conflicts on numerous occasions, hoping to encourage the IDPs to leave North Sulawesi. In one meeting, the official in charge of handling forced migrants concluded his discussion with IDPs from North Maluku by saying: "If you [the IDPs] do not go back to North Maluku, in ten years my children will kill your children, since this is our homeland, not yours." In early May 2003, those tensions erupted into violence in Bitung, when an argument between local youth and IDP youth turned into a large-scale conflict that lasted several days, necessitating the intervention of the army.[34]

To help those who had decided to stay, the provincial government instigated a "termination" program in April 2003.[35] Each family that stayed was supposed to receive a so-called "termination package." Acceptance of the package meant that the family in question relinquished IDP status and any claims to future aid. These people then became registered members of the local community. The "termination package" came in different forms; for example, those who accepted could choose the "trading stall" option, in which a family received a glass-fronted cabinet and a small amount of goods to sell. Another choice was the "bakery" option, through which former IDP families received bakery equipment and baking supplies. IDPs protested this termination package program, because they argued that the central government had promised them more.[36] They were promised Rp.3.5 million in cash to assist them in becoming self-sufficient (*uang saku/uang modal*), as well as Rp.5.5 million to build or purchase a house. In their protests, as usual, they complained of corruption in the Department of Social Affairs, and as usual officials denied the allegations.[37] People who accepted these termination packages reported that they did not receive a sufficient amount of aid to live independently of other aid or assistance, particularly after the officials deducted a large percentage for "distribution and administration."

These termination programs failed to resolve completely the "problem" of IDPs in North Sulawesi; several hundred families still lived in camps in Manado and Bitung in March 2007. To the dismay of city officials, these families continued to live in former IDP camps long after the aid had been stopped. Some even remained after the local government turned off the electricity and water. Interviews conducted in IDP camps in July 2006 found that people stayed for a variety of reasons. Some claimed to be waiting for their children to finish classes in local schools. Others said

---

[34] "Bentrok Massa, Wangurer Nyaris Rusuh," *Komentar*, May 6, 2003; "FSK Desak Pengungsi Dipulangkan," *Komentar*, May 6, 2001; "Pemkot Harus Tegas," *Manado Post*, May 6, 2003; and "Pengungsi Bentrok dengan Warga Wangurer: 2 Korban Luka Parah, Warga Minta Mereka Dipulangkan," *Manado Post*, May 6, 2003.

[35] The national government instituted a similar program in 2004, in which each IDP/refugee family was supposed to receive Rp.3,750,000 to move out of the camp and establish a self-sufficient household. See "Pemerintah Akan Laksanakan Program Terminasi Pengungsi," *Sinar Harapan*, June 22, 2004.

[36] "Pengungsi Maluku Utara di Manado Berunjuk Rasa," Liputan6.com, February 26, 2003. Similar claims and demonstrations were also made by IDPs elsewhere in Indonesia; see "Mensos Disambut Unjuk Rasa Pengungsi Poso," *Sinar Harapan*, July 30, 2002; and "Setelah Memblokir Bandar Udara Polonia Pengungsi Aceh Mogok Makan," *Kompas*, March 14, 2003.

[37] Subsequent events vindicate the IDPs' claims; see "Tiga Pejabat Mengutil Dana Pengungsi Manado," *Koran Tempo*, November 8, 2003.

they were waiting on the completion of new homes. Some admitted they were simply taking advantage of the free housing as long as they could. One man in Manado joked that if he waited long enough the entire place would be his. Some had already taken houses in Pandu or in other settlements but wanted to remain in the camps as long as they could due their central location in the city. A few simply had nowhere else to go and had little option but to continue living in the camps. There were claims that city governments would finally close the camps, but IDPs quickly pointed out that officials had been declaring deadlines for the closure of the camps since as early as 2002.

Many Christian IDPs have also decided to stay in Tobelo. Tobelo was the final destination for thousands of IDPs from all over the province during the conflict. Many have been there for more than five years and see no reason to go home; this is particularly true of Christian IDPs from Muslim-majority areas such as Ternate, Tidore, and southern and central parts of Halmahera. During the conflict, some had been forced to flee through the island's forested interior, at times making journeys of several weeks, and they did not want to have to repeat that ordeal if violence broke out again. One of the largest groups of IDPs that appears to be staying consists of Christian IDPs from Payahe in what was formerly the Oba subdistrict, in central Halmahera. They say they do not feel comfortable going home again and cite their minority status as the primary reason. Those who have made trips to Payahe claim that the Muslims in the Payahe region are still aggressive and they cannot do anything about it. Some of them report that local Muslims continue to work their coconut and spice groves that were seized during the conflict and refuse to return them. As one IDP said: "They [the Muslims] can do whatever they want. If they want something from you, they can just take it. What can you do? (*Ngana mau bikin apa?*)" Enough IDPs from Payahe still live in Tobelo that people now refer to a neighborhood on the outskirts of town as the "Payahe Complex." Tobelo was different than North Sulawesi and Ternate in that people in Tobelo generally welcomed the presence of Christian IDPs. In particular, the Tobelo elite welcomed the continued presence of IDPs because they were motivated by a desire to build up the region and eventually overshadow Ternate as the urban center of the province.

The social changes that have taken place amongst the IDPs themselves have also been a major factor in some of their decisions not to return home. IDPs from rural areas who fled to the urban centers of Manado, Bitung, Ternate, or Tobelo no longer want to live in rural areas. Several years of living in urban settings have changed their perceptions and their goals in life in such a way that returning to work in their coconut and spice groves no longer seems a desirable option. Some have married into local families while waiting for the conflict to stop and now wish to remain in North Sulawesi or elsewhere. Others have created new social networks (e.g., made up of church congregations, school friends) that they now value more than previous relationships in their places of origin.

A SITUATION IN FLUX

In the end, the Indonesian government's plan to end the country's conflict-induced displacement by the end of 2002 proved unrealistic. The government consistently pushed back the deadline in various parts of the country, as the initial goal proved unattainable. However, in 2004, regardless of the actual return, relocation, or integration rates of IDPs, the government declared that all IDPs, with the exception of those in Ambon and Central Sulawesi, no longer had IDP status.[38] Officially there are no longer any IDPs in North Maluku or North Sulawesi, but in reality thousands of displaced people still live in both provinces. More than six years after the cessation of hostilities in North Maluku, many communities and families must still deal with issues of displacement. The situation changes constantly as people move around, investigating various locales before deciding to settle in one village or town. Oftentimes these decisions are tentative, and the families or individuals eventually move elsewhere. Many who swore never to return to their pre-conflict homes have gone back, and others may still change their minds. Some are returning to stay, while others are simply tying up loose ends before they move elsewhere. As mentioned above, in March 2007 there were still IDPs living in camps in North Sulawesi, and the same was true for Ternate. Regarding the latter, however, many of the IDPs still in the camps are Christians who moved from camps in North Sulawesi to Ternate, where they are waiting to receive compensation for their destroyed homes. Many of these IDPs say they will move on once they receive compensation, but surely some will decide to stay and rebuild their lives in Ternate. This situation will continue to be in flux for some time to come as economies recover and intra-group relationships improve or deteriorate across the province.

As many have noted in contexts outside of Indonesia, the problems and challenges of displacement do not end once people have gone home or moved out of an IDP camp.[39] Even after the camps are empty and the last aid has been distributed, the proper handling of former IDPs remains important. The reintegration or integration of displaced people into post-conflict communities remains crucial to the continuing stability and economic development of post-conflict regions. During the height of the IDP crisis, some government officials worried that tensions between IDPs and their host communities could lead to violence.[40] They should be equally concerned with the reintegration of ex-IDPs and the potential for conflict surrounding this process. The failure to fully reintegrate the formerly displaced into post-conflict communities can sow the seeds for future violence as perceived wrongs and injustices mount and rekindle old animosities or create new ones (not necessarily based on religious differences). On the other hand, if done properly, the reintegration or integration of IDPs can speed the process of reconciliation and, one hopes, prevent future outbreaks of communal violence.

---

[38] Bakornas PBP, *Follow-up Workshop on the Management of IDPs*, p. 27. Refugees from East Timor residing in East Nusa Tenggara were also not affected by this decision. In Maluku the deadline was pushed back until the end of 2005. See "Penyelesaian Pengungsi Maluku Diundur Akhir 2005," Radio Vox Populi [Ambon], September 13, 2005.

[39] Tania Ghanem, "When Forced Migrants Return 'Home': The Psychosocial Difficulties Returnees Encounter in the Reintegration Process," Oxford: Refugee Studies Center Working Paper No. 16 (October 2003); Gaim Kibreab, "When Refugees Come Home: The Relationship between Stayees and Returnees in Post-Conflict Eritrea," *Journal of Contemporary African Studies* 20,1 (2002): 53–80; and Tim Allen and Hubert Morsink, eds., *When Refugees Go Home* (London: James Currey, 1994).

[40] Duncan, "Unwelcome Guests," pp. 39–41.

Spontaneity, Conspiracy, and Rumor: The Politics of Framing Violence in Central Kalimantan

Hélène Bouvier and Glenn Smith

Anti-Madurese riots in Kalimantan in 1996–1997, 1999, and 2001 were marked by displacements, killings, and brutality on a scale not seen in Kalimantan since the military-orchestrated 1967 anti-Chinese violence.[1] In Central Kalimantan alone, in the space of several weeks in 2001, over 150,000 Madurese were forced out of the province and at least 500 were killed. Though very little discussion has focused on the precise chain of events leading up to and continuing through the massacres, much discussion in the press and in scholarly writings on these events has dwelled on the various motivations thought to have driven Dayak and Malays to vent their anger on the Madurese. These motivations range from background causes, such as ecological and economic change, the history of disempowerment suffered by native groups during the New Order regime, and resentment of the relative success of migrant groups, including the Madurese, to proximate and triggering causes, such as rivalry between youths and gangs from the different ethnic groups, failures in the response of the security apparatus, and politicization of ethnicity[2] and government instability in Jakarta.

The explanation most often given by Dayaks, and the official position adopted by Dayak academics and spokespersons, is that the Madurese, imbued with a

[1] This article is based on fieldwork conducted on several occasions between 2002 and 2005 in Madura (both authors) and in 2002 in West and Central Kalimantan (first author). The opinions expressed are solely the authors', unless otherwise noted. The authors presented some of the information here in separate papers at the Southeast Asian Conflict Studies Network Conference 2004, in Penang, Malaysia, on January 12–15, 2004; and an earlier version of this paper appeared in a special issue of the *Asian Journal of Social Science* ("Violence in Southeast Asia") under the title "Of Spontaneity and Conspiracy Theories: Explaining Violence in Central Kalimantan" 34,3: 475–91. The authors thank the editor and anonymous reviewers for their helpful advice on improving the present text.

[2] Stanley J. Tambiah, *Leveling Crowds: Ethnonationalist Conflicts and Collective Violence in South Asia* (Berkeley, CA: University of California Press, 1996), p. 22.

"culture of violence"[3] and criminality, and incapable of adapting to local customs, were opposed by exasperated Dayaks, who spontaneously rose up in the face of a planned Madurese "power play" and bombing campaign in the town of Sampit, Central Kalimantan. The Madurese view, which has received little attention, is that they were forced out of Kalimantan by groups that hoped to take over the assets and employment that they had obtained by the sweat of their brow. Conspiratorial and stereotypical thinking—rightly or wrongly—has thus imbued much commentary on these events.

It is striking the extent to which various Madurese points of view have been absent from commentaries on the events in Central Kalimantan, particularly as the Madurese were the principal victims. Most reports of the violence were based entirely on interviews with Dayaks in Central Kalimantan,[4] and it is primarily from these that the chronology of fateful events leading up to the tragedy is reconstructed. Adding the accounts of Madurese internally displaced people (IDPs) from Sampit and other areas of Central Kalimantan provides a more accurate, or at least more complete, rendition of the events.[5] Thus, after offering a brief background introduction to the conflicts, we begin by piecing together the accounts of the events leading up to the Sampit massacres, events that to this day remain a focus of contestation. The accounts demonstrate the role of rumors in the prelude to violent confrontations.[6] Two competing conspiracy theories, in fact, emerge from comparisons of the Dayak and Madurese accounts. We evaluate various elements of these theories and identify their weaknesses, and conclude that a conspiracy—or at least preplanning—cannot be ruled out. That there was a determined and politically effective effort by Dayak elites to frame the conflict, both before and immediately following the physical clashes, is beyond dispute. The discussion then turns to the reasons for the wide dispersion and the tacit acceptance of the Dayak account (that the violence was the result of a spontaneous and defensive uprising). In closing, we show how this acceptance had an impact on government policy because it justified

---

[3] Dayaks, like most other Indonesians, regard Madurese society as violent and Madura Island to be racked by factionalism and frequent revenge killings.

[4] One study was based on four to six weeks of research in each province and repeated research trips conducted to verify data in 2002 in Madura, East Java, and Central Kalimantan. See Claire Q. Smith, *The Roots of Violence and Prospects for Reconciliation: A Case Study of Ethnic Conflict in Central Kalimantan, Indonesia*, Social Development Papers, Conflict Prevention and Reconstruction Paper No. 23 (Washington, DC: World Bank, 2005). As to the chronology of the violence and the underlying causes for it, the study's conclusions appear to have been reached without input from Madurese.

[5] A recent work using such an approach is Rochman Achwan, Hari Nugroho, and Dody Prayogo, with Suprayoga Hadi, *Overcoming Violent Conflict*, Vol. 1: *Peace and Development Analysis in West Kalimantan, Central Kalimantan, and Madura*, ed. Glenn Smith (Jakarta: Crisis Prevention and Recovery Unit; United Nations Development Programme, LabSosio and BAPPENAS, 2005). See http://www.conflictrecovery.org/bin/Kalimantan-final[1].pdf; the Kalimantan page at www.conflictrecovery.org has links to or copies of some of the other documents cited in this chapter.

[6] Rumors are frequently mentioned in writings on ethnic conflict as elements of discourse, organizing images, and triggers for violence. See Paul Brass, *Theft of an Idol: Text and Context in the Representation of Collective Violence* (Princeton, NJ: Princeton University Press, 1997); Veena Das, *Mirrors of Violence: Communities, Riots, and Survivors in South Asia* (New Delhi: Oxford University Press, 1990); Donald L. Horowitz, *The Deadly Ethnic Riot* (Berkeley, CA: University of California Press, 2000); and Ashutosh Varshney, *Ethnic Conflict and Civic Life: Hindus and Muslims in India* (New Haven, CT: Yale University Press, 2002).

the decision to evacuate Madurese and how it affected the manner of post-violence reconciliation and return of IDPs.

THE EVENTS OF DECEMBER 2000 TO FEBRUARY 2001

Recognizing the complexity of the Kalimantan conflicts, analyses of the causes leading up to them often distinguish between structural, proximate, and trigger causes.[7] It seems clear that fundamental structural causes for all of the conflicts would have to include the evolutions in the legal framework, which—through the 1960 Basic Agrarian Law, the 1967 Basic Forestry Law, and the 1979 Village Government Law—effectively facilitated the award of thousands of hectares of land traditionally owned by Dayak and other indigenous groups to Jakarta-based plantation, forestry, and mining interests, or to government transmigration projects. The laws also established the priority of national over traditional, or *adat*, law, providing for state or private ownership of forests, and, in many cases, preventing indigenous access to land where such access had been guaranteed by *adat* law.

Although government-sponsored transmigration has frequently been cited as another background cause for the Kalimantan conflicts, for the most part violence has not occurred in or near transmigration settlements, though seizure of land for such schemes has led to the expression of Dayak grievances. The vast majority of Madurese in Central Kalimantan were born there or came on their own. Many Madurese were involved in urban trading, logging, mining, and road building, sectors where they were highly visible to indigenous groups, and sometimes in direct competition with them. This could have explained the growing resentment focused on the Madurese, who were seen to represent the state's monopoly over land and resources and its disregard for the laws and prerogatives of the indigenous people (even if the Javanese more accurately represent the state's monopoly). The Madurese, meanwhile, considered it within their rights as Indonesian citizens to make a living in any part of the archipelago.

Dayak political and ethnic empowerment cannot be ignored as key factors behind the violence,[8] and localized political events should be acknowledged as proximate causes. Indeed, the first killing of a Madurese family in Sampit occurred on the day before the Sampit district head was to install officials, in compliance with the new decentralization law, none of whom were Dayak, or at least none of whom represented the main Dayak organization, Lembaga Musyawarah Masyarakat Dayak dan daerah Kalimantan Tengah (LMMDD-KT, Dayak and Central Kalimantan Representatives Association). A local Dayak forestry official who was slated to lose his position due to this reorganization was later arrested in connection with the killing (he was released following extended Dayak protests).

Central Kalimantan Dayak leaders could not have ignored the fact that previous attacks on Madurese in West Kalimantan had resulted in substantial political gains for Dayaks and Malays. Security sector rivalry, with the military seen to be supporting the Dayak while the police were perceived to be more closely allied with Madurese, was also part of the equation. This was a very volatile period, with

---

[7] Ibid., all titles.

[8] Gerry van Klinken, "Indonesia's New Ethnic Elites," in *Indonesia in Search of Transition*, ed. Henk Schulte Nordholt and Irwan Abdullah (Yogyakarta: Pustaka Pelajar, 2002), pp. 67–105 (see www.knaw.nl/indonesia/transition/workshop/chapter4vanklinken.pdf).

tensions running high. As explained below, the unfolding events were to put Sampit on a hair-trigger footing.

Chronologies of the riots in Central Kalimantan in 2001 usually begin with the killing of a Dayak man by the name of Sendong by three Madurese on December 15, 2000, in a karaoke bar in a brothel complex near the town of Kereng Pangi in the district of Kotawaringin Timur, about one hundred kilometers from the provincial capital of Palangkaraya. In retaliation for the killing and the flight of the three Madurese, Dayaks burned homes, cars, and motorbikes as well as four buses belonging to Madurese, causing some one thousand Madurese to flee into the surrounding forest and others to seek protection at the local police post. Eventually 1,335 Madurese were taken back to Madura Island, in East Java.[9]

In January 2001, tensions were high among the Madurese, who feared that the violence in Kereng Pangi could spread to Sampit, the main economic hub of Central Kalimantan province and one of the few towns in which Madurese made up a large percentage of the population: an estimated 60 percent.[10] On December 20, 2000, an explosion in a home in Sampit killed two Madurese and seriously burned four others in another house, the blast causing panic in an already tense population. Dayaks saw this as evidence for rumors that had been circulating that the Madurese were stockpiling bombs, even though the police chief in Palangkaraya quickly announced that, according to preliminary investigations, the blast had been caused by the explosion of firecracker materials *(bahan baku mercon, petasan)*,[11] probably stockpiled for use during the Lebaran festivities. In the following days, there were reports of rudimentary bombs being found in Sampit homes, and the military began to search passengers on ships arriving from Java. New rumors circulated and reverberated in the regional press that "the financiers for the homemade bombs are all the migrant leaders who are living it up in Sampit and the outskirts," and that their plan was to blow up "an extremely vital bridge on January 5th."[12]

The standard account outlined above is well known and has been repeated in many accessible documents. Not well known are the Madurese views[13] of these events; thus the rest of this section will present both versions and highlight their differences. First we examine the Kereng Pangi incident. There is some confusion as to what role exactly was played by the Dayak victim, Sendong, and uncertainty about the exact events of that fateful evening. Sendong has been identified variously as a Dayak militant involved in a riot the year before, a drunken miner,[14] or the son

---

[9] International Crisis Group (ICG), *Communal Violence in Indonesia: Lessons From Kalimantan*, ICG Asia Report No. 19, June 27 (Jakarta & Brussels: ICG, 2001), pp. 3–4.

[10] Prior to the conflict in 2001, the Madurese made up about 6 to 7 percent of Central Kalimantan's population.

[11] "Ledakan di Sampit Tewaskan Dua Orang" (Kompas, 20 December 2000); see http://www.library.ohiou.edu/indopubs/2000/12/20/0078.html

[12] "Arus Balik Bakal Diperiksa," *Banjarmasin Post*, January 3, 2001; see http://www.indomedia.com/bpost/012001/3/metropa/metro4.htm. The Sampit police chief denied the rumors.

[13] Not all details of the Madurese view presented here are necessarily recognized by all Madurese, though few of the many dozens of Madurese of all social backgrounds interviewed in West and East Madura, while they resided in IDP camps and with receiving families, would argue with the general outline. Many elements are confirmed, however, by a non-Madurese source from the conflict area who prefers to remain anonymous.

[14] Van Klinken, "Indonesia's New Ethnic Elites," p. 13.

of a neighborhood chief. According to one Madurese source, in a newspaper interview a family member was quoted as stating that, on the day of his murder, Sendong was picked up at his home in Buntok, Barito Selatan, and driven off in an unknown sedan. This was unusual, as he habitually took a minibus to get to Kereng Pangi. A Madurese version of the events in the karaoke bar has Sendong repeatedly jabbing one of the Madurese with the butt of a stick (a cue stick?) to provoke him before he, Sendong, was mortally attacked. Then, according to many Madurese IDPs, a very short time elapsed between the killing and the appearance of a large group of Dayaks in red headbands; given the quickness of their response, these avengers must have been organized prior to the killing, according to the Madurese. Evidence for both these interpretations of events is ephemeral. The exact newspaper reference has been forgotten, and the article could not be located (even if true, it proves nothing by itself). The stick detail is impossible to verify. The precise chronology of the incident and the Dayak response is unclear. But for many Madurese, this version of the story adds fuel to the sentiment that at Kereng Pangi they were being provoked in order to elicit a response.

A number of IDPs see the burning of Madurese homes and vehicles in Kereng Pangi, following the murder of Sendong, as the first major provocation, to which the Madurese responded by fleeing the area. On December 30, 2000, a second event occurred that the Madurese interpreted as a provocation: five migrants' (read: Madurese) homes were set afire on Jalan Tjilik Riwut, Km. 35, Kecamatan Bukit Batu, Kelurahan Tangkiling, Palangkaraya.[15] Again, cooler heads prevailed, and the Madurese did not respond. Events would be different when what Madurese IDPs call the third provocation occurred in Sampit, six weeks later.

This third provocation took place on Sunday, February 18, 2001. Shortly after midnight, on the eve of the ceremony installing new district government officials following district reorganization, a family of five Madurese in Baamang-Sampit were killed in their sleep.[16] Madurese immediately surrounded a nearby house, in which the killers were thought to have holed up. When the police intervened to take the suspects into custody, the Madurese vented their anger by burning one or more Dayak houses, killing a family that was caught inside one. Madurese then went on the offensive and killed up to twenty-four Dayaks.[17] For the next two days, according to the Dayak version of events, the Madurese "controlled" Sampit, parading around on motorbikes and shouting inflammatory statements like "Dayaks are cowards." Banners appeared with provocative titles proclaiming Madurese ownership of the town (at least one renaming the town "Sampang 2," after the Madura Island town). Enraged Dayaks at first fled Sampit, then returned with hinterland supporters beginning on February 20 and commenced killing Madurese and burning their homes in Sampit.[18] Bombs were discovered in vacated Madurese houses, seemingly confirming earlier rumors that the Madurese were stockpiling bombs with intent to

---

[15] *Banjarmasin Post*, January 2, 2001; http://www.indomedia.com/bpost/012001/2/depan/depan6.htm

[16] It was claimed Sendong's killers were hiding in the house, or variations of that claim (e.g., see http://www.earthisland.org/borneo/news/articles/010208article.html).

[17] The most often cited figure is up to eighteen dead and eight structures burned down, though the official figures show only 13 Dayaks killed out of 469 for the entire conflict.

[18] ICG, *Communal Violence in Indonesia*, pp. 4–5.

use them as weapons.[19] The killing and ethnic cleansing then began in the hinterlands, in the capital, Palangkaraya, and throughout most of the rest of the province. Dual discourses—that the Madurese were somehow less than human, and that they posed a threat to Dayak lands—were widely encouraged (see Fig. 1 and 2); they served to fuel the horrific violence that descended on the Madurese, including mass beheadings and looting of assets (see Fig. 3).

Figure 1: Madurese effigy, street corner, Palangkaraya. The writing says, *Orang Madura ... Hukum Mati* (Madurese ... Death Penalty). (Photo by Gerry van Klinken, March 2001)

---

[19] This chronology, essentially followed by subsequent outside researchers and including mystical glorification of the Dayak *"gerilyawan,"* appears in many Internet postings, notably two sent by "Svperstar" on May 13, 2001 to the *apakabar* listserv:
http://www.library.ohiou.edu/indopubs/2001/05/13/0006.html and
http://www.library.ohiou.edu/indopubs/2001/05/13/0009.html

Figure 2: Graffiti in Palangkaraya: "Stay away from Madurese, because Madurese smell like cows"; "Let us drive out the Madurese from free Dayak land!!!" *Tanah* (or *Bumi*) *Iseng Mulang* is a Dayak nationalist term for Central Kalimantan province.
(Photo by Gerry van Klinken, March 2001)

Figure 3: Looted Madurese home, Palangkaraya. (Photo by Gerry van Klinken, March 2001)

The accounts of several Madurese who were present in Sampit at the time add some detail to the above view—the generally accepted view—of the early killings in the town. Their reports also challenge the notion that the Madurese ever sought to "control" Sampit, and, if substantiated, would suggest that the Dayak attack on Sampit was planned well before the first five Madurese were killed on February 18.[20]

The West Kalimantan riots between Madurese and Dayak in 1996–1997, and between Madurese and Malay and later Dayak in 1999, had raised fears that Central Kalimantan would be next to explode. An embryonic multi-ethnic consultative group, chaired by the head of the Central Kalimantan Madurese Family Association (IKAMA, Ikatan Keluarga Madura Kalteng), Haji Marlinggi, had been set up to prevent or at least provide early warning of such an eventuality, but it was not yet fully operational in 2001. Haji Marlinggi, who owned one of the province's main stevedoring companies, was one of the leaders accused by Dayaks of stockpiling homemade bombs. Tensions in the Madurese community increased further in February, in fact, when rumors began circulating that groups of Dayak from neighboring provinces and the hinterlands of Kalimantan Tengah had been regrouping in camps on the outskirts of Sampit as early as two weeks before the first killings. On Thursday, February 15, 2001, a group of fifty Dayak leaders from West, East, and Central Kalimantan were received by Dayak leaders in Sampit, and they proceeded to occupy the house where the suspected killers would later take refuge in the early morning of February 18. Given the atmosphere in Sampit, the arrival of such a group raised suspicions among nervous Madurese. One Madurese leader approached the *bupati* (district head) of Kotawaringin Timur with the news that one of the *bupati*'s own deputies was among the group of men stationed in the house; he was told not to worry, that the Dayak were there only to carry out a ceremony, and that he, the *bupati*, had sent his deputy there to verify their intent. When he left the *bupati*'s office, this same Madurese leader went to alert Haji Marlinggi. Marlinggi warned him to keep quiet and not succumb to provocation. Saturday morning, February 17, this same leader received a phone call from a Dayak village head he knew well, a friend from earlier years when he had been a major trader in Kereng Pangi. The Dayak friend told him that he should prepare to evacuate his family. In the village head's words: "When the town's lights first go out, you run!" His friend told him that Dayak residents in Kereng Pangi were being asked to contribute Rp.50,000 each to a special force of six hundred fighters who were ready to initiate an attack on Sampit. The Madurese leader again contacted Marlinggi, this time by telephone, and was again told not to spread such information or do anything provocative. Thus, according to this Madurese, before any killings had occurred in the tense but still "peaceful" town of Sampit, a large group of Dayak were massing to attack the town.

The killing of the five Madurese in the early morning of Sunday, February 18, confirmed the worst fears of the Madurese elite in Sampit. A group of Madurese armed with sickles had surrounded the house where the Dayak leaders, and presumably the killers, were holed up. Marlinggi went with the district police chief (*kapolres*) and a small police force to try to persuade the Madurese not to be drawn into a conflict. The Madurese refused to stand down, and Marlinggi returned home after calling on the police to shoot any Madurese involved in actions against the

---

[20] Based on interviews in Surabaya and Madura with Madurese and non-Madurese leaders from Sampit in November 2003.

Dayak.[21] The Madurese persisted in demanding revenge and threatened to burn the house down to force the occupants out. The police then intervened and loaded all the occupants of the house into police trucks to bring them into custody as suspects. One suspect fell from the truck he had boarded and was killed by the Madurese. Enraged Madurese also tried to scale the trucks, but were shot at by police. They then focused their rage on several Dayak homes (from three to eight depending on the source), leaving up to eighteen Dayak dead, according to Madurese estimates.

At a meeting Sunday evening at the bus terminal, all the Madurese and their leaders came to an agreement that they must put an end to the violence now at all cost; the survival of their community depended on it. At the meeting the leaders reiterated Haji Marlinggi's earlier call on the police to shoot any Madurese involved in violence. Contrary to the accepted view of events, which holds that the Madurese had "the run of the town" or "controlled" Sampit from Sunday to Tuesday, Madurese IDPs from Sampit interviewed in Madura say that, during this period, various groups, usually multi-ethnic teams including Dayaks, were manning lookout posts in their neighborhoods as usual, though, admittedly, they were in a heightened state of alert due to the extreme apprehension of the townspeople. It is known that Dayaks were evacuating Sampit by then, but the Madurese version adds an important, but as yet unverified, claim: that the evacuation of Dayak families to Palangkaraya *preceded* the events of February 18. Asked about the provocative banners, the Madurese vehemently deny any knowledge of or responsibility for such displays. They say that such an action would be "stupid," "crazy," or "suicidal" for a small minority group such as theirs, and could only have been the work of the Dayak, intended to provoke and thereby mobilize their own fighters to "retake" Sampit.[22] Professing no knowledge of the youths on motorcycles who allegedly taunted Dayak ("the Dayak had all left Sampit by then," "Sampit was calm [after Sunday's incidents]"), some concede the possibility that "a few Madurese kids who didn't understand anything" might have been goaded by the sight of the banners into parading around.

On Monday, the word was out that Hotel Rahma, a Dayak-owned hotel, was full of Dayak warriors. The warriors delivered an ultimatum to the Madurese: Dayaks have completely surrounded Sampit; the Madurese must evacuate Sampit immediately, leaving their belongings behind, and in return they will be given safe passage. Marlinggi and, presumably, others refused to submit to this ultimatum. Marlinggi and his family were taken into protective custody by the police and later evacuated to Jakarta, where he was held for questioning. On Tuesday, the security forces instituted a "sweep" in Sampit to confiscate sharp weapons, according to most accounts. Several Madurese claim that the sweep only concerned Madurese and was effected by teams each composed of three Dayak men, a policeman, and a soldier. It was announced that the Dayaks from outside who were gathered in town had been invited to tour Sampit "just to check." At dawn on Wednesday, according to the

---

[21] Interviewed in Surabaya in 2003, Haji Marlinggi claimed that, after the Kereng Pangi incident, he paid a police team several million rupiah out of his own pocket to go to Madura in search of Sendong's killers, following reports that the killers had fled there. The team returned empty-handed.

[22] One cannot help being reminded of the rumors circulating in Bosnia that "Foca was going to be the new Mecca." People were marked for death, the rumors went, and the only choice was to attack first in order to preempt the attack. Stuart J. Kaufman, *Modern Hatreds: The Symbolic Politics of Ethnic War* (Ithaca, NY: Cornell University Press, 2001), p. 3.

Madurese, the Dayak leader Professor Usop announced that a peaceful resolution was no longer possible. Another Dayak leader, Ranang Baut, called for neighborhoods to be emptied in advance of a Dayak attack scheduled for ten o'clock the next morning.

In sum, the Madurese are convinced that the incidents in Kereng Pangi and especially Sampit were planned in advance to force them out of Kalimantan. Most feel they were "stupid" or "blind" not to have understood what was up. One said it was only once he was in Madura that certain preliminary details become clear to him. He said that a year before the troubles, a close Dayak friend asked why he would not consider selling off everything in Kalimantan and moving back for a comfortable retirement in Madura. He is convinced now that this Dayak was privy to information and was hoping he, as a friend, could be spared.

BETWEEN CONSPIRACY AND SPONTANEITY: EVALUATING VERSIONS OF EVENTS

The two versions of events, in pure forms, actually represent two competing conspiracy theories. In one, a conspiracy by Madurese to seize control of the province by force is crushed by the Dayaks rising up in spontaneous defense of their communities. In the other, Dayaks conspire to create a climate of tension and provoke attacks and counterattacks that justify an orchestrated campaign of violence and ethnic cleansing that will provide assets and employment for their disaffected youth, all in the absence of any provocation from peace-loving Madurese.

Conspiracy theories about the Sampit massacres can even come to resemble those spawned to explain the assassination of John F. Kennedy on November 22, 1963, in Dealey Plaza, in Dallas, Texas. In both, evidence is cherry-picked or emerges after the fact. Dayaks describe Madurese youths having the run of the town and proclaiming "Sampang 2," but they neglect to mention the Sunday meeting of Madurese community leaders at the bus terminal. Tantalizing reports of Dayak families evacuating Sampit before February 18 and other precursor details remain unproven.

When the rationale for an event is unclear, conspiracy theories often posit high-level scheming or dark motives; often these interpretations are post hoc embroideries on the facts or logically inconsistent with them. Evidence that Dayak fighters, military, and police all profited in some way from the Madurese evacuation is taken to show they were somehow "involved." On the other side, arguments are advanced claiming that a tiny Madurese minority had been poised to take over the entire province. Moreover, by interlocking coincidental or unusual events in a wider, more sinister, puzzle, conspiracy theories provide satisfaction and justifications to those who "understand." The fact that Sendong used an unusual form of transport that day means he must have been sent to provoke an incident in Kareng Pangi. The explosion in Sampit (at the "firecracker factory") was proof that Madurese were stocking bombs for a terror campaign. Prominently figuring in Dayak accounts of the Sampit massacres are outlandish claims—of flying swords, invulnerability—and self-aggrandizement that should be enough to cast serious doubts on the evidentiary value of whatever is put forth.[23]

---

[23] The equivalent among JFK assassination buffs would have to be Robert Morrow, though his James Bond-esque feats do not include wielding magical powers or invulnerability to bullets and arrows. See footnote 18, above, and Ulric Shannon, "First-Hand Knowledge: A Review,"

The main problem with conspiracy scenarios is that they propose observations that fit their theories rather than allow the theories to follow from the data.[24] Usually, characterizations of both parties are simplified to establish clearly innocent victims and conniving villains. To give simple examples: JFK was a "saint" murdered because he intended to withdraw from Vietnam;[25] Madurese had no problems whatsoever with their Dayak neighbors (according to the Madurese); or the Dayaks are a peace-loving people (according to the Dayaks). In each case, misbehavior by one's own group is portrayed as naïve, spontaneous, or, at most, the actions of uncontrollable rogue elements, while the misbehavior by the other group is said to have been orchestrated as part of a sinister, premeditated scenario.

Despite problems with applying conspiracy theories to the Sampit massacres, regarding them as clear-cut ethnic or communal disputes is too simplistic as well. We now have a number of well-researched reports and academic studies that suggest the massacres were not, or at least not only, the result of long-standing "horizontal disputes" and spontaneous communal reaction to initial incidents, but were largely, if not solely, based on well-organized and well-financed efforts to sustain and expand the conflicts to further local economic and political agendas.[26] There is a need to shift the focus to people who do violence and why, and away from questions of identities, religion, and ethnicity, since at a certain point somebody, or a small group of powerful individuals, takes decisions.[27] The capacity to commit violence (through organizations, weaponry, and techniques) is there waiting for the call; there is a reservoir of violence within society (institutions such as the army, criminal organizations, groups of thugs, vigilantes, or even members of sports clubs) composed of people whose careers are based on the use of physical violence, provocation, and terror. This violent complex constitutes the effective mechanism for past and potential violent conflicts.

Some Madurese adopt a behaviorist perspective, determining causality by outcomes, and see economic opportunism or collusion by security forces as two possible explanations for the massacres. There were likely many disadvantaged Dayaks who considered the economic success of the Madurese unfair. They could have been swayed into action by overt or tacit promises that they would receive Madurese property or assets in exchange for participation. And, in fact, Madurese

---

The Fourth Decade 1,1 (November 1993): 21–24 (see www.maryferrell.org/mffweb/archive/viewer/showDoc.do?docId=48678&relPageId=23).

[24] The well-documented effort by Gerry van Klinken, "Indonesia's New Ethnic Elites," is an exception. His contribution, which traces the history of ethnic mobilization and elite interventions in the run-up to and in the wake of the Sampit massacres, seriously undermines Dayak arguments that there was no preplanning.

[25] This theory, of course, received a wide audience through Oliver Stone's blockbuster film *JFK*, though evidence for this and other conjectures have not escaped challenge. See http://mcadams.posc.mu.edu/context1.htm; and Vincent Bugliosi, *Reclaiming History: The Assassination of President John F. Kennedy* (New York, NY: W. W. Norton, 2007). Cinema has also reinforced popular beliefs regarding Madurese violent society, notably the Indonesian film *Carok* (Duel), which played for a few weeks before it was outlawed in 1986. The film portrays a Madurese attending college in Java who interrupts his dissertation on the sociology of violence in order to return home and avenge the murder of his elder brother.

[26] ICG, *Communal Violence in Indonesia*; Van Klinken, "Indonesia's New Ethnic Elites."

[27] Robert Cribb, "Legal Pluralism, Decentralization, and the Roots of Violence in Indonesia" (paper presented at the LIPI-MOST UNESCO-CNRS Conference, "Conflict in Asia-Pacific: State of the Field and the Search for Viable Solutions," Jakarta, October 22–25, 2003).

homes and orchards were taken over during the years after the violence by Dayak warriors and disaffected youth. Some Madurese see in this development proof of a Dayak conspiracy to obtain economic benefits at their expense, though the Dayak accounts of the violence seem to suggest that the issues of fear and hatred were the more important factors fueling mobilization.[28] Fear and hatred may have been easier to stir up where there was a certain degree of ethnic segregation,[29] though Madurese IDPs dispute this notion that they were isolated from their Dayak neighbors by pointing to intermarriage, adoption, shared cultural practices, and religious practice, and the protection afforded the Madurese by other community members.

The role of the security forces has always been cited as an important factor in the Kalimantan violence. It has been said in their defense that the security forces were overwhelmed by the number of warriors involved, were not given clear orders, or received orders too late to stop the violence. Madurese IDPs, for their part, speak of deliberate apathy and nonintervention on the part of the police and army during the events,[30] as well as unwarranted reassurances given them by their own leaders, who were afraid that, by acting on the alarming clues provided by sympathetic Dayak friends, they would be succumbing to provocation and thus help trigger violent confrontations. Others go so far as to declare they are willing to testify before a judicial inquiry that security forces were well aware of the regrouping of warriors around Sampit prior to the massacres. From this point, it is easy to take the next step and see security sector inaction as the result of ulterior motives. Indeed, some security forces did profit from the precipitated departure of IDPs and the fire sales of their vehicles; the scramble for spoils might have been a factor in the shooting that occurred between army and police personnel in the port of Sampit on February 27, 2001. Although the police and perhaps the army may have been aware of mobilization before the attacks began in Sampit, there is no evidence to show that their inaction was due to anything more than fear of being outnumbered.

Timing and the perception that violent acts would go unpunished do seem to have made a decision to attack the Madurese easier to take. The Madurese had little support in Jakarta. The president at the time, Abdurachman Wahid, whose presidency and party were supported by most Madurese, was outside of the country. For months he had been at loggerheads with his vice president, Megawati Soekarnoputri, leader of the party supported by most Dayaks. Wahid's reforms were not popular among the security forces at that time. One does not need to engage in speculation as to the motives of political elites in Jakarta, beyond that they must have had a sense of being overstretched, with continuing troubles in Maluku, Central

---

[28] Dayaks sometimes do criticize Madurese for a tendency to display their wealth through home improvements or jewelry, a practice considered ostentatious or arrogant.

[29] Their living in a "segregated ethnic environment" was seen as a background cause for the West Kalimantan violence of 1996–97 and 1999. See Nancy Lee Peluso and Emily Harwell, "Territory, Custom, and the Cultural Politics of Ethnic War in West Kalimantan, Indonesia," in *Violent Environments,* ed. Nancy Lee Peluso and Michael Watts (Ithaca, NY: Cornell University Press, 2001), pp. 83–116.

[30] The Sampit events mirrored this account from South Asia where " ... violence (in part at least planned and directed) is committed by large 'impersonal' crowds and frequently acquiesced in by significant segments of the police force (who collude in the violence or passively watch it). In these circumstances, it is virtually impossible, or made impossible, to arrest offenders or expect offenders to be arrested. If arrests are made, they are simply token acts, and the offenders are soon released." Tambiah, *Leveling Crowds,* p. 329.

Sulawesi, and elsewhere to contend with. A likely scenario would have had local ethnics reasoning that the response from Jakarta to disorder would be neither swift nor firm so long as the attack was aimed against Madurese. Attacking the Javanese, on the other hand, could have triggered a very swift response from the security sector, many of whose senior leaders were Javanese. The Dayak needed the Chinese as business partners and to bankroll attacks against other groups, so they were not inclined to attack the Chinese.[31] But perhaps the most important reason for attacking the Madurese, as one Dayak elite in Central Kalimantan explained, was because the Madurese, unlike the other groups, would eventually respond to violence with violence. In hindsight, it appears the target and the moment were well chosen if the goal was to make a "shock and awe" political statement with minimum risk of central government response.

Figure 4: Propitiatory ritual posts marking the first anniversary of the February 25, 2001 massacre in Parengean, Central Kalimantan. A convoy of trucks evacuating men, women, and children from the region was stopped, and the occupants were led to this spot and to the football field across the road. Officially, 118 Madurese were killed. Many more escaped into the surrounding forest only to be hunted down or die from exposure. (Photo by Hélène Bouvier)

THE SILENCE OF THE VICTIMS

Causes of the conflict may be debated, but few would dispute that the Madurese version of events in Sampit has been largely neglected. Although there was nothing particularly difficult about questioning Sampit Madurese in Madura, few officials, reporters, or scholars seem to have done so. Perhaps one reason for this was the

---

[31] Though forced to contribute, Chinese often did so reluctantly due to their dependence on hardworking Madurese in their shops.

existence of widespread negative stereotypes of the Madurese. These stereotypes of the hot-tempered, vengeful Madurese are steeped in history and shared by most Indonesians even today.[32] Certainly the existence of entrenched stereotypes concerning the Madurese has done little to help critical thinking with regard to the conflict, leading observers to conclude they must have, at least to some extent, brought the conflict down on themselves. Those who accept this theory feel no need to confirm such an obvious fact. Even today, many Indonesians are afraid to go to Madura, believing that revenge killings are an everyday occurrence there, even if the region's contemporary statistics on violent crime hardly differ from statistics for the rest of Indonesia.

Another reason is, no doubt, the fact that Dayak communities maintain tighter networks among themselves and with the outside world than do the Madurese. The Madurese community was divided in its appreciation of the dangers in the run-up to the violence in Sampit, as we have seen earlier. Community elites were unsuccessful in marshalling support from other groups in Kalimantan or from Jakarta elites. Intra-ethnic divisions continued in Madura, where leaders of poor local communities demanded to receive the same food aid given to IDPs. In Madura's Sampang district, allegations would be made in 2005 that a Kalimantan Madurese NGO in league with local criminal elements was siphoning off part of the lump sum provided IDPs for return and reinstallation.[33] In terms of networking, the Madura–Dayak dissimilarity is exemplified most strikingly in the digital divide. An Internet search for "Sampit" or "Kereng Pangi" turns up hundreds of commentaries on websites and listserves, dated just after the conflict and virtually all pro-Dayak. Dayak cultural associations, academics, and NGOs are vastly better interconnected than their Madurese counterparts. Dayaks have for many years worked closely with Indonesian and international NGOs, including WWF (World Wildlife Fund) and the Ford Foundation, in the areas of environmental advocacy, forestry, biodiversity, microfinance, and culture. No comparable capacity building has been accomplished in Madura. Thus, while hungry, dazed, penniless, and often injured Madurese IDPs were shuffling through towns and reception centers in East Java, Dayak activists were demonstrating their proficiency in drafting reports and disseminating talking points.

The media advantage was crucial to shaping public opinion in the immediate aftermath of the conflict. The narrative portraying the local Madurese as a group armed to the teeth and on the verge of taking over Central Kalimantan when the Dayak forces intervened fails to explain why the five hundred to several thousand dead, the thousands injured, and the over 150,000 IDPs were almost exclusively Madurese.[34] In the press and on the Internet, this imbalance could be explained by

---

[32] Latief Wiyata, *Carok: Konflik kekerasan dan harga diri orang Madura* (Yogyakarta: LKiS, 2002); Glenn Smith, "Émotions et décisions violentes: le cas madourais," in *Asie-Europe: Les Émotions,* ed. Adam Kiss (Paris: Harmattan, 2000), pp. 145–99; and Huub de Jonge, "Stereotypes of the Madurese," in *Across Madura Strait: The Dynamics of an Insular Society,* ed. Kees van Dijk, Elly Touwen-Bouwsma, and Huub de Jonge, Proceedings of the Koninklijk Instituut voor Taal-, Land-, en Volkenkunde 2 (Leyden: KITLV, 1995), pp. 7–24.

[33] On the modalities of this aid and the allegations of its misuse, see Achwan et al., *Overcoming Violent Conflict,* pp. 64–66.

[34] The Madurese failed to use whatever arsenal they had allegedly amassed. Perhaps as convenient evidence of Madurese offensive intentions, bombs were "discovered" in some of their vacated houses. By early March, the official number of persons killed in the region had reached 469, among whom 456 were Madurese. See *Tempo,* March 11, 2001, p. 21; ICG,

the exceptional courage of the Dayak fighters, the longer length of the traditional Dayak *mandau* sword compared to the Madurese sickle, the magical ability of *mandau* to fly great distances, or the Madurese inability to handle their explosives. University researchers who were sent out to conduct research in the days following the violence (from February 26 to March 3, 2001) documented the "spontaneous" uprising of Dayaks, their patience worn thin by the "violent culture" of the Madurese; these findings appeared in the *Buku Merah* (Red Book) published and sent to the Indonesian president on March 8. After most Madurese were expelled from Central Kalimantan, a number of postings appeared on Internet sites reiterating the Dayak version of the events and calling for the release of Dayaks who were in police custody. Over one hundred postings to listserves at the time were forwards of similar or identical texts claiming that the Madurese had instigated the massacres in Sampit as revenge for the destruction in Kereng Pangi. Whatever the weaknesses in these arguments, they were passed on with little or no commentary by individuals and organizations sympathetic to the Dayak due to their past victimization by transmigration and development programs, logging, and mining conglomerates. In a few cases, the support came from groups concerned about the position of Indonesia's Christian minorities, though religion was not a primary factor in this conflict (about half of the Dayaks in Central Kalimantan are Muslim; in West Kalimantan most are Christian).

CONFLICT UNDERSTANDINGS AND PEACEMAKING

Discourse and perceptions of the causes and chronologies of the Sampit massacres had a definite impact on government policy, including: the decision to evacuate nearly all Madurese from Central Kalimantan rather than defend them in safe havens in Kalimantan; decisions concerning the manner in which peace conferences were run; and the decision to avoid government involvement in the repatriation of Madurese to Kalimantan in 2004 and 2005. They also had an impact on the work of non-governmental organizations helping IDPs and promoting reconciliation in Kalimantan.

Peacemaking activities following the 2001 Dayak–Madura conflict produced little in the way of concrete results for the Madurese IDPs until early 2004. Before then, only some seven thousand of the IDPs were able to return to safer areas of Central Kalimantan on their own. Until early 2004, the Dayak were unwilling to allow for a general return of the Madurese to Kalimantan unless their return was subject to terms unacceptable to most Madurese. The Dayak refused to permit the return of those who owned no land in Kalimantan, those who could not prove a certain number of years of prior residence, those without Dayak family ties, Madurese intellectuals, and those thought to have been involved in the conflict. The most difficult requirements to accept were the demands that the Madurese apologize for a conflict in which they were the primary victims and promise to leave the region again if they were involved in unspecified future conflict.

When the Madurese finally decided to return in large numbers to Central Kalimantan, they did so without help from the government, in early 2004, when

---

Communal Violence in Indonesia, p. 5. Most observers in Madura, and in Kalimantan, for that matter, doubt the official figures and estimate anywhere from one thousand to seven thousand Madurese were killed. One local official in Central Kalimantan said he spent long days and nights collecting and burying the bodies of Madurese who were hunted down in his village and in the surrounding forests or who died in their hiding places from starvation or wounds.

long-term humanitarian aid was replaced with a lump sum for return and reinstallation. They had no choice but to return quickly to Central Kalimantan on their own, through a process dubbed "natural" (*alami*). By mid-2005, some 80 percent of the Madurese from Central Kalimantan had returned. Those who had somewhere to return to could negotiate with the inevitable squatters (mostly young, unemployed Dayak fighters) to regain use of their homes and fields. Others could avail themselves of offers to settle in new areas under the protection of Dayak elites who invited them in order to increase their voting base in advance of elections.[35] Less fortunate were those who had no homes to return to, or whose former jobs had been taken over by others. According to some Madurese who made the effort to return to Central Kalimantan but then retreated again to Madura in 2005, some areas and some employment opportunities are now off limits to Madurese in Kalimantan, they have to pay millions of rupiah to get their property back, and they are frequently harassed. In short, Madurese who return are treated as "second-class citizens," to borrow the term one IDP used.[36] Research into the conditions of Madurese returnees is urgently needed to determine to what extent such portrayals are accurate. What limited information we could obtain at a distance suggests that the desire for peace has taken hold now, almost a year after most people returned, and most problems returnees were facing have since been resolved, though often through payoffs.

Madurese regarded the peacemaking process as one in which their representatives were largely powerless to address the main issues: how to implement the speedy return of refugees to Kalimantan and determine the root causes of the conflict. It appeared that many aspects of the conflict—and the possible involvement of ethnic elites, military, police, militias, and thugs—were considered too complex or too untidy to deal with at a peace conference. Peacemaking thus followed a "no fault" path of least resistance and, accepting the notion that cultural incompatibility was responsible for the conflict, the national and provincial government hosts of the peace conferences in Jakarta and East Java advocated projects to increase cross-cultural dialogue and respect for differences, and at least one international advocacy group (Search for Common Ground) developed an educational program in Kalimantan and Madura specifically targeting the youth.[37]

Common Ground's project was designed to provide, through the use of comic books, awareness of the dangers of ethnic stereotyping and education for IDPs concerning proper behavior in a migration setting.[38] The delicate nature of any program aimed at teaching perpetrators—and especially victims—that their behavior needs adjustment soon became clear: the comic books were well received in some areas, but elicited a strong negative reaction from Madurese in others. Under

---

[35] Ironically, one such Dayak elite who provided guarantees of safety for returning Madurese was widely considered a key instigator of the Sampit massacres.

[36] Arguably, the Madurese have always been second-class citizens in Indonesia as a whole. The IDP quoted here no doubt meant that the Madurese of Central Kalimantan, whether they had been living humble lives or, on the contrary, had amassed fortunes before the massacres, would be returning to occupy the bottom rung on the socioeconomic ladder, starting again from scratch. Many of the more successful Madurese have decided against returning and trying to restart or reclaim their businesses.

[37] See http://www.sfcg.org/programmes/indonesia/indonesia_kalimantan.html

[38] This web page, though not updated, describes the aims of the comic book project: http://www.sfcg.org/programmes/indonesia/indonesia_comic.html

pressure from Madurese associations, Common Ground had to recall all copies of the early comics and undertake to make changes in them.

In West Kalimantan, where the same arguments against Madurese and their culture had been heard since the first violence broke out in 1996, some Madurese themselves were advocating what can only be described as an "extreme makeover." A vast program run by several Madurese associations encouraged IDP parents to send their children to Islamic boarding schools in Java so they could "abandon their Madurese culture and Madurese language and all the negative aspects of it" and, as a result, could better adapt to future migrations ("*Allahamdullilah karakter hilang,*" one parent described it, "God willing, their [Madurese] character will disappear"). Among the negative traits that were to be rooted out were "touchiness" and "loud talking." Approximately one thousand children were sent to these schools between 1999 and 2002. All communication between children and their parents was monitored. Children's letters were systematically opened, and any letters containing a plea from a child to be allowed to return home were not forwarded to the parents. That Madurese associations could support such a program demonstrates the lack of educational alternatives for IDP children. This is perhaps an understandable response of parents to the culture-based threats to this particular minority, but also a chilling outcome of biased culturalist discourse.

CONCLUSION

This article has attempted to sift through the wheat and chaff of different accounts of the violence in Central Kalimantan in early 2001, contributing little-known Madurese perspectives to the discussion. What emerge are competing conspiracy theories supported by reference to different incidents and timelines; logical and evidentiary weaknesses can be found in both of these theories, as in the widely diffused narrative that describes a spontaneous uprising caused by cultural incompatibility. Perhaps as a way of avoiding a choice between the first two theories, government and NGOs worked on the assumption that fundamental cultural incompatibilities were responsible for the violence, and that addressing those incompatibilities could pave the way for a solution to the crisis. In this politics of framing, the Dayak were much better equipped to see that their version of the conflict prevailed. The cost–benefits were also favorable to them. There was little risk of punishment, and substantial benefits accrued to them as a result of removing most of the Madurese from the province. Numerous local factories, businesses, and shops transferred ownership to Dayaks, at least for the duration of the exile. Dayaks occupied Madurese plantations not destroyed during the riots and sold the harvests for three or four years, and then demanded and received final cash payoffs from the returning Madurese. Many Madurese-owned properties and businesses (including the late Haji Marlinggi's stevedoring company) remain in the hands of Dayak and other ethnic groups since most elite Madurese have elected not to return. The precipitated evacuation and four to five years of resettlement on Madura Island ensued, but its high cost failed to spur government action on IDP returns, an issue largely left to local and sometimes suspect initiatives. It is unclear to what extent the events of 2001 have led international aid organizations to examine the unintended consequences of capacity-building programs that have the effect of disproportionately empowering specific ethnic groups in multi-ethnic contexts.

Eventually, the two sides did agree on a return process, an accomplishment that has so far been impossible for the opposing sides in West Kalimantan. Resettled in Central Kalimantan, where they are trying to rebuild their lives, few Madurese (or Dayaks, for that matter) want to dwell on the past. In a region where contentious and unresolved histories have often been resurrected and replayed, putting the past behind them will be a major challenge for everyone involved.

Back to the Barracks: *Relokasi Pengungsi* in Post-Tsunami Aceh[*]

Eva-Lotta E. Hedman

[The] Chief of the Indonesian Military asked that the relocation process be accelerated because it relates to the dignity of Indonesia.
    (Pendopo Meeting Minutes, Banda Aceh, January 9, 2005)

The government's relocation plans don't make sense ... The government needs to decide if it represents the government or the people.
    (Mukhim Elder and IDP, Lhok Nga, February 2005)

When you have seen one, you have seen them all.
    (UN-OCHA Report on Relocation Barracks, Aceh Barat, March 2005)

INTRODUCTION

Within days of the December 26, 2004 tsunami that killed at least 127,000 people and left more than 30,000 missing and some 500,000 displaced from their homes in Aceh, the Indonesian government announced that international humanitarian assistance was needed for the emergency relief and reconstruction efforts. The tsunami, it soon emerged, had left in its wake massive destruction to infrastructure, livelihoods, and homes, especially along the west and northwest coasts of Aceh. It had also served to rupture the virtual closure of Aceh to the outside world achieved by the Indonesian government's implementation of martial law and a state of military emergency on May 18, 2003.[1]

Unsurprisingly, the issue of relocation of those displaced from their homes due to the tsunami quickly surfaced as a central concern of Indonesian government

---

[*] An earlier version of this essay appeared in the journal, *Indonesia*. See Eva-Lotta E. Hedman, "Back to the Barracks: *Relokasi Pengungsi* in Post-Tsunami Aceh," *Indonesia* 80 (October 2005): 1–19.

[1] This virtual closure remained largely unaffected by the formal "upgrade" to a state of civil emergency one year later, which remained unchanged until President-elect Susilo Bambang Yudyohono introduced a new framework for so-called "civil order" and "adjusted" security in Aceh on May 18, 2005 (Regulation 38/2005).

authorities, displaced persons themselves, and international humanitarian organizations. As suggested by the brief excerpts above, and the discussion to follow, however, the government's announced *relokasi pengungsi* program[2] raised many troubling questions, including questions concerning the role of the military, the rights of displaced persons, and the intervention of international humanitarian organizations in areas of protracted conflict. In this regard, the Indonesian authorities' evident enthusiasm at the time for so-called *barak-barak* (barracks)— against the expressed wishes of internally displaced persons (IDPs), as well as the considered opinions of international nongovernmental organizations (I/NGOs)— seemed to merit particular scrutiny, not least because of the military operations (*Operasi Terpadu*, Integrated Operation) that had featured forced displacement of civilian populations as a deliberate counterinsurgency strategy in Aceh.[3]

This chapter recalls something of the lived experience of displacement in the aftermath of the tsunami, whether in areas marked by "deep" militarization and conflict or in areas located closer to the provincial capital, with all its myriad manifestations of an internationally recognized "complex humanitarian emergency." To a considerable extent, research for this paper draws on observations, informal interviews, reports, and other material collected during visits to Aceh in February 2005, and again in January 2006. Since that time, there has been a proliferation of post-tsunami Aceh assessments, including numerous reports on humanitarian assistance, reconstruction, peace negotiations, and elections, as well as a growing scholarly interest in related issues, which, for the most part, remain beyond the scope of this chapter. The analysis here remains focused on the extraordinary conjuncture of events that saw the rupture—and yet also the rapid (re)deployment—of forms of (contested) governmentality in the most militarized area in Indonesia at the time. This snapshot of the immediate aftermath of the tsunami in a militarized conflict zone thus highlights the significance of the bio-politics of so-called "complex humanitarian emergencies." It also points to certain powerful enduring effects of the humanitarian discourse that gained wider circulation in the early post-tsunami period. Finally, it directs attention to the role of displaced persons themselves in challenging, through collective action, the very terms of engagement with "IDPs" and, thus, refocusing attention on the (contested) place of the internally displaced in the body politic.

A ROADMAP FOR RELOCATION

On the drive up from Medan, large tents along the main road to Lhokseumawe were the first signs of the massive displacement of tsunami survivors in Aceh. Of course, there had been other haunting reminders of displacement along the east coast, where conflict and violence left a landscape scarred by countless empty

---

[2] *Pengungsi* is used interchangeably in Indonesian to denote "refugees" (who have crossed an internationally recognized border) and internally displaced persons, or IDPs. See the UN Guiding Principles on Internal Displacement for the rights and protection guarantees of IDPs, as well as the role and obligations of local and national governments.

[3] For an early assessment, see Lukman Age, "IDPs Confined to Barracks in Aceh," *Forced Migration Review* (Special Issue, July 2005): 22–23. For brief overviews of conflict and displacement, see the papers by Ali Ramly Aulia and Eva-Lotta E. Hedman in *Aceh under Martial Law: Conflict, Violence, and Displacement*, ed. Eva-Lotta E. Hedman, Working Paper No. 24 (Oxford: University of Oxford, Refugee Studies Centre, July 2005).

buildings, with gaping holes instead of windows, doors, and roofs, marked by graffiti and tattered Indonesian flags in places. The expansion of military and paramilitary presence in Aceh in recent years contributed to extensive displacement as the accommodation of such forces had anticipated the construction of new facilities—ranging from roadside shacks to entire compounds—as well as the appropriation of former lumber yards, electric power plants, agricultural lands, and family homes.

Acehnese elder at roadside tent camp near Geudong, south of Lhokseumawe.
(Photo by Eva-Lotta E. Hedman)

The tarpaulin structures by the roadside near Geudong, south of Lhokseumawe, were still a long ways from the utter devastation visited upon entire communities on the west coast, including the provincial capital of Banda Aceh, where most international relief efforts and media attention were focused in the aftermath of the tsunami. They sheltered some 250 internally displaced persons from two fishing and farming communities (*kampung*), including one *dayah* (local Koranic school). When the waves hit these small communities on December 26, those who could fled inland, seeking shelter on the grounds of the nearby mosque (*masjid*) or local public school. As the scope of the destruction to homes and livelihoods in these communities became clear, local authorities moved survivors into tents, marked by the *Departemen Sosial RI* insignia, along the main road, readily visible to passersby, as well as to soldiers manning the nearby TNI (Tentara Nasional Indonesia, Indonesia's armed forces) post.

In the early phase of the massive international humanitarian assistance efforts in Aceh, when convoys of trucks with relief goods were roaring past this site in the direction of Banda Aceh on the west coast, this comparatively small roadside tent camp outside Geudong attracted some attention, as evidenced by the water cisterns with the *MSF—Medecins Sans Frontiers* logo prominently displayed in front. Unfortunately, the water from these cisterns was "no good," according to camp residents, and they did not dare to drink it on account of its murky appearance and strange smell. The one instance of direct delivery of relief goods to this tent camp, which also took place in the early days, had prompted local government officials to send a clear message that IDPs were not to accept any such international assistance, but should instead refer any erring do-gooders to the subdistrict office (*kantor kecamatan*). According to one of the village elders, he was roughed up by a man who accompanied visitors from the subdistrict office when this message was delivered; ever since, all international relief goods to reach the tent camp had been channeled through local government authorities. As a result, residents claimed, there had been no distribution of milk and only very small amounts of sardines, as well as a limited supply of bottled water, provided. It was suggested that such supplies had been hoarded and perhaps sold or otherwise traded locally.

While many children living in the tent camp were once again attending their old school by this time, for the adults life remained, in many ways, on hold. With homes and livelihoods destroyed or severely damaged and their futures uncertain, survivors struggled to return to their communities to begin clearing up, rebuilding, and perhaps fishing during the day, but found this very difficult due to a lack of resources and assistance. The distance of about five kilometers from the camp to their old communities posed a real problem, as passage between these locations cost Rp. 5,000 by local transport, each way, and there were few opportunities to earn cash.

Young Acehnese woman in tent shelter, near Geudong, south of Lhokseumawe.
(Photo by Eva-Lotta E. Hedman)

In this situation, it was perhaps unsurprising that residents of this tent camp were eager for their next relocation, this time into the so-called *barak-barak* reportedly under construction within one kilometer from their old communities. The tent camp residents viewed the barracks as a temporary arrangement, preferable to living under the tarpaulins along the main road during what they envisaged as an interim period for reconstructing their homes and rebuilding their villages. As of February 2005, they had not been informed of any target dates for completion of or relocation to the barracks. No other alternatives appeared to be under consideration by local government officials, whom the camp residents identified as the source of all available information about relocation. At no point had these IDPs themselves been invited to voice their concerns or to participate in any aspect of the decision-making process about the relocation and reconstruction of their communities. In addition, no IDPs had been involved in the actual construction of the barracks to date, despite the obvious importance of finding gainful employment and earning some much needed cash for these communities, a necessity repeatedly emphasized by camp residents.

On our arrival in Lhokseumawe in February 2005, we found another, much larger, tent camp of tsunami-displaced people by the mosque, near Pusong. With their tents stretching out along the shore line, at a safe distance from the sea and yet within sight of their old homes, this community of fishermen and their families had suffered considerable loss to life, property, and livelihoods due to the tsunami. Some of this destruction was readily visible even in the twilight, and, as the call to the *magrib* prayer sounded through the neighborhood, survivors pointed out partially destroyed homes or the gap left by a missing house that had been severed from its neighbors and carried out to sea by the waves. Stopping to chat on their way back from evening prayers, people from this community also spoke, with a knowingness and humor suggestive of a certain urban sensibility or savvy, of their experiences with local government officials and others in the aftermath of the tsunami. While most of the international humanitarian assistance and attention had passed them by, as truck convoys or airlifts loaded with relief goods headed straight for Banda Aceh, this community had become a beneficiary of the national political party, PKS (Partai Keadilan Sejahtera, the Prosperous Justice Party), which was making up for the shortcomings of local government by providing a steady supply of fresh drinking water. In contrast to the tent camps along the main road, this settlement seemed to be of little interest to the local military; no soldiers could be seen in the immediate vicinity. (The military presence remained quite visible in other parts of Lhokseumawe, however, not least along the main strip near the Pusong market, where heavily armed soldiers in combat boots, fatigues, and unmarked T-shirts kept moving in and out of sidewalk eateries during the evening. This kind of display, while not lost on anybody present, also remained studiously ignored, as if nothing was out of the ordinary, thus effecting the very state of exception, or emergency, that had become the rule in Aceh.)

On the road to Bireuen (Bireuen district), *barak-barak* lined the main highway, past Jeunieb (Bireuen). The structures had yet to be completed, but there could be no mistaking these timber-framed, tin-roofed, and, yes, barrack-shaped buildings. Half a dozen were in various stages of near completion, although there appeared to be little activity for a construction site. At the time, the closest neighbors to these barracks were TNI and Brimob (Brigade Mobil, paramilitary police mobile brigade units) posts, with precious few others in near proximity.

Barracks under construction along the main highway near Jeunieb (Bireuen).
(Photo by Eva-Lotta E. Hedman)

A short distance ahead, tsunami survivors from five *kampungs* were encamped under tarpaulin structures located along the main road across from a TNI post and a handful of small, adjacent houses, none of which pre-dated the martial law era in Aceh. Indeed, Batee Geulungku had remained primarily a military *posko* (command post), with a Brimob post around the bend of the road. Perhaps unsurprisingly, this IDP camp also appeared, at least in part, to be inscribed within the local arrangements and common practices that had emerged "on the ground," as government soldiers and civilian populations encountered each other in the context of "civil emergency" in Aceh during the early months of 2005. Thus, TNI soldiers required and camp residents supplied information about the identities of the 713 survivors displaced from these five villages, without any discernible intermediary role reserved for civilian government officials. Similarly, IDPs awaited and TNI soldiers provided updates on the next relocation into the barracks, which were under construction in the near vicinity of—or possibly even on the grounds of—a new battalion-sized military compound located on an otherwise empty stretch of elevated land stretching along the main road. There were trickles of crossroads visitations, in both directions, involving village elders (*teungku)*, accompanied by other men from the IDP community, seeking to make representations to the local officer in charge, and also involving soldiers, one-on-one, or in pairs, strolling around the tent camp, automatic weapons slung across their shoulders. Under the tarpaulins, a boy of almost three was cradling his most priced post-tsunami possession—a piece of wood in the rough shape of an automatic weapon, with a rope to hang around his little neck.

At the last stop in Bireuen district, another tent camp was scattered across an open area stretching out between the main road and a bend in the river near Batee Iliek. Located opposite a military command post and a larger TNI compound also visible—although just barely—from the road, this IDP camp featured a large tent designated for the twenty-odd troops stationed there from *Posko Kemanusiaan Terpadu TNI-AD, Yonif-742/SWY.* Soldiers, in full combat gear, could be seen walking around the camp, as well as in and out of the tents where IDPs were housed. According to one student volunteer in this camp, the soldiers did not appear to be tasked with assisting IDPs in any way other than, perhaps, to receive deliveries of fresh water and food from international humanitarian organizations and to accompany any other would-be visitors to this site. Upon their first arrival to this camp, the student volunteers had been asked to provide rice for these troops, a request they seemed to regard with a mixture of feelings ranging from "what-do-you-expect?" to "I-can't-believe-it." They did oblige, however, and thus remained a presence in this camp, the only one that was neither military nor IDP.

Acehnese tsunami survivors at roadside tent camp in Batee Geulungku (Bireuen).
(Photo by Eva-Lotta E. Hedman)

"Integrated Humanitarian Command Post": TNI *Posko*/IDP tent camp at Batee Iliek (Bireuen).
(Photo by Eva-Lotta E. Hedman)

The location of this IDP camp also made it a destination, as well as a transit point, for a certain amount of "social" interaction and activities by soldiers stationed at the TNI posts across the road. Thus, the grounds surrounding the camp continued to be used by these troops for games of football and for access to what appeared to be a popular spot on the river for water play, with a rope strung across the current to an old bridge foundation. Across the new bridge, there was also a Brimob post, marked by graffiti in a way reminiscent of the skulls-and-bones aesthetics of Guns 'n Roses, as if belonging to a bizarre cult rather than a branch of the state security forces. (Countless Brimob posts along the way similarly suggested, from the outside, tropical adaptations of the urban jungle rock club or, perhaps, crack house, thus marking certain areas as "bad neighborhoods" of a kind. Heavily armed Brimob troops stalking to market in Grong-Grong [Pidie] also appeared not so much in mufti as in an oddly stylized display of bandanas, dark sunglasses, and unmarked T-shirts, as if making a fetish of a certain "bad boy" imaginary.)

DAN ... BILA ESOK DATANG

In Banda Aceh in February 2005, the devastation wrought by the tsunami lingered everywhere—in stories of loved ones lost to the deadly waves, in obituaries with photographs placed in the local newspaper, in the rubble of entire neighborhoods crushed under a wall of water. The sheer scale of the loss in lives remains difficult, perhaps impossible, to comprehend. In some of the worst affected areas, there were disproportionately fewer women, and almost no children, among the survivors. The damage to homes and livelihoods, public infrastructure and government offices, military complexes and two crowded prisons, was also massive, and readily visible. As the waves effectively redrew the shoreline in certain places, some areas, including former residential neighborhoods, remained under water.

From Peunayong to Kampung Mulia, Lambaro Angan, and Kampung Lampriet in Banda Aceh, the trail of destruction left in the wake of the tsunami was overwhelming and the desolate landscape of rubble disorienting. Here and there, scattered houses were still standing in the midst of this wasteland, a few seemingly untouched by the force of the elements, many more with gaping holes or entire walls ripped out to reveal the debris of a life world swept away in the waves, buried under the rubble, and partially excavated by rescue teams and survivors. Among this debris lay scattered a pair of women's shoes, a man's KMP (*kartu merah putih*) identity card, a child's toy, a photograph of a young female student, a piece of paper with a handwritten poem in Indonesian ... *Dan ... Bila esok datang* ... (And ... If tomorrow comes ...). Among the survivors, two middle-aged men who had lost their wives and children surveyed adjacent properties, clearing up amidst the rubble, arranging some furniture in front of their houses, in a forlorn display of lives turned inside out. Nearby a couple of teenage boys were hard at work collecting "scrap metal" from the rubble, standing knee deep at times in the foul waters of the ditches lining the "roads" in this post-tsunami topography. In the background, one of the many large fishing boats hurled across these former neighborhoods by the towering waves had come to rest on a half-collapsed house. Further south, on the west coast, only the mosque was left to break up the bleak, vast horizon that had opened across a seemingly endless stretch of destruction in Lhok Nga (Lhoknga). A couple of kilometers inland, a single house could be spotted, evidently severed from its own foundation, squatting precariously on another.

Barracks under construction in Banda Aceh, with crews counting "returnees"
from the Klang Valley, Malaysia. (Photo by Eva-Lotta E. Hedman)

These were but brief glimpses of (former) neighborhoods in some of the tsunami-affected areas in Banda Aceh and Lhok Nga in early 2005, no longer recognizable even to survivors who once lived and worked there, nor easily negotiated, especially for those displaced to tent camps or elsewhere at some considerable distance.[4] Instead, most of the activity and traffic in such areas stemmed from clean-up operations, camp visitations, and field surveys conducted by one of the many I/NGOs, UN affiliates, and foreign military missions present in the area after the tsunami.[5] In many ways, the areas emptied of former residents by the tsunami thus remained, in no small measure, illegible and inaccessible to survivors some six weeks after their destruction. Meanwhile, the newly arrived international humanitarian workers and others who lacked prior local knowledge of Banda traversed a terrain mapped out by the "Humanitarian Information Center" (HIC) of the United Nations Office for the Coordination of Humanitarian Affairs (UN-OCHA), based on information supplied by the Australian Army. The Banda Aceh city map produced by HIC and dated February 22, for example, featured some twenty new "offices" of I/NGOs, UN affiliates, and donor institutions, crowded in a comparatively narrow stretch of the city. It was at these offices, and those of Indonesian government agencies and administrative departments, that some forty "sectoral working group

---

[4] In Banda Aceh, the tsunami reportedly left Ule Lhee village with an area of 54 ha, compared to the pre-tsunami measurement of 67 ha, a decrease that was due to sinking. Republic of Indonesia, "Master Plan for the Rehabilitation and Reconstruction of the Regions and Communities of the Province of Nangroe Aceh Darussalam and the Islands of Nias, Province of North Sumatera" (April 2005), II-9. See www.reliefweb.int/rw/rwb.nsf/ db900SID/SODA-6BFAHE?OpenDocument.

[5] An "Organization List" prepared and distributed by the Humanitarian Information Centre (HIC), Sumatra, identified 320 such organizations. Dated February 24, 2005, author's file.

meetings" per week were held at the time,[6] thus effecting a certain regularity in the circulation of people and information, including considerable crosstown traffic to reach these destinations, not least by means of chauffeured four-wheel-drive vehicles in the case of the larger (UN) agencies. By contrast, in the so-called "tsunami-affected areas," colored green on the same map mentioned above, only three locations were marked: a gas station, a BPN (Badan Pertanahan Nasional, National Land Agency) government building, and a Brimob post, as if nothing else of interest or import remained.[7]

Indeed, the massive influx of international humanitarian assistance into Banda Aceh in the aftermath of the tsunami, including some of the world's most experienced emergency relief workers, had itself changed the face of the city, for the time being. Having first emerged as an emergency tent-camp in its own right, the "UN Compound" on Jl. Jendral Sudirman promptly expanded to incorporate not only UN-OCHA, but also the World Food Program (WFP) and the "Joint Logistics Center" (JLC), as well as the HIC-administered information and communications tents, complete with networked computers, for visitors permitted entry by the security guards at the main gate. The International Organization for Migration (IOM), which was the first "IO" to be granted official access by the Indonesian government to IDP populations and camps in the martial-law era, was prominently located just across the street from the UN Compound. By contrast, the United Nations High Commissioner on Refugees (UNHCR), which, across the Straits in Malaysia, had played a critical role in spotlighting the plight and protection needs of Acehnese refugees, had an office tucked away in a residential area of Banda Aceh (by March 2005 it was requested to dismantle its admittedly compromised mission in Aceh altogether).[8]

Meanwhile, a different kind of re/mapping was underway with local and national, military, and civilian government officials taking stock of the situation in the province formerly known as Aceh (officially renamed Nanggroe Aceh Darussalam [NAD] under the Special Autonomy Law). In what appeared to be record time for organizational responses to complex humanitarian emergencies, Bappenas (Badan Perencanaan dan Pembangunan Nasional), the Indonesian government national planning board, in collaboration with key international donors, made public two "technical" reports on January 19, 2005 to provide a "Blueprint" that expressed their intention "to start making decisions on setting priorities and considering how to develop a strategy for reconstruction."[9] While the Jakarta government's own so-called "Master Plan" for the rehabilitation and reconstruction of Aceh and other affected areas was not released until April 2005, draft versions of this document, or certain aspects thereof, were in circulation at least as early as

---

[6] See, for example, "Sectoral Working Group Meeting Forecast," HIC, February 25, 2005, author's file.

[7] The BPN was the government authority tasked to assess land holdings and to issue new ownership certificates to affected populations in the aftermath of the tsunami.

[8] The UNHCR was subsequently invited to return to assist the government in the recovery and rehabilitation of the province of Aceh, as outlined in a "Memorandum of Understanding" dated June 10, 2005.

[9] Bappenas (Government of Indonesia), *Indonesia: Preliminary Damage and Loss Assessment/The December 26, 2004 Natural Disaster* (Jakarta: The Consultative Group on Indonesia, January 19–20, 2005); and *Indonesia: Notes on Reconstruction/Assessment/The December 26, 2004 Natural Disaster* (Jakarta: The Consultative Group on Indonesia, January 19–20, 2005).

February of the same year, thus anticipating, perhaps in crucial ways, its eventual release in April (see further below).[10] Indeed, a series of government statements, reports, and initiatives focused on the reconstruction of Aceh seemed to reflect—and reproduce—the state's resolve to maintain strict control of the relief efforts, as these documents included repeated public calls for centralized coordination and official registration of all concerned actors and activities. The government's vision contrasted sharply with the early *reformasi*-like flurry of humanitarian assistance provided by volunteers—arriving from other provinces, with Islamic groups, NGOs, medical and humanitarian organizations, even political parties and private corporations—found on the street corners of Banda Aceh in the early post-tsunami weeks.[11]

While in many ways unsurprising and arguably "legitimate," the Indonesian government's push for a kind of hypercentralization of humanitarian relief and reconstruction efforts also revealed a pervasive concern with control and surveillance in Aceh, "Special Autonomy" notwithstanding.[12] As it was only in the aftermath of the tsunami in early 2005 that Aceh re-emerged from the virtual lock-down effected by the declaration of martial law in May 2003, Indonesian civilian and military officials displayed considerable anxiety about the arrival and activities of international humanitarian organizations, other I/NGOs, foreign volunteers, reporters, and militaries. This anxiety was evident in countless statements—and clarifications—from civilian and military officials about the presence and role of such foreign missions on Indonesian territory. As early as January, "deadlines" for the withdrawal of foreign military assistance were made public. By February 2005, all international humanitarian and other organizations were required to register their personnel and/or volunteers for the issue of an official ID card to be worn at all times, with an expiration date prominently printed on the front. (Beyond this date, their continued presence and activity in Aceh was subject to government approval of an extension; as a result, the issuance of these cards served as a warning sign of the future for many I/NGOs.) In March of the same year, some organizations, including the UNHCR, were closing their offices in Aceh, with large unspent allocations remaining in their budgets and much unfinished business left behind. By April 2005, the month when the Indonesian government's Master Plan was finally made public, organizations whose work the local authorities did not find to be sufficiently focused on, or needed for, the reconstruction phase of the disaster-relief efforts were unlikely to remain operational in Aceh.

As for affected local populations, there was also evidence of old habits of control and surveillance intruding on and shaping the nature and direction of government (and other) interventions in early post-tsunami Aceh. If the tsunami waves served to unravel the "KMP regime" introduced under martial law in Aceh, civilian and military officials were remarkably quick to call for the official registration of individual tsunami survivors and the overall mapping of IDP camp or shelter locations. Of course, the tasks of identifying and locating displaced populations were

---

[10] Republic of Indonesia, "Master Plan."

[11] See Edward Aspinall, "Indonesia after the Tsunami," *Current History* (March 2005): 105–109.

[12] On the dynamics of centralization and its powerful effects in Aceh, see especially Tim Kell, *The Roots of Acehnese Rebellion* (Ithaca, NY: Cornell Modern Indonesia Project, 1995); and Geoffrey Robinson, "*Rawan* is as *Rawan* Does: The Origins of Disorder in New Order Aceh," *Indonesia* 66 (October 1998): 127–156.

integral to humanitarian assistance efforts, and, moreover, to the governance and administration of post-tsunami Aceh. However, the drive of official authorities to restore the capacity for "seeing like a state" could not but recall the widespread practices associated with military or paramilitary checkpoints, roadblocks, and so-called "sweeping" operations that had been used to establish the identity, movement, and, invariably, affinity of local populations during recent counterinsurgency campaigns.[13]

The government also moved with great speed to announce its *relokasi pengungsi* program, with particular emphasis on temporary "barracks" rather than the rehabilitation or construction of permanent housing. Having first identified a target number of twenty-four barracks camps that would be constructed to house some 35,000 IDPs in "phase one" of this project, the government promptly revised these figures upwards, to thirty-nine such temporary relocation sites built to accommodate 35,000 households, or some 140,000 displaced persons.[14] The swiftness and ease with which the Indonesian authorities involved UN agencies and NGOs in a "Joint Liaison Unit" to further this project also appeared remarkable, not least in the face of considerable apprehension in humanitarian circles regarding the encampment of displaced populations. As for local populations, there was evidence of concern and even outright opposition to the proposed barracks solution from the outset.[15] Indeed, against the backdrop of recent counterinsurgency campaigns in Aceh, which had featured large-scale forced displacement of civilian populations, sometimes as a deliberate strategy of war under martial law, it was hardly surprising that, in the immediate aftermath of the tsunami, there was little rush to join in the barracks relocation initiative.

There were also early and recurring reports to indicate that some of these same old habits for maintaining control and surveillance, further compounded by the predatory political economies that had long flourished in Aceh, resurfaced in regard to the distribution of humanitarian relief and assistance. At the daily briefing meetings held with Indonesian government officials at the Governor's Palace in Banda Aceh, TNI representatives frequently requested to receive more information on such assistance, including calls for regular "distribution coordination meetings"

---

[13] In the words of Indonesian Army Chief, Maj.-Gen. Bambang Darmono: "If the people live in the resettlement while we are working with the reconstruction, I think [it is] much easier to deliver food to them. Much easier to give them everything. And of course, also very easy to secure them from the GAM side." Interview with Sarah Ferguson, "The Fortunes of War," *ninemsn*, February 13, 2005.

[14] See especially Bakornas PBP, *Bulletin*, No. 32 (January 25, 2005) and No. 39 (January 31, 2005). See also Bakornas PBP, "Report of Joint Government/United Nations/NGO Rapid Assessment Mission of New Relocation Sites," www.humanitarianinfo.org/sumatra/assessments/doc/GoI_UN-joint_assessment_report_on relocation_ sites.doc) (dated January 2005). Bakornas PBP stands for the National Disaster Management and Refugee Coordinating Board.

[15] See, for example, "Indonesians Wary of Relocation Centers," *Washington Post*, January 31, 2005. At Kreung Sabe, south of Calang on the West Coast, for example, villagers were reportedly "determined to go back and rebuild as soon as possible and … don't want to go into camps," according to UNHCR Asia-Pacific Bureau director, Janet Lim, cited in "Indonesia: UNHCR Tailoring Shelter Solutions to Meet Aceh Needs," *UNHCR Update*, February 4, 2005. For a related report, see "Satlak Aceh Timur tak akui pengungsi Kuala Idi Cut," *AcehKita*, March 9, 2005.

at a military hangar.[16] Anecdotal evidence also indicated that the practice of stockpiling or warehousing relief goods in military hangars allowed for considerable irregularities in the distribution, ranging from the skimming of such goods to benefit troops and their families, to the withholding of deliveries from displaced persons of alleged separatist sympathies (in several cases, IDPs who resisted relocation to barracks were accused of being separatists).[17] As suggested by the large banners greeting humanitarian relief convoys and others traveling across the main road from Medan to Banda Aceh, there was evident anxiety about predatory practices even within the military: *Jangan memberikan apapun…! Kepada aparat keamanan selama perjalanan anda. (Koplihkam 2005)* (Don't give anything … To [members of the] security apparatus at any point on your journey.)[18] Of course, the billion-dollar budgets associated with the reconstruction of Aceh suggested greater opportunities for graft and corruption than the pilfering of relief goods, opportunities that included, for example, participation in the building of relocation barracks and the awarding of contracts to military businesses or corporations with strong links to government and (former) military officials.[19]

While this drive for a hypercentralization of tsunami relief and reconstruction efforts in early 2005 had powerful and perhaps lasting effects, it never formed a seamless web for representatives of the Indonesian government, international humanitarian organizations, or, indeed, affected local populations. Other competing dynamics also influenced the parameters of interventions in early post-tsunami Aceh. First of all, Indonesian political processes and institutions—ranging from the rivalry between the president and his vice president to the expanded legislative powers of the parliament and the enduring influence of the military (including in business corporations)—exerted critical influence on the nature and direction of

---

[16] See, for example, Pendopo meeting, Banda Aceh, January 16, 2005 (source: UN-OCHA HIC, Banda Aceh), author's file.

[17] Author's interviews. See also "Aceh Working Group Concern over TNI Monopoly," *AcehKita*, January 8, 2005. (The monopoly in question here concerns aid distribution, and, according to Rafendi Djamin at Imparsial, "has created corruption and bureaucracy." Ibid.) For reports on the linking of humanitarian assistance to (alleged) IDP political sympathies, see, for example, this article from Aceh Timur: "Refugees Accused as GAM if Reject the Relocation" *AcehKita*, February 23, 2005.

[18] The banner quoted here appeared a few kilometers away from another one displayed near Idi Cut on the east coast, which read: *Apabila ada masalah mampir ke pos TNI. Kami siap membantu. (Satgaspur I Yonif 2001 Raider)* (If there is a problem go to a TNI post. We're ready to help.) "Satgaspur" refers to Satuan Gabungan Tempur (Joint Operations Force); "Yonif 2001 Raider" to Batalyon Infantri 2001 Raider; and "Koplihkam 2005" to Komando Pemulihan Keamanan 2005.

[19] In Bireuen, for example, every barrack project reportedly involved the military at each stage of the construction: in supplying wood, workers, and security. Author's interviews. As for large reconstruction projects, the Jakarta-based Artha Graha bank and business conglomerate, in which the Indonesian military is reported to have significant stakes, has been linked to the West Coast of Aceh. The current bank chairman is retired major-general Kiki Syahnakri, indicted in absentia by a UN war crimes tribunal for his role in East Timor. His former close associate in East Timor, Colonel Geerhan Lantara, who is now Korem commander on the West Coast of Aceh, provides an "organic" link of sorts to some of the hardest hit areas, including Calang and Meulaboh. See "Beradu Cetak Biru," *Tempo*, February 13, 2005; and Aspinall, "Indonesia after the Tsunami." See also, "Military Business Amidst GAM Hunting" (parts 1 and 2), *AcehKita*, May 2 and 7, 2005; and the illuminating comments by George J. Aditjondro in "Aceh Damai, Bagaimana Nasib Bisnis Militer?" *Radio Nederland,* Juli 19, 2005.

responses to the disaster. Moreover, while mindful of their respective official mandates, and the limitations thereof, international humanitarian organizations at times demonstrated considerable capacity for constructive engagement with (local) official authorities, and, as a result, perhaps gained a surprising measure of discretion in implementing relief and reconstruction assistance. Finally, the relative weakness of organized civil society in pre-tsunami Aceh notwithstanding,[20] there was early evidence of considerable activism among survivors, who found themselves in a peculiar place where they had, on the one hand, lost nearly everyone and everything, and thus perhaps felt that they had little left to lose, while, on the other hand, they had gained renewed recognition as "internally displaced persons" with specific rights and needs under international humanitarian and human rights law. In this regard, the return to Aceh of some of the best and the brightest, who had left during the brutal repression of student, human-rights, and other civil society movements in 2000–01, further added to the "social capital" available for local affected populations in post-tsunami Aceh.

Roadside banner near Idi Cut (Aceh Timur): "Apabila ada masalah mampir ke pos TNI. Kami siap membantu." (Satgaspur I Yonif 2001 Raider). Translation: "If there is a problem, go to a TNI post. We're ready to help." (Photo by Eva-Lotta E. Hedman)

CLOSE ENCOUNTERS OF THE THIRD KIND

Some of these rather more complicated dynamics could be glimpsed during a meeting of invited representatives from the Indonesian government, international humanitarian organizations, local affected populations, and NGOs in February 2005. Organized and hosted by Mercy Malaysia in its "model" shelter camp along Jl. Jenggala in Lhok Nga (the district [*kecamatan*] to the immediate south of Banda

---

[20] See Aguswandi, "Breaking the Deadlock: Civil Society Engagement for Conflict Resolution," in *Aceh under Martial Law*, pp. 45–52.

Aceh), this meeting was to be chaired by representatives for UN-OCHA (Banda Aceh), with other internationals present, ranging from Medecins Sans Frontiers to Pompiers Sans Frontiers. In numerical terms, the largest representation at this meeting was comprised of local people, who included the head of a cluster of five villages (*mukhim*), the leader of one devastated *kampung*, a female high-school teacher, a college student (also working for UNICEF in the area), a female NGO worker, and also several of the IDPs living in the camp itself. Among the Acehnese and Indonesian participants, there were also one or two medics and a few associates of a corporate conglomerate who had set up Posko Jenggala in a neighboring *kampung*. The single most important presence at this meeting, however, was the subdistrict head himself, Mr. Rasidi, a recent Jakarta appointment dispatched to replace the former *camat* lost to the tsunami.[21]

On arrival at the shelter camp, the UN-OCHA staff was given a tour by the Malaysian medical doctor, Dr. Jumila, who was the real dynamo behind this particular Mercy project. A comparatively small camp, housing some six hundred displaced persons, many from the same *kampung*, it was indeed something of a showcase, featuring immaculate white tent structures for (extended, or adapted) individual households, proper wash- and bathroom facilities with clean water drawn from wells that the camp residents themselves had helped dig, and even a nursery where a dozen children listened in rapt attention to their teacher reading a storybook, while two young women, also from the *kampung*, looked on, as part of their assistant-teacher training. This camp was also home to a lovely little girl, aged three, whose extraordinary survival and eventual reunion with her father almost a month after the tsunami struck their home was already the stuff of legend. (It was said that she had been found curled up, and severely emaciated, in an open refrigerator, which, having served as her lifeboat in the furious waves, somehow was wedged stuck when the floodwaters receded, thus saving her, twice over, from being carried out to sea.[22])

Once the *camat* arrived, the meeting opened with a welcome address by Dr. Jumila and a round of introductions, flagging the names and concerns of participants' groups and organizations. The *camat* spoke of the destruction in Lhok Nga, where a total of eight villages were destroyed, leaving some eleven thousand survivors out of a pre-tsunami population of more than twenty thousand. He also underlined the damage to government buildings, pointing out that currently government officials could only work out of temporary offices. He expressed notable concern about what he identified as a lack of coordination in the distribution of humanitarian assistance, and, as a result, a perceived, wasteful overlap of efforts in Lhok Nga.

A flurry of comments followed that focused on the distribution of food and medical assistance, with the Posko Jenggala delegation identifying a number of problems attributed to the lack of "central coordination"; some camps had received

---

[21] According to a local newspaper reporter, such appointments had initiated the arrival of a growing number of non-Acehnese officials to fill the ranks of the local civilian government bureaucracy in the aftermath of the tsunami. Author's interview, Banda Aceh, February 24, 2005.

[22] An Associated Press picture of the emotional reunion of father and daughter traveled through the world media. See, for example, *International Herald Tribune*, January 25, 2005. The story was (re)told in the camp by Dr. Jumila of Mercy Malaysia in the presence of the little girl herself and her father, Mustafa Kamal.

an oversupply of foodstuff and other relief goods, resulting in the loss of perishable food, while other IDP locations had received insufficient deliveries and suffered from shortages. Participants wearing T-shirts with the imprint *Posko Jenggala Lhok Nga* also spoke of problems with consistency and follow-up in the medical assistance provided, warning that there was too much medication being made available to a local populace allegedly prone "to keep all medicines given." (The MSF representative in attendance, a doctor, suggested that patient cards be adapted to allow for comments only in English and Bahasa "so that other medics can read" the assessments and prescriptions of colleagues.)

Struggling to get a grip on a meeting they had been invited to chair, the UN-OCHA representatives eventually joined in by asking for more information about the so-called "watsan" (water and sanitation) situation among affected populations in Lhok Nga, and, in particular, the coordination of (or gaps hampering) humanitarian efforts meant to address this problem. The *camat* replied that "no mapping" of the watsan situation had yet been undertaken, and that government officials had no "mechanism" for finding out about this situation other than approaching, seemingly at random, if at all, "local NGOs" for such information. The UN-OCHA field representative, a young career officer newly arrived in Banda Aceh on dispatch from another assignment, who lacked any prior knowledge or experience of Indonesia, was clearly stumped, while her Bahasa-speaking colleague, who had arrived on his own initiative as a volunteer only a few days after the tsunami, was essentially relegated to acting as translator despite years of experience as a researcher in the country, including several visits to Aceh.

It was only at this point in the meeting, with the meta-discourse on "mapping" and "coordination" seemingly exhausted or in something of a tailspin, that members of the tsunami-affected communities in Lhok Nga added their own voices to those of the representatives of local government, business-backed *posko*, and UN-OCHA. As local high school teachers and village elders spoke, they focused attention on two critically urgent concerns of the displaced populations in Lhok Nga: the resumption of schooling for their children and the reconstruction of homes for their communities. With final exams scheduled in April, for example, the destruction of the (only) high school in Lhok Nga had left some three hundred surviving students and twenty-six surviving teachers (there had been five hundred students and forty-five teachers before the tsunami) without sufficient teaching materials and support. According to the female teacher at the meeting, neither the local government nor the I/NGOs had made any serious efforts to assist in improving this situation, even in the aftermath of the initial emergency phase, and with final exams fast approaching.

Speaking on behalf of the five-hundred-odd survivors of *kampung* Weuraya (Lhok Nga), with a pre-tsunami population of more than 1,700 people, village leader Md. Noor was the first person at this meeting to articulate the desire of IDPs to return home. "Everybody is committed to returning home," he repeated in a calm and steadfast voice as he looked around the table, as if to make sure that his message was not lost on anybody present. As if on cue, Dr. Jumila, whose Mercy camp was largely populated by people from *kampung* Weuraya and who had thus been working closely with Md. Noor and others from this community, picked up the thread. She recounted the plans and preparations in place for the initial construction of one hundred homes for IDPs from *kampung* Weuraya, a project that would draw on the residents' enthusiastic participation and material assistance from Mercy Malaysia. In the absence of government approval, however, this project, which enjoyed the full support of the affected community and generous financial backing from Mercy, remained moribund under the broader rubric of the existing Blueprint and the anticipated Master Plan for the reconstruction of Aceh. The game plan of Dr. Jumila, it appeared, was to woo the seemingly amiable Mr. Rasidi into giving special dispensation for the Mercy project to go ahead, perhaps in the hope that, as a new appointee, he would not be hampered by old conflicts in his area of jurisdiction, while at the same time he might be eager to seize opportunities to foster cooperation with local communities.[23] With her own departure imminent, she was also clearly eager to see some tangible and lasting "results" of the Mercy mission she had so energetically promoted over the course of several weeks.

If the need for special dispensation from the *camat* to allow for this specific reconstruction project was the ostensible reason for this meeting, the matter did not stop here. Indeed, there was no mistaking the intensity and urgency with which local representatives of displaced persons in Lhok Nga expressed a collective desire to return to rebuild their homes and communities. A wiry man with a weathered face, now lined deep with the sorrow of having lost everyone in his immediate family, Mr. Cipta, the head of a cluster of five *mukhim*, spoke without mincing words, his eyes fixed on the *camat*: "The government's plans don't make sense. There are twenty-one new sites for relocation, but they are all outside Lhok Nga. Go ahead and there will be another war. *The government needs to decide if it represents the government or the people.*"

Another participant, from a local NGO that pre-dated the tsunami, intervened to add that, in many instances, displaced people had already started going back on their own to rebuild their homes and communities together, without government or other assistance. In response, the *camat* referred to the lack of government guidelines to date and, at the same time, invoked the authority of the anticipated Master Plan on such matters, thus retreating into a position of "appointed officialdom, awaiting further instructions." Asked to clarify the length of time people from Lhok Nga would be expected to remain in temporary relocation shelters, or so-called *barak-barak*, the *camat* confirmed that it could last for one to two years.

This announcement sparked another burst of rapid-fire speech from Mr. Cipta, who argued that the government might now say that people would be able to return to their pre-tsunami homes and communities in one or two years time, but the issues of land-titles and property claims were already "getting murky." He told of bulldozers arriving in some places, leveling everything. As a result, he said, "there is no way of telling where the boundaries once were ... "

At this point, Mr. Rasidi returned to the "problem of coordination," which he identified as the real source of any concerns about property boundaries and their eventual disappearance. Claiming that this was not about "political will" or the lack thereof, the *camat* suggested that the bulldozing of rubble in certain places, whether by the Indonesian military or I/NGOs, reflected, again, the overall lack of central coordination, and, in particular, the failure to consult his office prior to these actions. Curiously, however, he also maintained that "the less bureaucracy, the better" in response to the call by Lhok Nga village elders for more comprehensive and

---

[23] There were reports of military activity in this area in the aftermath of the tsunami, with five people shot dead, all alleged GAM (Gerakan Aceh Merdeka, Free Aceh Movement) supporters, according to the Indonesian armed forces, a claim disputed by others displaced from the same *kampung*.

transparent efforts to promote land surveys and legal titling, which would involve local authorities at subdistrict and village levels. At this point, Mr. Cipta merely shook his head.

After the meeting, Dr. Jumila escorted the small UN-OCHA delegation on a pre-scheduled midday visit to a relocation camp in Lhok Nga, where the *camat*, having granted official permission for this "field trip," offered a quick guided tour. A mother and two young children were the only occupants to be found in a recently erected barrack. While showing visitors the room occupied by herself, her two children, her brother-in-law, and his surviving older son, she said very little, and seemed uneasy in the face of all the attention.

The room, which may well have met the 5-by-2-meters "official" requirement, appeared gloomy and stifling, with nothing but small mosquito-netted screens along the beams for light and ventilation, but it was neat and tidy, with two sacks of rice and some cooking oil and fresh water containers lined up against one wall, and sleeping mats, a few clothes, and other textiles against the other. Overall, this showcase relocation site, which had yet to be completed, was to include several barracks, each one measuring the approved 11-by-30 meters and containing twelve similar units. In addition, each barrack was to share one kitchen and two bathroom facilities, as well as a public hall for meetings and worship. None of these public facilities was on display during this official visit, presumably because they did not exist. There were also no provisions in place for water, sanitation, or electricity on this relocation site.

Nonetheless, the local government was already encouraging people to move in here, as evidenced by the mother-of-two chosen, unbeknownst to herself, as the public face and authentic voice of IDPs in this encounter with international humanitarian assistance officials. Speaking softly as the small international delegation moved on to the next pre-announced visit with the *camat*, she revealed that only two other units in this barrack were occupied by people displaced from her old *kampung*. The other occupants, all men, were unknown to her and her surviving (extended) family. Some of them, it seemed, had been recruited to work on the large relocation site across the road, where many more barracks were under construction. As a result, the social milieu of the already occupied relocation units and its immediate surroundings appeared not unlike that of a construction site, with workers living on site, in makeshift accommodations, for the duration of a project. The widow housed in the barrack in Lhok Nga rarely ventured outside, she said, and did not allow her young children, a boy of almost four and his five-year-old sister, to play beyond the landing outside the room where they now lived.

POSTSCRIPT

In the years that have passed since the December 2004 tsunami struck, leaving such devastation in its wake, Aceh's political and social landscape has undergone an extraordinary and far-reaching transformation beyond what was imaginable in early 2005. First of all, in June of 2005, the government of Indonesia lifted the civil emergency, thus paving the way for the Helsinki-brokered peace talks with its armed opposition, GAM (Gerakan Aceh Merdeka, Free Aceh Movement). These talks, moreover, resulted in the signing of a Memorandum of Understanding (MoU) in August of 2005. Under the provisions of the MoU, and under the auspices of an international observer mission (the Aceh Monitoring Mission, or AMM), a process involving the demobilization and disarmament of GAM, as well as government troop reduction and relocation, gained momentum throughout the remainder of the year, thus allowing for the wider demilitarization of Acehnese politics and society. Finally, once the Indonesian parliament, after much heated debate in Jakarta, adopted Law 11/2006 in August 2006, it became possible to hold local elections in Aceh as per the provisions included in the peace agreement. On December 11, 2006, Acehnese voters went to the polls and elected, by an overwhelming majority, candidates running on a GAM ticket to office in fifteen out of nineteen districts and, importantly, the former GAM-liaison to the AMM (Aceh Monitoring Mission), Irwandi Yusuf, to the post of provincial governor.[24]

In this context, it is all the more striking that the lives of IDPs have remained, in important respects, defined by their displacement. As documented by numerous reports, the process of rebuilding homes, communities, and livelihoods has left much to be desired from the perspective of displaced persons, whether in terms of local participation, project implementation, or social impact. Much less remarked upon, but worthy of note, are the powerful effects of the Indonesian government's promotion of the barracks and, at the same time, its circumvention of the IDP discourse in the early aftermath of the tsunami.

The Indonesian government's early post-tsunami efforts to identify preferred solutions and target populations—shaped at the time by its preoccupation with maintaining security in a highly militarized conflict zone—have had a lasting impact upon the nature and direction of humanitarian assistance and reconstruction in the region. On the one hand, despite evident concern for the issue of protection of displaced populations based on local knowledge and international expertise alike, the Indonesian government, in the context of civil emergency and large-scale troop deployment in Aceh, continued developing its barracks plans and, before long, also succeeded in lining up international agencies to provide for humanitarian needs (e.g., "watsan," or water and sanitation) in the barracks. Thus, the barracks served to reproduce a certain understanding of the very nature of the "problem" to which they were presented as a solution, with consequences extending well beyond the political conditions of their inception, as indicated by numerous reports.

On the other hand, despite the widespread circulation of the *UN Guiding Principles on Internal Displacement* in a Bahasa Indonesian translation among Indonesian government officials,[25] the Indonesian government has remained

---

[24] A reported, 86.9 percent of voters registered to vote, and the turnout on election day was 78 percent. The GAM–SIRA ticket of Irwan Yusuf and Muhammad Nazar captured 38.2 percent of the vote, which was more than twice that of their closest competitors. SIRA (Sentral Informasi Referendum Aceh, or Aceh Referendum Information Center) was founded in 1999 and gained widespread recognition for its role in mobilizing the largest rally in the history of Aceh, when an estimated one million people converged in Banda Aceh on November 9, 1999.

[25] *Mereka yang Mengungsi: Komik tentang Prinsip-prinsip Panduan Pengungsian Internal* (Jakarta: Baris Baru dan Oxfam GB, 2002). This booklet includes the "Guiding Principles on Internal Displacement," written in Bahasa Indonesia, in an appendix. The cover and the main section of the booklet are in the format of a comic book, featuring fleeing and frightened civilians, glimpses of ("disembodied") military boots and weapons, courageous human rights workers, and assorted perpetrators of violence, ranging from masked men with automatic weapons to local thugs engaged in intimidation and worse. In addition to Oxfam, this publication was sponsored by UN-OCHA (Indonesia), and Internal Conflict Monitoring Centre (ICMC), and it drew on contributions from a number of locally based human rights organizations, including in Aceh, Papua, Ambon, and Pontianak.

reluctant to recognize as internally displaced persons, or IDPs, the hundreds of thousands dislocated in the aftermath of the tsunami; in public discourse (including in meetings convened by the UN Office for the Coordination of Humanitarian Affairs [OCHA]), it instead referred to the "homeless," or to the "people who lost their homes because of the tsunami." As a result of the government's early attention to such "labeling,"[26] which then resonated among international agencies, this discursive shift pointed away from the concerns outlined in the *Guiding Principles*. In the context of Aceh—an area affected by natural disaster *and* protracted militarized conflict—it also served to distance from humanitarian and political consideration thousands of people whose displacement pre-dated the tsunami.

While the promotion of barracks and the circumvention of the IDP discourse in the early post-tsunami period left enduring legacies for displaced persons in Aceh, these efforts to confine and define IDPs have remained neither seamless, nor uncontested. Indeed, in the aftermath of the MoU, Aceh has also seen the collective mobilization of displaced populations as IDPs, inflecting familiar repertoires of protest with a rights-based IDP discourse in a new political context. Since the close of 2005, collective action has thus served in distinct ways to challenge the very terms of engagement with IDPs and has refocused attention on the (contested) place of displaced persons and communities in the body politic. As indicated below, collective action in the name of the internally displaced has involved (former) conflict IDPs mobilizing a mass march to the central highlands, thus invoking their right to return. Thousands of IDPs displaced by the tsunami have also demonstrated against new government resettlement regulations linking assistance provisions to predisaster property relations.

"Conflict IDPs and the Right to Return"

On December 10, 2005, after several unsuccessful attempts by individuals and families to return to their communities in central Aceh, a collective effort was launched by some 4,500 to 5,000 conflict IDPs in Pidie and Bireuen, two adjacent northern districts.[27] As transportation promised by local government officials failed to materialize on the day it was scheduled, IDPs turned this planned collective return into a protest march. Making their first stop at Abu Beureueh mosque in Beureuneun (Pidie), a prominent site of resistance and refuge alike in the social imaginary of many Acehnese, they continued some ten kilometers on to Lumputot (Bireuen). There, they eventually boarded trucks and buses headed for the interior highlands of central Aceh, accompanied by IDPs joining from other host communities in Bireuen, stopping to set up large makeshift tent camps by the mosques at two locations known as Km 60 and Ronga-Ronga.[28]

As it turned out, this collective attempt to return to the highlands met with considerable challenges. Contemporary reports tended to emphasize the

---

[26] For a wider discussion of the effects of "labeling refugees and other forced migrants," see Roger Zetter, "More Labels, Fewer Refugees: Making and Remaking the Refugee Label in an Era of Globalization," *Journal of Refugee Studies* 20,2 (2007): 172–192.

[27] According to the Center for Humanitarian and Social Development (CHSD), a local NGO in Pidie working with the IDPs, some five thousand names were collected at the outset of the return march. Author's interview, Pidie, January 11, 2006.

[28] See, for example, "Pengungsi Kembali ke Koloni," *AcehKita*, December 12–18, 2005, p. 10.

humanitarian nature of the difficulties encountered by these would-be returnees, including some sixty people who reportedly collapsed from exhaustion and starvation within the first week.[29] At the same time, however, there was evidence that political impediments also hampered the safe return of these (former) conflict IDPs, many of whom had fled their villages in the central highlands in 2000–2001 during a period of especially "high-intensity" conflict involving not only GAM and the Indonesian military, but also Javanese (trans)migrants and so-called anti-separatist militia groups.[30]

In the wider political context of this area, the requirement that would-be returnees had to produce formal verification of IDP status with the signatures of local government officials in the village where they had taken refuge and in their home village, without any commensurate government guarantees of security on their return, caught these (former) conflict displacees in something of a doublebind. Moreover, local civilian government officials also intervened in ways that seemingly aimed at silencing any collective IDP voice (for instance, by holding meetings without IDP leaders or other concerned parties present) and at undermining any united IDP front (e.g., by calling for further dispersals of IDPs to different subdistrict locations and individual villages).[31] In addition, there were reports of intimidation and assault at the hands of the Indonesian military and police. On January 8, military and police entered the makeshift camp at Ronga-Ronga, and IDPs were made to board buses and trucks as uniformed officials shouted out destinations: Timang Gajah, Rimba Raya, Pinto Rime Gayo, all in Bener Meriah. Finally, there were reports of violence targeting returning IDPs and/or their property, as well as cases of fighting with local youths or former militia, in places where local leaders refused to provide security guarantees. In a village in Ketol (Aceh Tengah), for example, eight IDPs trying to secure the signature of the village head were beaten up and had their motorbikes destroyed by local residents.

Having been displaced by conflict during the previous militarized campaigns of the counterinsurgency, IDPs who sought refuge with host communities had remained largely invisible in the wider context of early post-tsunami Aceh. While some 1,800 conflict IDPs were reportedly still in camps only days before the tsunami struck,[32] there was no corresponding figure for those who had sought refuge from militarization and violence with relatives or friends. This is not surprising, given the informality and fluidity of such arrangements compared to the official registration and regulation of IDPs in designated shelter areas. Nonetheless, conflict IDPs who had found shelter in host communities outnumbered by a considerable margin their encamped counterparts at that time.

---

[29] World Bank—DFS, "Aceh Conflict Monitoring Update, December 1–31, 2005."

[30] See, for example, Ali Aulia Ramly, "Modes of Displacement during Martial Law," in *Aceh under Martial Law: Conflict, Violence, and Displacement*, ed. Eva-Lotta E. Hedman, Working Paper No. 24 (Oxford: University of Oxford, Refugee Studies Centre, 2005), especially p. 18.

[31] Author's interviews with representatives from the Center for Humanitarian and Social Development (CHSD), the Aceh Monitoring Mission (AMM), the local government in Takengon, and with numerous conflict IDPs from Pidie and Bireuen at locations in Aceh Tengah, including at 60K, Ronga-Ronga, and Laut Tawar, as well as with other concerned observers in Banda Aceh. January 10–15, 2006.

[32] International Organisation for Migration, 2004, "Update on the IDP situation in Aceh," December 20, 2004.

Developments during the early implementation of the MoU highlighted the extent to which local political conditions shaped the horizon of "conflict IDPs" living in host communities. Not only did such conditions influence IDP efforts and prospects of recognition, but also their possibilities for return. For example, it was only in the aftermath of the peace agreement and its implementation—involving, notably, the demilitarization of host-community areas—that conflict IDPs in Bireuen and Pidie were able to organize their collective return to the central highlands of Aceh, a region formerly governed under a single administrative district, Aceh Tengah, which in 2003 had been divided by the (contested) creation of a second district, Bener Meriah. Moreover, since the Cessation of Hostilities Agreement (COHA) had broken down in 2002 following an attack on the Takengon local office of the international monitoring body, it was perhaps no coincidence that these conflict IDPs had remained displaced for so long. As noted above, their original flight from violent conflict had taken place as long ago as May to June 2001. Nor was it surprising that IDPs eventually seized on collective action in their efforts to secure a return to central Aceh, where so-called militia groups had gained particular notoriety. These groups were significantly not included in the MoU, but they still enjoyed the backing of local businessmen, as well as civilian and military officials.[33]

If the demilitarization of host-community areas allowed for new forms of collective action by (former) conflict IDPs in Pidie and Bireuen, a political campaign advocating the division of Aceh underscored the urgency of returning to the central highlands lest administrative remapping were to render the prospects for such return even more uncertain in the future. Indeed, the timing of the attempted collective return movement on December 10 followed on the heels of a December 4, 2005, rally in Jakarta, when seven local *bupati* unilaterally declared their secession from Aceh and their proposal to establish two new provinces: "Aceh Leuser Antara" (ALA), which would be forged out of the districts of Aceh Tengah, Aceh Tenggara, Aceh Singkil, Gayo Lues, and Bener Meriah, and "Aceh Barat Selatan" (ABAS), which would be formed from Aceh Barat, Aceh Barat Daya, Aceh Jaya, Nagan Raya, and Simeulue.[34] While less immediate, the scheduled termination of the EU-led Aceh Monitoring Mission in mid-March 2006 also threatened the prospects for safe return in what remained, in many respects, an unreformed outpost of the "new" Aceh.[35]

"Tsunami IDPs and Barracks Relocation"

In September 2006, with tens of thousands displaced by the tsunami still residing in so-called "temporary location shelters," it was the turn of IDPs living in such shelters, or barracks, to take collective action. On September 11, an estimated two thousand people joined in a major demonstration at the offices of the BRR (Badan Rehabilitasi dan Rekonstruksi [NAD-Nias], or the Rehabilitation and Reconstruction

---

[33] See, for example, Imparsial Team, "Report Post-MoU Monitoring on Aceh, Aug. 15–Oct. 15, 2005," October 2005. With the establishment of the Aceh Peace-Reintegration Agency (BRA) in February 2006, anti-separatist groups were included as beneficiaries eligible for government-funded reintegration programs, as were "conflict-affected persons" in general, and also GAM supporters who had surrendered prior to the MoU.

[34] "Pemekaran Aceh Idak Jadi Prioritas," acehkita.com, December 7, 2005.

[35] In mid-March, the AMM cut back its staff of 220 monitors by almost two-thirds, but also agreed on a three-month extension with the government. After a further extension, the AMM finally departed from Aceh in December 2006.

Board) in Banda Aceh to refocus attention on the situation facing the IDP barracks population. According to reports, this first demonstration remained entirely orderly and resulted in a negotiated agreement to review BRR regulations affecting the resettlement of what, in fact, has remained a considerable proportion of the barracks population—renters, squatters, and the landless.[36]

On September 19, and continuing until the following day, the BRR once more became the target of a major demonstration focused on government regulations and the resettlement of barrack IDPs. This time, the demonstrations, which again involved an estimated two thousand people, also featured a blockade of the BRR. As the police moved in to disperse the crowds, some protesters reportedly threw rocks in their direction, damaging a police car.[37] According to the BRR, three attempts at negotiating a settlement with the leaders of the second demonstrations failed, as demands had escalated "to include unrealistic requests," including the transfer of money into an NGO account. However, aside from "some loud, well-orchestrated cheering and chanting," the BRR concluded in its update on these events, "both demonstrations have been conducted peacefully."[38]

These demonstrations emerged against the backdrop of new regulations on resettlement issued by the BRR in June 2006. In brief, these regulations made new provisions for displaced populations not covered by the resettlement schemes developed for those who had owned their land before the tsunami, that is, for renters, squatters, and the landless. According to contemporary estimates, these groups composed the majority of the 70,000 to 100,000 people displaced by the tsunami who were still living in some 150 government barracks located across different parts of Aceh.[39]

As the new government regulations of June 2006 served to "unpack" and differentiate between the displaced on grounds of pre-tsunami property relations, they also, invariably, set into motion new forms of contestation over the nature and direction of post-tsunami resettlement. In important respects, they thus reflected and reproduced a shift away from the "humanitarian needs" discourse and practice within which the barracks—and their residents—had remained inscribed since the early post-tsunami months of 2005. That is, as the new regulations made distinctions among different categories of displaced persons, many of whom had encountered each other, "equally," as "IDPs" in the context of the barracks, it was not merely "confusion" and a "simmering crisis" that resulted, but also the opening up of a space for a new politics of recognition.[40]

---

[36] See, for example, BRR International Update, "Demonstrations at and Blockade of BRR in Banda Aceh," September 20, 2006.

[37] See, for example, "Protesters Attack Aceh Tsunami Reconstruction Office," *Reuters*, September 20, 2006. According to Banda Aceh deputy police chief Dede Setyo, the police "decided to disperse the crowd because they had been staying outside the BRR offices beyond the timeline that we gave them." Ibid.

[38] BRR International Update, "Demonstrations at and Blockade of BRR in Banda Aceh."

[39] In September 2006, BRR cited the figure 70,000 (in BRR," Special Unit on Barracks") and 100,000 (in "BRR International Update"). See BRR International Update, "Special Unit on Barracks," September 2006.

[40] The "confusion" and "simmering crisis" are noted in Oxfam International, "The Tsunami Two Years On: Land Rights in Aceh," *Oxfam Briefing Note*, November 30, 2006, p. 7.

Representation and Recognition: From IDP to Citizen in the New Aceh?

This new politics of recognition gained momentum as a result of the local elections on the horizon and the voter registration drive underway in 2006, including among IDPs in barracks and elsewhere. In the context of a highly contested election campaign, with local parties and so-called "independent candidates" running against the national party machines of Golkar and others, widespread collective action re-emerged, with local communities and groups further expanding an already impressive repertoire of protest. Such protests have focused on a range of reconstruction-related issues, and have targeted not only the BRR, as noted above, but also the BRA (Aceh Peace-Reintegration Agency), which was established in February 2006, with government funding to establish reintegration programs whose beneficiaries would include (former) militia groups, GAM supporters who had surrendered prior to the MoU, and "conflict-affected persons" throughout all rural communities.[41] Protests have also directed attention to the electoral process and, in places, the outcome of the elections.

While it is hardly surprising that the BRR and the BRA—the key coordinating and implementing government agencies focused on post-tsunami and post-conflict reconstruction—have been targeted by IDP protests, it is noteworthy that, in the post-election months of 2007, the local parliament in Banda Aceh has emerged as a new site of collective action in the name of the internally displaced. Within days of another round of protests involving hundreds of IDPs and, once again, Forak (the Inter-Barrack Communications Forum) at the BRR on April 9, 2007, the Acehnese Alliance of Youth and Students (Alee) called for an international audit of the BRR in a demonstration at the parliament in Banda Aceh. A few months later, on July 30, the parliament building was occupied for some thirteen hours by (former) conflict IDPs from Bener Meriah and Aceh Tengah, where tensions over the mismanagement of reintegration benefits by the BRA have remained acute, and where the elections were marred by comparatively high levels of fraud and violence.

As the broader political landscape underwent such dramatic transformation in the aftermath of the December 2004 tsunami, some of the earlier concerns for the protection and the rights of internally displaced persons may have seemed to have been unwarranted in the first place, or, at the very least, now appeared dated to observers and practitioners. However, as suggested above, the Indonesian government's promotion of barracks and its circumvention of the IDP discourse in early post-tsunami Aceh pointed towards certain (and away from other) understandings of the nature of the "problems" of displacement and the displaced. As the "international humanitarian community" was drawn into the orbit of various "solutions" to these "problems" presented by the Indonesian government, moreover, those solutions gained added momentum with, for example, the institutionalization of needs assessments and aid delivery focused on barracks. At the same time, the disregard for conflict IDPs and, indeed, for the complexity of—recurring, multiple, and/or secondary—displacement in a conflict-disaster zone remained pervasive in

---

[41] Although the politics of reconstruction and aid delivery demands more careful attention than is possible here, the assessments produced by donors and "partners" frequently mention the following "problems": the slow pace of delivery, the lack of transparency in identifying recipients, the absence of checks on contractors, and the corruption of funds.

international humanitarian practice into the post-MoU period in Aceh, and also served to reflect and reproduce official government discourse.

Inasmuch as the discursive practices and enduring legacies of humanitarian interventions in "complex emergency situations" merit further attention, in Aceh and elsewhere, the contestation of such practices and legacies by actual existing IDPs points to a critical research agenda focused on questions of representation, recognition, and displacement. For example, such an agenda may include more systematic research into the barracks as a form of "carceral institution" and the effects thereof upon the formation of solidarities and collective action among residents, ranging from those comparatively more confined to such living conditions to others with opportunities for visiting families and communities (a pattern noted in Aceh). Moreover, future research might also focus on the barracks as a kind of "vote bank" and the implications thereof for the public articulation of IDP "interests and grievances," and the politicization of reconstruction and reintegration efforts in the wider context of local elections, money politics, and political machines. Finally, as suggested in this postscript, there is much to learn from a more systematic scrutiny of the challenges to official IDP discourse and practice in Aceh, including from close-up political ethnographies and structured comparisons of protest. Indeed, even these brief glimpses indicate that as people who had found themselves "internally displaced" by natural disaster and/or militarized conflict challenged, through collective action, the effects of such discourse and practice, they also demanded their rightful place as national citizens in the body politic, thus pointing the way out of "displacement" as a lived experience.

GHOSTS WITH TRAUMA:
GLOBAL IMAGINARIES AND THE
POLITICS OF POST-CONFLICT MEMORY

Nils Bubandt

Narratives about spiritual revenge in the form of witchcraft attacks and ancestral anger have become widespread in North Maluku in the wake of violent communal clashes that ravaged the province between 1999 and 2001. In a novel twist of semantic adaptation, these spirit attacks have recently become associated with the global therapeutic concept of trauma and the occult figure of the Dracula (*drakula*), which takes its name from Count Dracula, a fictional vampire. This chapter traces the genealogy of these changes. It follows the accounts of one such vengeful ghost, who in the form of a female *drakula* terrorized locals and IDPs in the post-conflict town of Tobelo in early 2004.[1] The spiritual revenge of the *drakula*, which was popularly associated with the death of at least five people, was said to have been caused by *trauma*.

Both *trauma* and *drakula* are recent additions to the North Malukan vocabulary. Although the *drakula* has a long history in Indonesia (particularly in Java) of embodying political terror, the figure was only made available to the North Malukan popular imagination by soap operas and returning IDPs some time after 2002. The concept of trauma has similarly only recently become part of popular discourse in this part of Indonesia. It was introduced to the region by the media as well as by the NGOs and international relief organizations that rallied to help in the reconciliation process after the conflict. The dissemination of both concepts was characterized by two features. Firstly, the spread of the concepts closely mapped onto the movements

---

[1] IDP, or "internally displaced person," refers to people who have been forced to leave their homes and to flee into domestic exile as a result of violent conflict. In early 2000, more than one million Indonesians were classified as IDPs. The violent conflict in North Maluku forced over 200,000 people into exile into neighboring districts or provinces. Slowly, after 2002, the IDPs began returning home as part of a government-sponsored program of repatriation. See Christopher Duncan, "Unwelcome Guests: Relations between Internally Displaced Persons and Their Hosts in North Sulawesi, Indonesia," *Journal of Refugee Studies* 18,1 (2005): 25–46; and Jana Mason, *Shadow Plays: The Crisis of Refugees and Internally Displaced Persons in Indonesia* (Washington, DC: US Committee for Refugees, 2001), pp. 1–44, available at: www.unhcr.org/cgi-bin/texis/vtx/home/opendoc.pdf?tbl=RSDOCI&id=3ae6a5856

of internally displaced people, who at the height of the conflict in North Maluku made up around a quarter of the population. It was to a large extent with the IDPs that these concepts traveled and took on new meaning. Secondly, the popular reception of both concepts points to the space where the spiritual becomes political and the political becomes spiritual. It is within this space of spiritual politics that witchcraft has always existed in North Maluku, and it is within this same conceptual space, I argue, that trauma and Draculas were fused with local ideas of spiritual revenge.

Tracing the political history of the global concepts of the Dracula and trauma in eastern Indonesia and the semantic marriage of the two concepts in the post-conflict town of Tobelo, I provide an ethnographic example of the forms of reenchantment that the global discourses and practices of trauma enable. I argue that the North Malukan narratives about spiritual revenge seize upon the occult logic inherent in the political figure of the *drakula* and the global concept of trauma to make sense of the aftermath of conflict. In the process, the concepts are made to function within a North Malukan social rationality. The concept of trauma, in particular, is altered radically. It is thus inscribed within a memory politics very different from the global psychological discourse in which the concept originates.[2]

TRAUMA AND VAMPIRES IN CONTEXT

The ease with which trauma is incorporated into a local politics of thinking about past violence highlights the constituent plasticity of the psychological concept of "trauma." As "trauma" is disseminated by NGOs as part of a new global system of governance and development to become an accepted diagnostic device on a world-wide scale, the concept, as I will show, is lodged within local horizons of understanding violence. This semantic detachment from the global values and cosmology of the trauma discourse may help explain the successful dissemination to many parts of the world of the concept of "trauma." In the process of being globalized, however, trauma is dissociated from the global therapeutic paradigm and the science of the self on which the concept of "trauma" is founded, and made to serve other ways of remembering and talking about violence. Rather than being a disturbance in individual minds, trauma in North Maluku becomes an event that takes place in the social intersection between spirits and humans. Arguing that spirits are central vehicles of memory, I will show how the incorporation of trauma and the Dracula into an understanding of spiritual revenge is related to local ways of thinking about the past in North Maluku. The narratives about traumatized spirits in this way become positioned ways of speaking about violence, self, and social morality.

The need for studies of the symbolic, moral, and socio-political contexts in which post-conflict trauma occurs has often been emphasized,[3] and a number of good

---

[2] See Ian Hacking, *Rewriting the Soul: Multiple Personality Disorder and the Sciences of Memory* (Princeton, NJ: Princeton University Press, 1995). Allan Young, *The Harmony of Illusions: Inventing Post-Traumatic Stress Disorder* (Princeton, NJ: Princeton University Press, 1995).

[3] Michael Kenny, "Trauma, Time, Illness, and Culture," in *Tense Past: Cultural Essays in Trauma and Memory*, ed. P. Antze and M. Lambek (New York, NY: Routledge, 1996), pp. 151–71; Derek Summerfield, "A Critique of Seven Assumptions Behind Psychological Trauma Programmes in War-Affected Areas," *Social Science and Medicine* 48 (1999): 1449–62; and Patrick Bracken, *Trauma: Culture, Meaning, and Philosophy* (London: Whurr Publishers, 2002).

ethnographies of trauma outside of the West already exist.[4] Most of these studies, however, focus on the international treatment of trauma victims within organized therapeutic settings, and so far little attention has been paid to the ways in which the discourse of trauma has diffused beyond the clinic around the world. As Bracken and Petty have emphasized, "the language of trauma has become part of the vernacular—it is accessible and familiar in contemporary Western culture."[5] This chapter provides an ethnographic example of how this diffusion of trauma into popular discourse and political imagination also occurs outside the Western world. Attending to the ethnographic details of this global diffusion is important because it takes analysis beyond fruitless debates about whether or not trauma is a cultural phenomenon. A truly comparative perspective on the globalization of trauma should instead seek to analyze the contexts where discourses and practices about trauma, which are simultaneously political, cultural, global, local, and real, emerge in particular ways in particular historical circumstances. This chapter offers such an ethnography of "trauma in context" by tracing the emergence and vernacularization of the global trauma discourse in North Maluku.[6] The localized adoption of the scientific and therapeutic discourse of trauma functions, so I argue, in conjunction with the local assimilation of the occult figure of the Dracula promoted by a globalized media- and ideoscape, to confirm and reinvent the North Malukan spirit world and make it locally relevant to contemporary political realities.[7]

---

[4] Vanessa Pupavac, "Pathologizing Populations and Colonizing Minds: International Psychosocial Programs in Kosovo," *Alternatives* 27 (2002): 489–511; Lidija Milic, "From Serbia With Hate: A Case Study in Globalization, Trauma, and Language," *Dialectical Anthropology* 27 (2003): 331–53. Jennifer Cole, "Painful Memories: Ritual and the Transformation of Community Trauma," *Culture, Medicine and Psychiatry* 28 (2004): 87–105; Fransisco Ferrándiz, "The Body as Wound: Possession, *Malandros,* and Everyday Violence in Venezuela," *Critique of Anthropology* 24,2 (2004): 107–33; Clara Han, "The Work of Indebtedness: The Traumatic Present of Late Capitalist Chile," *Culture, Medicine and Psychiatry* 28 (2004): 169–87; Erica Caple James, "The Political Economy of 'Trauma' in Haiti in the Democratic Era of Insecurity," *Culture, Medicine and Psychiatry* 28 (2004): 127–49; and Christina Zarowsky, "Writing Trauma: Emotion, Ethnography, and the Politics of Suffering among Somali Returnees in Ethiopia," *Culture, Medicine and Psychiatry* 28 (2004): 189–209.

[5] Patrick Bracken and Celia Petty, "Introduction," in *Rethinking the Trauma of War,* ed. P. Bracken and C. Petty (London: Free Association Books, 1998), p. 1.

[6] On the concept of vernacularization, see Nils Bubandt, "Vernacular Security: The Politics of Feeling Safe in Global, National, and Local Worlds," *Security Dialogue* 36,3 (2005): 275–96.

[7] The analytical neologism of the –scape is coined by Arjun Appadurai to describe the global flows that constitute the building blocks of the "historically situated imaginations of persons and groups around the globe." See Arjun Appadurai, *Modernity at Large: Cultural Dimensions of Globalization* (Minneapolis, MN: University of Minnesota Press, 1996), p. 33. Appadurai argues that five, inherently perspectival, dimensions of cultural flows make up the landscape of globalization: ethnoscapes, technoscapes, financescapes, mediascapes, and ideoscapes. I employ the latter two concepts to describe the most important interrelated global flows in my ethnographic case. "Mediascapes" thus refers to the narratives and images distributed globally for local consumption by the printed and electronic media, while the notion of "ideoscapes" describes the global circulation of political images, narratives, and keywords. The Dracula is, as I will show, part of a global mediascape but has in Indonesia been incorporated into a nationalized ideoscape. Appadurai's list of flows is useful in order to point to the perspectivalism of the cultural dimensions of globalization, but it can be faulted for being somewhat idiosyncratic and incomplete. As a testimony to the theoretical power and analytical imperfection of Appadurai's approach, a host of additional "scapes" have emerged from anthropologists inspired by Appadurai. I will add my own neology to this list and argue that "science-scapes" is a useful concept to describe the global circulation of scientific concepts

OLD SPIRITS, NEW NAMES

In February 2004, the provincial town of Tobelo was haunted by the presence of a cannibal witch, or *suanggi*. For almost two months, the normally bustling streets of Tobelo fell completely silent, as people stayed at home and transport ground to an unusual halt after nightfall. Rumors of the *suanggi* quickly spread throughout most of North Maluku, and parents of children who attended school in Tobelo either sent money for them to leave town or admonished them not to go out at night. The story was eventually picked up by the weekly North Malukan newspaper, *Aspirasi*:

> Don't think this [*suanggi*] comes out of a book of fairy tales. For a month now, each night as the sun sets, a hush descends over Tobelo, the district capital of North Halmahera. The swarms of children in the town streets and the noise of play from the house fronts have now disappeared as if they have been swallowed up by the earth.[8]

A *suanggi* is a witch spirit known and feared in most parts of eastern Indonesia, where it has been a constant menace to social existence at least since the sixteenth century, when Portuguese discoverers described it shortly after their arrival as the first Europeans to the region.[9] The *suanggi* appears in a variety of local forms and is in Tobelo known as *o tokata*. The *o tokata* is a malevolent spirit of the dead whose danger is associated with its incomplete transformation into an ancestor spirit.[10] Often this dangerous spirit who exists between the living and the ancestors is related to violent death and the lack of a proper ritual burial. The *suanggi* is said to "tempt" (*menggoda*) and possess human beings who have been overly preoccupied with greed, gluttony, or social envy. Once they have succumbed, these "possessed" people lead dual lives, in which they carry out their normal existence during the daytime, but at night the head of such a person pulls free from his or her sleeping body (*cabut*). The disembodied head, its entrails dangling from the neck, then flies through the night in search of victims, usually people against whom the possessed person holds a grudge. The victim is attacked, and its liver eaten. The shadow or "image" of the victim (*bayangan* in Indonesian and *o gurumini* in Tobelo) is also

---

and narratives. These concepts function by claiming to be "nonpolitical" and to merely offer neutral, and scientifically based, devices for social improvement. The alleged nonpolitical character of these science-scapes is particularly reinforced when they are lodged with the "anti-politics machine" of development discourse. See James Ferguson, *The Anti-Politics Machine: "Development," Depoliticization, and Bureaucratic Power in Lesotho* (Cambridge: Cambridge University Press, 1990). The global dissemination of the concept of trauma is, I believe, a good illustration of a science-scape. Like other scientific concepts that have had a global impact, trauma has, however, also become an intrinsic part of a global ideoscape in the process of becoming globalized. This chapter seeks to trace the ethnographic path to North Maluku of the concept of trauma along such global flows of science, media, and politics.

[8] Asri Fabanyo, "Awas! Suanggi Pemakan 'Burung'" [Beware: A Witch on the Loose Eats Genitals], *Aspirasi*, February 5–11, 2004, p. 13.

[9] Hubert Th. Jacobs, *A Treatise on the Moluccas (c. 1544). Probably the Preliminary Version of António Galvão's Lost História das Molucas* (Rome: Jesuit Historical Institute, 1970), p. 181. See also Nils Bubandt, "Warriors of the Hornbill, Victims of the Mantis: History and Embodied Morality among the Buli of Central Halmahera" (PhD dissertation, The Australian National University, Canberra, 1995).

[10] Jos Platenkamp, "Tobelo: Ideas and Values of a North Moluccan Society" (PhD dissertation, University of Leiden, Leiden, 1988), p. 81.

damaged or replaced by that of the *suanggi*, and if the victim is not properly attended to by a local healer (*sow-sow*), these spiritual injuries almost inevitably lead to death.

In a number of ways, however, this particular cannibal spirit that haunted Tobelo town in early 2004 broke with convention. The female spirit would propose to young men, particularly teachers who, like other underpaid public servants, frequently made an extra income driving a taxi motorbike (*ojek*) in the evening. If the *ojek* driver accepted her sexual advances, the spirit would assault him and consume his genitals. This explicitly sexual and phallic nature of the attacks was new. Also new was the fact that only men seemed to be targeted. The newspaper article describes four encounters between the *suanggi* woman and young men, two of which ended with the death and emasculation of the man. The success of the female witch was ascribed to her reported beauty that easily lured her victims. Beauty was another unusual characteristic, the conventional *suanggi* being a terrifying and ugly monster.

Yet these innovations were overshadowed by two other novelties. Preferring to focus on the supposedly traditional nature of the episode, the newspaper report never mentions what was, in popular accounts of the *suanggi*, its fourth and most distinguishing novel feature: namely that the enticing woman in the moment of her attack would turn into a *drakula* with long fangs. Whereas the *suanggi* normally eats the liver of its victim, this female *drakula* would drink the victim's blood after biting him on the neck. This modus operandi clearly emulated the protagonists in the hugely popular vampire movies that were shown regularly on the commercial satellite channels to which most villagers had gained access in recent years.

In addition to the explicitly sexual and gendered character of the *drakula*'s attacks, one last feature was new. This was the first time that anyone could remember that the revenge of a ghost appeared to be motivated by trauma.

DRACULA, TRAUMA, TERROR

Two versions of the *drakula* story dominated the accounts I collected. The first maintained that the *drakula* was the daughter of a Tobelo village leader. She had been raped by a group of young men during the conflict in 1999–2001. After their assault, her attackers had killed her and dumped the body in a ravine, a place of hiding that often appears in myths. For six months she had been missing, until a diviner had dreamed of the ravine and alerted others to the possible significance of this vision. Indeed, the body had been found in the indicated spot and been given a proper burial. But as often happened in cases of violent and "bad" death, the spirit of the girl had turned into a dangerous and vengeful ghost. The difference in this case was that the ghost had taken the form of a vampire and was seeking out her attackers to enact her revenge.

Like other spirits, the *drakula* could assume a variety of forms in order to deceive the living. Once she had been cornered by villagers and taken to the police station. On route, so the story goes, she had transformed herself into a small girl, and the police, disbelieving the villagers' accusations against what appeared to be an innocent girl, had let her go. But unlike other spirits, the *drakula* described in this account had come into existence because of the trauma experienced by the raped woman, a trauma that she took with her into the spirit world and which now motivated her attacks.

A second account held the *drakula* was a woman who had joined the conflict as an active participant after her husband had been killed. According to this version, the woman came from Morotai, an island just off the northern tip of Halmahera that is regionally renowned for its black magic (*ilmu hitam*). Her husband had been killed in the region between Galela and Tobelo during a large-scale massacre in December 1999 and January 2000 that had shocked the entire Indonesian nation. As a result of these and later clashes during 2000, at least 10,000 Muslim people from the Tobelo area had, according to local UN figures, sought refuge on Morotai. According to this version of the narrative, the *drakula* was among these IDPs on Morotai. Having arrived back in her home region as an IDP, she had vowed to avenge the death of her husband, and she had joined in the communal conflict on the side of Laskar Jihad.[11] As part of this effort, so the story went, she had begun to study the black magic of the area, particularly magic that would guarantee invulnerability and bravery in battle. This was in no way unusual. During and after the conflict, North Maluku was abuzz with rumors about the use of such magic. Bravery was said to be ensured by taking medicinal herbs that made the protagonist "forget death" (*lupa mati*), and there were numerous stories of opponents who would launch themselves into suicidal attacks with a courage and apparent foolhardiness that were attributed to their use of magical herbs. Many people were quite candid about having used such "fighting magic" themselves, even though these admissions attracted criticism both from the Protestant Church and from reformist Islam.[12]

An excessive use of such herbs is considered to be dangerous, however, because the magic they contain is "owned" by dangerous spirits, who are eager to sway people to their side. The ingestion of excessive amounts of magical concoctions could thus be seen as one reason why the woman from Morotai had become a dangerous spirit. It was also said that her transformation into a vampire had occurred because she had experienced *trauma* from the death of her husband, as well as from her engagement in the fighting. Although the two accounts differed in the narrative details, they both agreed that the *drakula* was a traumatized ghost.

---

[11] Laskar Jihad is the paramilitary wing of the conservative Islamic organization, Forum Komunikasi Ahlu Sunnah wal-Jama'ah (FKAWJ), whose leader, Ja'far Umar Thalib, preaches a puritanical, Salafi form of Islam. Laskar Jihad was launched in early 2000 in direct response to massacres on Muslim communities in Tobelo. At mass rallies in Jakarta, attended by thousands of demonstrators, Ja'far Umar Thalib decried what he described as a genocidal attack on Muslims. He called upon the faithful to defend Islam and accused President Abdurrahman Wahid of siding with the Christians. The Tobelo massacre provided for Thalib welcome proof of what he saw as an ongoing Western and Zionist campaign to marginalize Islam in Indonesia, and for which the process of democratization was also merely a cover-up. Despite the importance of Halmahera in the formation of FKAWJ, very few Laskar Jihad ended up in North Maluku. It is estimated, however, that between three thousand and ten thousand volunteers were sent to Maluku. See Michael Davis, "Laskar Jihad and the Political Position of Conservative Islam in Indonesia," *Contemporary Southeast Asia* 24,1 (2002): 12–32; and Noorhaidi Hasan, "Faith and Politics: The Rise of the Laskar Jihad in the Era of Transition in Indonesia," *Indonesia* 73 (2002): 145–69. For a study of Laskar Jihad, see Noorhaidi Hasan, *Laskar Jihad: Islam, Militancy, and the Quest for Identity in Post-New Order Indonesia* (Ithaca, NY: Cornell Southeast Asia Program Publications, 2006).

[12] See Nils Bubandt, "Sorcery, Corruption, and the Dangers of Democracy in Indonesia," *Journal of the Royal Anthropological Institute* 12,2 (2006): 413–31.

THE MEDIASCAPE OF THE DRACULA

The newspaper article, cited above, about a vengeful ghost in Tobelo was sandwiched between a business report from a local chicken farm that discussed the profitability of industrial-style chicken farming and a list announcing the political candidates for seats in the regional parliament in the upcoming election. The 2004 election was the first truly democratic election in Indonesia for more than thirty years, but it was also anticipated with some trepidation, since many observers, both foreign and domestic, worried that the election might be derailed by violence instigated by groups from within the military or the former regime. For North Maluku, it was also the first election to take place after the region had become a separate province in late 1999 only to be catapulted into a drawn-out and violent conflict. The sectarian violence cost over 2,000 people their lives, resulted in a virtual collapse of local infrastructure, and led to a massive population displacement of more than 200,000 people. The human costs of the conflict for a province of only 800,000 were enormous. Indeed, most people in the regions of North Maluku affected directly by the conflict knew someone who had either been killed or who had disappeared in mysterious circumstances.

Tobelo was one of the areas most severely affected by the violence in North Maluku. While as many as 100,000 Muslims from Tobelo and villages to its south fled to the island of Ternate (and Morotai) during early 2000, the region itself received around 45,000 Christian IDPs from other parts of Halmahera.[13] Smaller streams of IDPs from the Tobelo area trickled to Christian villages in central Halmahera or further afield to Sorong, Biak, or Manokwari in the province of Papua. Although around 70 percent of those displaced from Tobelo had returned,[14] social anxieties were in early 2004 still palpable, both among the many recently returned IDPs and among those who had chosen to stay behind. In the aftermath of a conflict that had radically disrupted most people's lives and fostered countless forms of loss, the image of an undead vampire was an eerie reminder of the unresolved fate of many of the victims whose bodies had never been found or identified.

However, not all was bad in 2004. Compared to Maluku, its sister province, where sporadic fighting continued into 2002, North Maluku had recovered relatively quickly from the fighting. In the aftermath of the conflict, the region had received substantial amounts of aid, and a contingent of NGOs, national and international, had arrived to channel that aid to the needy. According to an unofficial estimate by a UN consultant, the international agencies and NGOs poured some twenty million US dollars into the regional economy annually.[15] Political autonomy had also proven a windfall to North Maluku, which now stood to receive the lion's share of profits from the vast natural resources of the region. In large part due to its mineral and timber exports and aided by the financial infusion from the international post-conflict industry, the province had experienced an economic growth in 2003 of more than 3 percent, and despite a drop in the economy of more than 20 percent during the conflict, economic forecasts for the region were bright.[16] The story about the

---

[13] Duncan, "Unwelcome Guests," p. 32.

[14] Bakornas, *Follow-Up Workshop on the Management of IDPs in Indonesia, Sukabumi 19–20 June 2003* (Jakarta: Bakornas PBP in cooperation with UN OCHA Indonesia, 2003), p. 14.

[15] Interview conducted July 2, 2003.

[16] Anonymous, "Pertumbuhan Ekonomi Malut 2003 Naik 3,08 Persen" [North Malukan Economy Grows by 3.08 Percent in 2003], *Mimbar Kieraha*, May 22, 2004, p. 5.

vampire therefore circulated in an atmosphere where economic optimism alternated with political anxiety and where the memory of recent violence divided the population along social, ethnic, and religious lines more sharply than ever before.

The economic upturn also had an impact on consumption and media habits. Throughout the region, small business was booming. Many of the internally displaced people, especially young men, now made a living as *ojek* drivers or as petty traders in sharp competition with a growing number of migrants from poorer parts of eastern Indonesia who flocked to the area to take advantage of the economic boom. A growing segment of the population could afford to ride *ojeks* to the market with their produce rather than transport it by foot or by ox cart. The cash income from which a growing portion of the population now benefited as civil servants, small-scale traders, or wage laborers in timber or mining companies also made the acquisition of TVs and VCD (video compact disk) players, two of the most desired consumer goods, possible for many people.

Diana, who worked in the small VCD rental shop in Tobelo, told me that vampire movies were highly popular. The shelves in her shop featured a number of movies in this genre. Apart from the Hollywood blockbuster movie, *Interview with a Vampire,* starring Tom Cruise, the tiny shop also stocked a number of American B-grade vampire movies. Indonesian vampire movies were the most popular, however. According to Diana, the most popular rental movie featuring vampires was an old Indonesian movie called *The Haunted Lake* (*Telaga Angker*). Evoking reports of the alleged reason for the appearance of the *drakula* in Tobelo, the blurb on the VCD package read: "She returns with lust and vengeance in her heart. You'd better pray that you never hurt her."[17] Feeling her job made her somewhat of an expert in the field of vampire, Diana even claimed to know that the name of the Tobelo *drakula* was Ida Farida. Although Farida is not an uncommon name, it is striking that the name is closely associated with the hugely popular TV series (*sinetron*) called *The Mystery of Mount Merapi* (*Misteri Gunung Merapi*). The leading actress of the TV series that has run continuously since 1998 is Farida Pasha. The story of the series is set in the historical period of the Mataram kingdom, and Farida Pasha plays the evil witch, Mak Lampir, who creates havoc in the empire. In particular, the witch is determined to break up the relationship between the hero, Sembara, and his love, Farida. For the millions of Indonesian viewers, including those in North Maluku, Farida therefore has the dual connotation of being both the real name of the popular actress playing the witch and the name of the fictional heroine in the series. The Tobelo *drakula* appeared to be a real manifestation with a fictional-yet-real name.

The newspaper article about the attacks directly addresses this relationship between media horror and real horror in Tobelo. The article begins by issuing a warning to the would-be sceptic:

> Better beware! A *suanggi* on the loose eats your penis. Terrifying scenes appear on TV as part of horror stories. But in Tobelo a *suanggi* is actually eating its victims. The genitals of the victims mysteriously disappear.[18]

---

[17] The Indonesian text of the blurb is: "Dia datang kembali dengan nafsu dan dendam di hati. Berdoalah semoga Anda tidak pernah menyakitinya."

[18] Asri Fabanyo, "Awas! Suanggi Pemakan 'Burung,'" p. 13.

TV programs, B-movies, and VCDs insert themselves seamlessly into everyday life in North Maluku and come to function as meaningful comments on and confirmation of a social life in which magic and modernity intersect. Commercial Indonesian TV channels that are brought to most North Malukan villages via the now ubiquitous satellite dishes frequently air highly popular "reality" programs about the mystical. One commercial channel broadcasts a late-night "documentary style" program called *Silet* that focuses on the supernatural; in it, a well-known "psychic" investigates "actual" instances of "supernatural" events. These instances often involve vampires and *drakulas*. Vampires and *drakulas* also appear on a regular basis alongside "traditional" Indonesian ghosts, such as the *tuyul* dwarf spirit or the

left: Two *drakula*. The fangs of the *drakula* are curved like the tusks of a wild boar. The text between the two figures reads: "Devils and ghosts are the same thing, okay?"
Drawing by Dorci Guslaw, May 2004.
right: Representation of a "traditional" witch. Witches are said to prey on their victims by hiding in the rafters of houses, waiting for the victim to fall asleep.
Drawing by Carolin Guslaw, May 2004.

female *pontianak* spirit, in Indonesian mystery "soap operas" on prime-time TV. The commercial success of TV shows that market the mystical as an object of capitalist and postmodernist fascination is therefore closely related to their ability to color the stories with recognizable Indonesian themes and characters. At the same time, the televangelism of self-confessed "mystics" is part of a global "turn to enchantment," in which the borders between magic and modernity are increasingly blurred.[19] As the global fascination with the occult feeds into local forms of magic,

---

[19] Jean Comaroff and John Comaroff, "Millennial Capitalism: First Thoughts on a Second Coming," *Public Culture* 12,2 (2000): 318. See also Birgit Meyer and Peter Pels, *Magic and*

the narratives disseminated by modern media have come to fertilize the social imaginary of North Maluku, in some cases cementing and augmenting its reality. During my stay in the region in 2004, the semantic appeal of the televised figure of the *drakula* was such that when I asked a group of school girls to draw pictures of the *suanggi*, they all produced drawings of beautiful women with protruding fangs as often as they drew conventional pictures of flying heads or shaggy figures.

A conventional witch (*suanggi*). Drawing by Fanda Kapita, May 2004.

Global media flows and their portrayals of modern forms of the occult appear to have allowed the reality of local spirit beliefs, which during the New Order were unilaterally stigmatized as backward and pagan, to be reconfirmed. Through global mediascapes, magic and modernity have found new forms of common expression.

Modernity: Interfaces of Revelation and Concealment (Stanford, CA: Stanford University Press, 2003).

PARANOID POLITICS AND THE POLITICAL GENEALOGY OF THE VAMPIRE

So far, I have described how the figure of the *drakula* percolated from media representations into North Malukan social reality in early 2004. In other parts of Indonesia, however, the Dracula has an older and intensely political pedigree. Thus, on Java the *drakula* had moved from the arts into political reality several decades earlier, a transformation that was closely associated with the political history of the New Order. As James Siegel has described, the figure of the *drakula* appeared in Javanese *wayang* theatre plays for the first time in 1969.[20] By the 1980s, the figure of the *drakula*—a Western horror figure that paralleled the ghosts of the Javanese spirit world—had become a popular figure in Javanese dramas. This popularity, which could be attributed to the ghost's foreign character,[21] foreshadowed the entry of the *drakula* into the electronic media. Appearing regularly in plays performed on Thursday night (*malam Jumat*), when the spirits are most active, the *drakula* entertained and frightened theatre audiences by both unsettling and confirming the good manners of Javanese society upon which the social politics of the New Order regime had been built.[22] As a foreign character, it seemed, the *drakula* was able to articulate a political critique that would otherwise not have been possible. The essentially foreign character of the Dracula was also evident in the first reported *drakula* attacks in Indonesia. During 1981, Indonesian newspapers reported several *drakula* attacks on foreign construction workers and airline pilots in both Java and Bali.[23] The cross-breeding between the *drakula* as a drama figure and as a socially real figure was intensified as the *drakula* came to act as an ambivalent figure of horror in Indonesian political discourse. This political genealogy is worth tracing briefly because it was in part responsible for making the *drakula* available to the North Malukan imagination by the early 2000s.

During the early 1990s, the figure of the *drakula* became a popular political metaphor used by critics and political reform groups to portray the Suharto regime. Suharto was frequently described as a vampire who was exploiting the people.[24] After the fall of the New Order, however, the figure of the *drakula* appeared to multiply in political rhetoric. In the political vacuum left by Suharto, it seemed as if every politician had become a vampire. The metaphor of "the political Dracula" could be applied by anyone to his or her political opponent and was frequently invoked to portray corruption and political graft in political circles. Calling someone a *drakula* was used as a generic slur if one wanted to portray that person as being against "the people" (*rakyat*) and against reform.

In its January 2000 edition, the tabloid *Demokrat*, for example, called Amien Rais, the leader of the Muslim reformist party PAN (Partai Amanat Nasional, National Mandate Party), "Indonesia's political vampire" (*Vampir Politik Indonesia*). The allegation of the tabloid was accompanied by a front cover featuring Rais as a Dracula with a blood-smeared mouth. *Demokrat* was a publication controlled by

---

[20] James T. Siegel, *Solo in the New Order: Language and Hierarchy in an Indonesian City* (Princeton, NJ: Princeton University Press, 1986), p. 91.

[21] Ibid., p. 92.

[22] Ibid. See also Saya Shiraishi, "Silakan Masuk. Silakan Duduk: Reflections on a Sitting Room in Java," *Indonesia* 41 (April 1986): 89–130.

[23] Siegel, *Solo in the New Order*, p. 321.

[24] Mary Margaret Steedly, "Virtual Enigma: Why We Can't Understand Indonesia," *Harvard Asia Quarterly* 4,2 (2000).

Taufiq Kiemas, the husband of Megawati Sukarnoputri, the leader of PDI-P (Partai Demokrasi Indonesia–Perjuangan, The Indonesian Democratic Party of Struggle). In the early stages of a battle over who was to become the next president, a battle Megawati was to win in 2001, the tabloid story was broadly perceived to be a direct political attack. The response was therefore vociferous. "We reject the representation of Amien Rais as a political Dracula," said the leader of PAN's legal team. The team accordingly threatened to sue the tabloid unless Taufiq Kiemas publicly apologized on behalf of his publication.[25]

A recurring figure in political rhetoric in post-Suharto Indonesia, the *drakula* assumed a more ominous political form as violent conflict spread across the nation in the early 2000s. In Papua, the killing of outspoken Papuan leader Theys Eluay, in November 2001, by a group of Kopassus officers was preceded by rumors in the capital of Jayapura about a roaming Dracula, who was said to have killed two children. As news of the monster spread to surrounding towns near Jayapura, people began to stay indoors at night.[26] Several observers claimed that the rumor about the Dracula had been deliberately planted in the local newspaper, *Cenderawasih Pos,* by the elite military unit, Kopassus, in order to terrorize people into staying indoors at night and thereby insuring an absence of witnesses to the murder.[27] The critical magazine *Tempo* alleged that this was part of a general political tactic. According to the magazine, the murder of Papuan independence activist Arnold Ap, in 1984, had been preceded by rumors about a roaming spirit, rumors that by all accounts had also caused widespread panic.[28]

Whether or not these allegations concerning the deliberate incitement of public fears are true, it is clear that political terror in Indonesia involves a politics of suspicion that is at once transparent and occult. In post-Suharto Indonesia, paranoia has become a distinct kind of political discourse, one in which politicians, military officers, journalists, and reformers equally engage. In this paranoid politics, the Dracula is simultaneously a political metaphor, a political tool, and a political reality. As a political metaphor, the Dracula is used to critique those in power. As a political tool, the Dracula is seemingly employed with the intention to terrorize citizens and shroud political crimes in obscurity; and as a political reality, the Dracula is able to cause social anxiety and empty town streets. This composite nature of the Dracula appears to both reveal and conceal the power of political intrigue. Because the monster is at once fake and real, the different manifestations of the Dracula demonstrate how mystery, rumor, and the occult are constituent parts of political terror in Indonesia. This political ambivalence, where the occult simultaneously appears to obscure and reveal the machinations of political intrigue, lends a paranoid quality to Indonesian politics.

In Tobelo, as it turned out, no prominent activist was killed in the days and weeks following the spread of the *drakula* rumor, and no evidence that the accounts

---

[25] Indomedia, "DPP PAN Adukan Suami Megawati" [PAN Sues the Husband of Megawati], *Indomedia,* January 29, 2000.

[26] Wens Manggut and Cunding Levi, "Theys's Death and the Vampire," *Tempo,* April 2–8, 2002.

[27] ELSHAM [Lembaga Studi dan Advokasi Hak Asasi Manusia], "Preliminary Report: The Abduction and Assassination of Theys Hiyo Eluay was Premeditated and Politically Motivated" (Jayapura: ELSHAM, 2001).

[28] Wens Manggut and Cunding Levi, "Theys's Death and the Vampire."

of the *drakula* had been deliberately circulated became evident. In fact, I never heard anyone even entertain the notion that the *drakula* was merely a shadow cast by an intentionally planted rumor (*isu*). Too many people had seen the *drakula* for her to have been a tactical figment of the army's imagination. The *drakula* was a reality in Tobelo that even ministers, bank employees, and military officials could not deny. And it was a reality both before and after a partial account of its activities was featured in a local newspaper. The paranoid politics embodied by this *drakula* (and its very real effects in Tobelo) do therefore not seem to be reducible to an act of deliberate instigation. It was a politics generated not by instigation and simple motives, but by memory, sociality, and morality that allowed the Tobelo *drakula* to emerge. The *drakula*s in North Maluku and in Papua clearly emerged in two different political circumstances. Since there was no organized secessionist movement and no general consensus on who or what had caused the 1999 conflict, it was much harder to point to clear political heroes and villains in North Maluku than in Papua. The decentralization process was, by all accounts, proceeding well, and it was generating optimism and anxiety at the same time.[29] Without a clear counter-hegemonic political discourse of the kind that has developed in Papua and with a future that appeared both bright and troubled, it was harder to harness the Tobelo *drakula* to any particular political cart. In the aftermath of an unresolved and violent political past, but with some grounds for optimism about the future, the Tobelo *drakula* seemed, in other words, to have a political will of its own.

Despite their different political heritages, however, the two *drakula*s were probably related. For whatever the truth about the rumors in Jayapura in November 2001, they were part of the political genealogy of the Tobelo *drakula*, because many of the roughly four thousand IDPs from Halmahera who had sought refuge in Papua during the violence in North Maluku would have heard about these rumors and could easily have brought them back to Tobelo when they were repatriated during 2002 and 2003. Perhaps they had learned that stories of Draculas were sometimes deliberately instigated by shadowy military figures, but this in no way detracted from the reality of the *drakula*; it only gave it a multi-dimensionality that contributed to its terror. As the Dracula slipped back and forth between the popular and the political imagination, each manifestation confirmed the reality of the other.

So far, I have shown how the discursive landscape in which the Tobelo *drakula* appeared in early 2004 was constituted by horror movies on VCDs and television, by rumors associated with the occult politics of state assassinations, and by the proliferation in post-Suharto Indonesia of political metaphors about "vampires." Using the vocabulary of Appadurai, one might say that the global "scapes" of modernity had provided new reality to local spirits by allowing them to be given new, legitimate names.[30] Global mediascapes disseminated the Dracula in order to cater to the modern fascination with the magical, while the national ideoscape was infused by an occult political logic in which the Dracula was both an actor and a sign. The confluence of these flows provided people in North Maluku with a new concept with which to reflect upon recent violence in locally meaningful ways. The last—and important—strand in the genealogy of the Tobelo *drakula* derived from the notion that this particular *drakula* was traumatized.

---

[29] See also Nils Bubandt, "Sorcery, Corruption, and the Dangers of Democracy in Indonesia."

[30] Appadurai, *Modernity at Large*.

GLOBAL DISCOURSE AND THE VERNACULARIZATION OF TRAUMA

Although "trauma" as a clinical concept can be traced back to the late-nineteenth century,[31] trauma is a new concept to most Malukans. It was introduced by media accounts of "traumatized communities" and by the "psychosocial" counseling programs of NGOs that attempted to remedy the negative effects of the 1999–2001 conflict in the region.

Following the economic crisis in 1997 and the political collapse of New Order rule in May 1998, Indonesia witnessed the outbreak or intensification of seven prolonged internal conflicts. While each of the conflicts in Papua, East Timor, Maluku, North Maluku, Central Sulawesi, Kalimantan, and Aceh had its own complex local history, they were also viewed by both national and international commentators as part of a tragic political legacy of thirty-two years of New Order rule.[32] In keeping with a new agenda of global governance in which conflict resolution and development had become increasingly intertwined, and in which conflict intervention had come to be seen as an effective tool for political engineering and democracy building,[33] the UN and its various agencies headed a large contingent of NGOs that rushed to provide humanitarian aid, ensure effective peace-building, and rebuild society in the areas affected by conflict.[34]

Trauma figured centrally in this international reconciliation work in Indonesia. The interest in the emotional state of the population of war-affected areas was a central tenet of a new international therapeutic paradigm that had come to govern global responses to internal conflict since the mid-1990s.[35] This was also the case for reconciliation work in North Maluku. Already in one of the first reports on the conflicts in Maluku and North Maluku, jointly authored by the government of Indonesia and a range of UN agencies, concern was expressed that "no local expertise to provide trauma counseling" existed in the two provinces. The report urged that the main hospital in North Maluku should be "strengthened to handle additional local trauma cases."[36] By 2001, the main focus of the UNICEF emergency assistance to Indonesia was on Maluku and North Maluku. As part of this focus, the agency supported the training of sixty counselors in specialist trauma counseling

[31] Young, *The Harmony of Illusions*.

[32] Benedict Anderson, ed., *Violence and the State in Suharto's Indonesia* (Ithaca, NY: Cornell Southeast Asia Program Publications, 2001); Geoffrey Robinson, "People's War: Militias in East Timor and Indonesia," *South East Asia Research* 9,3 (2001): 217–318; Robert Hefner, "Global Violence and Indonesian Muslim Politics," *American Anthropologist* 104,3 (2002): 754–765; and Jacques Bertrand, *Nationalism and Ethnic Conflict in Indonesia* (Cambridge: Cambridge University Press, 2003).

[33] Outi Korhonen, "International Governance in Post-Conflict Situations," *Leiden Journal of International Law* 14,3 (2001): 353–72; Roland Paris, "International Peacebuilding and the 'Mission Civilisatrice,'" *Review of International Studies* 28,4 (2002): 637–56; and Roland Paris, *At War's End: Building Peace After Civil Conflict* (Cambridge: University of Cambridge Press, 2004).

[34] Among the UN agencies present in North Maluku were the UNDP (United Nations Development Programme), UNICEF (United Nations International Children's Emergency Fund), OCHA (Office for the Coordination of Humanitarian Affairs), and WFP (World Food Programme).

[35] Vanessa Pupavac, "War on the Couch: The Emotionology of the New International Security Paradigm," *European Journal of Social Theory* 7,2 (2004): 149–70.

[36] GOI, *The Maluku Crisis: Report of the Joint Assessment Mission by the Government of the Republic of Indonesia and International Agencies* (Jakarta: Government of Indonesia [GOI], 2000), p. 18.

methods, and it was estimated that they could provide treatment for eleven thousand children and "female caregivers" per year. In response to increasing requests from health services and affected communities for trauma support programs and to local assessments that indicated "widespread and serious trauma," the agency in 2002 set aside 990,000 US dollars from its Indonesian budget of around six million dollars for "psychosocial" support in eastern Indonesia. The psychosocial support efforts, which also received financial support from Japan, Australia, and Holland, involved the training of several hundred school teachers in trauma counseling and trauma therapy. In addition, 29,000 children in Maluku, North Maluku, and West Timor participated in "recreational and expressional activities" in order to help them overcome their trauma experiences of the conflict.[37]

Of particular concern in this work were the around 1.4 million people who had become internally displaced by the conflicts in Indonesia. The official record notes that the conflict in North Maluku alone had created 220,000 IDPs, some 25 percent of the population.[38] All organizations agreed that trauma was widespread among the IDPs, and since the majority of the internally displaced were children and women, these two groups were seen as being in special need of trauma treatment. While some estimates indicated that 60 percent of IDPs were affected by some kind of trauma,[39] media reports often suggested that all IDPs were traumatized. At the same time, as trauma appeared to be endemic in the region, it also became distinctly gendered, being associated in particular with women. Most programs were targeted at women, who were perceived as especially important because they were both victims of trauma themselves and caregivers to traumatized children. The surveys that sought to diagnose trauma also centered on women as particularly vulnerable. Thus, a livelihood survey among IDPs in Indonesia funded by the World Food Programme (WFP), which attempted to fix the level of "emotional trauma" on the district level, chose to ask only female respondents whether they had observed "indications of emotional trauma," such as "sadness," "boredom," "nightmares," "drinking," or "worry" in themselves, their husbands, or their children.[40] Trauma in North Maluku was, in other words, linked to refugees and to female IDPs in particular. In this context, it is perhaps no accident that the *drakula* in Tobelo was a woman, traumatized, and either an IDP or the victim of gendered violence.

According to the global therapeutic paradigm, trauma treatment is essential for a return to normalcy in communities affected by violent conflict. This is so because trauma relief and reconciliation are regarded as mutually linked. Since trauma grows out of and is seen to perpetuate conflict, true peace can only be achieved, according to this paradigm, through the psychological treatment of trauma.[41] As one UNICEF report on North Maluku has it: "Many IDPs and conflict-affected communities would be able to reintegrate into society and sustain productive livelihood if support

---

[37] UNICEF, *A Humanitarian Appeal for Children and Women: January–December 2002. Indonesia* (Jakarta: UNICEF, 2002).

[38] Duncan, "Unwelcome Guests," p. 31.

[39] Nugroho Abikusno, "Reproductive Health Services for Internally Displaced Families in Indonesia," *The Journal of the Indonesian Medical Association* 3,1 (2002): 274.

[40] WFP, *Internally Displaced Persons (IDPs) in Indonesia: Livelihood Survey: Synthesis Report, Findings and Strategy Options* (Jakarta: World Food Programme, 2002), p. 56.

[41] Pupavac, "War on the Couch."

were provided to address their trauma and stress."[42] The same report, which was part of UNICEF's humanitarian appeal for women and children affected by violence in Indonesia, tells the following story of Anya:

> Anya (not her real name) is twelve years old. She lives in an orphanage in Tobelo on the island of Halmahera in North Maluku Province, Indonesia. In October 1999 her parents were killed in front of her in a horrifying wave of inter-ethnic violence that swept through her village on the outskirts of Tobelo. Although several orphanages were built to cater to the thousands of children left without one or both parents, staff at the orphanages are only able to provide for their basic needs, not their emotional or psychological pain. Anya herself is deeply disturbed by the incident and was diagnosed as suffering from severe Post Traumatic Stress Disorder (PTSD).
>
> Anya's case was brought to the attention of the UNICEF consultant, an expert practitioner in a range of therapies including Eye Movement Desensitization and Reprocessing (EMDR) and play therapy. A limited programme of treatment for Anya was immediately designed. After just a few treatment sessions, there was a marked improvement in Anya's ability to cope with her loss. Through allowing Anya to express her fears and pain through colour and play, a small spark of hope and recovery returns to her shattered life.[43]

This account of Anya's case illustrates how useful are narratives of personalized suffering to conflict alleviation programs. Using what is portrayed as "sophisticated psychological therapies" to treat trauma, the international agencies claim that they not only alleviate the effects of previous conflict but also prevent future conflict. Trauma discourse is thus related to a novel social theory about conflict in which the cause for the "new wars" that characterize the post-cold war era is psychologized.[44] The basic idea is that violence generates trauma, which in turn generates renewed violence. This idea was turned into development policy when the WHO (World Health Organization) in 1998 established a framework called "Health as a Bridge to Peace" and used it as a main approach in North Maluku.[45] The treatment of Anya's PTSD was thus, in the words of the UNICEF report, a way of "'piggybacking' conflict reduction and prevention strategies into assistance activities."[46] In this way, the science of trauma became a new and legitimate tool to carry out social engineering. Feldman describes how this political use of trauma entails a "trauma-aesthetic" characterized by a universal and homeostatic perception of self and society.[47] Trauma is believed to destabilize a static sense of self, just like violence destabilizes a presumably peaceful society. Trauma and conflict, in other words,

---

[42] UNICEF, *A Humanitarian Appeal for Children and Women*, p. 2.

[43] Ibid., p. 14.

[44] See Pupavac, "War on the Couch," p. 158; and Mary Kaldor, *Global Civil Society: Answer to War* (Cambridge: Polity Press, 2003).

[45] For an account of the Health as a Bridge to Peace (HBP) concept, see the WHO website at www.who.int/hac/techguidance/hbp/about/en/

[46] UNICEF, *A Humanitarian Appeal for Children and Women*, p. 5.

[47] Allen Feldman, "Memory Theaters, Virtual Witnessing, and the Trauma-Aesthetic," *Biography* 27,1 (2004): 185.

become signs of abnormality that psychosocial and social recovery programs seek to remedy in order to ensure the return to the "normal" state of individual mental health and communal peace.

All the major international NGOs working in the area were quick to address the perceived need for treatment of trauma and stress. The Dutch-Scandinavian organization CARDI (Consortium for Assistance and Recovery towards Development in Indonesia) and the French medical organization MSF (Médecins sans Frontières) carried out emergency psychosocial work in both Maluku and North Maluku, as did Christian organizations like World Vision International, Action by Churches Together, and International Catholic Migration Commission. The psychosocial approach of the international agencies also heavily influenced the Indonesian relief efforts in Maluku, such as the trauma therapy and assessment programs conducted by staff from the Faculty of Psychology at the University of Indonesia. Thus, the logic of "the psychosocial"—which promised to mend society by treating the psychological trauma of individuals—did not arrive in North Maluku as a purely global idea. Rather, the psychosocial technologies of trauma assessment and trauma therapy were, to a large extent, "Indonesianized" by the Indonesian NGO staff, trauma counselors, and psychologists who peddled the new idea of trauma with the same zeal that Indonesian authorities had promoted the ideas of "development" and "progress" in the past.[48]

With the combined efforts of international agencies, NGOs, and the Indonesian authorities, people in Tobelo had plenty of opportunity to learn about trauma. They heard about trauma in schools; they could read about trauma in the local media and listen to talk about trauma on the local radio stations. Alternatively, they could visit one of the four "Happy Houses" set up by World Vision International in Tobelo to treat orphaned and traumatized children. If they belonged to the roughly one quarter of the population that had been displaced by the conflict in the region, they had likely been enrolled in a therapy or peace-building program in which trauma was a central concern. Through NGO work and media attention, *trauma* had become a household concept in Tobelo by 2003.

The 1999–2001 conflict was certainly violent and had a hugely disruptive effect on social life in North Maluku. It was, however, far from being the first conflict in the region. Known in Europe as the Spice Islands, the region had attracted mercantile competition and colonial attention since the Renaissance because of its clove and nutmeg. Colonial interest had meant that North Maluku had been embroiled in recurrent violent conflict over the past centuries. As a result of this history, ethnic identity in the region always involved the active cultivation of collective memory of these conflicts, which often turned into self-aggrandizing myths of heroism in the service of one of the dominant sultanates, Ternate and Tidore.[49] Just as ethnohistoriography very much focused on conflict, so personal memory was often calibrated by reference to some wider conflict in which the community had been involved, whether it be the Second World War, the 1958–1959 Pemesta rebellion, or the Indonesian political campaign to absorb Papua in the early 1960s.

---

[48] See Ariel Heryanto, "The Development of 'Development,'" *Indonesia* 46 (October 1988): 1–21.

[49] Nils Bubandt, "The Odour of Things: Smell and the Cultural Elaboration of Disgust in Eastern Indonesia," *Ethnos* 63,1 (1998): 48–80; Nils Bubandt, "Genesis in Buli: Christianity, Blood, and Vernacular Modernity on an Indonesian Island," *Ethnology* 43,3 (2004): 249–70. See also Jos Platenkamp, *Tobelo: Ideas and Values of a North Moluccan Society*.

North Malukan memory was, in short, already full of conflicts. The conflict that began in 1999 was, however, the first regional conflict associated with trauma. It was also the first conflict in which the actions of a spirit were said to be motivated by "trauma." That the traumatized spirit was female and, according to the most widely believed version of the story about the *drakula*, internally displaced was, in this context, not coincidental. The traumatized *drakula* provided for people in North Maluku a new way of talking about why cannibal spirits haunted their lives. It did so, I will argue, because the global enchantment of trauma could easily be fused with local ideas about spirits and the self in North Maluku.

THE ENCHANTMENT OF TRAUMA

Derek Summerfield argues that the success of PTSD as a diagnostic label—post-traumatic stress being the one psychiatric diagnosis "that anyone like[s] to have," according to an editorial in the *American Journal of Psychiatry*—is the result of a contemporary shift in the perception of the person.[50] Related to an ideology of individualism that has risen to dominance at the same time that confidence in both religion and authorities has declined, the success of PTSD grows out of a cultural understanding of the self in which notions of individual rights and personal injury are seen as increasingly naturalized and legally protected "psychological properties." PTSD, so Summerfield claims, "is the diagnosis for an age of disenchantment."[51]

Patrick Bracken has followed this line of analysis to argue that PTSD—a syndrome that gained scientific recognition in the early 1980s in the wake of the political struggle to socially rehabilitate Vietnam war veterans, and which is said to arise out of a breakdown of meaning in the victim's life as a result of extreme distress—has become an apt kind of syndrome for a postmodern age preoccupied with the dangers of the loss of meaning and increasing uncertainty. Citing Anthony Giddens, Bracken argues that under the social conditions of late modernity, the self has become the main, but fragile, source of meaning. In a seemingly secular age, the psychologized self has assumed the position of vulnerability once occupied by the Christian soul. Because the self is fragile, a person must constantly labor to achieve self-realization, and this modern project of establishing one's own identity goes hand in hand, so Bracken argues, with a scientific interest in the realm of internal subjectivity.[52] The late-modern preoccupation with the undermining of meaning makes PTSD an apt illness of late modernity. PTSD, the master trope of the trauma discourse, is, Bracken asserts, a cultural syndrome of the late-modern West.[53]

Bracken's critique of the trauma discourse is in many ways highly perceptive and pinpoints the inherent ethnocentrism of its institutionalized globalization. As Joshua Breslau points out, the global expansion of the trauma discourse as part of international conflict resolutions policies "has been possible because of the fit

---

[50] Derek Summerfield, "The Invention of Post-Traumatic Stress Disorder and the Social Usefulness of a Psychiatric Category," *British Medical Journal* 322 (2001): 96.

[51] Ibid.

[52] Patrick Bracken, "Post-Modernity and Post-Traumatic Stress Disorder," *Social Science and Medicine* 53 (2001): 740.

[53] Ibid., p. 741.

between this diagnosis and the agendas existing within global institutions."[54] Trauma provides, in Arthur Kleinman and Robert Desjarlais's words, an occasion to re-inscribe political violence and displacement within a psychological narrative. As a treatable diagnosis, trauma lends itself to be used as a handle for political intervention in post-conflict situations by translating violence into biographical form.[55] The account of Anya's PTSD illustrates this move from the social to the personal. As a consequence of this slippage, the global proliferation of the discourse of trauma has been criticized for being neo-liberal and for being Eurocentric.[56] Bracken suggests that the discourse on trauma, with its focus on the "intrapsychic," is a child of "the European Enlightenment and its concern with reason and interiority."[57] While the trauma paradigm might provide appropriate technical solutions for distress in a Western context, Bracken argues, "when exported to Third World or non-Western societies, [the idea of trauma and the proposed psychological solutions to it] become confusing and problematic."[58]

It is here, I think, that Bracken's otherwise perceptive analysis becomes derailed. While the critique of the politics of modern subjectivity provided by Bracken and others explains the scientific rise and popular acceptance of the trauma discourse in a Euro-American context and the political motivation behind its global expansion, the theory of modernity implicit in these analyses is too narrow to explain the local success of the global trauma discourse in North Maluku and elsewhere. At least, it is not enough to explain why spirits have begun to be traumatized in North Maluku after 2002. The reception and adoption of *trauma* as a concept in North Maluku, I argue, has not been "confusing and problematic," as Bracken suggests. Instead, the introduction of *trauma* to North Maluku has given rise to new forms of meaning that make perfect sense to people, even if they are patched together from global flows of media narratives and development practices. Trauma may have grown discursively from the European Enlightenment and been given political significance in a social context where people believe themselves to be disenchanted, but its globalization is not imprisoned by this heritage. Rather, the plasticity or "labiality" of trauma as a concept makes its globalization a heterogeneous and unpredictable process of appropriation.[59]

My second problem with the critique of trauma by Bracken and others relates to its allegedly disenchanted quality. The globalization of trauma is thus not the story of how a "disenchanted" and "(post)modern" concept was exported to traditional "non-Western societies" to damage and confuse their cultural horizons, as Bracken

---

[54] Joshua Breslau, "Cultures of Trauma: Anthropological Views of Post-Traumatic Stress Disorder in International Health," *Culture, Medicine and Psychiatry* 28 (2004): 114.

[55] Arthur Kleinman and Robert Desjarlais, "Violence, Culture, and the Politics of Trauma," in *Writing at the Margins: Discourse between Anthropology and Medicine*, ed. A. Kleinman (Berkeley, CA: University of California Press, 1995), pp. 173–89.

[56] See Vanessa Pupavac, "Pathologizing Populations and Colonizing Minds: International Psychosocial Programs in Kosovo," *Alternatives* 27 (2002): 489–511; and Derek Summerfield, "A Critique of Seven Assumptions behind Psychological Trauma Programmes in War-Affected Areas," *Social Science and Medicine* 48 (1999): 1449–62.

[57] Patrick Bracken, *Trauma: Culture, Meaning, and Philosophy* (London: Whurr Publishers, 2002), p. 42.

[58] Ibid., p. 220.

[59] On the "labiality" of trauma, see Feldman, "Memory Theaters, Virtual Witnessing, and the Trauma-Aesthetic," p. 185.

seems to imply. Without wanting to downplay the institutional and discursive relations of power that drive the globalization of the trauma discourse, I suggest that reducing the local appropriation of trauma to a matter marked by confusion, invasion, and damage perpetuates what Marshall Sahlins has called the "tristes tropes of Western hegemony and local anarchy" and sets up an unbridgeable gap between a modern West and a fragile, non-modern rest.[60] Positing this great divide assumes not only that the non-West is essentially non-modern, but also runs the danger of affirming conventional social theory by equating modernity with disenchantment. Bracken's "postpsychiatry," with its emphasis on ethics and contextualized understanding, is, in many ways, an important corrective to a universalist and cognitivist idea of trauma.[61] Bracken's contextualization of trauma retreats, however, into cultural relativism because it is based on a categorical distinction between the modern and the traditional (inspired in equal measure by Giddens and Heideggerian phenomenology)—a distinction that runs counter to a process-oriented and relational understanding of both globalization and modernity.

Trauma, I argue, is, in its "Western" context, not a symptom of disenchantment but of reenchantment, because it is associated with a morality and a set of practices and technologies that establish "the self" as a new center, that project new utopian ideas about the subject and about society, and that promise new magico-technological ways of achieving these utopian goals. The association of trauma with the "occult" world of vampires, divination, and vengeful spirits in North Maluku is therefore not surprising. As Michael Kenny has pointed out, there are clear parallels between the social morality inherent in witchcraft and the morality of theories of traumatic memory that seek to represent an existing pathology as being caused by hidden (i.e., repressed or forgotten) acts of evil that took place in the past.[62]

The global spread of trauma as a concept, in other words, carries with it multiple forms of enchantment as well as reason. The global trauma discourse cannot therefore be reduced to a Western "export" that the "non-West" buys lock, stock, and barrel, reaping only confusion and problems as a result. Rather, the global concept of trauma is co-produced regionally when local forms of enchantment are given new strength by engaging and retextualizing the enchantment inherent in the global trauma discourse. This retextualization allows trauma to become a new kind of magic for old problems.[63] The fact that a cannibal witch spirit in Tobelo was believed to have been produced by the experiences of a traumatized, female IDP is only one instance of this phenomenon. Just as the line between magic and modernity is blurred in global media representations of the Dracula, the magic of modernity finds new expression in the North Malukan reception of trauma. To flesh out this argument, I will need to return one last time to the Dracula in Tobelo.

---

[60] Marshall Sahlins, "Goodbye to Tristes Tropes: Ethnography in the Context of Modern World History," in *Assessing Cultural Anthropology*, ed. R. Borofsky (New York, NY: McGraw-Hill, 1994), p. 381.

[61] Patrick Bracken, *Trauma: Culture, Meaning, and Philosophy*, p. 223.

[62] Michael Kenny, "Trauma, Time, Illness, and Culture," in *Tense Past*, pp. 151–71. See also Jean La Fontaine, *Speak of the Devil: Tales of Satanic Abuse in Contemporary England* (Cambridge: Cambridge University Press, 1998).

[63] Jean Comaroff and John Comaroff, "Occult Economies and the Violence of Abstraction: Notes from the South African Postcolony," *American Ethnologist* 26,2 (1999): 279–303.

TERROR: SPIRITUAL, COLONIAL, AND MODERN

Johannes is a well-respected man in Tobelo. He is not rich, but he earns a decent living as a coconut farmer and has managed to send three of his children to the Christian seminary to become ministers. Johannes is not a man who believes in witchcraft. He is a man of God who has left pagan superstitions behind. And yet he has seen the *drakula* on several occasions and claims he is one of the lucky few to have seen the *drakula* without being attacked. Johannes's ambivalent relationship to the local spirit world reflects a general ambivalence in North Malukan Christianity. Since the first Dutch missionaries arrived to North Maluku in the 1860s, most traditional beliefs relating to spirits have been either frowned upon or actively opposed. This has changed somewhat in recent years. In the new political climate of post-Suharto Indonesia, localism has thus received a new political status, and with it, traditional beliefs have come to be valued again. Although this political shift has played a role, I think that for a convinced modernist Christian like Johannes, this new political climate would not be enough, in itself, to vindicate traditional beliefs. More relevant for him was the fact that this particular ghost appeared—outwardly at least—to be anything but traditional. As he described his encounters with the *drakula*, it became clear that it was its modern trappings, its vampire appearance, and its trauma that made its reality convincing.

Johannes lives on the outskirts of Tobelo, in the center of what used to be a Dutch colonial coconut plantation, the *Morotai Klapper Cultuur Maatschappij*. The area is still today called by the acronym of the plantation: MKCM. It was in this former colonial plantation, now run by the Protestant Church, that the *drakula* first appeared in Tobelo. Fearing the area because of this manifestation, *ojek* drivers would refuse to ride alone through the plantation, gathering instead in small groups outside the well-lit gates of the barracks of the adjacent district military command center.

Being a man of modern convictions, Johannes had tried to provide his own form of illumination to the darkness that seemed to attract the vampire to the plantation. He had hung an electric bulb from a pole on the side of the road, and it was here that he first saw the *drakula*. Her wailing had woken him and his neighbors one night in February 2004. It was an eerily loud howling, Johannes remembered, as if "she was crying into a megaphone." The analogy is interesting since the megaphone is a simple but effective tool of political propaganda, frequently employed by government officials, and in the lead-up to the approaching national election in early 2004, megaphones had become even more prominent in Tobelo. The *drakula*, it seemed, had a political statement to make.

The plantation and the military command center lie in a zone just north of Tobelo that was the scene of the horrific massacres that killed more than eight hundred people in late 1999. During the massacres and the ensuing clashes between 1999 and 2001, the command center of the Infantry Battalion 732 (Yonif 732) had played a key role. Troops from the battalion had manned the strategic and intensely mistrusted check-point called "Stone Door" (*Pintu Batu*) a few kilometers to the north, which separated the Muslim "white" forces around Galela from the Christian "red" forces who controlled Tobelo.[64] All-powerful during the New Order, the

---

[64] Already in the first phases of the conflict in central Maluku, opposing groups would identify themselves through the use of colored headbands. In a process of religious self-identification, Christian combatants adopted red headdresses, while their Muslim opponents donned white headbands. As a consequence, supporters of the Christian groups were referred to as the "red side" (*pihak merah*), while Muslims were referred to as "the white side" (*pihak putih*). This mode

military had become thoroughly discredited after the fall of Suharto, and during the North Maluku conflict the military was suspected—with good reason—of bias by both sides. There were thus numerous instances in which the military played an active role in the fighting, usually with the territorially stationed troops on the side of the Muslims and the tactical mobile police units (*Brimob*), who were called in for support, on the side of the Christians. Since the *drakula* was found plying her deadly trade in a dark, colonial plantation not far from a military checkpoint that had been at the center of violent conflict, both her choice of venue and the public consensus that she was avenging past wrong-doing appeared to speak to an array of memories in which colonialism, suspicions of state-military treachery, and a recent violent past all played a part.

Johannes remembered that the *drakula* was dressed in white as she walked backward—as cannibal witches (*suanggi*) are wont to do—along the road toward Tobelo. Johannes had grabbed a stone and thrown it at the figure, but was then himself seized by panic and had retreated to his house. The wailing had continued for three nights, before the *drakula* disappeared as suddenly as she had arrived. The white dress of this *drakula* was seemingly establishing a new fashion among witches. A few months later another witch appeared in the region dressed in a similar garment. In May 2004, a photograph circulated through the town of Ternate. It portrayed a young man with a gym bag over his shoulder; behind him, a weird greenish figure hovered. It was clearly a woman, her long black hair draping onto a white gown. In the picture, she has large green eyes with no pupils; every shuddering person who saw the picture in Ternate recognized her as a *suanggi*. This picture, which was circulated via mobile phone among the Ternatan middle class, was accompanied by a story. According to this story, the young man was visiting one of the springs in Ternate, half a day ride by car from the town of Tobelo, for a picnic when the photo was snapped. He had returned home from the picnic in good health, but when the photograph was developed and the young man saw the figure behind him, he immediately fell ill and soon died. In the aftermath, so the story continued, the photographer had also fallen ill and his fate remained uncertain. Amid some speculation that the photograph might be a fake and remarks that the figure resembled a vampire that figured in a weekly horror show on TV, people also agreed that no *suanggi* had ever been photographed before and that this kind of aberration had to be a result of the violent excesses perpetrated during the conflict.

REVENGE, TRAUMA, AND MORALITY

Spirits can be traumatized in North Maluku because they, like humans, are historical beings. The Tobelo *drakula* was as a historical being intimately bound up with the recent conflict. In one version of her story, she was a traumatized IDP who was driven to magical excess; in another, she was the raped and killed daughter of a village leader out for revenge (*balas dendam*). In both cases, the *drakula* was avenging particular historical offences perpetrated during the conflict. Both versions relate to the widespread sense that post-conflict society remained mired in the transgressions of its violent past. In this sense, the actions of the *drakula* resembled many other forms of spiritual revenge (*nyawa menuntut*) that haunted North Malukan life in the

---

of identification and self-identification was followed when fighting broke out in North Maluku in late 1999.

years after the conflict. In 2003, a woman was rumored to have turned up at a local health clinic (*puskesmas*) in the town of Ternate with a horribly disfigured face. The facial distortions seemed to be growing worse as time passed, until she came to have the face of a pig. Her disfigurement, it was said, was spiritual punishment for having insulted someone killed during the violence. Another story reported that the face of a man had, in a similar way, been transformed into that of a monkey. Another account related the story of a man called Mahmood, who had been rushed to the hospital after he had cut his own throat and tried to pull out his windpipe. He had been sewn up, but died after he cut open his throat again. "These were not the acts of a crazy person," Om Mahdi, who related the story to me, emphasized. "There have been many incidents like that one after the conflict." For instance, there was the woman who, for no apparent reason, threw herself onto her stove and let herself burn to death, a seemingly impossible feat on a slow-burning petroleum stove. Disfigurement, suicidal rages, witch attacks, and roaming *drakula*s are all part of the same pattern: a pattern of revenge wreaked by spirits who had been wrongfully killed.

These attacks are often mimetic. The man who cut someone's throat is driven by the spirits to cut his own repeatedly; the woman who participated in the burning of other people throws herself onto a burning stove; and people who shame others by calling them monkeys or pigs turn into these abominable animals themselves. Although nobody I talked to ever mentioned the possible mimesis entailed by the cannibalism and blood-drinking of the *drakula*, rumors of cannibalism circulated widely in North Maluku after the violent conflict. I heard several stories about how blood or parts of the liver of a slain enemy had been consumed by members of the "red," or Christian, side in Tobelo and Kao, emulating pre-Christian practices that sought to incorporate the "image" or "shadow" of the slain enemy through the consumption of these substances.[65] Similarly there were rumors that some members of the "white," or Muslim, side carried large quantities of lemon with them, suggesting that they intended to chop up their victims and eat them raw with the lemon juice in the same manner that people sometimes eat fish raw (*makan mentah*).[66] In the North Malukan imaginary, allegations of such blood rituals played an important part in the post-conflict narratives. In light of such allegations, the *drakula*'s drinking of blood and consumption of the genitals assume a strikingly mimetic significance.

The relationship between conflict and memory that the *drakula* establishes is therefore not unique. In North Maluku, spirits are always "central vehicles for memory."[67] The ancestors (*nenek moyang*) play an important role in all North Malukan communities, whether they are Muslim or Christian, as do various kinds of spirits (*jin, moro, meki, pontianak, setan*). In traditional Tobelo society, the ancestors (*o gomanga*) had to be ritually produced after death through a spiritual cleansing of the three aspects that make up human beings. The ritual transformation of the three aspects or components—the body (*o roëhe*), the shadow (*o gurumini*), and the "spirit" (*o nyawa* or *o gikiri*)—had to be wrested from the possession of witch beings (*o toka*) to

---

[65] See Platenkamp, *Tobelo: Ideas and Values of a North Moluccan Society*, p. 144.

[66] For the significance of blood, see also Nils Bubandt, "Genesis in Buli: Christianity, Blood, and Vernacular Modernity on an Indonesian Island," *Ethnology* 43,3 (2004): 249–70.

[67] Michael Lambek, "The Past Imperfect: Remembering as Moral Practice," in *Tense Past*, p. 241.

transform the *nyawa* spirit into a clean ancestral spirit and prevent it from becoming a smelly (*ma dorou*) spirit, a witch.[68] A similar pattern of ideas about smell, spirits, and ancestors exists throughout North Maluku,[69] but of special interest here is the idea of *nyawa*. In Tobelo, *nyawa* as a lexeme is associated with life utterances, like the ability to move and breathe. *Nyawa* denotes "life," the very fact of being alive.[70] It is this quality or aspect of the deceased that takes revenge (*menuntut*) upon those responsible for the death of a person. The idea of spiritual revenge (*nyawa menuntut*) is variously expressed in ritual throughout North Maluku. In Tobelo, this revenge also crosses generations. Thus, the descendants of an ancestor who has killed others may themselves be punished by the spirits of these slain people. The living inherit, as Platenkamp suggests, the "moral responsibility" for their ancestor's deeds.[71] The ancestors, in turn, may seize the bodies of their descendants and act through them.

Although this is a worldview that has come under increasing attack from reformist Islam and the Protestant Church, the living and the spirits maintain a close and interlinked relationship in North Maluku. This relationship has to be honored by the living lest they be punished through illness or misfortune. Large-scale violence, such as the recent conflict, is therefore bound to have social consequences if revenge can be enacted beyond the limits of death. In this sense, it is no coincidence that the *drakula* in Tobelo was so intimately tied to specific acts of violence that had supposedly occurred during the conflict.

Apart from the conjecture that the *drakula* could have been a raped girl or a woman who ingested excessive amounts of magic, a third account circulated. It claimed that the *drakula* was the spirit of a beautiful and mysterious Christian woman who had appeared during the conflict in the predominantly Muslim town of Ternate. She had jumped off one of the passenger ferries at the dock and onto a telephone pole, where she had taunted local inhabitants, daring them to kill her. I was told by people who claimed they had either witnessed or participated in the event that neither spears nor homemade guns had any effect on her. Eventually she had been brought to the ground by the religious prayer (*dikir*) of a devout Muslim who had performed the pilgrimage to Mecca (*haji*), and she had been set upon with machetes and spears. Even after her throat had been cut, however, she still taunted her attackers: "Cut me all you want, I cannot die, and soon I will return to avenge myself." Even though the body had been chopped into small pieces and stuffed into the septic tank of an outdoor toilet, the account implied that she had returned as a *drakula* to avenge herself.

The *drakula* figure was a terrifying presence in early 2004 that allowed for the retelling of a number of narratives that hinted at the horrors of the recent North Malukan past. All narratives speak to a kind of sociality where human subjectivity is closely associated with the subjectivity of spirits. The life of a person does not end when that person is killed; instead, it turns into a new kind of agent. The morality of this agent is highly ambivalent. The *drakula* is, on the one hand, motivated by a strong sense of justice. Yet she is also a highly reprehensible and immoral being. For

---

[68] Platenkamp, *Tobelo: Ideas and Values of a North Moluccan Society*, p. 170.

[69] Leontine Visser, *My Rice Field Is My Child: Social and Territorial Aspects of Swidden Cultivation in Sahu, Eastern Indonesia* (Dordrecht: Foris Publications, 1989); and Bubandt, *Warriors of the Hornbill, Victims of the Mantis*.

[70] Platenkamp, *Tobelo: Ideas and Values of a North Moluccan Society*, p. 13.

[71] Ibid., p. 106.

this reason, the *drakula* could be either adopted as an in-group hero or rejected as an out-group villain. On the mainly Muslim island of Ternate, the *drakula* was the spirit of a Christian woman, a taunting witch-like presence, even when she was alive. For Udin, a Muslim man in Tobelo, the *drakula* was Muslim—he referred to her as the "veiled dracula" (*drakula berjilbab*)—the just avenger of her husband's death and her own struggle as a refugee. For Yansen, a Christian Tobelo man, she was a Christian woman, raped and killed by Laskar Jihad, who had rightly enacted her revenge. One man's unjust act of revenge, as Derek Summerfield has pointed out, "is another's social justice."[72]

Her identity opaque, her religious affiliation contested, her origin and motives uncertain, the *drakula* became a polyvalent vehicle for thinking and talking about the conflict. The conflict in North Maluku has frequently been described as either religious or ethnic, a portrayal that locals mainly contest. The polyvalence of the *drakula* certainly cuts across these conventional divides and suggests that post-conflict memory and identity are more complex. Striking in this polyvalence is also how the ideas of morality, subjectivity, and sociality that emerge from the narratives about the traumatized vampire differ from those political ideas of the self associated with (post)modern trauma. Revenge (*tuntutan*) is not morally wrong in itself, as it would be in the psychosocial discourse on trauma. In a region of Indonesia where local identity and history are defined to a large extent by past conflicts, revenge is a socio-spiritual fact of life. Indeed, it is the constituent element of human beings associated with "life" and with being (*nyawa*) that enacts revenge. Instead of being an event that takes place in individual minds,[73] trauma in North Maluku is an event that takes place in the intersection between spirits and human beings. In Tobelo, trauma has shifted from being a discursive concept in a science concerned with the individual self to becoming tied to a cosmology in which human beings and spirits—whether they assume the form of witches, ancestors, or Draculas—partake in the same cycle of being. This makes for a very different relationship between politics and the self than that which dominates the global therapeutic paradigm of trauma.[74] The result is a local form of "memory politics," in which past violence revisits the present through the actions both of humans and spirits.[75] The stories of the *drakula* demonstrate how it is sometimes not enough to make peace with the living. In the post-conflict imaginary in North Maluku, peace with the living cannot be achieved unless one brings about peace with the deceased because the spirits of the dead are traumatized and are in search of revenge.

By April 2004, all sightings of the *drakula* in Tobelo had ceased, and as people in the town reclaimed the night, narratives of the *drakula* joined the host of tales about other spiritual apparitions that haunted Halmahera before, during, and after the violent conflict.[76]

---

[72] Derek Summerfield, "Effects of War: Moral Knowledge, Revenge, Reconciliation, and Medicalised Concepts of 'Recovery,'" *British Medical Journal* 325 (2002): 1105.

[73] For a critique of this notion, see Patrick Bracken and Celia Petty, *Rethinking the Trauma of War* (London: Free Association Books, 1998).

[74] See Pupavac, "War on the Couch"; and Allan Young, *The Harmony of Illusions."*

[75] On memoro-politics, see Ian Hacking, "Memory Sciences, Memory Politics," in *Tense Past*, pp. 67–87.

[76] See Nils Bubandt, "Violence and Millenarian Modernity in Eastern Indonesia," in *Cargo, Cult, and Culture Critique*, ed. Holger Jebens (Honolulu, HI: University of Hawai'i Press, 2004), pp. 92–116.

CONCLUSION

This chapter has attempted to outline the mediascape, ideoscape, and "science-scape" that made the *drakula* available to the North Malukan social imagination. Tracing the various strands that make up its political and social genealogy, I have argued that the ideas about trauma and spiritual revenge that are associated with the Tobelo *drakula* speak to the ways in which global and local imaginaries merge in post-conflict North Maluku. Global flows of horror images and multinational rehabilitation activities have combined with the paranoid style of Indonesian politics and regional imaginaries brought by the movements of IDPs to make the concept of trauma and the figure of the Dracula available to post-conflict communities in North Maluku.

The trauma paradigm is a truly global phenomenon.[77] The concept of trauma is disseminated around the world as part of a scientific discourse about memory and conflict and embedded in the economic and political practices of an assemblage of powerful global institutions.[78] But this does not lead to a "global trauma concept" to which all local practices and ontologies simply bend. Similarly, the global figure of the Dracula, disseminated in movies and soap operas, has become a potent political metaphor in Indonesia—a specter of state power.[79] Although these global and national flows have taught the victims of and witnesses to the North Malukan conflict to think about violence through trauma and about politics through the Dracula, both concepts entail their own forms of enchantment that speak directly to the reality of the North Malukan spirit world. Images of horror and the magical character of psychosocial concepts are easily adapted by people in North Maluku to give local magical realities new explanatory power and legitimacy.

Trauma and the modern occult figure of the Dracula have coalesced with vengeful spirits so as to provide new reality to local ways of imagining conflict and its aftermath. Thus people in Tobelo seem to ascribe trauma as much to the spirits as to themselves, and to understand trauma as closely associated with the general notion of spiritual revenge. Ghosts and spirits in North Maluku are real, social agents that articulate a social morality. The concept of trauma is therefore appropriated to provide a new and (through its association with Western scientific discourse) legitimate reason why ghosts and spirits haunt social life after conflict. The revenge of these spirits both traverses and upholds the ethnic and religious divisions that the conflict produced. The attacks are seen to be revenge for acts that go back to the

---

[77] Michael Fischer, "Emergent Forms of Life: Anthropologies of Late or Postmodernities," *Annual Review of Anthropology* 28 (1999): 455–78.

[78] Joshua Breslau, "Globalizing Disaster Trauma: Science, Culture, and Psychiatry after the Kobe Earthquake," *Ethos* 28, 2 (2000): 174–97; and Joshua Breslau, "Cultures of Trauma: Anthropological Views of Post-Traumatic Stress Disorder in International Health," pp. 113–26.

[79] On the magicality of Indonesian statecraft, see also Ariel Heryanto, "Where Communism Never Dies: Violence, Trauma, and Narration in the Last Cold War Capitalist Authoritarian State," *International Journal of Cultural Studies* 2,2 (1999): 147–77; Joshua Barker, "State of Fear: Controlling the Criminal Contagion in Suharto's New Order," in *Violence and the State in Suharto's Indonesia*, pp. 20–53; Tim Lindsey, "The Criminal State: Premanisme and the New Indonesia," in *Indonesia Today: Challenges of History*, ed. G. Lloyd and S. Smith (Singapore: Institute of Southeast Asian Studies, 2001), pp. 283–97; and James Siegel, "Suharto, Witches," *Indonesia* 71 (April 2001): 27–78.

conflict and thus tend to run along religious lines of opposition. Yet both religious communities feel equally obliged to come to terms with the anger of the spirits. The spirit attacks make any clear apportioning of guilt impossible, since in any given instance it is unclear whether the spirit attack is morally right or wrong. In all cases, moreover, the activities of the *drakula*—for some a just avenger, for others a reprehensible presence—are the result of traumatization. As the notion of trauma is dislocated from its psychological context and brought into the orbit of a North Malukan spirit world, local ways of speaking about violence, self, and social morality gain new legitimacy. In the end, these narratives of vengeful spirits may hold their own promise for a restoration of social coexistence.

CONTRIBUTORS

Lorraine Aragon is an Adjunct Associate Professor in the Department of Anthropology at the University of North Carolina, Chapel Hill. She is author of *Fields of the Lord: Animism, Christian Minorities, and State Development in Indonesia* (Hawaii, 2000) and other publications related to religion, art, and the state. In addition to articles and chapters on Sulawesi's Poso conflict, Dr. Aragon's other recent research concerns intellectual property rights law and regional arts.

Edward Aspinall is a fellow in the Department of Political and Social Change, Research School of Pacific and Asian Studies, Australian National University. He is the author of *Opposing Suharto: Compromise, Resistance, and Regime Change in Indonesia* (Stanford University Press, 2005) and a forthcoming book on the history of the Aceh conflict.

Hélène Bouvier is researcher at the Southeast Asia Center (LASEMA-CASE), French National Center for Scientific Research (CNRS). She received her doctorate in ethnology at the Ecole des Hautes Etudes en Sciences Sociales, Paris, and has researched and written extensively on performing arts, migration, and conflict in Indonesia since 1985.

Nils Bubandt is an associate professor in anthropology at Aarhus University. Since 1991, he has conducted fieldwork in eastern Indonesia for a total of some forty months. His publications include "Sorcery, Corruption, and the Dangers of Democracy in Indonesia," *Journal of the Royal Anthropological Institute* (N.S.) 12,3 (2006); and "The Politics of Feeling Safe in Global, National, and Regional Worlds," *Security Dialogue* 36,3 (2005).

Richard Chauvel teaches at Victoria University, Melbourne. He has published widely on Australia's relations with Indonesia, as well as the history and politics of Papua and Maluku. His study of the Republic of the South Moluccas rebellion was published as *Nationalists, Soldiers, and Separatists* (KITLV Press). He is working with colleagues at CSIS in Jakarta on a research project concerning governance in the central highlands of Papua. Prior to joining Victoria University, Dr. Chauvel taught at the University of Indonesia, 1987–1992.

Jamie S. Davidson is Assistant Professor of Political Science at the National University of Singapore. His research interests range from ethnic violence and law and politics to infrastructure development. He is co-editor of *The Revival of Tradition in Indonesian Politics: The Deployment of* Adat *From Colonialism to Indigenism* (2007); and author of *From Rebellion to Riots: Collective Violence on Indonesian Borneo* (2008).

Christopher R. Duncan is an assistant professor in the Department of Religious Studies and in the School for Global Studies at Arizona State University. He is currently writing a book about communal violence in Indonesia, focusing on North Maluku. He also does research on social and religious change among the Forest Tobelo, a group of forest-dwelling foragers in North Maluku.

Eva-Lotta E. Hedman is Senior Research Fellow at the Refugee Studies Centre, University of Oxford. She is the author of *In the Name of Civil Society: From Free Election Movements to People Power in the Philippines* (Honolulu, HI: University of Hawai'i Press, 2006).

Geoffrey Robinson is an Associate Professor of History at UCLA. He has written and taught extensively on questions of political violence, popular resistance, and human rights in Southeast Asia. His major works include: *The Dark Side of Paradise: Political Violence in Bali* (Cornell University Press, 1995); and *East Timor 1999: Crimes Against Humanity* (Elsam & Hak, 2006).

John T. Sidel is Professor of Politics at the London School of Economics (LSE). He is the author of *Riots, Pogroms, Jihad: Religious Violence in Indonesia* (Cornell University Press, 2006) and *The Islamist Threat in Southeast Asia: A Reassessment* (East-West Center, 2007).

Glenn Smith is researcher, writer, and consultant on livelihoods and conflict. Educated at the University of California, Berkeley, and the Ecole des Hautes Etudes en Sciences Sociales, Paris, he manages ConflictRecovery.org. He currently leads a joint UNDP–Indonesia peace-building project in Aceh.

SOUTHEAST ASIA PROGRAM PUBLICATIONS
Cornell University

Studies on Southeast Asia

Number 45   *Conflict, Violence, and Displacement in Indonesia*, ed. Eva-Lotta E. Hedman. 2008. ISBN 978-0-87727-745-3 (pb.)

Number 44   *Friends and Exiles: A Memoir of the Nutmeg Isles and the Indonesian Nationalist Movement*, Des Alwi, ed. Barbara S. Harvey. 2008. ISBN 978-0-877277-44-6 (pb)

Number 43   *Early Southeast Asia: Selected Essays*, O. W. Wolters, ed. Craig J. Reynolds. 2008. 255 pp. ISBN 978-0-877277-43-9 (pb).

Number 42   *Thailand: The Politics of Despotic Paternalism* (revised edition), Thak Chaloemtiarana. 2007. 284 pp. ISBN 0-8772-7742-7 (pb).

Number 41   *Views of Seventeenth-Century Vietnam: Christoforo Borri on Cochinchina and Samuel Baron on Tonkin*, ed. Olga Dror and K. W. Taylor. 2006. 290 pp. ISBN 0-8772-7741-9 (pb).

Number 40   *Laskar Jihad: Islam, Militancy, and the Quest for Identity in Post-New Order Indonesia*, Noorhaidi Hasan. 2006. 266 pp. ISBN 0-877277-40-0 (pb).

Number 39   *The Indonesian Supreme Court: A Study of Institutional Collapse,* Sebastiaan Pompe. 2005. 494 pp. ISBN 0-877277-38-9 (pb).

Number 38   *Spirited Politics: Religion and Public Life in Contemporary Southeast Asia,* ed. Andrew C. Willford and Kenneth M. George. 2005. 210 pp. ISBN 0-87727-737-0.

Number 37   *Sumatran Sultanate and Colonial State: Jambi and the Rise of Dutch Imperialism, 1830-1907*, Elsbeth Locher-Scholten, trans. Beverley Jackson. 2004. 332 pp. ISBN 0-87727-736-2.

Number 36   *Southeast Asia over Three Generations: Essays Presented to Benedict R. O'G. Anderson*, ed. James T. Siegel and Audrey R. Kahin. 2003. 398 pp. ISBN 0-87727-735-4.

Number 35   *Nationalism and Revolution in Indonesia*, George McTurnan Kahin, intro. Benedict R. O'G. Anderson (reprinted from 1952 edition, Cornell University Press, with permission). 2003. 530 pp. ISBN 0-87727-734-6.

Number 34   *Golddiggers, Farmers, and Traders in the "Chinese Districts" of West Kalimantan, Indonesia*, Mary Somers Heidhues. 2003. 316 pp. ISBN 0-87727-733-8.

Number 33   *Opusculum de Sectis apud Sinenses et Tunkinenses (A Small Treatise on the Sects among the Chinese and Tonkinese): A Study of Religion in China and North Vietnam in the Eighteenth Century*, Father Adriano de St. Thecla, trans. Olga Dror, with Mariya Berezovska. 2002. 363 pp. ISBN 0-87727-732-X.

Number 32   *Fear and Sanctuary: Burmese Refugees in Thailand*, Hazel J. Lang. 2002. 204 pp. ISBN 0-87727-731-1.

Number 31   *Modern Dreams: An Inquiry into Power, Cultural Production, and the Cityscape in Contemporary Urban Penang, Malaysia*, Beng-Lan Goh. 2002. 225 pp. ISBN 0-87727-730-3.

Number 30   *Violence and the State in Suharto's Indonesia*, ed. Benedict R. O'G. Anderson. 2001. Second printing, 2002. 247 pp. ISBN 0-87727-729-X.

Number 9   *Southeast Asian Capitalists,* ed. Ruth McVey. 1992. 2nd printing 1993.
220 pp. ISBN 0-87727-708-7.

Number 8   *The Politics of Colonial Exploitation: Java, the Dutch, and the Cultivation
System,* Cornelis Fasseur, ed. R. E. Elson, trans. R. E. Elson, Ary Kraal.
1992. 2nd printing 1994. 266 pp. ISBN 0-87727-707-9.

Number 7   *A Malay Frontier: Unity and Duality in a Sumatran Kingdom,* Jane
Drakard. 1990. 2nd printing 2003. 215 pp. ISBN 0-87727-706-0.

Number 6   *Trends in Khmer Art,* Jean Boisselier, ed. Natasha Eilenberg, trans.
Natasha Eilenberg, Melvin Elliott. 1989. 124 pp., 24 plates.
ISBN 0-87727-705-2.

Number 5   *Southeast Asian Ephemeris: Solar and Planetary Positions, A.D. 638–2000,*
J. C. Eade. 1989. 175 pp. ISBN 0-87727-704-4.

Number 3   *Thai Radical Discourse: The Real Face of Thai Feudalism Today,* Craig J.
Reynolds. 1987. 2nd printing 1994. 186 pp. ISBN 0-87727-702-8.

Number 1   *The Symbolism of the Stupa,* Adrian Snodgrass. 1985. Revised with
index, 1988. 3rd printing 1998. 469 pp. ISBN 0-87727-700-1.

SEAP Series

Number 23   *Possessed by the Spirits: Mediumship in Contemporary Vietnamese
Communities.* 2006. 186 pp. ISBN 0-877271-41-0 (pb).

Number 22   *The Industry of Marrying Europeans,* Vũ Trọng Phụng, trans. Thúy
Tranviet. 2006. 66 pp. ISBN 0-877271-40-2 (pb).

Number 21   *Securing a Place: Small-Scale Artisans in Modern Indonesia,* Elizabeth
Morrell. 2005. 220 pp. ISBN 0-877271-39-9.

Number 20   *Southern Vietnam under the Reign of Minh Mạng (1820-1841): Central
Policies and Local Response,* Choi Byung Wook. 2004. 226pp. ISBN 0-0-
877271-40-2.

Number 19   *Gender, Household, State: Đổi Mới in Việt Nam,* ed. Jayne Werner and
Danièle Bélanger. 2002. 151 pp. ISBN 0-87727-137-2.

Number 18   *Culture and Power in Traditional Siamese Government,* Neil A. Englehart.
2001. 130 pp. ISBN 0-87727-135-6.

Number 17   *Gangsters, Democracy, and the State,* ed. Carl A. Trocki. 1998. Second
printing, 2002. 94 pp. ISBN 0-87727-134-8.

Number 16   *Cutting across the Lands: An Annotated Bibliography on Natural Resource
Management and Community Development in Indonesia, the Philippines,
and Malaysia,* ed. Eveline Ferretti. 1997. 329 pp. ISBN 0-87727-133-X.

Number 15   *The Revolution Falters: The Left in Philippine Politics after 1986,* ed.
Patricio N. Abinales. 1996. Second printing, 2002. 182 pp. ISBN 0-
87727-132-1.

Number 14   *Being Kammu: My Village, My Life,* Damrong Tayanin. 1994. 138 pp., 22
tables, illus., maps. ISBN 0-87727-130-5.

Number 13   *The American War in Vietnam,* ed. Jayne Werner, David Hunt. 1993.
132 pp. ISBN 0-87727-131-3.

Number 12   *The Voice of Young Burma,* Aye Kyaw. 1993. 92 pp. ISBN 0-87727-129-1.

Number 11 *The Political Legacy of Aung San*, ed. Josef Silverstein. Revised edition 1993. 169 pp. ISBN 0-87727-128-3.

Number 10 *Studies on Vietnamese Language and Literature: A Preliminary Bibliography*, Nguyen Dinh Tham. 1992. 227 pp. ISBN 0-87727-127-5.

Number 8 *From PKI to the Comintern, 1924–1941: The Apprenticeship of the Malayan Communist Party*, Cheah Boon Kheng. 1992. 147 pp. ISBN 0-87727-125-9.

Number 7 *Intellectual Property and US Relations with Indonesia, Malaysia, Singapore, and Thailand*, Elisabeth Uphoff. 1991. 67 pp. ISBN 0-87727-124-0.

Number 6 *The Rise and Fall of the Communist Party of Burma (CPB)*, Bertil Lintner. 1990. 124 pp. 26 illus., 14 maps. ISBN 0-87727-123-2.

Number 5 *Japanese Relations with Vietnam: 1951–1987*, Masaya Shiraishi. 1990. 174 pp. ISBN 0-87727-122-4.

Number 3 *Postwar Vietnam: Dilemmas in Socialist Development*, ed. Christine White, David Marr. 1988. 2nd printing 1993. 260 pp. ISBN 0-87727-120-8.

Number 2 *The Dobama Movement in Burma (1930–1938)*, Khin Yi. 1988. 160 pp. ISBN 0-87727-118-6.

Cornell Modern Indonesia Project Publications

Number 75 *A Tour of Duty: Changing Patterns of Military Politics in Indonesia in the 1990s.* Douglas Kammen and Siddharth Chandra. 1999. 99 pp. ISBN 0-87763-049-6.

Number 74 *The Roots of Acehnese Rebellion 1989–1992*, Tim Kell. 1995. 103 pp. ISBN 0-87763-040-2.

Number 73 *"White Book" on the 1992 General Election in Indonesia,* trans. Dwight King. 1994. 72 pp. ISBN 0-87763-039-9.

Number 72 *Popular Indonesian Literature of the Qur'an*, Howard M. Federspiel. 1994. 170 pp. ISBN 0-87763-038-0.

Number 71 *A Javanese Memoir of Sumatra, 1945–1946: Love and Hatred in the Liberation War*, Takao Fusayama. 1993. 150 pp. ISBN 0-87763-037-2.

Number 70 *East Kalimantan: The Decline of a Commercial Aristocracy*, Burhan Magenda. 1991. 120 pp. ISBN 0-87763-036-4.

Number 69 *The Road to Madiun: The Indonesian Communist Uprising of 1948,* Elizabeth Ann Swift. 1989. 120 pp. ISBN 0-87763-035-6.

Number 68 *Intellectuals and Nationalism in Indonesia: A Study of the Following Recruited by Sutan Sjahrir in Occupation Jakarta*, J. D. Legge. 1988. 159 pp. ISBN 0-87763-034-8.

Number 67 *Indonesia Free: A Biography of Mohammad Hatta*, Mavis Rose. 1987. 252 pp. ISBN 0-87763-033-X.

Number 66 *Prisoners at Kota Cane*, Leon Salim, trans. Audrey Kahin. 1986. 112 pp. ISBN 0-87763-032-1.

Number 65 *The Kenpeitai in Java and Sumatra*, trans. Barbara G. Shimer, Guy Hobbs, intro. Theodore Friend. 1986. 80 pp. ISBN 0-87763-031-3.

Number 64 *Suharto and His Generals: Indonesia's Military Politics, 1975–1983*, David Jenkins. 1984. 4th printing 1997. 300 pp. ISBN 0-87763-030-5.

Translation Series

Volume 3	*The Japanese in Colonial Southeast Asia,* ed. Saya Shiraishi, Takashi Shiraishi. 1993. 172 pp. ISBN 0-87727-402-9.
Volume 2	*Indochina in the 1940s and 1950s,* ed. Takashi Shiraishi, Motoo Furuta. 1992. 196 pp. ISBN 0-87727-401-0.
Volume 1	*Reading Southeast Asia,* ed. Takashi Shiraishi. 1990. 188 pp. ISBN 0-87727-400-2.

Language Texts

INDONESIAN

Beginning Indonesian through Self-Instruction, John U. Wolff, Dédé Oetomo, Daniel Fietkiewicz. 3rd revised edition 1992. Vol. 1. 115 pp. ISBN 0-87727-529-7. Vol. 2. 434 pp. ISBN 0-87727-530-0. Vol. 3. 473 pp. ISBN 0-87727-531-9.

Indonesian Readings, John U. Wolff. 1978. 4th printing 1992. 480 pp. ISBN 0-87727-517-3

Indonesian Conversations, John U. Wolff. 1978. 3rd printing 1991. 297 pp. ISBN 0-87727-516-5

Formal Indonesian, John U. Wolff. 2nd revised edition 1986. 446 pp. ISBN 0-87727-515-7

TAGALOG

Pilipino through Self-Instruction, John U. Wolff, Maria Theresa C. Centeno, Der-Hwa V. Rau. 1991. Vol. 1. 342 pp. ISBN 0-87727—525-4. Vol. 2., revised 2005, 378 pp. ISBN 0-87727-526-2. Vol 3., revised 2005, 431 pp. ISBN 0-87727-527-0. Vol. 4. 306 pp. ISBN 0-87727-528-9.

THAI

A. U. A. Language Center Thai Course, J. Marvin Brown. Originally published by the American University Alumni Association Language Center, 1974. Reissued by Cornell Southeast Asia Program, 1991, 1992. Book 1. 267 pp. ISBN 0-87727-506-8. Book 2. 288 pp. ISBN 0-87727-507-6. Book 3. 247 pp. ISBN 0-87727-508-4.

A. U. A. Language Center Thai Course, Reading and Writing Text (mostly reading), 1979. Reissued 1997. 164 pp. ISBN 0-87727-511-4.

A. U. A. Language Center Thai Course, Reading and Writing Workbook (mostly writing), 1979. Reissued 1997. 99 pp. ISBN 0-87727-512-2.

KHMER

Cambodian System of Writing and Beginning Reader, Franklin E. Huffman. Originally published by Yale University Press, 1970. Reissued by Cornell Southeast Asia Program, 4th printing 2002. 365 pp. ISBN 0-300-01314-0.

Modern Spoken Cambodian, Franklin E. Huffman, assist. Charan Promchan, Chhom-Rak Thong Lambert. Originally published by Yale University Press, 1970. Reissued by Cornell Southeast Asia Program, 3rd printing 1991. 451 pp. ISBN 0-300-01316-7.

Intermediate Cambodian Reader, ed. Franklin E. Huffman, assist. Im Proum. Originally published by Yale University Press, 1972. Reissued by Cornell Southeast Asia Program, 1988. 499 pp. ISBN 0-300-01552-6.

Cambodian Literary Reader and Glossary, Franklin E. Huffman, Im Proum. Originally published by Yale University Press, 1977. Reissued by Cornell Southeast Asia Program, 1988. 494 pp. ISBN 0-300-02069-4.

HMONG

White Hmong-English Dictionary, Ernest E. Heimbach. 1969. 8th printing, 2002. 523 pp. ISBN 0-87727-075-9.

VIETNAMESE

Intermediate Spoken Vietnamese, Franklin E. Huffman, Tran Trong Hai. 1980. 3rd printing 1994. ISBN 0-87727-500-9.

* * *

Southeast Asian Studies: Reorientations. Craig J. Reynolds and Ruth McVey. Frank H. Golay Lectures 2 & 3. 70 pp. ISBN 0-87727-301-4.

Javanese Literature in Surakarta Manuscripts, Nancy K. Florida. Vol. 1, *Introduction and Manuscripts of the Karaton Surakarta.* 1993. 410 pp. Frontispiece, illustrations. Hard cover, ISBN 0-87727-602-1, Paperback, ISBN 0-87727-603-X. Vol. 2, *Manuscripts of the Mangkunagaran Palace.* 2000. 576 pp. Frontispiece, illustrations. Paperback, ISBN 0-87727-604-8.

Sbek Thom: Khmer Shadow Theater. Pech Tum Kravel, trans. Sos Kem, ed. Thavro Phim, Sos Kem, Martin Hatch. 1996. 363 pp., 153 photographs. ISBN 0-87727-620-X.

In the Mirror: Literature and Politics in Siam in the American Era, ed. Benedict R. O'G. Anderson, trans. Benedict R. O'G. Anderson, Ruchira Mendiones. 1985. 2nd printing 1991. 303 pp. Paperback. ISBN 974-210-380-1.

To order, please contact:

Cornell University
Southeast Asia Program Publications
95 Brown Road
Box 1004
Ithaca NY 14850

Online: http://www.einaudi.cornell.edu/southeastasia/publications/
Tel: 1-877-865-2432 (Toll free – U.S.)
Fax: (607) 255-7534

E-mail: SEAP-Pubs@cornell.edu
Orders must be prepaid by check or credit card (VISA, MasterCard, Discover).